Critical Arc|

Critical Architecture examines the relationship between design and criticism in architecture. Placing architecture in an interdisciplinary context, the book explores architectural criticism with reference to fields such as art, cultural and literary criticism, and considers how critical practice in design operates through a number of different modes: buildings, drawings and texts.

With 36 chapters by an international cast of leading academics and designers, organised under four thematic headings, *Critical Architecture* brings together a diverse range of projects and writings that challenge the view that the terms 'design' and 'criticism' should be divided.

Introducing key debates in contemporary architectural criticism through text and designs, this accessible single-source publication is ideal for undergraduates and postgraduates studying the practice and theory of art and architecture, as well as all those interested in contemporary architectural discourse.

Jane Rendell is Professor of Architecture and Art and Director of Architectural Research at the Bartlett School of Architecture, University College London. **Jonathan Hill** is Professor of Architecture and Visual Theory and Director of the MPhil/PhD by Architectural Design programme at the Bartlett School of Architecture. **Murray Fraser** is Professor of Architecture at the University of Westminister in London. **Mark Dorrian** is Reader in Architecture at the School of Arts, Culture and Environment, University of Edinburgh and Co-Director of Metis.

CRITIQUES: Critical Studies in Architectural Humanities

A project of the Architectural Humanities Research Association

Series Editor: Jonathan Hale (University of Nottingham)

Editorial Board:
Sarah Chaplin (Kingston University)
Mark Dorrian (University of Edinburgh)
Murray Fraser (University of Westminster)
Hilde Heynen (Catholic University of Leuven)
Andrew Leach (University of Queensland)
Thomas Mical (Carleton University)
Jane Rendell (University College London)
Adam Sharr (Cardiff University)
Igea Troiani (Oxford Brookes University)

This original series of edited books contains selected papers from the AHRA Annual International Conferences. Each year the event has its own thematic focus while sharing an interest in new and emerging critical research in the areas of architectural history, theory, culture, design and urbanism.

Volume 1: Critical Architecture
Edited by: Jane Rendell, Jonathan Hill, Murray Fraser and Mark Dorrian

Volume 2: From Models to Drawings: On Representation in Architecture
Edited by: Marco Frascari, Jonathan Hale and Bradley Starkey

Volume 3: The Politics of Making: Theory, Practice, Product
Edited by: Mark Swenarton, Igea Troiani and Helena Webster

AHRA provides an inclusive and comprehensive support network for humanities researchers in architecture across the UK and beyond. It promotes, supports, develops and disseminates high-quality research in all areas of architectural humanities.

www.ahra-architecture.org.uk

Critical Architecture

**Edited by Jane Rendell, Jonathan Hill,
Murray Fraser and Mark Dorrian**

LONDON AND NEW YORK

First published 2007
by Routledge
2 Park Square, Milton Park, Abingdon, Oxon OX14 4RN

Simultaneously published in the USA and Canada
by Routledge
270 Madison Ave, New York, NY 10016

Routledge is an imprint of the Taylor & Francis Group, an informa business

© 2007 Selection and editorial matter, Jane Rendell, Jonathan Hill, Murray Fraser and Mark Dorrian;
individual chapters, the contributors

Typeset in Univers by Wearset Ltd, Boldon, Tyne and Wear
Printed and bound in Great Britain by The Cromwell Press, Trowbridge, Wiltshire

British Library Cataloguing in Publication Data
A catalogue record for this book is available from the British Library

Library of Congress Cataloging in Publication Data
Critical architecture / edited by Jane Rendell ... [et al.].
   p. cm. – (Critiques–critical studies in architectural humanities)
   Includes index.
   1. Architectural criticism. 2. Architectural design. I. Rendell, Jane, 1967–
   NA2599.5.C75 2007
   720.1–dc22   2007002166

ISBN10: 0-415-41537-3 (hbk)
ISBN10: 0-415-41538-5 (pbk)
ISBN10: 0-203-94566-2 (ebk)

ISBN13: 978-0-415-41537-8 (hbk)
ISBN13: 978-0-415-41538-1 (pbk)
ISBN13: 978-0-203-94566-7 (ebk)

Contents

Contents

Illustration credits

Maria Theodorou (2002) 73

Laura Ruggeri (1997) 106; (2006) 108

Patrick Keiller (2003), insets courtesy of the BFI (1902) 116, 118

HAPPENinc. (2004) 126 (all), 127 (all)

Nigel Green and *The Architects' Journal* (2002) 130

Warren and Mosley (2002) 132 (all)

Katja Grillner (2004) 137

Sharon Kivland (2002–6) 143; (2005) 149

Penelope Haralambidou (2005) 158

David Cross of Cornford & Cross (2006) 159

Yeoryia Manolopoulou (2004) 172, 175

Philippe Rahm Architects (2005) 184 (all), 185, 186, 187 (all); (2006) 188

The Alvin Boyarsky Memorial Trust, London (1985) 191

Igor Marjanovic (2004) 197

Marie Carlsson (2004) 201–3

Warta Kota (2003) 216 (all), 217 (middle and bottom)

Stephen Cairns (2005) 217 (top)

Cedric Price Archive, Collection Centre Canadien d'Architecture/Canadian Centre for Architecture, Montréal 220, 221 (all), 222

Marianne Mueller, Mueller Kneer Associates, Architects 223 (top)

SHoP Architects (2003) 223 (bottom)

Penelope Haralambidou (2004) 229

The Louvre Museum, Paris, and Philadelphia Museum of Art (1998) 233

Victoria Watson 242, 243

Frode Larsen (2005) 272

Nils P. Lotherington (2003) 274

Gini Lee (2002) 280, 282, 283, 284, 284, 285, 287

A+URL 291

City Mine(d) through Tom Deforce, Barcelona 297

Atelier Feichang Jianzhu (2006) 304 (top)

OMA/AMO Rotterdam (2006), © OMA/Rem Koolhaas, Ole Scheeren 304 (bottom)

Paul Smoothy (2001) 309, 312 (all), 313, 314 (all), 315, 316, 317

Fluid (2002) 319 (bottom); (2003) 320; (2004) 319 (top), 321, 322; (2005) 323 (all)

Hélène Binet (2004) 322 (all)

Domino Press (1975) 326

The Zionist Archive 327

Ganit Mayslits Kassif and Udi Kassif 329

Don Koniak, Karina Tollman, Philipp Misselwitz and Philipp Thomanek; photograph: Jorg Glascher (2004) 330 (1)

Galila Yavin and Tamar Zacharovitz 330 (2)

Gaston Zahr, Noa Pasharel-Haim, Alasdair Ross Graham, Oded Kidron, Birgit Glaetzel and Omer Weissbein 330 (3)

Tamar Navon, Ifat Hollender-Emmer and Michael Ilan 330 (4)

Roee Hemed and Jonathan Dror 330 (5)

Maor Roytman and Oren Ben Avraham 330 (6)

Peter Barber Architects, Donnybrook Quarter, London (2006) 336–7

Contributors

Tim Anstey is an architect and researcher. He studied at the University of Bath and the British School at Rome and has taught and lectured at architecture schools in the UK, Sweden and North America. Until recently he was a Senior Lecturer at the Department of Architecture, Royal Institute of Technology (KTH), Stockholm, and is now at the University of Bath. Tim has published widely in both academic and practice contexts, including *RES Journal of Anthropology and Aesthetics*, *Albertiana*, *Journal of the Societée International Leon Battista Alberti*, *RIBA Journal*, *The Architects' Journal* and *Building Design*. With Katja Grillner and Rolf Hughes he is co-editor of *Architecture and Authorship* (2007).

Daniel Barber is an architectural historian and theorist with interests in historical and contemporary discussions of architecture and environmentalism. He has taught at the School of Visual Arts, New York, the Yale School of Architecture, and the Graduate School of Architecture, Planning and Preservation at Columbia University. He is currently a PhD Candidate at Columbia University, working on relations between architecture, government policy and culture in post-war Europe and the Americas. Barber lives and works in New York City and Dolores, Colorado.

Andrew Benjamin is Professor of Critical Theory in Design and Architecture at the University of Technology, Sydney. His recent books include *Style and Time: Essays on the Politics of Appearance* (2006), and *Disclosing Spaces: On Painting* (2004).

Ana Betancour is an architect. Her practice work ranges from architectural and urban design through to academic research, multidisciplinary/cultural/new media projects. An Associate Professor at the Department of Architecture, Royal Institute of Technology, Stockholm, she runs A+URL (Architecture + Urban Research Laboratory). She has taught and researched at various international institutions: the Bartlett School of Architecture, UCL, University of East London and University of Catalonia among others. She has published and exhibited widely, and is a member of international networks, most recently in collaboration with City Mine(d), an independent organisation based in Brussels, London and Barcelona.

Katarina Bonnevier is an architect and PhD candidate at the Department of Architecture, Royal Institute of Technology, Stockholm. In her dissertation, *Enactments of Architecture*, she investigates how building constellations constitute gender performativity. Earlier work includes 'A Queer Analysis of Eileen Gray's E.1027', in Hilde Heyen and Gulsum Baydar (eds), *Negotiating Domesticity: Spatial Productions of Gender in Modern Architecture* (2005).

Stephen Cairns teaches architectural design and theory at the University of Edinburgh. He has published on postcolonial themes, contemporary theorisations of the city, aesthetics and representation in architecture. He edited *Drifting: Architecture and Migrancy* (2004), and has contributed essays to such journals as *Postcolonial Studies*, *The Journal of Architecture* and *Urban Studies*.

David Cunningham teaches at the University of Westminster and is an editor of the journal *Radical Philosophy*. He is co-editor of *Adorno and Literature* (2006) and a special issue of *The Journal of Architecture* on post-war avant-gardes (2001). Other work has been published in *Architectural Design*, *New Formations* and *SubStance*. He is currently writing a monograph on modernism and abstraction, as well as co-authoring a book on the theory of the metropolis.

Mark Dorrian is Reader in Architecture at the School of Arts, Culture and Environment, University of Edinburgh and co-director of *Metis*. His books include (with Gillian Rose) *Deterritorialisations: Revisioning Landscapes and Politics* (2004) and (with Adrian Hawker) *Metis: Urban Cartographies* (2003). His work has been published in *Architecture and Ideas*, *Architectural Research Quarterly*, *Artifice*, *Chora: Intervals in the Philosophy of Architecture*, *The Journal of Architecture*, *The Journal of Narrative Theory* and *Word & Image*. He is currently working on the cultural history of the aerial view.

Kim Dovey is Professor of Architecture and Urban Design as well as Head of Architecture at the University of Melbourne. He has a PhD from the University of California, Berkeley, and has published a broad range of social critiques on architecture and urban design. Recent books include *Framing Places: Mediating Power in Built Form* (1999) and *Fluid City: Transforming Melbourne's Urban Waterfront* (2005). His current work is focused on constructions of place identity and urban 'character'.

Murray Fraser is Professor of Architecture at the University of Westminster in London, where he is Coordinator for Postgraduate Studies and Research. He is a qualified architect with many years in practice, and a PhD in architectural history from UCL. His research and teaching work spans design, history and theory, cultural studies and advanced digital techniques. He has written widely on the subject of cross-cultural relationships and post-colonial theory in architecture, and is about to publish a book with Joe Kerr titled *Architecture and the 'Special Relationship'*, looking at the influence of America on post-war British architecture and urbanism.

Katja Grillner, MArch, PhD, is an architect and critic based in Stockholm, Sweden. She is a Senior Lecturer, Director of Research and PhD-Studies, and Director of AKAD at the Department of Architecture, Royal Institute of Technology, Stockholm. She is a member of the board of the Swedish Architecture Museum. Her research on architecture and landscape combines theoretical, historical and literary strategies. She is author of *Ramble, Linger and Gaze – Philosophical Dialogues in the Landscape Garden*, Stockholm: KTH (2000), editor of *01-AKAD – Experimental Research in Architecture and Design* (2005) and co-editor of *Architecture and Authorship* (2007).

Penelope Haralambidou PhD is an architect, researcher and Lecturer in Architecture at the Bartlett School of Architecture, UCL. Her work investigates spatial perception, imagination and representation and she sees architectural drawing as a critical method. Her projects have been distinguished in international competitions and exhibited in Europe and the United States: for example, domoBaal, London (2006 and 2007), Slade Galleries, London (2004), Museum of Contemporary Art, Athens (2002) and the 7th Biennale of Architecture, Venice (2000). She was a founding member of Tessera, a collaborative architectural practice, who addressed issues of contemporary public space and designed 'Athens-Scape', RIBA, London (2003).

Hilde Heynen is Professor of Architectural Theory at the Katholieke Universiteit Leuven, Belgium. She is author of *Architecture and Modernity: a Critique* (1999) and her articles have been published in *Assemblage*, *Archis*, *Harvard Design Magazine* and *The Journal of Architecture*. In 2001, with André Loeckx Lieven De Cauter and Karina Van Herck, she co-edited an anthology in Dutch of major twentieth-century texts on architecture, and in 2002, with Hubert-Jan Henket, she co-edited *Back from Utopia: the Challenge of the Modern Movement*. Other co-edited volumes include, with David Vanderburgh, *Inside Density* (2003), and with Gulsum Baydar, *Negotiating Domesticity: Spatial Productions of Gender in Modern Architecture* (2005).

Jonathan Hill, an architect and architectural historian, is Professor of Architecture and Visual Theory and Director of the MPhil/PhD by Architectural Design programme at the Bartlett School of Architecture, UCL. He is the author of *The Illegal Architect* (1998), *Actions of Architecture* (2003) and *Immaterial Architecture* (2006). Jonathan is the editor of *Occupying Architecture* (1998), *Architecture: the Subject is Matter* (2001) and the 'Research by Design' issue of *The Journal of Architecture* (2003). Galleries where he has had solo exhibitions include the Haus der Architektur, Graz, and Architektur-Galerie am Weissenhof, Stuttgart.

Rolf Hughes, a writer, researcher and critic, holds a PhD in Creative and Critical Writing from the University of East Anglia (UK). He is co-editor of *The Book of Models* (1998, reprinted 2003), *Hybrid Thought* (2003), *Architecture and Authorship* (forthcoming, 2007), *Second Nature* (forthcoming, 2007), and publishes prose poems, fiction and drama as well as scholarly essays on design methodology. A Senior Researcher at the Department of Architecture, Royal Institute of Technology, Stockholm, he also teaches at Konstfack University College of Art and Design, and is a member of the board of AKAD.

Ganit Mayslits Kassif studied at the Bezalel Academy and then gained a Diploma in Architecture with Distinction from the University of Westminster, London. She has taught at the Bartlett School of Architecture, UCL, and the Technion, Haifa. Combining practice and research, she is interested in architecture as a cultural and sensual construct and investigating new strategies for urban regeneration. Since 1994, she has been co-partner in Mayslits Kassif Architects based in Tel Aviv, which deals with major public projects such as the redevelopment of the Tel Aviv Port and regeneration of various city centres such as Herzliya, Ashdod and Karmiel.

Udi Kassif graduated from the Bezalel Academy with distinction and later gained his Diploma from the Architectural Association, London. He worked at John Pawson's office in London as well as with Raoul Bunschoten. In his practice and research, he is interested in the development of new architectural methodologies and multi-disciplinary tools that correspond to the dynamic contemporary urban condition. Since 1994, he has been co-partner in Mayslits Kassif Architects based in Tel Aviv, which deals with major public projects such as the redevelopment of the Tel Aviv Port and regeneration of various city centres such as Herzliya, Ashdod and Karmiel.

Patrick Keiller studied architecture at the Bartlett School of Architecture and fine art at the Royal College of Art. His films include *London* (1994) and *Robinson in Space* (1997), a study of the UK's landscape and economic geography later extended as a book. He is a Research Fellow at the Royal College of Art, where his most recent project is *The City of the Future*, an exploration of the landscapes of early film. Other publications include contributions to *The Unknown City* (2000), *This Is Not Architecture* (2002), *Re:CP* (2003) and *London: from Punk to Blair* (2003).

Sharon Kivland is an artist and writer, Reader in Fine Art at Sheffield Hallam University, and Research Associate of the Centre for Freudian Analysis and Research, London. She is currently working on a series of three books, titled *Freud on Holiday* (2006 and 2007); she is also co-editor of *Transmission: Speaking and Listening* (2001–6) and *The Rules of Engagement* (2004–7). Her work is represented by domoBaal Contemporary Art, London, and Galerie Bugdahn & Kaimer, Düsseldorf. She is Visiting Fellow in the Institute of Germanic and Romance Studies, University of London (2006–8).

Andrew Leach is a UQ Postdoctoral Research Fellow in Architectural History at the University of Queensland, Australia. He has published widely on Manfredo Tafuri (1935–94), including his book *Manfredo Tafuri: Choosing History* (2007), and on the architectural history of New Zealand. He co-edits, with Deidre Brown,

Fabrications: the Journal of the Society of Architectural Historians, Australia and New Zealand, published by the University of Queensland Press. His other publications include *Frederick H. Newman* (2003) and *Campus Confessions* (2004), and essays in *Architectural Theory Review*, *The Journal of Architecture*, *Mosaic* and *Oase*.

Gini Lee is a landscape architect and interior designer who lectures in spatial design and cultural landscape studies at the Louis Laybourne Smith School of Architecture and Design, University of South Australia. She recently completed her PhD by Design Project at RMIT University in Melbourne, entitled *The Intention to Notice: the Collection, the Tour and Ordinary Landscapes*. In this study she investigated ways in which landscapes can be understood and incorporated into cultural readings of individuals and communities. The research proposes new curatorial models involving interiors, gardens and architectural spaces through which we can understand, access and care for landscapes.

Steve McAdam is a founder and director of Fluid. An architect with extensive experience in urban regeneration and masterplanning, he has led major urban-regeneration projects in London, the Midlands and Merseyside. In 2003 the London Development Agency appointed him to direct pre-submission stakeholder consultation, public-sector engagement and responsive masterplanning for the 2012 Olympic and Legacy masterplans in the Lower Lea Valley. He is involved in several Housing Market Renewal projects and in advising local authorities on consultation strategies for Local Development Frameworks. Steve is a consultant to the Council of Europe, and Senior Lecturer at London Metropolitan University.

Igor Marjanovic is Assistant Professor of Architecture at Washington University in St Louis. Together with Katerina Ruedi Ray, he is a principal of *ReadyMade Studio*, an interdisciplinary art and design practice. His current research focuses on the historical role of Alvin Boyarsky in architectural education and practice. He has co-authored two books: *The Portfolio* and *Practical Experience*. Marjanovic graduated summa cum laude from the University of Belgrade and completed his diploma thesis at the Moscow Architectural Institute. He received a Master of Architecture degree from the University of Illinois at Chicago.

Ben Nicholson studied architecture at the AA, Cooper Union and Cranbrook Academy. He is an Associate Professor of Architecture at The School of the Art Institute, Chicago, and lives and works in New Harmony, Indiana. His publications include *The Appliance House* (1990), a CD-Rom, *Thinking the Unthinkable House* (1997), and a satire, *The World: Who Wants It?* (2002). He has exhibited at The Canadian Center of Architecture, The Cartier Foundation, The Whitney Museum and The Museum of Science and Industry, Chicago. He is currently writing *Horror Vacuii* that reveals number, geometry and labyrinths through beans, sand drawing and walking.

Alona Nitzan-Shiftan is an architect and Senior Lecturer at the Faculty of Architecture and Town Planning, Technion, Israel Institute of Technology. She studies the politics of architecture in the context of post-WWII architectural culture, particularly in Israel and North America, and in relation to nationalism, postcolonialism and globalisation. She holds a PhD and an MArch from MIT, and was recently the Mary Davis Fellow and the Kress Postdoctoral Fellow at the Center for Advanced Study in the Visual Arts (CASVA) at the National Gallery. She is currently working on a manuscript *Designing Politics: Architecture and the Making of 'United Jerusalem'*.

Philippe Rahm, DipArch, studied at the Polytechnic School of Lausanne and Zurich. Until 2004 he was an associate of Décosterd & Rahm. Philippe has exhibited in Archilab (2000), SF-MoMA (2001), Museum of Modern Art, Paris (2001), 8th Architecture Biennale, Venice (2002), Valencia Biennial (2003), Graz Biennial (2003), CCA Kitakyushu (2004), Mori Art Museum (2005), Frac Centre, Orléans, Centre Pompidou, Beaubourg (2003–6) and CCA Montréal (2007). Philippe teaches at the Architectural Association, London and is Professor at ECAL Lausanne and was Visiting Professor at the Ecole Nationale Supérieure de Beaux-Arts, Paris (2003) and Mendrisio Academy of Architecture, Switzerland (2005).

Jane Rendell, BA (Hons), DipArch, MSc, PhD, is Professor of Architecture and Art and Director of Architectural Research at the Bartlett School of Architecture, UCL. She is author of *Art and Architecture* (2006), *The Pursuit of Pleasure* (2002); co-editor of *Spatial Imagination* (2005), *The Unknown City* (2001), *Intersections* (2000), *Gender, Space, Architecture* (1999), *Strangely Familiar*, (1995); on the editorial board of *ARQ* and a member of the AHRC Peer Review College. In 2006 she was a Visiting Research Fellow at CRASSH, University of Cambridge and received an honorary degree from University College of the Creative Arts.

Charles Rice is Senior Lecturer in the School of Architecture at the University of Technology, Sydney. He has also taught in the histories and theories programme at the Architectural Association, London. He is author of *The Emergence of the Interior: Architecture, Modernity, Domesticity* (2007). His recent work is also published in the anthologies, *Negotiating Domesticity: Spatial Constructions of Gender in Modern Architecture* (2005), *Walter Benjamin and History* (2005) and *Capitales de la modernité: Walter Benjamin et la ville* (2005), as well as in journals including *The Journal of Architecture* and *Home Cultures*.

Laura Ruggeri, MA Spatial Culture, the University of Middlesex, United Kingdom, and *Dottore* in *Semiotica*, University of Bologna, Italy, was born in Milan. Since 1997 she has been living in Hong Kong where she teaches Theory of Design and Research Methods in the MA and BA programmes at The Hong Kong Polytechnic University and devotes her time to the exploration of Hong Kong infraspaces and the scrutiny of the ideologies and forces that shape her environment. She is co-editor of *HK Lab2*, Map Books (2005), and her articles and critical essays have appeared in a number of international publications and can be sampled on her website, www.spacing.org.

Paul Shepheard studied architecture at the Architectural Association, graduating in
1973. He has three books published with the MIT Press: *What is Architecture?*,
on landscapes, buildings and machines (1994), *The Cultivated Wilderness*, on
the dynamics of landscape strategies (1997), and *Artificial Love,* on machines
and architecture (2003). He was Visiting Professor at the University of Texas at
Austin from 1996 to 2002, and in 2006 he was artist in residence at the
Adademie van Bouwkunst in Amsterdam. He is currently working on a critical
proposition summed up as 'How To Like Everything'. More details can be found
at www.paulshepheard.com.

Naomi Stead, BArch, University of South Australia, PhD, University of Queensland, is
a Senior Lecturer in Architectural Theory, Philosophy and Cultural Studies at the
University of Technology, Sydney. She is a prominent architectural critic in
Australia, contributing regularly to professional journals such as *Architecture
Australia*, *Monument*, *Architectural Review Australia*, *Pol Oxygen* and *[Inside]*.
Her other research interests include the history and theory of museums,
representations of architecture and the metropolis, concepts of authorship in
architecture, intersections between architecture and the visual and performing
arts, and queer space.

Teresa Stoppani, MArch, IUAV University of Venice and PhD Arch&UD, University of
Florence, taught architectural design and theory at the IUAV, 1995–9, and at the
Architectural Association in London, 2000–2. Since 2000, she has been Senior
Lecturer in Architecture at the University of Greenwich, London, where she is
Co-ordinator of Histories and Theories. Recent publications include chapters in
Urban Space and Cityscapes, 2006, and *Haecceity Papers*, 1, 2 (2006), and the
edited monograph *Antipodes/Measuring the World*, *Haecceity Papers*, 2, 2
(2006).

Maria Theodorou, architect, PhD (AA), Postgraduate Diploma (La Sapienza), is Head of
the Architecture Network, Greece. She was a Fulbright Visiting Fellow at the
University of Princeton in 2005, adviser to the Minister of Culture, Greece
(1996–2004), the Cultural Olympiad (2001–4) and a Council of Europe expert
(2003). She was the editor of the Athens D.O.E.S. series, on the *Archis* advisory
board (2000–4), and juries of international architecture competitions. She is the
founding member and director of the SARCHA non-profit organisation. She
lectures and publishes on architecture theory and her current research focuses
on architecture and activism.

Elisabeth Tostrup, Professor at the Oslo School of Architecture and Design, was a
practicing architect for many years during which she won prizes in several
important architectural competitions in Norway. She is also an experienced
researcher and received her doctorate in 1996 for the thesis *Architecture and
Rhetoric: Text and Design in Architectural Competitions, Oslo 1939–1990*. In 1993
she won first prize in the international essay competition organised by the EAAE.

She has held a number of academic appointments and published widely on Nordic twentieth-century architecture. Her latest book is *Norwegian Wood: the Thoughtful Architecture of Wenche Selmer* (2006).

Igea Troiani PhD is a Senior Lecturer at Oxford Brookes University. She was educated and lectured in Australia prior to moving to the United Kingdom. Until 2005 she was a partner with Andrew Dawson in HAPPENinc, a collaborative studio based in Brisbane, which produced architectural competitions, theatre set designs, exhibitions and architecture. She has published in *The Journal of Architecture* and *Architecture Australia*. She is interested in alternative methods of 'writing' architectural history relating to her production of architectural history documentaries: *Building Mayne Hall* (2004) and *CGA: 12 Decades of Design* (2005).

Victoria Watson PhD is the director of The Big Air World, an association formed to develop and promote the phenomenon of Air Grid, published as articles and exhibited in the United Kingdom, the Netherlands, Germany and Czechoslovakia. Her current research involves exploring the deployment of Air Grid in the manufacture of an architectural apparatus: *The House Of Miniscule Impressions.* An architect, Victoria studied architecture at the Bartlett School of Architecture, UCL, and the Polytechnic of Central London. She is Senior Lecturer in Architecture at the University of Westminster.

Sarah Wigglesworth is the founder director of Sarah Wigglesworth Architects. Her practice has produced a sequence of award-winning buildings, most recently the highly acclaimed new studios for the Siobhan Davies Dance Company. Her prominent role in the wider architectural debate, particularly in relation to the role of women, was recognised with the award of an MBE in 2003. She is Professor of Architecture at the University of Sheffield, where she directs the PhD by Design programme; she is one of the few high-profile UK architects to retain an active role in education and theory.

Robin Wilson is a writer on art, architecture and landscape. He contributes regularly *to The Architects' Journal.* He recently completed his PhD at the Bartlett School of Architecture, UCL, and teaches at the Bartlett School of Architecture and The Bristol School of Architecture, University of the West of England.

Jianfei Zhu studied architecture in China (Tianjin) and the United Kingdom (The Bartlett School of Architecture, UCL). He is currently Senior Lecturer at the University of Melbourne. Author of *Chinese Spatial Strategies: Imperial Beijing 1420–1911* (2004), and 'Criticality in between China and the West' (*The Journal of Architecture*, November 2005), his research concerns social, political and formal issues of architecture and urbanities in late imperial, modern and contemporary China, and includes an experimental use of Western social theories in the Chinese context. He is currently working on Beijing of the 1950s and theories of the 'metropolis' examined in Chinese/Asian terms.

Acknowledgements

The editors would like to thank the British Academy and the Bartlett School of Architecture for their financial support of the 'Critical Architecture' conference held at the Bartlett School of Architecture, University College London, 2004. This is the event that launched this project, and we are grateful to all those who attended the conference and helped in its organisation, especially Ana Araujo, Aslihan Senel and Rachel Stevenson. Financial support for the production of the resultant book – the present volume – was received from the Architecture Research Fund of the Bartlett School of Architecture, University College London, the University of Westminster and the University of Edinburgh.

Since 'Critical Architecture' was the first of an annual series of conferences to be held in association with the newly formed AHRA (Architectural Humanities Research Association), thanks are due to Jonathan Hale of the University of Nottingham for his far-sightedness in initiating AHRA and his continuing hard work and enthusiasm in promoting and directing it. This volume initiates a new book series that will be based on the AHRA conferences. We would also like to thank Caroline Mallinder of Routledge for supporting both the current and prospective volumes.

The image on the front cover is an original artwork by the artists Cornford & Cross, commissioned by the editors. The artists also kindly provided us with ideas for the visual identity of this book and the series as a whole. We would also like to thank all those who have given permission to reproduce texts and images in this collection. Every effort has been made to contact copyright holders for permission to reprint material in this book. The publishers would be grateful to hear from any copyright holder who is not acknowledged here and will undertake to rectify any errors or omissions in future editions of the book. Each image is given full attribution in the relevant figure caption, but we would like to make a special acknowledgement here to Ben Marcus who has kindly allowed us to reproduce parts of his prose poem.

Throughout the editorial process our research assistant, Nick Beech, has provided rigorous and conscientious input as well as wit and cheer, we thank him most warmly. And finally, we extend our gratitude to all the authors – architects, artists, critics, film-makers, historians, theorists and writers – for their contributions. Their often differing but always stimulating demonstrations of what critical architecture means to them work together here to indicate a challenging, engaging and expanded redefinition of the relationship between criticism and design in architectural practice.

Introduction

Critical architecture: between criticism and design

Jane Rendell

The chapters in *Critical Architecture* include papers presented at the 'Critical Architecture' conference held in November 2004 at The Bartlett School of Architecture, University College London. The conference was organised by Jane Rendell and Jonathan Hill of the Bartlett, and was held in association with AHRA (Architectural Humanities Research Association) represented by Murray Fraser of the University of Westminster and Mark Dorrian of the University of Edinburgh.

From the early stages of developing the conference to the numerous letters written in response, it became clear to us as organisers that the papers presented at the 'Critical Architecture' conference had challenged a view closely held by the architectural community in the United Kingdom and elsewhere, that the terms 'design' and 'criticism' should be divided – design should take place through the production of buildings, while criticism should be performed by critics who 'judge' buildings by writing essays. 'Critical Architecture' questioned this assumed division between design and criticism and proposed instead that, as forms of architectural critical practice operating within an interdisciplinary context, their relationship could be rethought. So what I would like to do here briefly, for purposes of clarification, is to define how I understand the terms 'interdisciplinary' and 'critical architecture' to operate within the context of this debate.

Given the recent appropriation of the term 'interdisciplinarity' in much of the literature concerning research in academe and higher education, where the word is now used in place of multidisciplinarity, it seems important to briefly outline how an interdisciplinary approach can be distinguished from a multidisciplinary one. Long before its adoption and redefinition as part of recent research assessment and funding council terminology in the United Kingdom, the term 'interdisciplinary' had been theorised and practised in critical discourse.[1] As a term associated with a desire to produce political critique, interdisciplinary research calls into question the ideological apparatus that structures the terms and methods of specific disciplinary practices.[2] The writings of Julia Kristeva and Homi K. Bhabha among many others make this point clear.[3] The aim of such work is to question dominant processes that seek to control intellectual and creative production, and instead generate new resistant forms and modes of knowledge and understanding. It seems to me that the need for interdisciplinary research, as I have defined it, is crucial. It does not, I argue, reflect a desire to work to existing standards, rather it is the kind of transformative activity that intellectual and creative life requires to critique and question such 'norms'.

Architecture is a subject that includes history, theory, criticism and design as well as urban, technological, social and professional studies. As such, architecture embraces knowledge, understanding and modes of operation particular to a number of disciplines ranging from the sciences through to the arts and humanities. It is possible to identify architectural design as a specific discipline within the subject of architecture. Defined in this way, architecture can be described as a multidisciplinary subject. However, it is also possible for those various disciplinary approaches brought together – or which have yet to be brought together – within architecture to exert critical pressure on one another; I would describe the moments, projects and practices where this occurs as interdisciplinary. In situations when researchers from architecture work with those from other subjects to form multidisciplinary research teams, it is only when this research aims to critique the modes of operation of those disciplines involved that it should be described as 'interdisciplinary'. So architecture is a multidisciplinary subject, which can operate in an interdisciplinary way.[4]

What of the term 'critical architecture'? In 2003, when Jonathan Hill and I first talked about our ambitions for the conference, we both wished to hold an event that would stimulate a discussion concerning the relationship between criticism and design in architecture and related disciplines. The term 'critical architecture' emerged as a short-hand for critical architectural practice and as a simple way of marking a place between criticism and design in architecture. In tracking back through the key turns in the debate around the critical and post-critical in architecture, starting out with 'Critical Architecture: Between Culture and Form' (1984) by K. Michael Hays,[5] it became apparent that this had been, to date, a conversation dominated in the most part by voices from the United States. Through its substantial publishing industry, the United States has been able to export ideas globally, but it has perhaps been less than efficient in importing relevant work from elsewhere. For us, the conference marked a desire to discover an understanding of the critical and post-critical in architecture informed by the work of theorists and practitioners from around the world.

It is worth briefly noting the main aspects of the post-critical debate so far, and how they relate to *Critical Architecture* here, as framed in this book. In his paper, Hays argues that critical architecture is possible and operates between two poles, resisting cultural determinism on the one hand and recognising that autonomy is required for engagement on the other; the work of Mies van der Rohe is cited as an example. Many of the chapters in this volume also explore critical architecture as a form of design practice, which occupies the territory between form and culture, and others agree with Hays' aspiration, stated at the end of his paper, that both architectural design and architectural criticism should be critical: 'If critical architectural design is resistant and oppositional, then architectural criticism – as activity and knowledge – should be openly critical as well.'[6]

If we turn now and look at the post-critical position, it is around Robert Somol and Sarah Whiting's paper, 'Notes around the Doppler Effect and Other Moods of Modernism',[7] that the debate revolves. Somol and Whiting advocate an architecture linked to 'the diagrammatic, the atmospheric and cool performance' as an alternative to the critical project which they describe as indexical, dialectical and as 'hot representation'.[8] Their approach is grounded in a rejection of a disciplinarity that is autonomous and a dialectic that is oppositional, as represented by the work of Hays and also Peter Eisenman. Given their lack of interest in social critique, it is easy to see why they reject Hays' dialectic of culture and form, but it seems strange that they are adverse to the work of Eisenman. Perhaps it is because, while Eisenman's focus on an autonomous aesthetics is close to the Somol and Whiting project, his interest in autonomy, defined in terms of disciplinary purity, does not fit comfortably with their aspirations for an architectural design that engages with other disciplines. While many of the contributors to *Critical Architecture* diverge in opinion from much of the Somol and Whiting rhetoric, they do not in general support Eisenman's position either. And some of the features attributed to a post-critical architecture by Somol and Whiting, namely that we should move from architecture as discipline to performance or practice, and regard the participation of users as integral to architectural production, echo in positions expressed in *Critical Architecture*. However, many authors published here, including this editor, contra Somol and Whiting, strongly believe that the social and the cultural are highly relevant aspects of architectural practice. Given the disastrous changes to the Earth's climate caused by carbon dioxide emissions, along with the intensification of imperialist aggression by oil-dependant nations as demand outstrips supply, it is not possible to go along with corporate capitalism in a pragmatic mode without critique – to do so would be to support without question the inequalities that are integral aspects of this economic system.

The special issue of *Perspecta* in which Somol and Whiting's paper was published also contained articles in support of the critical architecture project. Diane Ghirardo, for example, argued that as well as believing that architectural resistance to capitalism was impossible, architectural critic and historian Manfredo Tafuri had also noted that there was 'an architecture which attempted to redistribute the capitalist division of labour' and that this was evident in the work of Raymond Unwin, Ernst May and Hannes Meyer among others.[9] While, in an interview with the editors, Hays asserted that for him the term 'critical' derived from critical theory and could be summed up as 'the constant imagination, search for, and construction of alternatives', so claiming creativity and productivity for the critical and effectively neutralising the post-critical position.[10] A number of articles have been published subsequently, in the *Harvard Design Review* and elsewhere, that take up various positions around the post-critical, from those who are somewhat disbelieving of the post-critical, to those who support the call by a younger generation to engage with market forces and reject theory.[11]

Rather oddly, given the title of this *Perspecta* issue, *Mining Autonomy*, autonomy remains one of the least explored terms of the debate. And it is really here that any interrogation of the critical in architecture needs to begin. An understanding of autonomy in terms of disciplinarity alone certainly seems inadequate, whether this is desired, as the post-critics state of Hays and Eisenman, or rejected, as in the work of the post-critics themselves. The definition of so-called autonomous practice and its relation to the economy, to social and cultural relations, to aesthetics and to self-reflection needs further investigation. Chapters in *Critical Architecture* by Mark Dorrian, Andrew Benjamin, David Cunningham, Kim Dovey, Hilde Heynen, Charles Rice and Jianfei Zhu rise to this challenge and in different ways explore architecture's autonomy.

The relationship between criticism and design in terms of critical practice is another area of the debate developed here in ways that go beyond the terms of the North American discussion. If, following Raymond Geuss (in turn following Marx), critical theory can be defined in terms of self-reflectivity and the desire to change the world,[12] then when criticism and design take on the task of self-reflection and evidence a desire for social change both can be described as critical (as forms of critical practice here rather than critical theory). However, criticism has a specific purpose, which is to provide a commentary (a social and historical context, a judgement, an explanation, a discriminating point of view, a response, or even a point of departure) on a cultural work – art, literature, film or architecture. If criticism is defined by a demand to give an account of a work, to evaluate it, position it – culturally and critically – then does this stop criticism from being understood in terms of critical practice? I would argue that it does not, and that criticism, if it expresses the qualities of critical theory outlined above, can be understood as a particular form of critical practice, one which always has an 'other' in mind. However, it is precisely at this point that disagreement often ensues, with commentators refusing to see how criticism, since it does not usually produce 'buildings', can be thought of in terms of design, or how design, since it does not operate through 'writing', can be thought of as criticism – to think the two together is to make a muddle.[13] Instead I maintain that to think design and criticism together is productive, and demands that we call into question the definitions and assumptions that underpin both modes of activity.

Criticism is certainly an action; it is worth noting that the verb 'to criticise' is also associated with critique. While some have located critique as a sub-set of criticism – that critique is a social form of criticism – I would rather take the line of thinking adopted by David Cunningham in this volume, who notes that in Immanuel Kant's *Critique of Pure Reason* (1781) 'critique comes to denote a specific reflection on the essential *conditions* and *limits* of possible knowledge'. While Cunningham goes on to state that critique only becomes self-reflective in G.W.F. Hegel's reworking of Kant, Peg Rawes has argued that it is in Kant's *Critique of Judgement* (1790) that critique becomes embodied.[14] Taken together, these two viewpoints allow a concept of critique to emerge – self-reflective and embodied – that comes close to practice, so bridging the split between design as a material, subjective and embodied process, and criticism as an abstract, objective and distanced one.

Roland Barthes' reminder that 'to *criticize* means *to call into crisis*' is also helpful to remember.[15] The phrase places emphasis on a particularity of criticising that can be shared by both criticism and design. And, in discussing the relationship between literature and literary criticism, Jacques Derrida has argued for the possibility of a lack of distinction between the two:

> These new distinctions [between literature and literary criticism] ought to give up on the purity and linearity of frontiers. They should have a form that is both rigorous and capable of taking account of the essential possibility of contamination between all these oppositions [...].
>
> (Jacques Derrida, *Acts of Literature,* edited by Derek Attridge, London: Routledge, 1992, p. 52)

I agree with Derrida's position, and suggest that we give up the frontier and cease drawing lines to separate design and criticism, that we look instead to sites of contamination – perhaps of interdisciplinarity – for these call into question existing definitions and demand instead new forms of critical and creative work.

Critical Architecture brings together a range of this new work, which taken as a whole demonstrates what happens when criticism and design are both understood as part of an interdisciplinary field of activity.[16] For the 'Critical Architecture' conference, each editor focused on a specific way of negotiating the relationship between criticism and design in architecture and we used these to generate the four themes, as follows: 'Criticism/Negation/Action' (Mark Dorrian), 'Architecture-Writing' (Jane Rendell), 'Criticism by Design' (Jonathan Hill) and 'The Cultural Context of Critical Architecture' (Murray Fraser). We have decided to use these four themes to structure this edited volume, using the form of a short editorial to introduce the contributions and main areas of concern within each section.

Mark Dorrian's interest in the intellectual developments that have taken place in critical theory over the last thirty years led him to ask how the idea of criticism in architecture should be understood today. In the first section, 'Criticism/ Negation/Action', chapters explore whether criticism still has pertinence or whether we have moved, as some have argued, into a 'post-critical' condition. Authors examine the limits of the so-called post-critical condition, the potential for new models of criticism, and the terms upon which contemporary criticism might be mounted. The first section investigates the adequacy of existing historical models and asks whether we need to imagine new kinds of reconfigured critical practices. The chapters put forward suggestions for what these new practices might be like and how they integrate with questions of action.

In the second section, 'Architecture-Writing', I explore new ways of writing architectural criticism. I take as my starting point discussions in art criticism concerning art writing and examine how these have opened up possibilities for new writing practises and for rethinking the relationship between criticism and critical practice in the visual and performing arts. This debate questions objectivity and judgement, and introduces instead considerations of subjectivity, positionality, textuality and materiality in criticism and writing. The contributors explore how the potential offered by this debate influences architectural criticism and, through theoretical essays, works and projects, speculate upon the relation of creative and critical practice in architecture-writing.

The history and status of the architect are interwoven with those of design, a term which comes from the Italian *disegno*, meaning drawing, suggesting both the drawing of lines on paper and the drawing forth of ideas. Jonathan Hill took this as the basis for the third section, 'Criticism by Design', asking his contributors to respond to the following series of questions: What is the relationship of designing to building? Is there a role for the design project that is critical but not intended to be built? Can a design, whether drawn or built, question existing conditions and propose alternatives? Is the dependence of designing on drawing positive? Are other means of design more effective in developing a critical architecture?

Finally, in the fourth section, 'The Cultural Context of Critical Architecture', Murray Fraser suggests that the term 'critical architecture' creates problems. Fraser states that critical architecture is usually understood to refer to a mode of architectural practice that opposes dominant economic and cultural strands, instead hinting at an alternative form of practice that does not reproduce prevailing values. Yet he wonders whether it would not be more useful to recognise a complex and negotiated concept of critical architecture that depends on cultural context. Contributors to the fourth section examine variations between rural, suburban and urban conditions within developed countries and how globalisation and cultural diversity influence critical discourse in architecture. In different ways, the chapters suggest, somewhat provocatively, that from a cultural perspective critical architecture is relative, a luxury enjoyed in Western countries, yet urgently needed elsewhere.

In sum, *Critical Architecture* is an attempt to examine the relationship between design and criticism by placing architecture in an interdisciplinary context and considering its various activities as forms of critical practice. The volume investigates the potential of this suggestion in different ways, exploring modes of critical practice that operate in architecture through buildings, drawings, texts and actions, and bringing together not just the 'stars' of architecture, but a more diverse mix of voices, from established academics and practitioners to those currently engaged in doctoral research or setting out in art and architectural practice for the first time. The contributors come from theory and practice, from inside and outside architecture, and each one addresses the term 'critical architecture' according to their own particular position, negotiating the relation between criticism and design in ways that vary according to specific research interests and modes of working.

As the proceedings of a conference that was organised into four strands, it is of course possible to read the book in sections, but one can also look out for the themes that work across these. The discussion of autonomy has already been noted and takes place over a number of sections in *Critical Architecture*, while Walter Benjamin's writings on the experience of architecture as distraction – a potentially useful way for rethinking the role of the critical in architecture – are discussed by both Katja Grillner and Charles Rice. Artist Sharon Kivland and architectural theorist Stephen Cairns engage with a particular tense that they associate with the critical – the future anterior – what will have been, while Penelope Haralambidou and I, for example, explore the role of the enigma through allegory and psychoanalysis focusing on the production of spatial and material configurations that blend writing and drawing, criticism and design.

I feel the publication of this co-edited volume is timely for a number of reasons. First, in terms of the emerging interest in design as a form of so-called practice-based and/or practice-led research, *Critical Architecture* makes clear that design is a mode of enquiry that is capable of generating new ways of knowing and understanding the world through creative processes and the production of artefacts, but also that designers are able to offer critiques of their own mode of practice, both self-reflective and politicised. Second, and in relation to contemporary discussions concerning criticism as a form of practice, it is important to note that criticism, although it usually works through the medium of writing, can, as demonstrated here, operate through other media, and although it always has an 'other' in mind, criticism can be understood as a mode of critical practice in its own right. Finally, with respect to the current debate concerning 'post-criticism', I strongly argue for the possibility of criticism and design as vital forms of intellectual and creative labour, which aim to lay bare social, cultural and ethical concerns at the heart of contemporary aesthetic and spatial practice and experience today. In a world that currently remains in the grips of an unjust corporate and imperialistic capitalism, critical architecture is urgently required.

Notes

1 I would like to refute the position put forward by Peter Carl that 'The term "interdisciplinary" comes from trying to find respect in research-driven universities [...]'. See Peter Carl, 'Practical Wisdom and Disciplinary Knowledge', *Architecture Research Quarterly*, 9, 1, 2005, pp. 5–8, p. 5.

2 This is a response to Felipe Hernández's provocation that 'interdisciplinary research' might only be 'the reserve of the wealthier schools of architecture in larger urban centres'. See Felipe Hernández, 'The Scope of Critical Architecture', *Architecture Research Quarterly*, 9, 1, 2005, pp. 8–9, p. 9. I argue that since the practice of interdisciplinary activity is a political necessity not a material luxury, it does not make sense to align interdisciplinary research with affluence; rather, it should be understood to emerge from the desire for political critique.

3 See for example Julia Kristeva, 'Institutional Interdisciplinarity in Theory and Practice: An Interview', Alex Coles and Alexia Defert (eds), *The Anxiety of Interdisciplinarity, De-, Dis-, Ex*, v. 2, London: Black Dog Publishing, 1997, pp. 3–21. Homi K. Bhabha has described the moment of encounter between disciplines as an 'ambivalent movement between pedagogical and performative address'. See Homi K. Bhabha, *The Location of Culture*, London: Routledge, 1994, p. 163.

4 For a longer discussion of this argument, see Jane Rendell, 'Architectural Research and Disciplinarity', *Architecture Research Quarterly*, 8, 2, 2004, pp. 141–7.

5 K. Michael Hays, 'Critical Architecture: Between Culture and Form', *Perspecta*, 21, 1981, pp. 14–29.

6 Hays, 'Critical Architecture: Between Culture and Form', p. 27.

7 Robert Somol and Sarah Whiting, 'Notes Around the Doppler Effect and Other Moods

of Modernism', in Michael Osman, Adam Ruedig, Matthew Seidel and Lisa Tilney (eds), *Mining Autonomy,* a special issue of *Perspecta*, 33, 2002, pp. 72–7.

8   Somol and Whiting, 'Notes Around the Doppler Effect', p. 74.

9   Diane Y. Ghirardo, 'Manfedo Tafuri and Architectural Theory in the U.S., 1970–2000', in Michael Osman, Adam Ruedig, Matthew Seidel and Lisa Tilney (eds), *Mining Autonomy,* a special issue of *Perspecta*, 33, 2002, pp. 38–47, p. 40.

10   K. Michael Hays, Lauren Kogod and the Editors, 'Twenty Projects at the Boundaries of the Architectural Discipline Examined in Relation to the Historical and Contemporary Debates over Autonomy', in Michael Osman, Adam Ruedig, Matthew Seidel and Lisa Tilney (eds), *Mining Autonomy,* a special issue of *Perspecta*, 33, 2002, pp. 54–71, p. 58.

11   For a discussion that examines the relationship between critical and post-critical in terms of an intellectual genealogy, see George Baird, ' "Criticality" and its Discontents', *Harvard Design Magazine*, 21, Fall 2004/Winter 2005. For a paper that rejects the post-critical position, see Reinhold Martin, 'Critical of What? Toward a Utopian Realism', *Harvard Design Magazine*, 22, Spring/Summer 2005, pp. 104–9; and for one which supports it, see for example, Michael Speaks, *Architectural Record*, June 2005, pp. 73–5.

12   Raymond Geuss, *The Idea of Critical Theory: Habermas and the Frankfurt School,* Cambridge: Cambridge University Press, 1981, p. 2.

13   See Brian Hatton's review of 'Critical Architecture', *Architecture Research Quarterly*, 8, 4, 2004, pp. 105–8, where he argues against the bringing together of criticism and design.

14   See Peg Rawes, 'Critical Practice', *Architecture Research Quarterly,* 9, 1, 2005, pp. 9–10, and David Leatherbarrow's wonderfully rich discussion of conviction and critique, *Architecture Research Quarterly,* 8, 3/4, 2004, pp. 199–202.

15   Roland Barthes, 'Writers, Intellectuals, Teachers', [1971] in *A Roland Barthes Reader,* edited with an introduction by Susan Sontag, London: Vintage, 1982, pp. 378–403, p. 379.

16   Elsewhere I have termed such work 'critical spatial practice', see Jane Rendell, *Art and Architecture: a Place Between*, London. I.B. Tauris, 2006. See also Jane Rendell (ed.), *Critical Architecture*, a special issue of *The Journal of Architecture*, 10, 3, June 2005.

Criticism/Negation/
Action

Introduction

Criticism/Negation/Action

Mark Dorrian

The eight chapters that comprise this section are connected by an interest in the conditions of criticism in architecture and their relation to questions of action (or 'practice', or 'operativity'). The sequence in which the chapters are presented is intended to draw out the thematic linkages between them while, at the same time, highlighting the differences and tensions in the ways they deal with their material. And, although the thematic series arcs, broadly, from the legacy of Manfredo Tafuri, to the issue of autonomy, to considerations of activism, to the productivity of the gap between critical writing and architectural practice, this is only to scratch the surface: much else – as will be seen – is covered along the way.

The first three chapters in the section all engage with Manfredo Tafuri, and seek – albeit in different ways – to recover something of the value of the operative, of architectural practice, out of his work.

Andrew Leach's chapter examines the complex tension between operativity and criticality in Tafuri's writing. Recounting his analysis of the emergence of architecture's constitutive institutional conditions within the specific historio-cultural context of early Renaissance Tuscany, Leach describes how, for Tafuri, architectural theory arose at the outset as an intellectual, future-oriented activity legitimated through an appeal to an idealised (Roman) past that was pressed into service on behalf of the demands of the present. For the critical historian, the 'problem of history' that theory presents is how to counter history's ideological deployment and return to it its complex heterogeneity. Interestingly Leach shows how this will be as much a matter of form for Tafuri as it is of content, describing his experiments with the presentation of historical materials in ways (reminiscent of Walter Benjamin's notion of constellations) that avoided the positive and monological implications of narrative. Yet, at the same time, the dilemmas are apparent. At what point can the 'historical knowledge' that is returned to the present be said to begin, and how does the effort to maintain 'knowledge of the past on its own terms' meet with an avowed epistemological weakness (the contingent, approximate nature of all historical representations), this weakness itself being both an assertion of the independence of the past and a deflationary, prophylactic strategy against the operative?

The status and character of Tafuri's 'historical project' also preoccupies Teresa Stoppani, who considers his reference to ideologies as 'delirious representations' that historical analysis must unpick. Connecting her discussion to Rem Koolhaas' famous use of the term in his book, *Delirious New York*, she argues for a rethinking of delirium that would allow it to be conceptually reinserted and activated in a kind of reversed way within the open field of the historical project, a possibility she sees presaged in the work of certain women architectural theorists in the 1980s and 1990s, such as Diana Agrest, Jennifer Bloomer and Catherine Ingraham.

The third chapter that directly addresses Tafuri's legacy is David Cunningham's. Although broadly in agreement with Tafuri's diagnosis of the fate of contemporary architecture within capitalist modernity, he sees – even on the radically restricted terms available to it – a critical possibility that the totalising character of Tafuri's formulation tends to occlude. This would be the articulation and expression, within an architectural project, of the socio-economic and political contradictions that structure in advance the conditions of its own production. He argues that something like this is achieved in OMA's recent McCormick Tribune Campus Center at IIT in Chicago.

Cunningham's argument locates 'a certain autonomy' – a point of distantiation from the distortions of capitalist modernity – as the condition of possibility of critique. Autonomy is also a key issue in Andrew Benjamin's chapter, where it is mobilised in defence of a proper concern with form that is not formalism, but rather is the site of a critical transformation of architecture that emerges out of the terms of its own tradition. Benjamin begins by arguing that two orientations emerged out of the interaction between architecture and deconstructive philosophy. The first – exemplified by Frank Gehry's Bilbao Guggenheim – he characterises as an a-symbolic heightening of aesthetic content as a response to a contemporary absence of affect, a gesture that disengages affect from function and privileges appearance over programme. The second he discusses via Peter Eisenman's reading of Terragni's architecture, which – he argues – activates criticality by 'the twofold move of recovery and working through'. This institutionally destabilising production of alterity in repetition is conditional upon an already-constituted 'internality' – that is, autonomy – of architecture.

Beginning her chapter with a description of critical theory as a questioning of the way in which forms of social domination attain legitimacy, Hilde Heynen goes on to claim that much of the modern movement can be seen as 'an embodiment of the idea of critical architecture'. While acknowledging the necessity of an 'autonomous moment', at the same time she argues for the importance of maintaining the modern movement's commitment to architecture as a positive instrument of social change (against those, therefore, who suspect this commitment of being historically grounded upon a coercive social metanarrative and an authoritarian epistemology). Unlike Andrew Benjamin, Heynen reads the notion of criticality in Eisenman's work as having a primarily aesthetic – rather than cognitive/social – character. Glossing the recent 'post-critical' debate in the US, she argues that – despite its relation to popular cultural forms – it reproduces the terms of an elitist heroic modernism as opposed to a transgressive avant-garde (whose ideals she wishes to support) dedicated to 'overthrowing

the separation between art and the everyday'. In conclusion she defends the importance of utopian thinking as a liberative, critical and future-oriented social imaginary.

Daniel Barber's chapter analyses the 'post-critical' discourse as it has
developed in the US, focusing on its invocation of the work of Gilles Deleuze and Félix
Guattari. Barber argues that limitations in the post-critical theorists' reception and
mobilisation of this has resulted, not in the radical puncturing of architecture's disciplinarity at which it seems to aim, but in the solidification of a new disciplinary paradigm
concretised around a 'slightly expanded concept of design'. Against this, Barber argues
for what he describes – drawing the term from Antonio Negri – as a 'militant' architecture. This, which he sees as emerging in relation to a 'critical environmentalism', would
be insistent upon the transversal dissolution of disciplinary autonomy (significantly,
autonomy here is formulated not as a precondition of criticality, but rather as an obstacle to it) and strategically capable of grasping political possibilities within the complex
singularity of specific situations. The activist dimensions of Barber's argument are
clear, and he cites Paul Patton on 'the permanent possibility for piecemeal social
change'. This allows a useful vantage point from which to register the tension
between this argument and one such as that presented earlier by Cunningham who
discounts '*direct* or *immediate* political practice' in architecture as fantasmic: 'the
romantic revival of "hopes in design" recently resurrected...by a certain Deleuzianism.' There are a number of questions to be debated here, the first clearly being consequences of the transformation of the 'hopes in design' – as ironised by Tafuri – into
the hopes beyond design towards which Barber's a-disciplinary militant architecture
is directed.

Activism is a central concern in the chapter by Maria Theodorou, who
relates it 'to the desire and demand for change [that] seizes every opportunity available
to achieve its aim'. In her role as Head of the Architecture Network in Greece and
advisor on architecture for the 2001–2004 Cultural Olympiad, she facilitated a series of
urban events that took place in Athens. Her chapter reflects upon two of these. The
events were calculated to intervene in a very specific urban, cultural and political situation that she describes by analysing the Athenian citizens' relation to their city, as historically constructed and then transformed through a specific political and material
history (of immigration, of physical urban construction, of Church/State politics, of
national identity).

Finally, Naomi Stead's chapter considers and defends the role of the architectural critic, whose distinctive agency was – she suggests – collapsed by being
absorbed into architectural practice's 'theoretical turn' from the late 1970s. Taking one
of her own earlier essays – published in *Architecture Australia* – as a case study, Stead
reflects on responses to it, concluding that her respondents' perception of a 'crisis' in
Australian architectural criticism was less the registration of a malaise than a sympto-
matic response to the critic's work of interpretation: the inevitable – and productive –
non-identity of her discourse with its object.

Criticality and Operativity

Andrew Leach

Today's debate on the critical dimensions of architecture tends to advance one of two basic claims: that all practices in architectural culture either can be or are critical; or that we have entered a moment spurning critical theory's explicit contribution to architectural knowledge. This tendency is informed by critical theory itself, yet dubbed the 'post-critical' in order to make clear its claim to return the architectural work to centre-stage as the object of theory.[1] With this largely intergenerational, principally North American 'conversation', Manfredo Tafuri (1935–4) has returned to the discursive centre with renewed importance. Conducted over three decades, his relentless interrogation of the departments of architectural culture comprises one of the most sustained investigations ever of the 'problems' facing architecture's institutional composition. These problems have returned to the forefront as *Grey Room* confronts its *Assemblage* parents and *Oppositions* grandparents, as academics trade blows across generations in the pages of *Harvard Design Magazine* and *Perspecta*, and as a 'new pragmatics' publicly refines the terms of an architectural theory for architecture's sake. Although Tafuri's writing potentially thwarts a wide readership with its cloying Marxism, his earliest international audiences grasped with both hands the possibilities offered by his work to the architectural theory genre emerging in the 1960s. His thoughts on criticism, theory, history, and research are embedded in our current conceptualisation of architectural culture and the specific fields with which his work is preoccupied.

Tafuri's fourth monograph, *Teorie e storia dell'architettura* (1968), considers a range of architecture's historical intellectual relationships with knowledge of the past and the bearing of those dealings upon architecture's capacity to be critical in and of itself.[2] The book locates architecture's institutional foundations in post-feudal Tuscany, a setting fostering the intellectualisation of architectural practice and its historical bases. It argues that the workings of architectural theory – intellectual dimensions now inextricable from architecture as a practice of building and engineering – or architectural ideology, to invoke his closely related history *L'architettura dell'umanesimo* (1969), engender an operational distinction between architecture and its various contexts.[3] In this time and place, and from this moment onwards, architecture and its intellectuals make a heavy investment in the past as a source of values, not to mention as a repository of formal and architectonic precedent. He suggests, for instance, that, in Florence, the new city-state sought to overcome the immediate past; an idealised Roman antiquity offered a cultural standard for the Medici and their artists. At this moment, architecture negates the field in which it exists, defining that field as irrelevant or surpassable. No longer part of the medieval city, it projects the values of a non-existent past, relying upon the intellectual differentiation of architecture from that which is not architecture.

From this differentiation, which defers to homogenous ideal images of past life, emerges the architectural theory treatise as a projective intellectual pursuit that delineates and defends, from moment to moment, the boundaries of architecture's art and 'technique'. Defined thus, architectural theory's inherent forward focus, dependent upon a structural ideological rapport between future and past, introduces history to architectural culture as a 'problem'. For Tafuri, this problem is the proper domain of the architectural historian, whose concern is the relationship between past and present, and by implication the past's availability as representation, in the present, to architects and thus to the future.

To rephrase this thought in more explicitly temporal terms: the practice of architecture concerns not the perpetual present, but projection from that present into a future of the architect's making. The intellectual dimensions of this relationship between present and future, traceable in architectural practice, constantly test and redefine architecture as an art. Tafuri identifies that architecture is practised in the mode of the 'project', corresponding to the intellectualised future that conceives at once a world to come and the place of architecture-as-art therein. In other words, architectural practice occupies the theoretical space between the present, in which a future is conceived, and the future itself. The passage of time monitors the closure of the intermediary period between present and future, through which the projective future becomes present. However, this intermission allows the introduction of a host of complications. Abstract or practical, they transform the project's intellectual purity into a realised, but compromised, work of architecture.

Depending on the intellectualisation, in turn, of the 'realised work', the project's limitations are manifold and include building regulations, communication technology, media, representability, public exposure, client pressures, and institutional vicissitudes. Many argue that these constraints finesse the 'original' scheme. Nonetheless, what we might term as 'realised' corresponds to Boris Groys's notion of the project's documentation. In *The Loneliness of the Project* (2002), the document appears as that which gives insight into the project, which (as for Tafuri) is an idealised intellectual construction occupying a realm between present and future. The documentation is a trace, close or distant, of the project's intentions, but is compromised and ultimately distinct from the project itself. Groys suggests that the deformations the project sustains through its encounter with reality correspond to the confrontation of a utopian agenda with its present, to a 'traumatic' instant in which the distance between present and any conceivable future reduces to nought.[4]

We might understand Tafuri's apparent declaration of architecture's 'death' or its (or his) 'crisis' as an historical analysis of architecture's more recent denial of this intellectual mechanism. It appears in the modern movement. We find it also, he asserts, in the Renaissance. Yet what Leon Battista Alberti, Filippo Brunelleschi, and others consciously offered architecture-as-art, the modern movement suppressed.

Tafuri famously accuses the modern movement's historians (Sigfried Giedion, Nikolaus Pevsner, Bruno Zevi, Paolo Portoghesi) of maintaining too heavy an investment in architecture's future, describing them as 'instrumental historians' practising 'operative criticism'. They operate under the guise of historians while using the historian's media to extend their architectural practice. Like the architects proper of the modern movement, they anticipate utopia and actively pursue it into the future. One of Tafuri's points of argument, curiously, relates to the propriety of the media used by architects and historians respectively. His operatives do not design buildings or plan cities, but they legitimate – on false authority – those visions with which they concur by demonstrating their fulfilment of an historical trajectory. Tafuri holds that this sends a misleading signal to readers of Giedion or Portoghesi. Operative historiography, in one sense, is close to its earlier manifestation in architectural culture: negating that which falls outside the remit of architectural theory and empowering works and figures that are exemplary of that which architecture's intellectuals agree architecture to be. Rather than comprise a critical dimension in architectural culture, through which architecture takes part in a dialectical exchange with its various contexts, Tafuri observes that architectural culture had come merely to simulate a critical response to its surroundings, which it denies. Instead of provoking architecture's intellectual agents into a critical discourse, historians were compounding the problem. For Tafuri, this requires a new critical action against architectural theory, through which the instrumental historiography shaped by the intellectualisation of architecture would sustain the scrutiny of an audit, holding it accountable to the world beyond its present, and the past beyond its introspective historiography. This demands, it follows, a new kind of historian who would introduce the unmediated, heterogeneous historical knowledge that undermines the ideological, homogeneous histories authorising and legitimating architectural projection.

In *Teorie e storia*, Tafuri charts out the tradition of operative criticism from Bellori's *Vite* (1672) to Zevi and Portoghesi's *Michelangelo* (1964).[5] His course is somewhat naïve and, in terms of his audience and institutional objectives, instrumental in and of itself. Setting this aside, the basis of his criticism is simple: these historians offer a problematic inheritance to the present by using the historian's media – books, articles, lectures – to practise in a projective mode. Giedion's *Space, Time and Architecture* (1941) is unarguably a work of history.[6] However, it is produced within the theoretical borders of 'architectural knowledge' and defers unequivocally to the limits established by modernist architectural theory. For Tafuri, someone who looks like a historian would treat architectural theory as a target, would work to undermine the past's easy availability to the programmatic dimensions of architectural practice. Instrumental critics, conversely, reassuringly position the past as a long preface to the present, a path that reaches through the present and into the future; all the while, the values of both this past and future are shaped by the present. Conducting an architectural practice in a temporal sense, they represent the past in the present in order to project a future of their own making, which they vigorously seek to fulfil. Zevi and Portoghesi's vociferous defence of modern expressionism and its historical deference to mannerism and the baroque thus equally constitutes a project: in bringing the past into the present, they demand something of the future. Tafuri's implicit argument is that, while these are examples of historiography, they should not be. His point is that the new role required of the historian in architectural culture is to undermine this relationship with the future, to act against the architectural project.

Tafuri's 'La critica operativa' does not denounce architectural culture's tendency towards operativity in blanket terms. He advances several examples that demonstrate a 'proper' mode of operative practice, forms of analysis that do not purport, either through their content or media, to justify on historical bases the directions of architectural practice, but which nonetheless take a nuanced stance towards history as a dimension of the present.[7] In written form, he allows those types that have a blatantly instrumental mode: treatise, open debate, manifesto. However, he suggests that an instrumental depiction of architectural history might be better served by visual contextual analyses of the present. This requires a distinction between history as representation of the past and history as the past's endurance in the present. The latter would be the proper domain for this latter visual practice.

The translation of architectural photography from documentation (albeit loaded) to critical description through the editorial and architectural production of the Archigram collective (1961–74) and the journal *Carré bleu* (from 1958) offer analytical strategies that directly inform the future without suggesting a causal relationship between past and future — although he admits that neither example extends the principle as far as he can envisage.[8] Likewise, the typological approach to historical urban contexts found in the practices of Vittorio Gregotti, Carlo Aymonino, Alison and Peter Smithson, or in the methodology of the 'Buchanan Report' (1963), treats history as one element of a complex, heterogeneous present field, part of a complicated zero-degree upon which the architectural project builds.[9] He calls this 'typological criticism' insofar as these architects regard history as available through a taxonomy of types that explicitly relates to the world of history's reception rather than its production. It practises a criticism of the present, finding its justification of the project explicitly in the present (of which history is a part) rather than in a distorted account of the past.[10] Such practices would make no claim of an inoperative knowledge of the past, but their criticism of history, as manifest in the project, treats history as received in the present, not produced for their own ends.

Tafuri indicates, in other words, the possibility of an architectural appreciation of history that accepts the function of historiography to represent. It agrees that history is not the same thing as the past and that the historian's writing is only at best an approximation. (This latter point is at the heart of Tafuri's admiration of Carlo Scarpa, whose acceptance of the heterogeneity of the accumulation of pasts manifest in the present corresponds to Tafuri's own, even if he makes different 'uses' of that knowledge.)[11]

Instrumental history appears to offer an historically grounded logic to the direction taken by the present and immediate future of architecture. To that extent, it claims that history is the same thing as the past; from a history that offers a true account of the past, the present can draw its lessons. Tafuri demonstrates that, within architectural culture, one can either stand in the present looking back while looking forwards (the operative) or, from the present, look back in order to communicate the past to the present (the critic). While the former practice judges the present, the latter seeks to maintain knowledge of the past in its own terms, without forcing its actuality. What Tafuri and others call, in the preface to *La città americana* (1973), a 'critico-historical practice' regards the distant past as analysable in the present while forcing neither 'resolution' nor reconciliation with the present.[12] Simultaneously confronting the values of both past and present, this practice searches out – refining its tools constantly in relation to its materials – a mode of representation that renders these values and the values of historiography transparent. Its target is the ideological insularity propagated by testing architectural knowledge solely against architectural theory.

The obstacle that Tafuri encounters, though, is that this figure of the historian does not really exist except as a replica of Tafuri himself, an institutionalisation of all his biographical and contextual specificities. His Venetian Istituto di storia dell'architettura did not, therefore, send armies of these historians into architectural culture, even if it educated architects who understood history in a more nuanced way than their counterparts elsewhere. In order to take theory (understood as any form of intellectual or ideological insularity) as a target, the historian must be outside the bounds of architectural theory, beyond architecture's internally devised value system. Yet they must know (technically, methodologically) as much as the architect in order to engage the architect in a dialectical exchange. The students of Tafuri's 'Storia dell'architettura 2a' seminar would graduate as architects, as he had done, and not as historians with a specialised architectural knowledge (even if some went on to become historians, like Tafuri). We might suppose that Tafuri hoped that the position of his Istituto in the broader structure of the Istituto universitario di architettura di Venezia would simulate his disciplinary gamble: occupying a position within architectural culture but 'beyond' architectural ideology, even if not beyond, say, history's disciplinary ideologies.

In other words, we must accept Tafuri's case for the historian's new standing in architectural culture as an abstraction lacking a large number of obvious examples. What remains is a projective theory of the organisation of knowledge in architectural culture posing as a remedy. However, it remains a theory in the prescriptive sense: an image towards which Tafuri conscientiously worked in the confines of his immediate institutional and cultural settings. Even though Tafuri's historiography is thus highly operative relative to an internalised discussion in architectural history on its disciplinary limits, his instrumental reading of architectural culture as comprising operative and critical branches clearly lays out the function of different activities within architectural culture and both within and beyond architecture as a practice-cum-art defined intellectually.

Under these arrangements, historical research has an ethical dimension. In establishing the presentation of contemporary yet heterogeneous fields of evidence of the past in dialectical opposition to a homogeneous narration of that knowledge in order to make it useful for the present, Tafuri identifies the need for historians to undermine history's utility to architectural or theoretical problems in the present. His experimentation with the forms and structures of 'historical documentation' explains the tendency of his later histories away from narrative and towards the presentation of archives, documents, and artefacts. Perhaps logically, those books that fulfil this criterion most effectively have made the least impact on architectural thinking. Fewer architectural theoreticians deal with *Venezia e il rinascimento* (1985), *Storia dell'architettura italiana 1944–1985* (1986), or *Giulio Romano* (1989) than continue to engage Tafuri's more 'theoretical' histories, such as *Progetto e utopia*, *La città americana* (1973), or *Architettura contemporanea* (1976).[13] It makes sense that the more Tafuri refined his methodology of reporting historical research in a manner that undermined the utility of historical narrative, the less architectural discourse perceived his work as relevant to contemporary debate. This development is now simplistically, almost rhetorically, posited as Tafuri's withdrawal from the concerns of the present. The failure of his disciplinary theory to translate into a form of practice follows its failure to fully account for the complicated dualities that render many historiographical or architectural decisions at once critical and operative.

The case of Alberti, to take one instance, dogs him from *Teorie e storia dell'architettura* all the way to *Ricerca del rinascimento* (1992).[14] In the meantime, new Alberti scholarship had thoroughly undermined the simplistic image that Tafuri himself portrays in *L'architettura dell'umanesimo*, following Burckhardt, of an ideologue whose mental acuity enabled him to perform the intellectual moves assuring architecture's artistic autonomy. This move was substantially undermined by Franco Borsi's presentation of the Albertian *oeuvre* (1973). Tafuri registers his surprise at Borsi's Alberti in 'Discordant Harmony' (1979) by acknowledging the complexities and complicity of Alberti's 'ideology', which he then constructs as an ironic subscription to the artistic ideals of the city-state rather than as a wholehearted belief in humanist man.[15]

The struggle in Alberti between ideology's maintenance and its deconstruction, or (more architecturally) in Giovanni Battista Piranesi between the image and its disturbance, corresponds to the dialectics that Tafuri posits as a basic condition of historical research: evidence versus narrative, past versus history. How, his final monograph asks, can we practise history without exposing it to all the 'risks' bound up in its reception? Is there not a fundamentally disciplinary question that pertains to research itself rather than to its presentation or take-up? Problematising historical research and its publication within the field of architectural culture returns us to the distinction between operative and critical practices. Intention has little to do with the way that an architectural audience consumes, if at all, the research presented to a public. However, Tafuri implies that the historian can go some way towards assuring the reader that historical knowledge is ultimately un-useful in the present. It does not solve problems, and does not point the way forwards. Hence, the question of ethics: Tafuri assumed that, for the historian, operativity is ultimately misleading. Yet how far can one concerned with criticality, and with a critical project, 'return' knowledge to the present without rendering it operant in terms justified by history? The ongoing exchange between Tafuri's writings and seminars that explicitly raise the problem of historiography and those of his writings and lectures that document his historical research renders the irresolution of this particular ethical dilemma plainly evident.

These issues resonate with the present conceptual mobility of criticism. To what extent does present theorisation and reflection on criticism and criticality in contemporary architectural culture underpin criticism's emergent status as 'new theory', thus offering itself up as a new target to those who hold close to the Tafurian model of critico-historical practice, even if not its language or subject matter? What explains today's substantial interest in Tafuri's 'legacy'? The present emphasis placed on his attempt to found an autonomous history appears to support the transplantation of theory, as a written form of analysis, with critical (or theoretically astute) historiography. We might thus understand Tafuri's availability to architectural theory writing without searching his work for clues that will inform specific forms of architectural production. There are several cases where his 'ghost' conducts arguments at odds with his writing as read in the long-view. Such phenomena evidently belong to the notion of 'legacy', and require neither Tafuri's consent nor concurrence. However, as Mark Wigley has observed, learning from Tafuri involves undermining even the myths that gather around his name, in writing 'he no doubt would have hated', and challenging those turns in the organisation of architectural knowledge that his myth appears to endorse.[16] The result will seem foreign to the first generation of Tafuri's readers, as well as to those who have enlisted him towards ends played out in contemporary architectural theory. The clarity of the positions staked out in *Teorie e storia* has never been so diminished as in the present moment. What, today, are the function of critics and historians? What are the limits of operativity? These questions will endure the flak of post-criticality and return for as long as architecture is the subject of intellectual work and its practitioners look to the future.

Notes

1   See John Macarthur and Naomi Stead, 'The Judge is Not an Operator: Historiography, Criticality and Architectural Criticism', *Oase*, 69, 2006, pp. 116–39.

2   Manfredo Tafuri, *Teorie e storia dell'architettura*, Bari: Laterza, 1968, revised editions 1970, 1973, 1976, 1980.

3   Manfredo Tafuri, *L'architettura dell'umanesimo*, Bari: Laterza, 1969, especially 'Architettura e ideologia'. A better-known use of this term appears in 'Per una critica dell'ideologia architettonica', in *Contropiano*, 1, 1969, pp. 31–79.

4   Boris Groys, *The Loneliness of the Project*, Antwerp: MuHKA, 2002.

5   Giovani Pietro Bellori, *Le vite de' pittori, scultori et architetti moderni*, 1672, Bologna: Forni, 1977; Paulo Portoghesi and Bruno Zevi (eds), *Michelangelo architetto*, Turin: Einaudi, 1964.

6   Sigfried Giedion, *Space, Time and Architecture: the Growth of a New Tradition*, Cambridge: Harvard University Press, 1941.

7   See Monica Luca (ed.), *La critica operativa e l'architettura*, Milan: Unicopli, 2002, especially Daniel Sherer in 'Un colloquio "inquietante": Manfredo Tafuri e la critica operativa, 1968–1980', pp. 108–20.

8   Tafuri, *Teorie e storia*, pp. 188–90. He implicates his own experiments with critical photography and montage: Giorgio Picconato, Vieri Quilici, and Manfredo Tafuri, 'La città territorio: Verso una nuova dimensione', *Casabella-continuità* 270, 1962, pp. 16–25.

9   Colin Buchanan, 'Traffic in Towns', London: HMSO, 1963; Tafuri, *Teorie e storia*, p. 190.

10   Tafuri, *Teorie e storia*, pp. 190–6.

11   Manfredo Tafuri, *Storia dell'architettura italiana: 1944–1985*, Turin: Einaudi, 1986, especially chapter 6, 'Due "maestri": Carlo Scarpa e Giuseppe Samonà', pp. 139–43.

12   Giorgio Ciucci, Francesco Dal Co, Mario Manieri-Elia, and Manfredo Tafuri, *La città americana dalla guerra civile al New Deal*, Bari: Laterza, 1973, pp. v–xi.

13   Manfredo Tafuri, *Venezia e il rinascimento: Religione, scienza, architettura*, Turin: Einaudi, 1985; Manfredo Tafuri, Ernst Gombrich, *et al.*, *Giulio Romano: Architetto*, Milan: Electa, 1989; Tafuri, *Progetto e utopia: Architettura e sviluppo capitalistico*, Bari: Laterza, 1973; Manfredo Tafuri and Francesco Dal Co, *Architettura contemporanea*, Milan: Electa, 1976.

14   Manfredo Tafuri, *Ricerca del rinascimento: Principi, città, architettura*, Turin: Einaudi, 1992.

15   Franco Borsi, *Leon Battista Alberti: L'opera completa*, Milan: Electa, 1973; Manfredo Tafuri, 'Discordant Harmony from Alberti to Zuccari', *Architectural Design*, 49, 5/6, 1979, pp. 36–44.

16   Mark Wigley, 'Post-Operative History', *Architecture New York*, 25/26, 1999, p. 53.

Unfinished Business

The historical project after Manfredo Tafuri

Teresa Stoppani

> The historical project is an intermittent journey through a maze of entangled paths, one of the many possible 'provisional constructions' [...] The cards can be reshuffled and to them added many that were intentionally left out.
>
> (Manfredo Tafuri, 'Introduction: the Historical Project', in *The Sphere and the Labyrinth: Avant-Gardes and Architecture from Piranesi to the 1970s*, translated by Pellegrino d'Acierno and Robert Connolly, Cambridge, MA and London: MIT Press, 1990, pp. 1–21, p. 21)

The historical 'project'

From the late 1960s and through the 1970s, Manfredo Tafuri works towards the development of his 'historical project' through different strands of research. Tafuri's engagement with the present addresses contemporary architectural production – both theoretical and built – in its relationship with modernism and capitalism, challenging the distinction between an inside and an outside of architecture. There is no outside of architecture, affected as it is by the conditions of its production. Even the most exclusively theoretical and apparently self-referential forms of architectural criticism are not free of what Tafuri calls 'the multiple techniques of environmental formation'.[1]

The very notion of criticism is questioned in his work: the production of ideas in architecture – be it in the form of history or theory – is in itself a project, a form of making, rather than a discourse applied a posteriori to the architectural project.

In *Theories and History of Architecture* (1968),[2] the work of the architectural critic is sternly pictured as a walk on a tightrope. Later, as Tafuri unfolds his definition of the historical project, the construction reveals its discontinuous structure and uneven nature. The critic walks on the windswept tightrope on which s/he is asked to proceed through selections and exclusions, returns, simultaneity, lacunae and correspondences, and the line of investigation opens up to complications and multiplications of plural discourses – what Tafuri calls 'fasci' (bundles). Thus unfolded, the task of the historical project is to refrain from segmentation and from the instrumental definition of a definitive solution, a closed form – a history, a story. The project remains open, continuously re-engaging with the present.

Here I want to argue that Tafuri's historical project is more than just 'historical': if this history is inevitably a history of the present, history is embedded in the project. Still at work today, the historical project continues to offer rich possibilities for new lines of research, becoming not only a method for the production of histories, but also a generator of further projects – be they design, critical, or textual. In particular, I look here at the developments of some of Tafuri's key ideas in the corpus of discursive practices produced by the current generation of architectural feminist theorists, and focus in particular on the notions of 'delirium' and 'linearity' as they are explored, redefined and appropriated as tools for critical work in architecture.

Delirium

Historical work as defined by Tafuri is not a resolved, detached ex post-discourse on the past, but a soft shifting ground that interacts with the other forces at play, which are still active, or reactivated by the discourse itself. Implied with and inseparable from its materials, the historical work balances involvement and distance in a coexistence that is not a suspension – the impasse of architecture in the 1970s that Tafuri denounces – but the continuous re-engagement with the present.

At the same time, through the research he develops in New York at the Institute for Architecture and Urban Studies – a group with strong and significant links with the Institute of Architecture of the University of Venice, where Tafuri operates – Rem Koolhaas introduces the notion of delirium to architectural discourse. Delirium will remain active in it, and later voices in architecture – those I call here *mulieres delirantes* – will redefine and re-engage it in the historical project as a discourse of the present in architecture. Both delirium and the historical project inhabit the present and are implied in it. Both are at work together with their own materials, and constantly redefine themselves in their application to the specific. In this sense, they are projects.

In the 1970s, Koolhaas inaugurates his project on the contemporary city by focusing on Manhattan in his *Delirious New York* (1978).[3] The forces that produce Manhattan – unconsciously, claims Koolhaas – become the paradigm for the development of the contemporary metropolis, beyond and besides (and notwithstanding) modernism. It is these forces that Koolhaas calls upon to reactivate the production of an architecture capable of coping with the contemporary city. Koolhaas writes on Manhattan but produces his manifesto for the contemporary metropolis.

For Koolhaas, the true nature of Manhattan, beneath and within the orthogonality of its orderly grid, is delirious, that of 'an acutely disordered state of mind involving incoherent speech, hallucinations and frenzied excitement'.[4] Etymologically, the delirious is that which deviates from the straight(forward)ness of the *lira* (the ridge between furrows), the linearity of the modern *tabula rasa*, and its precepts of growth. In Koolhaas, the multiplicity of New York's 'blueprint' derails from the projected a priori straightness of the *lira* and can only be described and explained by an 'irrational activity'. Yet this derangement happens in keeping with the rules and regulations of the city's planned linearity. That is to say, the architectural delirium takes place within the control of – and it is indeed released by – the 'multiple techniques of environmental formation'[5] that are external to the architectural discourse. How much of this activity and its object, then, is really irrational? What is this delirium, and how does it operate on the city?

If we read delirium beyond its etymological sense of transgression from linearity, and consider it in Freudian terms as an intentional erasure and censorship, we can then argue that, in Koolhaas, this method becomes 'operative' in a Tafurian sense. Delirium here produces a closed project that remains active only if it is transferred (translated) from the written text to the practice of design. Only if the definition and modes of operations of delirium are opened, and delirium allows for a process of ongoing re-definition and adjustment of itself, is it then possible to return it to architectural discourse, while retaining its congenial interference, implication and imbalance with the architectural project.

Delirium in the historical project

For Sigmund Freud, 'Deliria are the work of censorship which no longer takes the trouble to conceal its operation; [...] it ruthlessly deletes whatever it disapproves of, so that what remains becomes quite disconnected.'[6] The ruthlessness and the determination of the delirium make it – already and intentionally – a project. At this point, it is Tafuri's explicit reference to Freudian delirious representations in his text on the historical 'project' that makes it possible to challenge delirium and incorporate it as an open instrument of analysis and reconstruction for the historical project.

Tafuri identifies 'ideologies as [socially produced] "delirious representations" [that] act as *dams* to restrain surging forces', and he places the task of historical analysis in 'the deconstruction of these *dams*'.[7] The role of the historical project is to go beyond a history as repression, and to refrain from segmentation and from the instrumental definition of a figure. Dams are deconstructed, and the historical project remains open. Here the delirious approach produces a 'determinate abstraction [that allows] to give a sense of direction to theoretical work',[8] but it constantly questions its limits, its relationship with its material and the nature and stability of the material itself; here analysis operates by erecting temporary and constantly re-definable barriers. The historical project moves forward by 'significant samplings' to seek solutions and modes for the present. In an attempt to avoid total erasures and maintain complexities, it absorbs and holds together differences: events are exposed and their 'fasci' ('groups' in the English translation, but more correctly 'bundles') are untangled, but links are never ignored, erased, severed.

Both delirium and the historical project retro-act on architecture and on the physical complexity of the city. But, while the delirium's erasures and superpositions imply its strategic and automatic translation into the practice of design, the tension between the historical project and the processes it investigates maintains the complexity of the relationships that concur in the production of architecture, developing an analysis capable of transforming itself and its own language together with the material it reactivates. Delirium, as a close and partial project, retro-acts on the city as an operative strategy that works by leaps and selective discontinuities, and translates itself into the necessary partiality of the architectural project. Nothing is more rational, intentional, controlled, structured than this form of delirium – in architecture.

The historical project, instead, remains an open system that operates by endless possible returns, by proximity and continuity (including filiation), to trigger a process of investigation that may or may not approach design. What is then, or what can be, the connection between the historical project and the design project, if Tafuri's intentions are clearly those of a re-engagement of architecture? The historical project defined by Tafuri addresses the impasse of architecture as a discipline through the 1960s and 1970s, and becomes not only a method for the production of histories, but also a generator of endless analysis and further projects (design, critical, textual).

The historical project is more then just 'historical': if its history is inevitably a history of the present, it is embedded in the project. And if we argue that architecture is that which occupies the space of the difference between delirium and historical project, delirium needs to be redefined once again. Then it is important to consider what delirium – a redefined delirium – and the historical project have in common, or – rather – what allows us to reconsider them jointly in their attempt to instigate non-modernist histories.

The *mulieres delirantes*

Is it possible to redefine delirium and incorporate it in the historical project, as a historical work in and of architecture, which becomes a proposition? A delirium that defies linearity but also – and mainly – uses erasure to unveil (possibilities) rather than delete, to accumulate complexities and re-value and dwell in the detail. This delirium is not that of the erasure but that of the erased, an open project rather than a closed, operative, sedated one: delirium not as deviation, or transgression, or censorship, but as placement of a re-examined past within the present. Voices of the delirium thus redefined as an open project can be found in what I would call – for the purpose of this argument – the work of the *mulieres delirantes*, that is, the corpus of discursive practices (and projects) produced in the 1980s and 1990s by women architectural theorists.

In an indirect but very relevant process of filiation from Tafuri's work, it is possible to see how delirium and its erasures can be reversed into a process of inclusion and continuation. The erasures of delirium and official history are thus never total and absolute, they always leave traces, marks, unsolved knots buried within. And it is the project of the new historical work to operate as a Tafurian 'litmus paper', to reveal, expose and reactivate these partially buried traces. In 'Architecture from Without: Body, Logic and Sex' (1971–87) Diana Agrest writes:

> The *refoules* [repressed] of architecture, the public, the negation all become
> the material of my fictional configuration. The (project) marks I make are
> organized through a contradiction – a negation through an affirmation. [...] It
> is the affirmation of the erasure of the city in order to reinstate its trace.
>
> (Diana Agrest, *Architecture from Without: Theoretical Framings for a*
> *Critical Practice*, Cambridge, MA: MIT Press, 1991, p. 193)[9]

Agrest's work moves within the discipline of architecture, from a 'without' that is
internal to it, but has long been silenced by the official histories and workings of architecture. 'Without' is not external by definition, but it is that which has been pushed
out, excluded; not outside, it does not 'take side out', but is forced into that position by
official erasures. For Agrest, instead, erasure becomes the recuperation of the erased:
nothing is dismissed. And yet Agrest's theoretical project remains interrupted, and can
seek its completion only in the practice of the architectural project.

In 'The Wicked Architect', Tafuri describes how Giovanni Battista Piranesi's
restitution of Rome's Campo Marzio combines archaeological knowledge with
absolute arbitrariness: 'History no longer offers *values* as such. [...] It is the experience
of the subject that establishes values.'[10] It is here that Tafuri asks a key question
for modernity:

> cannot this interest in 'what is hidden' in ancient architecture [caves, under-
> ground passages, substructures] be interpreted as a metaphor for the
> search for a place in which the exploration of the 'roots' of the monuments
> meets with the exploration of the depths of the subject?
>
> (Tafuri, 'The Wicked Architect', *The Sphere and the Labyrinth*, p. 38)

And, although Jennifer Bloomer argues otherwise, I would suggest that this is the
germ that generates (directly or indirectly), or the missing fragment that explains, the
coming into being of Bloomer's *Architecture and the Text: the (S)crypts of Joyce and*
Piranesi (1993), a study of Piranesi's etchings in relation to James Joyce's *Finnegans*
Wake, in which Bloomer defines her proposition of a feminine architecture.[11] More
generally, and more fundamentally, the relationship between Tafuri's 'project' and
Bloomer's study seems to reside in the method of writing history that she applies. In
Bloomer's work:

> [A] recognition of the conventions of historiography that demand a depend-
> ence upon primary and secondary documents, upon proof of hypothesis,
> upon bipolar logic and hierarchical, linear thinking – that is, the conventions
> of research founded in what is called 'scientific method' – has been aban-
> doned. But this, to a large degree, is not true. It is not the *recognition* of
> scientific-method-based research that has been forsaken but blind faith in it.
> Conventional method is called into question here. Thus, this is a work of
> critical analysis that began with a constellation of questions rather than
> a hypothesis.
>
> (Bloomer, 'A Priming', *Architecture and the Text*, p. 5)

And, as if continuing the arguments that provisionally close Tafuri's *The Sphere and the Labyrinth*, Bloomer wonders:

> Is there further research to be done on the relation between architecture and writing, research that goes beyond the pitfalls and dead ends of the arguments made over the last twenty years that depend upon semantic and syntactic translations between languages [...] and simple tropic analogies? [...] Are the configurations significant that describe the relations among language, literature, writing, drawing, building, and architecture? How might a consideration of the connections between theory and practice inform and be informed by these configurations? The relations of space and time? Those of nature and culture? If we reconstrue history and historical research in terms of a suspension of belief in the mutual exclusivity, or bipolarity, of these pairs of concepts, how might this inform and be informed by those configurations?
>
> (Bloomer, 'A Priming', *Architecture and the Text,* pp. 5–6)

Bloomer begins her work with 'a constellation of questions' that unfold into a complexly interwoven text, a non-linear web of intertextuality. Five years later, Catherine Ingraham's book, *Architecture and the Burdens of Linearity* (1998), focuses on the presence of the non-linear in the historically 'line-focused' discipline of architecture. Ingraham opens her book with – among much else – an analysis of King Lear's tragedy of daughters and lines, maps and traces, relations of knowledge and power,[12] in order to explore the relationship of architecture to the proper.[13] But what is proper to architecture, or, can architecture be 'improper'? For Ingraham 'The problem seems to be that the idea of an improper architecture makes no sense, for "to architect" is, in some way, "to make proper" '.[14] The architecture of the proper constructs within itself its own built history as the fixed interpretation of a historical event. But architecture imports a plurality of materials and knowledge from elsewhere, and this guarantees 'that architecture will be open, *especially* open [...] to the play and danger of "meaning" '. 'Yet,' continues Ingraham, 'what begins as the authoritative conjunction of different languages and foreign material very quickly becomes the exclusion of these differences.'[15] It is at this point – I argue – that architecture needs to redefine its delirium as that which opens up the space of the difference: between history and historical project, between erasure and undialectical suspension. Ingraham continues:

> one might be tempted to say that architecture comes into its own the moment the structure of the proper is destabilized; [...] a certain ground opens up then, and open ground is where architecture can sink roots and thrive.
>
> (Ingraham, *Architecture and the Burdens of Linearity*, pp. 28–9)

For Tafuri, the historical project is 'an intermittent journey through a maze of entangled paths, one of the many possible "provisional constructions" [...] The cards can be reshuffled and to them added many that were intentionally left out.'[16] Can we then consider the foregoing texts as fragments of the historical project that redefine, incorporate and use delirium? Rather than a deviation from linearity or a process that (in Freudian terms) 'ruthlessly deletes', delirium after the historical project is here both the erasure and the (trace of the) erased, a co(i)mplication of the line that holds together erasure/erased and becomes space – the space occupied by architecture.

Does this redefined delirium – not-deviation, not-transgression, not-censorship, not-erasure – need to be gender-identified as 'woman'? Is this only 'feminine architecture'? Can the placement of a re-examined past in the present be operated from within architecture and without identifying 'woman' as an opponent, or the marginal, the excluded?

The work of the *mulieres delirantes* provides a gendered take on a seminal text and ideas. This work is individual and yet choral, constructed within the complexity of the single text, as well as through the manifold web of connections between them. As a choral project it remains discontinuous, undeveloped, unresolved – and incomplete. But perhaps it can still open up possibilities for 'other' strains of action in architecture theory.

After the historical project

The work of these 'daughters of Tafuri' does not simply develop issues and ideas from Tafuri's project. The historical project is not a source of materials. Nor is it a method – it can not be just and simply applied. Every time it is re-enacted it needs to be designed, exposed and put in danger. It is in this latter sense that these works can be posited as active continuators of a project that is, by definition, endless. Like these, there are and there can be many other further developments, histories and stories, other 'others' in the discipline of architecture.

Tafuri's historical project unlocked – 'blasted' – the stasis of the isolation of the proper of architecture. But the question remains: can we have another Tafuri now? (And by Tafuri I mean his redefinition of history, and in particular of history in architecture.) Is another Tafuri possible, while the plurality of voices triggered by his call is still operating within (rather than on) the spoils of Tafuri's project? Do we need another Tafuri? A project that by definition invents itself as open, incomplete and endless is inevitably designed to slip away from the hands of its 'architect' and become plural. And while we do not need another Tafuri right now, we can *only* have many. With a cautionary warning.

After launching a historical project that, beyond the 1968 plurality of 'theories', also opens up a plurality of 'histories', Tafuri withdraws in the specificity of strict disciplinary research in architecture with his studies on the Renaissance. These are for him the tassels of a larger historical project, in which architecture is exposed in relation to political, economic and ideological forces. Having witnessed the wreckage of the catastrophe hurled at his feet – that of architecture through the 1970s – in this phase of his work Tafuri reactivates the time of the Renaissance and in particular of Renaissance Venice, but his message goes to contemporary architecture. In *Venezia e il Rinascimento* (1985)[17] the reactivation operated by the 'historical project' contains the not-so-hidden goal of constructing – at once – a historical method and a theory of the present: the appearance of the *novitas* in Renaissance Venice is investigated to reveal the city's malleability and capacity to react by appropriating and including the modified new in an anti-classical order that offers itself as a flexible paradigm for addressing the present. In *Ricerca del Rinascimento* (1992)[18] Venice becomes the moment and the place where certainties are questioned and produce a crisis that opens up the anxiety of the modern.

Two directions of work open up and can be identified here. On one hand is the work of the Department of Architectural History at the IUAV in Venice – the heir of the famous Institute – which embraces this 'message-by-examples' and develops, with Tafuri and after his death, a series of historical studies in architecture that seem to vindicate the need to readdress the discipline at its roots through the specific object of its investigation. In 1985, Paolo Morachiello, writing 'A Detailed Description' of the Department of Architectural History, can thus provide only a summary of the research in progress at the Department, including a comprehensive list of the different research topics, but refraining from offering 'a projection of aims' or from addressing issues of the 'project' role of the historian:

> The historian [...] must aspire to rigour in recounting what has happened and why it has happened. He must break down the construction, the sign, the text and the image and faithfully and tirelessly recover their causes, without idealising either the building or the drawing or still less the document. This is implicitly the historian's intent: his method, always supposing that one exists, depends upon his intent and the object of his study. This presentation of the work of the Department of Architectural History must therefore be in the form of a detailed description rather than a projection of aims.
>
> (Paolo Morachiello, 'The Department of Architectural History', in Luciano Semerani (ed.), *AD Profile 59: The School of Venice,* a special issue of *Architectural Design*, 55, 5/6, 1985, pp. 4–80)

Break down, recover the causes, describe: this is the vocabulary of a careful, rigorous – orthodox – history that seems to have forgotten the anxiety and the tension of its project.

On the other hand there is the 'delirious' work – delirious of a redefined delirium – of those I have identified as Tafuri's 'daughters', the *mulieres delirantes* whose emphasis on the provisional nature of history re-opens historical constructions to expose what had been 'intentionally left out': 'The importation of material from elsewhere,' writes Ingraham, 'the plurality of knowledge that accompanies the formation of architecture, is also a guarantee that architecture will be open, especially open [...] to the play and danger of "meaning".' [19]

And this is a 'project' in architecture.

Notes

1   Manfredo Tafuri, 'Introduction: the Historical Project', *The Sphere and the Labyrinth*, p. 2.

2   Manfredo Tafuri, *Theories and History of Architecture*, translated by Giorgio Verrecchia, London: Granada, 1980.

3   Rem Koolhaas, *Delirious New York: a Retroactive Manifesto for Manhattan*, New York: The Monacelli Press, 1994.

4   *The Oxford English Dictionary* defines 'delirium' as 'an acutely disordered state of mind involving incoherent speech, hallucinations, and frenzied excitement' (*The Oxford English Reference Dictionary*, second edition, edited by J. Pearsall and B. Trumble, Oxford and New York: Oxford University Press, 1996).

5   Tafuri, 'Introduction: the Historical Project', *The Sphere and the Labyrinth*, p. 2.

6   Sigmund Freud, *The Interpretation of Dreams* (Second Part), (1900–1901) in *The Standard Edition of the Complete Psychological Works of Sigmund Freud*, Volume V, translated by James Strachey, London: Vintage, 2001 (1953), p. 529, my emphasis.

7   Tafuri, 'Introduction: the Historical Project', *The Sphere and the Labyrinth*, pp. 9–10, my emphasis.

8   Ibid., p. 10.

9   This text, originally written in 1971, remained unfinished and was completed in 1987 for publication in *Assemblage*, 7, Fall 1988, pp. 28–40. It is now included in Diana Agrest, *Architecture from Without: Theoretical Framings for a Critical Practice*, Cambridge, MA: MIT Press, 1991, pp. 179–93.

10   Tafuri, 'The Wicked Architect', *The Sphere and the Labyrinth*, p. 38.

11   Jennifer Bloomer, *Architecture and the Text: the (S)crypts of Joyce and Piranesi*, New Haven and London: Yale University Press, 1993.

12   Catherine Ingraham, 'Dividing the Land: Lines of Identity and Descent', *Architecture and the Burdens of Linearity*, New Haven and London: Yale University Press, 1998, pp. 1–29.

13   Ingraham, 'What is Proper to Architecture', *Architecture and the Burdens of Linearity*, pp. 30–61.

14   Ingraham, *Architecture and the Burdens of Linearity*, p. 12.

15   Ibid., pp. 18–19.

16   Tafuri, 'Introduction: the Historical Project', *The Sphere and the Labyrinth*, p. 21.

17   Manfredo Tafuri, *Venice and the Renaissance*, translated by Jessica Levine, Cambridge, MA and London: MIT Press, 1989.

18   Manfredo Tafuri, *Ricerca del Rinascimento*, Turin: Einaudi, 1992.

19   But, continues Ingraham, simultaneously 'architecture formulates itself as a discipline, a field of expertise, and thus must establish boundaries [...] that give it an identity different from other disciplines' (Ingraham, *Architecture and the Burdens of Linearity*, p. 18).

Architecture as Critical Knowledge

David Cunningham

In a well-known passage in *Architecture and Utopia*, Manfredo Tafuri posits what he calls 'a simple truth': 'just as there cannot exist a class political economy, so too there cannot be founded a class aesthetic, art, or architecture, but only a class *critique* of the aesthetic, of art, of architecture, of the city itself.'[1] The 'negative' aspects of this argument have been widely remarked upon, and have often been taken to indicate an underlying 'structural pessimism' present throughout Tafuri's work. As the author himself acknowledged, his 'simple truth' would appear, to many, as the mere pretext for a thoroughly despairing articulation of 'apocalyptic prophecy', an 'expression of renunciation'.[2] Yet, while Tafuri's detailed response to such a reading may hardly be comforting in itself, this does not efface the need to engage what he identifies as its fundamental *error* – an 'isolation' of the 'architectural problems treated' from the 'theoretical context' that originally defined them. Tafuri's reference is to the journal *Contropiano*, and to the 'most advanced studies of Marxist thought' that informed it;[3] a context that situates his work within a broader attack on reformist attempts to operate within existing socio-political institutions common to the Italian Left of the time. At the same time, it manifests a more specific cultural suspicion of all forms of romantic aesthetic utopianism – one which Karl Marx himself inherited from G.W.F. Hegel's arguments concerning 'abstract freedom' – that underpins a vigilant deflation of any avant-gardist effort to anticipate 'by means of the image alone [...] the conditions of an architecture "for a liberated society" ';[4] an attempt that would yield 'historically created conditions of emancipation to fantastic ones'.[5]

Yet what of that which Tafuri apparently *does* allow for in his 'simple truth'; that is, the class *critique* of architecture? Given a more general analysis of the capacity for any criticism to see itself, in the context of advanced capitalism, 'overturned into a positive contribution [...] all the more positive because all the more dramatically critical and self-critical', how is the avowed potential for a 'critique of architecture' to be conceived?[6] Is this *simply* to be construed as a final giving way of practice to writing, of action to reflection?

In approaching such questions, one should start with what might otherwise be too quickly passed over – Tafuri's delimitation of such a critique in terms of the specific criticism of architectural *ideology*. While the concept of ideology has not fared too well in recent theoretical discourse, it needs to be retained here if only because it makes clear the reasons why critical writing on architecture can only begin from the social formations of capitalist modernity. For, whatever the preceding history that took place under this name up to the Renaissance and beyond, it is *only* with the emergence of capitalist modernity that architecture appears as such, in an institutional, professional or disciplinary sense; a sense stabilised around the late eighteenth century in the context of rapid urbanisation and an emergent bourgeois culture.[7] In this way, architecture's modern construction as more than *just* a matter of building design and production is also its necessary formation as an independent set of structures and discourses, internally and externally related to the totality of such structures within capitalist society as a whole, from education to law to political economy proper. A critical reflection upon architecture qua architecture must thus start not from an empirical analysis of built form, extending from ancient to contemporary, but from a historical account of what is entailed by its specifically modern status as an institution, which opens up an irreducible non-identity with regard to the actual material practices to which it relates. This is less about a 'pessimistic' judgement upon the socio-political potency of current architectural possibility as such, than it is about an account of the evolving ideological role that has historically generated the modern idea of the 'architectural' itself.

Now, this said, it should be clear that, surprising as it may seem, what Tafuri delimits as architectural ideology finds a certain corollary in Bernard Tschumi's equally influential affirmation of architecture as a particular form of *knowledge*: '[A]rchitecture itself goes beyond the mere process of building. The complex cultural, social, and philosophical demands developed slowly over centuries has made architecture a form of knowledge *in and of itself*.' If this defines its 'positive' terms, at the same time the *critical* potential of such knowledge is thus tied up with 'real conflicts' concerning the 'nature and definition of the discipline' *in and of itself*, as well as of its openness (or otherwise) to what Tschumi describes as 'social, spatial, conceptual concerns'.[8] While registering then – at the very least – evident differences of emphasis and tone in Tafuri's and Tschumi's formulations at this point, I want to suggest two things. First, that what is at stake here must be considered in terms of a *problematic of autonomy*; a problematic, the social (as opposed to merely aesthetic) nature of which has been widely misrecognised in architectural theory. Second, that, while Tschumi's claim has been largely absorbed into the bloodstream of recent architectural discourse as the basis for an expanding architectural *theory*, particularly within the academy, this has taken place, by and large, without adequate attention to the question of how exactly 'knowledge' – a term whose philosophical history is one of almost unparalleled complexity – should be understood here.

In the context of modern philosophy, of course, critique and knowledge belong inextricably together; a co-belonging that is most clearly cemented in Enlightenment thought in the second half of the eighteenth century – precisely at the moment at which architecture as ideology and institution is effectively constituted as part of a larger historical process of disciplinary separation and division. Such co-belonging is canonically set out in Immanuel Kant's *Critique of Pure Reason* (1781), in which, philosophically, critique comes to denote a specific reflection on the essential *conditions* and *limits* of possible knowledge, particularly as regards the natural sciences. It is, however, only with Hegel that a second broader sense of critique is clearly added to this Enlightenment idea, one which will come to denote reflection, not only on the supposedly universal and unchanging limits to knowledge, but on the historical restrictions placed upon knowledge by the *variable* structures of the social world. It is thus that critique is connected to the possible engendering of an emancipatory praxis that would work to free the subject from existing distortions and 'coercive illusions'; a dynamic historical process that is, in turn, the basis for the materialist critique of political economy arrived at in Marx.

It is from this Hegelian–Marxist understanding of critique that Tafuri derives his own critique of architectural ideology. Famously, it is also the basis for Max Horkheimer's 1937 definition of critical theory – his effective manifesto for the Frankfurt School. If all theory is 'stored-up knowledge', Horkheimer writes, by contrast to the 'idealist critique of pure reason', critical theory 'never aims simply at an increase in knowledge as such'.[9] Horkheimer's argument here is less with Kant himself than with the unreflective 'social conformism' resulting from early-twentieth-century positivism. As Simon Jarvis puts it: 'The putative pure description of positivism carries an ineliminable prescriptive moment within it. Positivism becomes the liquidation [. . .] of the possibility that the facts might change.'[10] For, while positivism's post-Kantian conception of critique restrictively defined it as a formal method of logic, any critique that willed emancipation had also, for Horkheimer and Theodor Adorno, to involve a reflection upon the conditions of knowledge entailed by the contradictions present within existing *social* reality – contradictions that require, therefore, more than merely logical resolution.

Insofar as architecture is, in its modern disciplinary sense, 'a form of knowledge in and of itself', Horkheimer's basic distinction suggests, then, two main ways in which the form of such knowledge might be construed. The first would present itself on the basis of the cognitive interests of a familiar technocratic model, realised in a disciplinary increase in scientific understanding of, and thus applied technical control over, the built environment on the part of the professional expert. In this sense, architectural knowledge always risks becoming a mere species of instrumental positivism, a rationalisation and 'consolidation' of existing social reality. Hence, for Tafuri, its ideological character; the intrinsic failure of architecture qua architecture to reflect upon the social conditions of its own institutional status and the divisions of labour sustaining it. Architecture's historical incapacity to operate critically can then be read as a problem inherent within the notion of a critical *architecture* – as opposed to a critique *of* architecture – as such: 'To search for an alternative within the structures that condition the very character of architectural design is indeed an obvious contradiction in terms.'[11] The problems within which architecture finds itself enmeshed are not themselves architectural, but the problems of an unfree *society*.

The essential truth of this is, I think, undeniable, and I have no wish to dispute it. Yet might it not also be the case that it is, precisely, the *exposure* of these 'intrinsic limits' of architecture, not only within critical writing but within architectural practice itself, that does, finally, allow for another critical possibility – a possibility that Tafuri's absolutised conception of the political, as the direct and total transformation of social relations, tends to sweep over all-too-quickly? This would, at least, imply a second kind of architectural knowledge, in which a critical (and self-critical) knowledge would be itself a form of intervention, however mediated; a species of reflection upon the *wider* social contradictions that determine and constrain praxis. This, at any rate, is what I want, in a very schematic fashion, to consider below. And it is in attempting to do so that I want to return to the question of autonomy.

The general significance of processes of autonomisation in the development of modern capitalist culture is by no means restricted to art, though it is, arguably, in art that such processes take a particularly accentuated form, as the 'illusion' of an absolute separation from social praxis that identifies it with a kind of intense fetishisation.[12] It is also in terms of its relation to the category of 'art' that the question of autonomy in *architecture* has tended to be broached by its theorists. As a result, perhaps unavoidably, the problematic of autonomy has been too readily reduced to issues concerning fundamentally *stylistic* modes of formalist aestheticism. However, despite widespread misunderstanding, the concept of autonomy, as developed by Adorno from within the terms of Frankfurtian critical theory, should not, in fact, be understood as naming either a simple option for cultural production or an inherent property of the object itself (as it is in Clement Greenberg, for example), but, rather, precisely as the basis for an historical analysis of art's unfolding *social* determination in capitalist culture, its production out of historically specific social relations. In this sense, as Adorno insists, *all* autonomy is an illusion – since it is, simultaneously, *both* autonomous *and* a social fact – and yet, paradoxically, all-too real, insofar as the social separation it marks determines art's place within the divided reality of capitalist modernity as a whole; a separation which, given that it *is* part of a larger social structure, art itself cannot simply overcome. Autonomy, that is to say, is not a straightforward choice, to be accepted or otherwise, but rather defines a 'situation' that art must work with under the conditions of capitalism.[13]

Nonetheless, given Adorno's own post-Kantian association of autonomy, as resistant to the demands of capital accumulation, with a certain 'purposelessness', it is quite understandable that there has been a general suspicion that such a category would not be relevant to a thinking of architecture. Indeed, this is something Adorno himself seems to struggle with in his one essay devoted to architecture, much of which is concerned with a reading of Loos' would-be separation of the purposeful from the purpose-free. Adorno's claim, in 'Functionalism Today', that architecture is 'in fact *both* autonomous and purpose-oriented', can seem a merely rhetorical solution.[14] Yet, as he argues, in capitalist society 'usefulness has its own dialectic'. For, paradoxically, the very possibility of a genuine 'functionality' or 'use' is – in a society 'bewitched' by exchange value (whereby 'new *needs*' are called forth 'according to the profit motive')

– dependent upon a moment of autonomy.[15] Functionalism, as Adorno writes, might 'like to break out of this entanglement [...] yet, it can only rattle its chains in vain as long as it remains trapped in an entangled society'.[16] It is in such a context that architecture's relation to the category of 'art' is mediated, far more generally, by a dialectic of autonomy and heteronomy at work in the formation of capitalist culture.[17] In no sense, then, can we simply parcel up different cultural forms into fixed separate categories of 'autonomous' and 'heteronomous', with, say, music assigned to the former and architecture to the latter.[18] A certain dialectic of form and function is immanent to the work, in *both* art and architecture, and mediates the dialectic *of* art and architecture, the 'autonomous and purpose-oriented', without thereby simply identifying the two: 'In any given product, freedom from purpose and purposefulness can never be absolutely separated from one another.'[19]

In principle, therefore, once we recognise the bases behind Tafuri's own argument concerning architecture's distinctively modern status as ideology – its constitutive non-identity to simple building production – we can see that, actually, this dual character *must* define such non-identity; that, in fact, the production of architecture qua architecture is impossible without it. Hence, as Adorno notes, the ineliminable aporia of functionalism – the will to pure use-value must run aground in a society in which a genuine use-value could only be projected into the utopian space of a qualitatively different future. At the same time, autonomisation is itself a process that can, of necessity, never be completed: 'Nothing exists as an aesthetic object in itself.'[20] As such, what might seem to be Tafuri's argument *against* any possible conception of an architectural autonomy – its inescapable imbrication with capitalist social relations and conditions of production – is, in an admittedly more accentuated form, only to remark the social character of all cultural autonomy itself. It is the *irreducible* dialectic of autonomy and heteronomy at work here that thus indicates what is, for example, inherently problematic about current would-be directly politicised discourses concerning architecture and the everyday. The notion of an *immediate* dissolution into the everyday risks becoming simply an ethico-sentimental avoidance of the realities of social division; a consolatory pseudo-democratisation of culture.

Of course, equally, one might ask, if all such ambitions are revoked, is it not the case that architecture can only retreat into the auratic consolation of what Tafuri calls 'form without utopia', a 'sublime uselessness' which dissolves it at another level?[21] Yet, this 'form without utopia' is ambiguous, and its 'sublime uselessness' is only useless in one sense. For, at another level, it is put to some pretty obvious *uses* within contemporary capitalism: as aesthetic 'cover' for development. This would mark a developing postwar functionalisation *of* art's autonomy itself, one that appears to have rapidly accelerated over the last two decades. As Peter Bürger rightly notes: 'Only an art that has become (relatively) autonomous can be harnessed. The autonomy of art is thus simultaneously the precondition for its later heteronomy. Commodity aesthetics presupposes an autonomous art.'[22] The cultural phenomenon of architecture as 'brand' – exemplified by Frank Gehry's recent buildings – operates, in all-too-obvious ways, within the terms of this dialectic. What, then, does this mean politically? In Adorno's terms:

> [Nothing] can smooth over the contradiction. On the one hand, an imagined
> utopia, free from the binding purposes of the existing order, would become
> powerless, a detached ornament, since it must take its elements and struc-
> ture from that very order. On the other, any attempt to ban the utopian
> factor, like a prohibition of images, immediately falls victim to the spell of
> the prevailing order.
>
> (Adorno, 'Functionalism Today', pp. 16–17)

The problem of the 'prevailing order' is not a 'design problem', which is why no 'instru-
ments of a different type of designing, or of a radical "anti-design" ', can resolve it.[23]
As Adorno continues:

> [Architectural work] is conditioned by a social antagonism over which the
> greatest architecture has no power: the same society which developed
> human productive energies to unimaginable proportions has chained them
> to conditions of production imposed upon them [...] This fundamental
> contradiction is most clearly visible in architecture.
>
> (Adorno, 'Functionalism Today', p. 16)

There is little, if anything, to be gained by evading the 'simple truth' of this impotence.
Yet it is what Adorno calls the particular *visibility* of 'contradiction' in architecture that
might be most productively focused upon at this point.

For Fredric Jameson the 'emblematic significance of architecture today
lies', via the dialectic between the architectonic object and urban organisation, 'in its
immediacy to the social, in the "seam it shares with the economic" '.[24] Now, in this
light, it would be in its capacity to *articulate* the tensions present within such a dialectic
that architecture has its critical social 'substance', laying bare, often 'unconsciously',
those very systemic contradictions through which it must emerge. And it is in fact only
by virtue of a certain autonomy that such visibility of contradiction can indeed be rendered as a form of critical knowledge, rather than *mere* social fact. For while it may
not, *as* architecture, positively resolve such contradiction – which would be the criteria
of judgement for any claim to be *directly* political – it does, by virtue of its very double
character, articulate the social, spatial demands that such irresolvable divisions
produce, interrupting, from within, the constraints imposed by the social relations of
technological production. In this sense, what Adorno, in *Aesthetic Theory*, defines as
the essential 'relation of art to society' – that the unresolved antagonisms of reality
return to it as immanent problems of form – is also true, in its own particular way, of
architecture, which is equally dependent upon the conflictual conditions of its realisation as *both* autonomous and purpose-oriented if it is not simply to deliver itself over to
the reproduction and extension of the status quo.

Formally, it is not, then, a question of magically resolving architecture's own
contradictions, a reconciliation under duress that could only ever occlude the violences
of its own social condition. It is a question of *pursuing* the contradictions themselves –
both practically and theoretically – as a means of critically articulating a social content

which is always in danger of being submerged. Such danger means that autonomy has to be constantly *renewed* through an immanently self-critical dynamic generated by its productive tension with the heteronomous. Without such a dynamic of renewal, propelled by its own social conditions of 'alienation', autonomy does indeed become aestheticism, in a form that is itself, ironically, open to 'functionalisation' in the service of capitalist development. If this is to be avoided, then it depends upon architecture's capacity to critically articulate the internal and external historically-variable relations that it has to other cultural forms to whose productive logics it is subjected – to 'art' certainly, but also to mass media, communication technologies, advertising, commodity design, retail display and so on. Not so as to dissolve itself completely into such forms, nor to make the impossible utopian claim to manage them in their entirety (the fantasy of total design), but so as to critically mediate and express existing forms of social conflict within itself, in a way which is, simultaneously, a critique of the very conditions which produce the contemporary character of that autonomy. It is thus not by the eradication of its autonomy – which to the degree that is socially determined is ineradicable outside of some larger social transformation – but by its incessant, critical-productive *re-formation* of this autonomy that architecture is able to articulate what Rem Koolhaas calls its historically variable 'web of umbilical cords to other disciplines',[25] as a condition of a critical reflection upon the contemporary possibilities of architecture itself.

This does not so much *refute* Tafuri's prohibitions on a critical architecture as posit a fragile and tenuous practice that might render visible the social contradictions that would define any such critique. Hence, of course, as opposed to the 'detached ornamentation' of brand architecture, the ceaseless ambiguity that accompanies someone like Koolhaas' various interventions into, and formal interpolations of, the emergent spatial logics of a global capitalist modernity. In itself this suggests a rather different reading of the 'politics' of such a practice than that propounded by currently influential 'post-critical' discourses. Consider the OMA design for the Illinois Institute of Technology McCormick Tribune Campus Center. By 'positioning each programmatic particle as part of a dense mosaic,' writes Koolhaas, 'our building contains the urban condition itself.'[26] In what does this 'containing' of the 'urban condition' consist? Clearly the building cannot itself *be* this urban condition, nor does it constitute any simple 'representation' of it. Rather, one might approach this through the specific relations that the design establishes with the existing structuring principle of the campus, Mies van de Rohe's 'grid', and the putting of a formal model that also references contemporary *social* systems of the network in tension with it. In this sense, OMA's project effects the transformation of a certain social system into the terms of a formal category, not so as to 'aestheticise' it (though this will always be a necessary risk), but in such a way as to mediate within itself the structures of relation and division that such a system manifests at the level of form. This seems more plausible – and, finally, less politically complacent – than to regard Koolhaas' work as the happily *positive* 'production and projection of new forms of collectivity', in the absence of any obvious broader *social* basis for such new forms (in any 'progressive' sense, at least).[27]

Compared with the seductive dream of a *direct* or *immediate* political practice – the romantic revival of 'hopes in design' recently resurrected by a certain Deleuzianism – what is at work in this may not seem like much. Yet, against the inevitable drift into an abstract utopianism that this seemingly inevitably entails, it does redeem the possibility of a critique, and production of architectural knowledge, beyond merely a historical displacement of architectural practice by an externalised critical writing (or by other practices that may mediate the urban problematic: photography, film, site-specific installations and so on). Or, rather, it argues for the reciprocal trans-disciplinary *mediation* of forms of critical practice and critical writing or other cultural forms, each impossible without the other. None of this is to deny what is most compelling in Tafuri's critique of architectural ideology. Rather, it is to suggest a different way of reading Tafuri himself, against the grain. In this sense, we would see his writings as what Adorno calls a 'second reflection'; a conceptual mediation that would be itself impossible without the *first* critical reflection provided by the historical–cognitive content of certain architectural practices themselves, which thereby give us a unique knowledge of our social relations and formations under capitalism. If nothing else, in this way Tafuri's own criticism is re-conceived in terms, not of a melancholic mastery over modern architectural history, but of an essential dialectical relation with it; a relation without which, indeed, no critique would be possible at all.

Notes

1   Manfredo Tafuri, *Architecture and Utopia: Design and Capitalist Development*, translated by Barbara Luigia La Penta, Cambridge, MA: MIT Press, 1976, p. 179.
2   Tafuri, *Architecture and Utopia*, p. viii.
3   Tafuri, *Architecture and Utopia*, pp. viii–ix.
4   Tafuri, *Architecture and Utopia*, p. 179.
5   Karl Marx and Friedrich Engels, *The Manifesto of the Communist Party*, Moscow: Progress, 1977, p. 70. See also David Cunningham, 'Architecture, Utopia and the Futures of the Avant-garde', *Journal of Architecture*, 6, 2, 2001, pp. 169–82.
6   Manfredo Tafuri, *Theories and History of Architecture*, translated by Giorgio Verrechia, New York: Harper and Row, 1980, p. xv.
7   I am indebted here to Anthony Vidler's paper, 'Disenchanted History/Negative Theories: Tafuri's Architectural Dream Book', delivered at the conference *Marx, Architecture and Modernity*, University of Westminster, May 2004, which the author was kind enough to send to me.
8   Bernard Tschumi, 'Architecture and its Limits I', in Kate Nesbit (ed.), *Theorising a New Agenda for Architecture: an Anthology of Architectural Theory 1965–1995*, New York: Princeton Architectural Press, 1996, pp. 152, 154, emphasis added.
9   Max Horkheimer, 'Traditional and Critical Theory', translated by M.J.O. O'Connell, in Paul Connerton (ed.), *Critical Sociology*, Harmondsworth: Penguin, 1976, pp. 206, 224.
10   Simon Jarvis, *Adorno: a Critical Introduction*, Cambridge: Polity, 1998, p. 88.
11   Tafuri, *Architecture and Utopia*, p. 181.
12   It is in these terms that the autonomy of art appears to assume a quite different form from that autonomy claimed by, say, medicine or 'pure' mathematics as modern disciplines.
13   This is why one cannot simply discard the category of autonomy in Adorno as a kind of obsessive 'preference' on his part, as Hilda Heynen suggests, while maintaining

from his thought an idea of something like a 'critical mimesis'. For the possibility of such mimesis is entirely dependent upon art (or architecture's) moment of autonomy. Otherwise, such mimesis is indistinguishable from affirmation of the existing order. Indeed, without the *dialectic* of autonomy and heteronomy through which it could be articulated, any idea of critical mimesis would be simply incoherent. See Hilde Heynen, *Architecture and Modernity: a Critique*, Cambridge, MA: MIT Press, 1999, pp. 191–2.

14   Theodor Adorno, 'Functionalism Today', in Neil Leach (ed.), *Rethinking Architecture: a Reader in Cultural Theory*, London and New York: Routledge, 1997, pp. 15–16.

15   As he puts it: 'If an advertisement were strictly functional, without ornamental surplus, it would no longer fulfil its purpose as advertisement' (ibid.).

16   Ibid.

17   See David Cunningham, 'A Seam with the Economic: Art, Architecture, Metropolis', in Marta Kuzma and Peter Osborne (eds), *Recuperating Political Radicality: Constructing the Political in Contemporary Art*, Oslo: Office for Contemporary Art Norway, 2006, pp. 131–66.

18   See Heynen, *Architecture and Modernity*, p. 191. This is not to say that architecture does not represent a certain *problem* for Adorno, insofar as it would seem, necessarily, to give a stress to the heteronomous pole of this dialectic in a manner qualitatively different to other art forms.

19   Adorno, 'Functionalism Today', p. 8.

20   Ibid.

21   Tafuri, *Architecture and Utopia*, p. ix.

22   Peter Bürger, *Theory of the Avant-Garde*, translated by Michael Shaw, Minneapolis: University of Minnesota Press, 1984, p. 113, note 8. Unfortunately Bürger fails to develop the historically new *dialectic* of autonomy and heteronomy at stake in post-war art and architecture that this suggests.

23   Tafuri, *Architecture and Utopia*, p. 179.

24   Frederic Jameson, *The Cultural Turn*, London and New York: Verso, 1998, p. 163.

25   Rem Koolhaas/OMA (with Bruce Mau), *S, M, L, XL*, Köln: Benedikt Taschen, 1997, p. 513.

26   See Koolhaas' comments at www.arcspace.com/architects/koolhaas/McCormick-Tribune/ (accessed 23 February 2006).

27   See Robert Somol and Sarah Whiting, 'Notes Around the Doppler Effect and Other Moods of Modernism', in Michael Osman, Adam Ruedig, Matthew Seidel and Lisa Tilney (eds), *Mining Autonomy*, a special issue of *Perspecta*, 33, 2002, pp. 72–7, p. 75.

Passing Through Deconstruction

Architecture and the project of autonomy

Andrew Benjamin

With the emergence in the 1980s of a series of architectural strategies that came to be grouped under the heading of deconstruction, a number of different tendencies were conflated. Analysing that conflation now is productive both in terms of acquiring a greater understanding of the differing directions at work within architecture during that period (and enduring up to the present) as well as reconfiguring what characterised that particular moment into something productive for contemporary design practice. Taken together, they will allow for a reworking of criticality. On one level what the term 'deconstruction' did was to legitimate an architectural practice that had broken the hold of symbols on the one hand and the ubiquity of certain modernist conceptions of form on the other. This occurred at the same time as a number of philosophers – most notably Jacques Derrida – became interested both in writing about architecture and in collaborative activity with architects. There is, however, a more complex background that needs to be noted. There are two initial aspects that should be addressed.

The first is that architecture has often sought justification or legitimation in that which is external to it. For Leon Battista Alberti this lay in the human body, for others in a commitment to architecture being the enactment or realisation of ideal geometries. Equally, there was a belief that architecture could be an instrument for social change. In all of these instances, not only was legitimacy addressed, at the same time a ground of judgement was established. While deconstruction provided such a possibility, there was nevertheless a fundamental difference. What was outside had entered architecture. This is the second aspect and it provides another important setting – one larger than deconstruction itself – in which architecture's relation to deconstruction needs to be situated.

Rather than seeking legitimacy in a series of external constraints, architecture's embrace of modernity – perhaps, the way the modern began to figure within architecture – was in terms of architecture's emerging autonomy. Autonomy should not be understood as involving architecture's separation from the social or the political. Rather, autonomy becomes a way of locating architecture's potential both for development and for criticality – these terms can be as much affirmed as they can be disavowed – within the practice of architecture. What this means is that architecture cannot be evaluated merely in terms of its symbolic value; evaluation has to do with its own internal operation and therefore in terms of its own self-conception. Before proceeding it is vital to be precise concerning the meaning of autonomy as it is positioned in relation to architecture. Discussing his early 'House' projects, Peter Eisenman argues for the displacing of autonomy. However he has a very specific formulation of the term in view. The sense of autonomy to be displaced is defined by him as 'the condition in which architectural meaning exists solely in the object'.[1] There is a move of fundamental importance from a conception of autonomy in which it is equated with the autonomous object to the autonomy of the discourse of architecture. Even if the former is abandoned by Eisenman, the latter is retained as the site of criticality.

Deconstruction had a similar relation to philosophy where the latter is conceived as an autonomous discourse (one with its own history). It was an intervention, initially at least, that operated within philosophy. Moreover, it took philosophy to be a practice with a series of internally defined activities linked to the evaluation and construction of philosophical texts. In addition, central to deconstruction's site of engagement was the presence of philosophy within institutions. Fundamental to deconstruction therefore was a twofold concern: in the first instance with philosophy's specifically textual presence, and in the second with its institutional one. It is not just that both these aspects are internal to philosophy and thus provide a critical sense of autonomy; they are concerned, in addition, with the way that philosophy constructs itself as a discipline. Deconstruction opened up as a question philosophy's self-construction and thus allowed philosophy's image to be a site of investigation and radical reappraisal. Deconstruction, therefore, made it possible to rethink the practice of philosophy and thus its construction in ways that attempted to eschew both novelty and the utopian. The former would insist on simple invention and thus neglect the already given situation – perhaps place – within which thinking and thus philosophy takes place. The latter, the utopian, equally neglects the same determinations reducing alterity to an image of the future.

Deconstruction is inextricably connected to the project of autonomy. However, the presence of that project within architecture differs importantly from the way it figures within philosophy. From a philosophical perspective, autonomy cannot be readily differentiated from questions of criticality. Within the philosophical, the critical can be linked to a sustained investigation of the possibility – perhaps the pretensions – of classical metaphysics. Autonomy within the philosophical locates the critical in a space other than one informed by simple instrumentality. Within architecture the stakes are different. The role of any discourse within a practice whose material presence involves the move from diagrams and plans to literal material presence will always have a different status to a form of practice that remains literally discursive. Within architecture, once autonomy is no longer directly linked to the autonomous building, then it opens in at least two directions. One direction leads towards an emphasis on the aesthetic (an emphasis in which the abandoning of any intentional interest in the project of autonomy, and thus the possibility of criticality and a politics of architecture, all figure as signs). Within this opening there is a retention of the relation of autonomy with the single building. The other direction retains the critical impulse identified within deconstruction as a philosophical project. In architecture these two directions, while real, were nonetheless conflated under the general heading 'deconstructivist architecture'.[2] As with any distinction – here it is marked by questions of direction – there will always be points of overlap and intersections. At certain moments differences blur. Nonetheless differing tendencies can still be detected.

The first direction retains the criticality inherent in the philosophical. The relationship between criticality and autonomy within any discursive practice – be it architecture or philosophy – has to do with a complex sense of continuity. Continuity cannot be avoided. Architecture, as with philosophy, continues. What the necessity of continuity sets up is the link any discursive practice has to its own history. The history of philosophy could be understood as the continual reposing of questions that rarely vary such that history is the continuity of the always the same. However, once a concern with the critical enters, then any practice, while continuing, does so with the recognition that continuity is itself an engagement with its own possibility. In other words, there cannot be simple continuity, nor can continuity be understood as the repetition of the same ideal elements. Continuity emerges therefore as a form of discontinuity. In regards to philosophy, this means that while writing still takes place and while books and academic articles still appear, the structure of their content and the topics addressed are more likely to have a disjunctive relation to a pervasive and idealised sense of tradition than one allowing for its simple repetition. In philosophy, deconstruction provided a means by which there could have been a transformation; one thought beyond the destructive hold of nihilism and thus enjoining what could be described as the continuity of discontinuity.

Clearly at work is a type of formalism in which the transformative potential of a particular practice is found in the way criticality is evidenced by the formal possibilities for continuity. Again, it is the continuity of discontinuity. This link to formalism – form as a site of continual transformation – provides the way into architecture. However, it is precisely the insistence on form that opens up the other dimension within autonomy, namely the recourse to a definition of the autonomous in terms of the aesthetic. Prior to pursuing the presence of a form as a site of transformation – and here it is possible, at least initially, to position such proper names as Eisenman and Libeskind – it is important to note the way autonomy and the aesthetic work together.

On one level, all architecture has an aesthetic dimension. It exerts an appeal. Having visual presence – both in terms of its projection into the urban fabric and in its creation of internal spaces – architecture is a site of affect. Architecture has an ineliminable affective component. Allowing for affect is to attribute a specific quality to space. Affect – in both sculpture and architecture – is the creation of spatial experience. In architecture, however, there is an important difference, since the aesthetic need not be present in terms of either beauty or attraction. An aesthetic response could be one of indifference. The reason for such a response – indifference –

being understood as aesthetic has to do with the inherent relation between aesthetics and experience. If the aesthetic is the site of experience, then it is always possible for there to be an experience that does not occur. In other words, what this allows for is a site of potential experience in which the object's presence, both in terms of appearance as well as functional possibilities, is so mute and thus unable to engender a connection, be it in terms of affect or more banally in terms of use, that it becomes possible to argue that the aesthetic is marked by its non-occurrence. What this means is that in a context of this nature, the aesthetic would be defined in terms of non-occurrence; the experience that does not arise with a corresponding absence of affect. (The question of how to evaluate this state of affairs could take its point of departure from Walter Benjamin's argument that within modernity architecture is often experienced in a state of 'distraction'.)[3] All possibilities will have been drained from the event.

Once this description is given to an aesthetic response marked by a type of emptiness, then one way of responding is to heighten the aesthetic content. Heightened content will always be positioned on the level of appearance. This will not take place in terms of ornamentation, since that would merely repeat post-modernism's indebtedness to the history of the symbol and thus to a type of ornamentation; rather, it will have two interrelated components. In architecture, as opposed to art, this means, in the first place, excluding the link between affect and function, while in the second, privileging appearance over programme. The connection between both these possibilities should be clear. While there is an obvious difficulty in that even though both function and programme will be retained – their retention marking the presence of architecture – the fact of their presence will not automatically be attributed architectural significance. Nor will they emerge as sites of research or experimentation. What matters will be appearance. One way of accounting for this position will be in terms of having provided form with a uniquely aesthetic characterisation. This will not be the same as defining architecture in terms of form, nor even in relation to form's ornamental presence. Ornament involves a relation to structure, while appearance – as a term situated within autonomy – is concerned with the affective nature of a structure's external projection.

If there is a clear example of this approach – the privileging of appearance and thus the aesthetic over the programmatic – then it resides in the work of Frank Gehry. While it is a late project in relation to the work of Gehry's that was identified with 'deconstructivist architecture', the 'Guggenheim Museum' in Bilbao dramatises the twofold move that characterises the aestheticisation of architecture. On the one hand there is the sustained failure of programmatic possibilities – the relationship between scale and exhibition was never properly analysed or resolved. And yet, on the other, the visual hold of the exterior gives rise to the building's clear success in terms of a visual urbanism. The building's appearance is what matters. The disjunction between programme and appearance evidences the aesthetic, since what is of significance is not affect in terms of programme – rather, the affective has to do with the relationship between the urban body and the appearance of the exterior (perhaps more

accurately the exterior as appearance). That relation defines the site of affect. If anything, it is the disjunction between the urban body and the body positioned by, and for,
an encounter with art – the project of the art museum in general – that reinforces the
necessity to view this instance of Gehry's work in terms of the aesthetic.

In sum, the argument is that in terms of the interconnection between affect
and programme – the possible encounter with art, an encounter that would define the
building's programme – then the building's operation remains problematic. However, in
terms of the building's visual urbanism, its role in the construction of the urban fabric
and thus the experience of being in the city, it is a clear success. While aesthetics
triumphs over programme, this instance of the centrality of the aesthetic needs to
be understood in terms of its being one possibility within the emergence of architectural autonomy.

Once deconstruction can be seen as involving that version of autonomy
that takes the specific and the complexity of its interiority as its point of orientation,
then its presence in architecture opens up in these two directions. The identification of
criticality with formal possibilities and the denial of criticality in the name of the aestheticisation of the architectural establish the two directions to which autonomy –
operating in part as deconstruction in architecture – gives rise. Taking this formulation
a step further necessitates showing in what way a form of architectural innovation –
operating as formal innovation – allows for this interconnection between autonomy and
deconstruction to emerge. The example here is the work of Eisenman. However,
instead of developing the argument in relation to a building, of greater interest, in this
context, is his analysis of architectural works by Giuseppe Terragni.[4] That analysis has
to be understood, at least at the outset, as a deconstruction of the tradition of the plan,
a tradition exemplified both in Rudolf Wittkower's redrawing of Palladio and then in
Colin Rowe's arguments that neither Mies van der Rohe nor Le Corbusier depart in a
sustained way from the structuring presence of the Palladian plan and elevation and
hence remain neo-Palladian. It should be noted from the outset that Eisenman redraws
Terragni. His approach therefore mimes Wittkower and Rowe. However, it is in the
miming that the transformation can be located. Drawing, perhaps redrawing, becomes
an instance of discontinuity as continuity.

When Derrida writes on Maurice Blanchot what is of interest to him is not
the move in which the strategies of metaphysics are identified and subject to the
process of deconstruction. Blanchot's writings have an importantly different relation to
any dominant tradition. There is a sense in which his texts do not invite deconstruction
because in the openings – and thus in the need to trace the work of those openings –
there is already a productive distancing from any simple repetition of the demands of
classical metaphysics. Derrida's writings on Blanchot have a different status than
those devoted to philosophical works and projects that fall readily within the domain of
logocentrism.[5] The space between the writings of Blanchot, and that domain, is identified and affirmed by the process of deconstruction. That affirmation becomes an
instance of criticality – where criticality is defined by the distance and the continuity of
discontinuity, both of which are internal to the operation of the philosophical. Decon-

struction in architecture, if the term is still to have real purchase, is not the application of Derrida's work to architecture but a reiteration within architecture, conceived as an autonomous discourse, of the identification of distance and the affirmation of openings that refuse their reincorporation within the dominant traditions operative within it. This formulation of the relationship between deconstruction and architecture identifies the centrality of Eisenman's engagement with Terragni as a pivotal site of investigation.

For Eisenman, the Casa del Fascio (1936) and Casa Giuliani-Frigerio (1942) are both 'critical architectural texts' – because, as he argues, 'the readings of their façades, plans and sections are not stable; they can be read as displacements from an architecture of hierarchy, unity, sequence, progression and continuity'.[6] What matters here is how 'displacement' is understood. Criticality enters because there is both a disruption of 'hierarchy' as well as an undoing of a sense of architectural continuity defined in terms of the repetition of the same. Repetition identifies both the continuity of architecture and the internality of architecture as the locus of intervention. Repetition therefore allows for the possibility of the interplay of continuity and discontinuity. What this means is that criticality has to assume architecture's internality – in sum autonomy – as its conditions of possibility. In his analysis of the Casa del Fascio, Eisenman uses the term 'transformations'. Again this term, as with the earlier 'displacement', signals a move within a formal vocabulary that attempts to break the hold of a certain tradition of the plan, while at the same time holding to architecture's own continuity.

There are two elements that need to be noted here. The first is that criticality concerns both formal invention – the invention of work and thus of having 'worked through' the tradition – and thus a definition of the critical as provided by autonomy.[7] The second is that Eisenman's argument, while concerning form, is not formalist. Formalism involves the refusal of architecture's affective nature. As will be noted, affect is fundamental to Eisenman's argument.

In regards to the first of these elements, what has to be argued is that Eisenman is recovering from Terragni's work that which makes it irreducible to the already-given conventions of architecture. To that extent, the approach mimes the one taken by deconstruction to texts that distance the hold of logocentrism. In other words, criticality is not mere invention; nor is it utopian speculation. The recovery of a project allows architecture to work through the hold of dominance. The twofold move of recovery and 'working through' defines more precisely the way in which criticality operates. For Eisenman, they are linked to ways of reading. Reading, however, cannot be divorced from the process of redrawing. (Hence what is at stake is architecture rather than philosophy.) This re-presentation involves shifts in rendering. Again there is the mime. Eisenman argues that rendering the southwest façade of the Casa del Fascio using one mode of representation rather than another opens up its possibilities. This is of course the opening of recovery. Eisenman argues that when:

> the volume is rendered white, it conceptually compresses the plan and the
> volume together [...] This condition in the front façade allows the solids and

the voids to become critical textual figures that undercut the traditional referential status of elements such as windows and columns so that these
elements are not merely read either functionally or aesthetically. In the face
of the notations produced by the juxtaposition of solids and voids, explanations engendered by rationalist mathematics and nostalgic metaphysics
begin to recede as persuasive, and other explanations become more
dominant.

(Peter Eisenman, *Giuseppe Terragni*, p. 55)

The detail of this position needs to be noted. The argument presented by Eisenman
involves a reading; a reading that amounts to the process of re-representing, thus
redrawing in order to recover (or establish) the project's criticality. The interest does
not lie in the object's appearance. Rather, it is found in the way of presenting the
object such that it is in the formulation of another plan and the emergence of a new
notation that not only is an earlier one distanced, but the ideational qualities inherent in
it are also overcome. The recovery of the object – recovery as redrawing – is, at the
same time, an affirmation of the distance inherent in criticality, as it signals the already-
present deconstruction of 'rationalist mathematics and nostalgic metaphysics'.

Affect for Eisenman is also linked to a type of reading. In regard to the
façades of the Casa del Fascio, he argues that a 'textual reading of these façades relies
on a perceptual approach different from our acculturated one'.[8] Perception is just that.
A 'critical textual reading' involves as much the object's physical presence as it does
its repositioning within a conceptual argument; a repositioning that, once again, would
be the result of a redrawing. Once the terminology of perception is introduced, then
what is at stake is affect. However, because affect is linked to programmatic expectation rather than simple aesthetics, it has a necessarily different quality. Furthermore,
since affect is at work and because it cannot be separated from programme, not only
is the aesthetic effectively distanced, the force of the difference between deconstruction in philosophy and deconstruction in architecture is announced.

Eisenman's is a deconstructive approach to Terragni. The deconstruction in
question involves the interrelationship between criticality and autonomy.[9] As opposed
to Gehry for whom autonomy emerged as an aesthetic concern, Eisenman's deconstruction is a replanning and therefore a reprogramming of architecture's possibilities.

Notes

1   Peter Eisenman, *House of Cards*, Oxford: Oxford University Press, 1988, p. 181.
2   It is now possible to see that the original exhibition that brought together a number of
     different architectural projects under the heading of 'Deconstructivist Architecture'
     did so by deferring to philosophy. What was not undertaken was the necessity of
     thinking how what pertained in philosophy could also come to pertain in architecture.
     While that may itself be a philosophical observation, it is one that insists on the limit
     of philosophy and thus on the emergence of a differing site of autonomous activity. In
     this instance this other site is the architectural. For the catalogues of the 1988 exhibi-

tion at the Metropolitan Museum of Art, see Philip Johnson and Mark Wigley, *Deconstructivist Architecture*, New York: The Museum of Modern Art, 1988.

3   I have developed an approach to this aspect of Walter Benjamin's work in 'Boredom and Distraction: The Moods of Modernity', in Andrew Benjamin (ed.) *Walter Benjamin and History*, London: Continuum Books, 2005.

4   Peter Eisenman and Giuseppe Terragni, *Transformations Decompositions Critiques*, New York: The Monacelli Press, 2003.

5   See, for example, Jacques Derrida's discussion of the problematic status of the term 'récit' in Maurice Blanchot's *La folie de jour*, in 'La loi du genre', in Jacques Derrida, *Parages*, Paris: Galilée, 2003, pp. 231–67. Derrida's introduction to this collection of his papers on Blanchot addresses the transformative effect Blanchot's writings have on attempts to write about him.

6   Eisenman, *Giuseppe Terragni*, p. 11.

7   The concept of 'working through' (*durcharbeiten*) forms a fundamental motif in psychoanalysis. See Sigmund Freud, 'Erinnen, Wiederhoilen und Durcharbeiten', in *Studienausgabe: Schriften zur behandlungstechnik*, Frankfurt: Fischer Taschenbuch Verlag, 2000, pp. 207–15. I have used this concept in developing a philosophical conception of repetition that involves a link between discontinuity and production. See Andrew Benjamin, *The Plural Event*, London: Routledge, 1993.

8   Eisenman, *Giuseppe Terragni*, p. 37.

9   A similar argument could be advanced in relation to Libeskind's *Jewish Museum*, Berlin, in which programme becomes formal creation understood as the project of 'replanning'.

A Critical Position for Architecture?

Hilde Heynen

The assumption that architectural theory and architecture itself should occupy a critical position has recently been challenged, especially in the United States. The 'critical assumption' relied on the acceptance of critical theory as the most legitimate theoretical framework for architects, theorists, and critics. There are reasons to believe in the continuing validity of this critical project.

Critical theory and critical architecture

According to Max Horkheimer, critical theory is that branch of humanities that is motivated by the tension between rationality and reality.[1] Critical theory does not wish to accept social reality as it is, but always questions its legitimation and justification: is it absolutely necessary that social reality is as it is, or are there possibilities to imagine – and realise – a more humane, a more just, a more emancipated society? Critical theory as initially embodied by the Frankfurt School (Horkheimer, Theodor Adorno, Herbert Marcuse) discussed all kinds of things with these questions as leading motivations. This critical tradition has been taken up by later developments, among them poststructuralism, feminism, and postcolonial theories.[2] The most important critical contribution of poststructuralism has to do with its striving to criticise all forms of essentialism: according to poststructuralist thought, one should be wary of all parties who claim to possess truth because they know the 'essence' of a certain matter – be it beauty, or justice, or violence, or architecture. Deconstructive thinking, for example, has been critical of all notions inherited from tradition regarding the 'nature' of architecture. Feminist theories have used this approach to question gender as a social and cultural construction, and to criticise the oppression that is effectuated in the name of the 'natural qualities' of either men or women. Postcolonial theories have criticised colonialist and imperialist discourses, showing us how they embody a series of unacceptable assumptions about the superiority of European culture, justified by claims about progress and moral values.

The processing of these theoretical contributions into architectural theory has led to the expectation that the most worthwhile architecture should be critical: architectural works should relate to their social condition in a critical manner. My book *Architecture and Modernity: a Critique*, can be read as such: it builds up an argument, relying on the critical theories of Benjamin and Adorno, which leads to the claim that architectural works, through their mimetic relation with programme, site, materials, historical, and social context, can critically reflect upon their social condition.[3] This critical reflection is possible because architecture has an autonomous moment – it is not entirely determined by heteronomous forces such as technical, functional, or economic requirements. The recognition of an autonomous moment in architecture is indeed a necessary but by no means sufficient requirement for a critical architecture. In every built work of architecture, social interests are also at stake. A critical treatment of social reality therefore inevitably operates at various levels simultaneously and cannot just be reduced to the packaging aspects of a building. Questions such as 'who is building and for whom?', 'what is its impact on the public domain?', or 'who will profit from this development?' are, and will continue to be, relevant in this connection. These questions too can be mimetically incorporated in the design, however, giving more weight to its critical aspirations.

Within this theoretical framework, it makes sense to see much of the architecture of the Modern Movement as an embodiment of the idea of critical architecture. Indeed, many modernist architects started from a severe criticism of the existing social situation and how it was sedimented in the built environment. They saw their own architectural proposals – especially in the field of housing – as accommodating a new way of living that offered an alternative to the exploitation and injustice of the status quo. Modern architecture thus equalled a social project, with utopian overtones, based upon a critical attitude towards the existing. The new architecture was seen by critics such as Benjamin or Karel Teige as prefiguring a future society to come, where openness and transparency would reign.[4] The new architecture with its bare interiors, its open plan and its rational kitchens would teach people that material belongings are less important than a social spirit, they would liberate women from the burden of too heavy domestic duties and they would act as perfect accommodations for a life that would be much more mobile and flexible. The most radical pursuers of this logic were the architects of Russian constructivism,[5] but many other leftist architects would surely subscribe to it. They all were convinced that there existed a clear connection between architectural patterns and social reality, and they conceived of their own work as contributing to a more just, better society.

This conception of 'critical architecture' as one that strives to improve social reality is nevertheless not the only one.[6] Michael Hays, who is very influential in the United States, works with a somewhat different notion. His 1984 article, 'Critical Architecture: Culture and Form', which discusses the work of Mies van der Rohe, stresses instead the autonomous moment of architecture, locating its criticality in its very autonomy:

> Distinguishing architecture from the forces that influence architecture – the
> conditions established by the market and by taste, the personal aspirations
> of its author, its technical origins, even its purpose as defined by its own
> tradition – became the objective of Mies. To achieve this, he placed his
> architecture in a critical position between culture as a massive body of self-
> perpetuating ideas and form supposedly free of circumstance.
>
> (K. Michael Hays, 'Critical Architecture: Between Form and Culture',
> *Perspecta: The Yale Architectural Journal*, 21, 1984, pp. 15–29)

For Hays, the operational terms describing the critical qualities of Mies's work are
resistance, opposition, silence, discontinuity, difference, displacement, and authorship.
Remarkably, architecture's social dimension is not a determining factor in establishing
its critical character. I would argue therefore that Hays, in leaving aside this crucial
issue (which would indeed make it difficult to label Mies' architecture as 'critical'), is
distancing himself from one of the most essential aspects of critical theory – its claim
to assess discourses and facts from the point of view of their relation to social reality.
In doing that, Hays prepares the ground for a free-floating, utterly disconnected, completely intellectualised discourse and practice of 'critical architecture', such as that of
Peter Eisenman, which seems quite remote from the intentions that inspired the work
of the original protagonists of critical theory.

Two avant-gardes

This twofold understanding of the notion of criticality in architecture – one more
socially motivated, the other more aesthetically – is reminiscent of a similar discrep-
ancy in the understanding of the avant-garde. Also in this discussion, there are basi-
cally two different ways of conceiving what the avant-garde is all about. The first –
heroic – one is based on the literal meaning of the word 'avant-garde', which refers
to the front part of a marching army, the scouts that first head into unknown territory. The avant-garde thus signifies progressive political and artistic movements,
which consider themselves to be ahead of their time. This is the notion of the avant-
garde that is dominant in the work of authors such as Matei Calinescu or Renato
Poggioli.[7] It understands the avant-garde as the 'spearhead', the most radical part of
modernist movements. More recently, however, a competing viewpoint stresses
instead the aspect of transgression. This viewpoint is theorised by Peter Bürger.
According to this author, the avant-garde movements in the first half of the twentieth century did not so much concentrate on purely aesthetical issues, but were concerned to abolish the autonomy of art as an institution.[8] Their aim was to put an end
to the existence of art as something separate from everyday life, of art, that is, as an
autonomous domain that has no real impact on the social system. Movements such
as futurism, Dadaism, constructivism, and surrealism acted according to the principle
of 'Art into Life!', objecting to the traditional boundaries that separate artistic practices from everyday life.

Andreas Huyssen has taken up this understanding of the avant-garde in order to differentiate between 'avant-garde' and 'modernist'. For him, the avant-garde is not the most radical 'spearhead' of modernism, but rather formulates an alternative to modernism. Whereas modernism insists on the autonomy of the work of art, is hostile towards mass culture and separates itself from the culture of everyday life, the historical avant-garde aimed at developing an alternative relationship between high art and mass culture and thus should be distinguished from modernism.[9] One can say that the 'American' notion of critical architecture, defended by Hays and Eisenman, is closer to the modernist, elitist outlook, whereas the more 'European' understanding that I tend to support is closer to an avant-garde ideal of overthrowing the separation between art and the everyday.

A post-critical condition?

The basic idea that architecture can and should be critical, however, has recently come under attack. Robert Somol and Sarah Whiting, for example, state that the days of 'critical architecture' are over, and that the stage should be given to 'projective architecture'.[10] They unequivocally understand critical architecture as the kind of architecture advocated by Michael Hays and Peter Eisenman. Their idea of 'critical architecture', which clearly favours its American manifestation, characterises it as indexical, dialectical, based upon ideas of 'representation' and 'autonomy'. The 'projective architecture', on the other hand, would be 'diagrammatic', based upon 'atmospheric interaction', aimed at 'cool performance', and concerned about 'multiple engagements', recognising a diversity of economies, ecologies, and social groups.

As George Baird observes, Rem Koolhaas seems to act as an obvious referent for those advocating a 'post-critical' architecture. Baird quotes Koolhaas, who in 1994 had already declared that 'there is in the deepest motivations of architecture something that cannot be critical'.[11] And of course Koolhaas' famous characterisation of the architect as a surfer on the waves of societal forces seems to support this argument. Nevertheless, as Baird points out, there are some problems with the unquestioned incorporation of Koolhaas into the post-critical party; Koolhaas, who advocated in *Delirious New York* the 'paranoid-critical' method practised by the surrealists, has also been known to have participated in several episodes of critical engagement. Baird mentions how Koolhaas chastised Andreas Duany for his involvement in the Disneyfication of Manhattan's 42nd Street, and blamed Chinese authorities for their cooperation in the destruction of Beijing's old quarters. Several OMA projects, such as the Seacenter for Zeebrugge, can moreover be analysed as critically interacting with their social and urban context,[12] which means that it is at least questionable to glorify Koolhaas as the protagonist of a post-critical practice.

The tendency to declare architecture to be in a 'post-critical' stage is, anyhow, far less visible in Europe. On the contrary, even. In April 2003, for instance, a colloquium was held in Brussels, organised by Nethca, and entitled 'Critical Tools'.[13]

During this colloquium, the majority of the speakers, who mostly came from France, Belgium and the United Kingdom, agreed that the critical project had to be paramount in architecture (although they rather disagreed about the exact meaning and implications of this shared assumption). Only one of the keynote speakers, Alejandro Zaero-Polo, started his lecture by referring to the North American discussion and the supposed fact of a 'post-critical' condition for architecture.

Another counter-example can be found in a recent publication brought out by NAi Publishers, *New Commitment*.[14] This publication is announced on their website like this:

> NAi Publishers has noted an increasing level of discussion in architecture and urban planning, in the visual arts, photography and design about social issues. Architects, artists, and designers are on a quest for legitimacy for their work and for socially relevant activities. Professional journals are calling for reflection and reconsideration of how one carries out one's craft. In other words, a debate is clearly underway about a new form of engagement by the design and visual disciplines toward the current problems of society.
>
> (www.naipublishers.nl/art/reflect01_e.html, accessed 15 August, 2006)

NAi thus clearly observes a renewed interest in architecture's critical potential. As does the magazine *32BNY*, a 'journal of architecture and urban culture' that 'draws on the spheres of design, theory, urbanism and art to create a progressive platform for the widening scope of architecture today' and that recently published a theme issue on 'Commitment'.[15]

It seems, however, that the 'projective architecture' advocated by Somol and Whiting and the return to 'commitment' are not mutually exclusive. In looking closely at the arguments developed by Somol and Whiting, for example, we see that they do not give up on the social dimension of architecture, that they do indeed stress architecture's relation to its social context as very important. Their strategy can be summed up in fact as a misrepresentation of the whole idea of 'critical architecture', by focusing on some of its marginal aspects and ignoring others, followed by an advocacy for a new kind of architecture – 'projective architecture' – that in many ways is simply a new disguise for the old idea of 'critical architecture'. One also recognises a typical motive in the whole strategy – that this is the outburst of a younger generation of critics who need to murder their fathers (Hays and Eisenman) in order to establish a legitimate position for themselves. As Reinhold Martin points out: 'the post-critical project is deeply Oedipal.'[16]

Taking up again the distinction between a heroic and a transgressive conception of the avant-garde, one could argue that the call for the post-critical follows the logic of the first. The impetus behind this position seems to coincide with the urge for the ever-new, with the idea that artists and architects always need to explore new territories and that worthwhile architecture has to be experimental and cutting-edge. The post-critical position can be seen as the next step in a series of moves that always necessitates the newer to take the place of the new. Calling for a continuation of the critical project, on the other hand, would instead coincide with the logic of a transgressive avant-garde. In this case the urge to criticise the existing social condition can be seen as equivalent to a desire to overcome the divide between high culture and down-to-earth everyday reality. The driving force behind this position is the indignation concerning the fact that social reality continues to be oppressive and unjust, and the conviction that, as long as this situation remains persistent, the need for critique remains as urgent as ever.

Colonialism and sexism

Postmodernism and later '–isms' have never succeeded in attaining a similar validity in social and critical terms as modernism did. That is why, in thinking about criticality, we should return to modernism and then ask ourselves where we stand today. It seems to me that there are two major concerns that are at stake if we question the critical relevance of modernism. These have to do with colonialism and sexism.

With colonialism, there is no denying that there exists a direct link between the universalist and progressive ideals of the Modern Movement on the one hand, and the colonial discourse that legitimated colonialism as a political practice on the other. From a post-colonial point of view, we should further investigate and criticise modernism's involvement with the colonialist project. The same goes for modernism's built-in tendency for sexism, which can be found at the level of discourses, practices, and spatial articulations.[17]

If colonialism and sexism were inherent to modernism – the most outspoken critical project of architecture of the twentieth century – we should wonder about their impact on today's architectural culture. Can we state that we have overcome these issues? Is present-day architectural culture blameless in these respects? I do not think so.

It is easy to find evidence for this. Take, for instance, Koolhaas' writings on Lagos.[18] He advocates Lagos as emblematic for the future of the city, as a kind of self-organising entity that proves that the rigid logic of architects and planners can be overcome by the reality of urban life itself, which succeeds in reaching a very high level of performativity, regardless of the rules and expectations of conventional planning schemes. Now, interesting and intriguing as his observations may be, they nevertheless remain observations by an outsider, a rich, white fellow who lands – out of the blue – in Lagos, spends a couple of weeks there venturing through the city in well-protected cars and with minimal contact with the ground (and with the people) and declares all well and fascinating. With Yorgos Simeoforidis, we should be willing to wonder about the ethical questions this attitude evokes:

What can we say to the people of Lagos who do not inhabit, who do not commute, and who do not possess our Western comforts? That their

> Megalopolis is beautiful because everything is drifting? That they have no
> problems because Lagos is a city that works? That this is how all the
> world's big cities will be in the near future? That there is no need to do
> anything?
>
> (Stefano Boeri and Yorgos Simeoforidis, 'Why Research?
> (Answers to Yorgos)', in Jennifer Sigler (ed.), *Hunch*, 6/7
> (The Berlage Institute Report), Summer 2003, pp. 99–104, p. 101)

As to the question of sexism, the continuing discrimination against women in the profession is well documented. Although women make up a very large part of the student
population, they nevertheless remain an underpaid and under-represented minority in
the profession itself. Women architects do not often rise to stardom, they usually
remain in the background of the office, helping out and performing a large part of the
less visible jobs. When the Berlage Institute recently asked a large amount of notorious architects and critics to have their say about the contemporary situation of architecture, its questions were answered by 95 men and 17 women – a fair depiction, one
might assume, of the present gender relations in the architectural field.[19]

For me, raising the critical issues of colonialism and sexism points forward
to the underlying issue of utopia. Indeed, criticising modernism and later tendencies
for their failure to counter colonialism and sexism can only be done when one
assumes that another condition is possible – when one believes, that is, that a kind of
utopian desire to realise a social reality without colonial or gender discrimination is not
intrinsically false or ultimately unattainable.

The question of utopia

For me it is indeed crucial that the role of utopian thinking be recognised in architecture. As I argued earlier, we should be aware that the force of utopian thinking might
be the most important legacy of the Modern Movement, for it harbours the capacity to
criticise the status quo, the courage to imagine a better world and the audacity to start
building it.[20] It seemed for some time that, with modernism, utopian thinking was
referred to the dustbin of history. I am glad to observe, however, some tendencies
that now point in the other direction.

An exhibition on the work of Zaha Hadid and Patrik Schumacher, for
example, was entitled *Latent Utopias*, its publicity stating: 'Every epoch needs its
utopias. A society that does not speculate about its future development is curiously
disquieting, even monstrous.' The way in which Okwui Enwezor organised *Documenta*
11 witnessed a certain utopian desire. His concept was based on the idea of a critical
methodology of interdisciplinarity that is appropriate to a global public sphere in which
critical models and ideas of artists and intellectuals can be presented and discussed.
One of the publications resulting from this effort was *Under Siege: Four African Cities*,
which explored 'the polymorphous and apparently chaotic logic of the postcolonial city'

in order to find 'the signs and new codes of expression of new urban identities in formation'.[21] In doing so, the authors look for transformative capacities hidden within the existing chaos.

It is also in this sense that I see the whole discussion regarding 'projective architecture': rather then label it 'post-critical', I would stress its transformative potentials. If you read 'projective' as 'embodying a project', it indeed contains a critical and even a utopian dimension. Utopia today cannot be about a singular, well defined, and straightforward concept for a future society. Utopia inevitably rests upon paradoxes and contradictions, and we have to work through them in order to transform the present into a future that might be somewhat better.

This attempt coincides with what the editors of a recent book – Amy Bingaman, Lise Sanders, and Rebecca Zorach – have termed 'embodied utopias'.[22] For them, this term refers to the act of imagining an alternative to the constrictive and discriminatory spaces of the present, and then enacting this vision in all its materiality. It refers to social transformation in the making – the effort to work through the possibilities of fragmentary change and incomplete, unfinished projects that harbour the desire for a better world.

Notes

1   Max Horkheimer, *Traditionelle und Kritische Theorie,* Frankfurt am Main: Fischer, 1970.
2   Iain Borden and Jane Rendell, 'From Chamber to Transformer: Epistemological Challenges and Tendencies in the Intersection of Architectural Histories and Critical Theories', in Iain Borden and Jane Rendell (eds), *InterSections: Architectural Histories and Critical Theories,* London: Routledge, 2000, pp. 3–23.
3   Hilde Heynen, *Architecture and Modernity: a Critique,* Cambridge, MA: MIT Press, 1999.
4   See Hilde Heynen, 'Modernity and Domesticity: Tensions and Contradictions', in Hilde Heynen and Gülsüm Baydar (eds), *Negotiating Domesticity: Spatial Productions of Gender in Modern Architecture,* London: Routledge, 2005, pp. 1–29.
5   See Victor Büchli, *An Archaeology of Socialism,* London: Berg, 1999, especially 'Revolution and the Restructuring of the Material World', pp. 23–40.
6   I am aware that the distinction I am drawing here between my own position and that of Michael Hays is similar to Reinhold Martin's depiction of a 'political' and an 'aesthetic' critique. See Reinhold Martin, 'Critical of What? Toward a Utopian Realism', in *Harvard Design Magazine*, 22, Spring/Summer 2005, pp. 104–9.
7   Renato Poggioli, *The Theory of the Avant-Garde*, London: Harvard University Press, 1982 (translated from *Teoria dell'arte d'avanguardia*, 1962); Matei Calinescu, 'The Idea of the Avant-Garde', in Matei Calinescu (ed.), *Five Faces of Modernity: Modernism, Avant-Garde, Decadence, Kitsch, Postmodernism,* Durham: Duke University Press, 1987, pp. 93–148.
8   Peter Bürger, *Theory of the Avant-Garde*, Minneapolis: University of Minnesota Press, 1984 (translation of Peter Bürger, *Theorie der Avant-Garde*, 1974).
9   Andreas Huyssen, *After the Great Divide: Modernism, Mass Culture, Postmodernism*, Bloomington: Indiana University Press, 1986.
10   Robert Somol and Sarah Whiting, 'Notes Around the Doppler Effect and Other Moods

of Modernism', in Michael Osman, Adam Ruedig, Matthew Seidel, and Lisa Tilney (eds), *Mining Autonomy,* a special issue of *Perspecta*, 33, 2002, pp. 72–7.

11   George Baird, ' "Criticality" and its Discontents', in *Harvard Design Magazine*, 21, Fall 2004/Winter 2005, pp. 16–21.

12   Hilde Heynen, 'A Tower of Babel', in Hilde Heynen (ed.), *Architecture and Modernity: a Critique*, pp. 209–18.

13   See users.swing.be/nethca/index2.htm (accessed November 2004).

14   Hans Aarsman *et al.*, *Reflect 01: New Commitment in Architecture, Art and Design*, Rotterdam: NAi Publishers, 2003.

15   See www.32bny.org (accessed 15 August 2006).

16   Martin, 'Critical of What? Toward a Utopian Realism', p. 105.

17   Heynen, 'Modernity and Domesticity: Tensions and Contradictions'.

18   Rem Koolhaas, 'Fragments of a Lecture on Lagos', in Okwui Enwezor *et al.* (eds), *Under Siege: Four African Cities – Freetown, Johannesburg, Kinshasha, Lagos*, Ostfildern-Ruit: Hatje Cantz, 2002.

19   See Jennifer Sigler (ed.), '109 Provisional Attempts to Address Six Simple and Hard Questions About What Architects Do Today and Where Their Profession Might Go Tomorrow', special issue of *Hunch* 6/7, 2003.

20   See Hilde Heynen, 'Coda: Engaging Modernism', in Hubert-Jan Henket and Hilde Heynen (eds), *Back from Utopia: the Challenge of the Modern Movement*, Rotterdam: 010 Publishers, 2002, pp. 378–99.

21   See the publisher's website: www.hatjecantz.de/controller.php?cmd=detail*and* titzif=00009090 (accessed November 2004).

22   Amy Bingaman, Lise Sanders, and Rebecca Zorach (eds), *Embodied Utopias: Gender, Social Change and the Modern Metropolis*, London: Routledge, 2002.

Militant Architecture

Destabilising architecture's disciplinarity

Daniel A. Barber

Do not think that one has to be sad in order to be militant.

(Michel Foucault, 'Preface', in Gilles Deleuze and Felix Guattari, *Anti-Oedipus: Capitalism and Schizophrenia*, Minneapolis: University of Minnesota Press, 1983, p. xiii)

The American architectural discourse has been in a special sort of turmoil for the last few years, one that bluntly challenges the accepted disciplinary boundaries of the field. This is on account of three primary factors: first, a quantum growth in the power of computational technology; second, a discursive engagement with theoretical concepts that problematise architecture's relationship to culture; and third, an interrogation of the ethics, on cultural and political terms, of architecture's operations (this last as a result of, on the one hand, new evidence of the symbolic power of architecture through the destruction and proposed re-creation of the World Trade Center, and, on the other, an increased cultural awareness of environmental pressures). These three factors have led many to propose a new potential for social engagement in architectural theory and practice. However, as I will indicate in what follows, the theoretical modes that have attempted to articulate new terms of architecture remain, despite their claims to the contrary, resolutely invested in familiar disciplinary assumptions.

In the United States, this new theoretical trend goes by the name of 'post-critical' architecture and theory, and has been developed most prominently by Robert Somol and Sarah Whiting, though other theorists and practitioners, including Stan Allen, Sylvia Lavin, and Michael Speaks, have made significant contributions.[1] Though different in their specific articulations, post-critical positions maintain the same basic principles, as follows: first, the post-critical rejects the concept of 'critical architecture' as reliant on a rigid conception of disciplinary autonomy and on a resistant stance towards cultural norms. Second, the post-critical sees indeterminate processes and multiplistic interdependencies as generative of a more flexible disciplinarity. It asserts that a theory of complexity – based in an interpretation of the work of Gilles Deleuze and Felix Guattari – allows for a productive engagement with technology, and together these allow new relationships between architecture and culture. Thus the discipline, the post-critical proposes, is more adaptable, its operations more malleable, its engagement with society more multifaceted. Third, the post-critical proposes that the result of these new relationships is the possibility of new, non-oppositional concepts of social engagement for architecture. The architect can now absorb multiple inputs, produce complex systems, and manage networked relationships in order to productively engage economic, cultural, and social conditions without sacrificing disciplinary integrity.

This post-critical discourse, especially its emphasis on the productive potential of technology, has come to infuse many conferences, journals, design studios, and theory courses throughout the United States. Where there is discussion of networks, production systems, or mass customisation, a theoretical position rejecting an architecture of resistance is often not far behind. Of course, this needs to be seen in the context of a culture of practice and theory dominated for decades by the 'critical' potential of formal operations; 'critical architecture' proposed that an architecture of autonomous formalism could disrupt social norms by producing defamiliarising spatial conditions, thereby creating a space for reflection upon consciousness.[2] In general, the North American discourse has welcomed the post-critical disruption to the critical imperative.

In what follows, I will argue against the post-critical position without recourse to the claims of critical architecture, asserting both the continued necessity of, and the new possibilities for, architecture as a cultural practice that opposes the status quo. I will argue on theoretical terms, rejecting post-critical theory's limited reading of Deleuze and Guattari and the impoverished concept of 'social engagement' it produces. In doing so, I will show that the post-critical claim for disciplinary flexibility is, in fact, merely a re-inscription of disciplinary autonomy oriented around a slightly expanded concept of design. I will then outline a political interpretation of Deleuze and Guattari, one that has been largely ignored in architectural theory, and indicate the relevance of this interpretation to a resolutely political, environmental, and activist resistance in architecture.

This other interpretation of Deleuze and Guattari reads their theoretical concepts as expanding the political relevance of architecture. Conceiving of the world in terms of networks, as this reading maintains, is an epistemological shift of historical significance, one that provides productive access to the chaotic interconnectedness of social and natural processes. Such a shift allows for an architecture that embraces the dissolution of its disciplinary boundaries and the radical contingency of its activities in order to maximise its ability to destabilise regimes of exploitation and oppression. This architecture, a militant architecture, takes advantage of complexity theory to find opportunities for social and political resistance everywhere.

I adopt the term 'militant' following Antonio Negri, who uses the term to describe the activity of being inside history, of 'doing, making, constituting history'.[3] Militancy, in this sense, is not based on duty and discipline, on fidelity to an ideal plan, but instead on the insistence that social conditions are constantly constructed with and by our everyday actions and formalised practices. Within architecture this concept has particular relevance: every project is based in specific social, political, and environmental conditions. The work of the militant architect is to identify and respond to these specific conditions rather than conform to a pre-existing model, to extract from these conditions the political goal most relevant to them. Militancy is the organisation of constituent power, power from below, 'capable of crossing all borders and reaching everywhere'.[4] This is the potential of complexity technology and theory, militancy as vigilant attention to the possibility for resistance in the radical singularisation of conditions.

The post-critical argument is not, it turns out, based on a rejection of the critical per se. Rather, post-critical theorists argue on the terms of autonomy and disciplinarity. Their attempt to surpass criticality is based in a de-legitimisation of the concept of architectural autonomy that has, for the past 30 years, provided the possibility for the critical model. As Somol and Whiting write in their article 'Notes Around the Doppler Effect and Other Moods of Modernism' (2002): 'If critical dialectics established architecture's autonomy as a means of defining architecture's field or discipline, a Doppler [post-critical] architecture acknowledges the adaptive synthesis of architecture's many contingencies.'[5] Similarly, in Michael Speaks' introduction to his series of 'Design Intelligence' interviews (2003), he opposes the twentieth-century vanguard – reliant on the certainty of architecture's autonomy – to the twenty-first-century post-vanguard, for whom disciplinarity is always in flux, and who are therefore 'better suited to prosper in the uncertainty created by the new global reality'.[6] Flexible disciplinarity is the foundation of the post-critical position.

This position has been articulated, in almost every case, through discussion of two concepts developed by Deleuze and Guattari: the *diagram* and the *virtual*. Somol and Whiting's 'Doppler Effect' article, arguably the best-known formulation of the post-critical position, will serve as my primary example here. Somol and Whiting define the diagram as the 'tool of the virtual',[7] referencing Deleuze and Guattari's *A Thousand Plateaus* as follows: 'the diagrammatic [...] does not function to represent, even something real, but rather constructs a real that is yet to come, a new type of reality.'[8] The claim for social engagement in post-critical discourse is based in the positive potential of the new. Complexity and multiplicity create, for Somol and Whiting, 'surprising plausibilities'[9] by organising 'the effects and exchanges of architecture's inherent multiplicities';[10] the diagram generates new relationships between architecture and the social.

But what are these relationships, and how are they generated? How, precisely, does the diagram organise multiplicity towards a 'real that is yet to come', and thereby allow the discipline of architecture to become more flexible? Somol and Whiting provide a coded glimpse into a response to these questions by proposing that post-critical architecture, through the diagram, creates a new realm of aesthetic effects, a realm they identify as 'qualities of sensibility, such as effect, ambiance, and atmosphere'.[11] Somol and Whiting's claim for new social engagement is in terms of the potential for 'qualities of sensibility' to impact culture in new, non-oppositional ways.

It is left unclear in the 'Doppler Effect' article why these qualities of sensibility are generative of the new, and why they have a positive social function. Somol and Whiting appear to have based their theoretical position on an article written by Brian Massumi for *Architectural Design* (*AD*) in 1998. In this article, 'Sensing the Virtual, Building the Insensible', Massumi outlines an interpretation of Deleuze based on the latter's writings on Henri Bergson, quoting Deleuze's assertion that 'architecture is a distribution of light before it is a concretisation of forms'.[12] Massumi then proposes that, in considerations of architecture, 'the separation between "primary" sensations (i.e. depth and forms) and "secondary" sensations (in particular colour and lighting) is untenable'. In other words, the atmospheric effects of a building – qualities of sensibility – are equal to formal qualities. Given this premise, Massumi wants to '-re-entertain questions about perception, experience, and even consciousness that have been anathema for some time now to many in architecture'. Qualities of sensibility, or, in his terminology, 'fogs and dopplerings', are, according to Massumi, produced through a diagrammatic design process, and are significant to perception and social experience.[13]

The diagram, in Massumi's reading, is a visual representation that places heterogeneous and conflicting registers on the same plane. The diagrammatic design process, he suggests, requires intuitive leaps between these registers; these leaps have analogues – specific impacts – on the concrete manifestation of the new spatial condition, though they are not manifest in any representational way.[14] These leaps Massumi identifies as 'the virtual', the unidentifiable 'newness' of spatial experience that results from processed complexity – the 'surprising plausibility' that captivates Somol, Whiting, and their colleagues. 'Fogs and dopplerings', disorienting perceptive experience of new spatial arrangements, are thus 'traces of the virtual', and demonstrate that 'the potential of a situation exceeds its actuality'.[15]

Many may recognise the basic formulations of the critical model on slightly different terms. Rosalind Krauss, in an essay on Peter Eisenman written in 1977, proposes that Eisenman's reading of formalism on linguistic terms allows him to produce architecture as a 'cognitive object [...] that had the power to cause in its reader or viewer reflection upon the modes of consciousness'.[16] Somol and Whiting produce a digitised formalism on the same terms, and with the same goals. The diagram and the virtual create new spaces and new spatial experiences, and in this experience of newness they, following Massumi, see new possibilities for architectural engagement with society. What I want to emphasise is that post-critical theory interprets Deleuze and Guattari exclusively as a theory for the production of new perceptual effects and that in this interpretation they demonstrate a reliance on a definition of design and its aesthetic products as the essence of architecture. In other words, the post-critical continues the project of an autonomous architectural formalism. Rather than using the diagram to destabilise architecture's disciplinarity, they use it to draw new boundaries around the field based on a slightly expanded concept of design. 'Design', they write, 'is what keeps architecture from slipping into a cloud of heterogeneity'; and further:

> When architects engage topics that are seemingly outside architecture's historically-defined scope – questions of economics or civic politics, for example – they don't engage those topics as experts on economics or civic politics but rather as experts on design, and on how design may affect economics or politics.
>
> (Somol and Whiting, 'Doppler Effect', p. 75)

The diagrammatic process is the tool through which the post-critical maintains architecture's consistent internal integrity, re-inscribing the position that it is *only through this internal integrity* that architecture can impact 'non-architectural issues'.

Somol and Whiting simply propose that the growing capacity of architecture to engage a broad range of social, political, economic, material, environmental, and other issues – the potential of complexity – results in the diachronic replacement of cognitive form with ambient effect, the de-familiarising space of the critical with the disjunctive fog of the post-critical. Thus they are repeating, rather than eclipsing, the withdrawal of critical architecture into a reliance on the autonomy of form; the disciplinary agenda inherent in their interpretation of Deleuze and Guattari blinds them to the anti-disciplinary force of this theory. In focusing on relationships *within* architecture, they have missed the more compelling opportunity, that of destabilising the relationship *between* architecture and its outside.

The other possible lesson of complexity theory is that the assumptions of autonomous disciplinarity that infuse architectural theory – critical, post-critical, or otherwise – need to be rejected. The task for architectural theory is to adjust the register of architectural activity from the autonomous realm of aesthetic effect to an expanded realm of multiple and unstable engagements with the social. The task for architectural practice is to find available openings to destabilise current regimes of production – continuously. The vigilance of this position requires a militant approach, finding opportunities everywhere for realising social desire in the production of the built environment.

There is, in other words, a politics of sensibility, a social relevance to the production of disjunctive experience, which the post-critical ignores. The theoretical concepts of Deleuze and Guattari are embedded in a philosophy of social formations, in which the experience of the new produces, precisely, an experience of, and the conditions for, the possibility of resistance. The diagram is thus a tool of the virtual because it creates a distinct alliance of forces, one that does not ossify into a regulated power structure but is defined by and only relevant to its moment of instantiation. Specific connections are organised towards specific purposes, allowing the capacity for radical difference to be inserted into material practices. In *What is Philosophy?*, Deleuze and Guattari lament the lack of recognition of the productive political potential of these connections: 'We lack creation,' they write, 'we lack resistance to the present.'[17] The virtual is the 'future form' of social relations; and the diagram is the tool of resistance, the projective realisation of that future in the present.

There are many Deleuzo–Guattarian concepts that emphasise the development of connections across and between heterogeneous registers, and that are available as conceptual tools for a militant architecture. The rhizome is perhaps the most familiar, a concept that describes relational systems with no centre. I want to briefly outline three concepts relevant to discussions of the diagram and to anti-disciplinarity as the politicisation of architectural processes: these concepts are the abstract machine, transversality, and micro-politics.

The multiplistic relationships of the rhizome are connected at a given time and towards a given purpose as an abstract machine, for which the diagram serves a piloting function. An abstract machine is a theoretical, technological, social, and material construct; a collection of individuals, techniques, tools, and processes that perpetually transforms itself to produce social relations. A machine is nothing more than the connections it makes; there is nothing essential to it, nothing to protect it from a 'cloud of heterogeneity' except its temporally and contextually defined purpose. Deleuze and Guattari insist that society is literally machinic; it is not *like* a machine but functions *as* a machine, and its problems and contradictions need to be addressed on these terms. An abstract machine coheres and maintains direction through the force of social desire. The diagram, in this sense, is the map of desire, the 'pilot' of a machinic assemblage, organising the capacities and directions of the assemblage. It does not, however, ossify into a permanent state, but perpetually re-scans and re-adjusts itself based on feedback and possibility.

The second concept is transversality, which elaborates on the scope of the connections on which the diagram and the abstract machine operate. Transversality is articulated most clearly in Guattari's *The Three Ecologies*, where he outlines three systems of processes with interpenetrating relationships: the personal or psychological, interpersonal social relations, and the processes that connect society to the 'external' processes of nature. There is an ecology within each set of systems, and an ecology between and amidst the systems. The task of political work is to think or act transversally, to propose connections between and through these three systems.[18]

The architectural production of qualities of sensibility and the individual experience of the new are relevant to social and political organisation; individual experience impacts thoughts and actions within and through these multiple registers. At the same time, prioritising specific issues in a built project itself produces sensible experience of the space, creating culture in terms of politics. Transversality insists that the production of built space is a significant personal, social, and environmental act.

The third concept is micro-politics. Micro-politics is articulated through the related concept of 'singularity', which emphasises the uniqueness of a given situation. Micro-politics proposes to singularise political goals in terms of the specifics of a given condition, rather than on the macro-political terms of, for example, 'socialism', 'feminism', or 'environmentalism', macro-models that lead to the replacement – rather than the destabilisation – of power structures. Micro-politics asserts that power is produced from below, 'within the very tissue' of social relations; it is distributed through network relations, and strengthened by virtue of the destabilisation of pre-existing distinctions.[19] Abstract, desiring machines, and the diagrams that pilot them, gain power from the specific qualities of a given condition rather than through conforming to preconceived organisational regimes.

The limited post-critical interpretation of complexity theory, coupled with the popularity of post-criticality within the current North American scene, threatens to restrict the potential of Deleuze and Guattari for architecture. It is on these terms that I have made this theoretical intervention, first demonstrating the restricted concept of architecture endemic to the post-critical position, and then briefly outlining other possibilities. What I hope to have demonstrated instead is that the theory of complexity allows us to reconsider the position of culture and society relative to architectural discourse. Rather than a prescriptive theory of architecture, Deleuzo–Guattarian concepts allow us to develop a theory of social formations relative to architecture, creating new models for architecture's interaction with a multiplicity of fields and concerns. In this context, the post-critical is nothing but regressive distraction.

The potential of indeterminacy and multiplicity, read through the abstract machine, transversality, and micro-politics, is to exaggerate complexity, to radically destabilise a stable disciplinary identity. Technological, theoretical, and ethical positions for architecture need to be negotiated on these terms. Architecture is already dissolving into practices with disparate professional and social emphases, from product design to Internet environments to urban planning; such a dissolution, albeit with the caveat of an insistence on architecture as design, has been crucial to the development of the post-critical notion. What is of concern is not this recognition of flexibility, but what is done with it; in this sense, relative to the anti-disciplinary potential of diagrammatic practices, the rejection of the critical is arbitrary.

The political reading of Deleuze and Guattari shows that the function of the diagram is to manifest what Paul Patton has called 'the permanent possibility for piecemeal social change',[20] a potential for which architecture, as an abstract machine prone to active experimentation across multiple disciplines, is well suited to actualise. In order to do so, architectural theory after critical architecture needs to dismantle, rather than reinforce, architecture's autonomous condition. Obsessively focused on the politics of sensibility – on the insistence that social and material conditions are constantly being constructed – militant architecture takes advantage of complexity theory to assert the resistant potential of its practices.

Coda: environmentalism and the diagram

Since this text was written in the summer of 2004, the characteristics it describes have not substantially changed. If anything, the post-critical wave has gained strength in North American architecture schools, at the same time that it has increasingly become clear that a misrecognition of the critical is at the heart of much of this popularity.[21] The question that arises, to paraphrase Bruno Latour, is: 'have we ever been critical?' If so how, and to what end? If these recent debates have contributed to architectural discourse, it has been in terms of highlighting deficiencies in our understanding of the critical project, of identifying the precise ways in which architecture, historically, has been a symptom of a series of impingements on political subjectivity, and how, in its present practice, it often attempts to – also symptomatically – remove itself from political considerations altogether. Without recourse to the design tropes or theoretical frameworks of 'critical architecture', then, we are left with a set of more general questions regarding the role of culture in political practices. Perhaps the post-critical has been a necessary phase to arrive at the urgency of these disciplinary interrogations.

Because of an enlarged post-critical scene in the schools, the third set of pressures mentioned at the beginning of this chapter, 'an interrogation of the ethics, on cultural and political terms, of architecture's operations', have significantly increased: the continued problems of rebuilding the World Trade Center, the failure of architects (aside from, of all people, the New Urbanists) to provide tangible proposals for rebuilding the Gulf Coast after Hurricane Katrina, and the increased awareness of environmental pressures that are now more explicitly debated in terms of national security. The post-critical position has, in this light, even more similarity to the critical practices it rejects, practices such as those of Peter Eisenman and Mario Gandelsonas who, in the 1970s, sought to insulate architecture from the vagaries of the social turmoil of that decade while, in effect, moving the theoretical discourse of the field away from its implication in emerging political concerns.[22] Post-criticality, then, emerges as a sort of pre-emptive strike against the productive possibilities of architecture's disciplinary diffusion, coupled with aesthetic practices and design tropes that claim 'contemporanaeity' as a cover for their increasing social irrelevance.[23]

To return, then, to the work of Deleuze and Guattari, the question for architecture has become: 'what is its diagram of operations, and how can productive interventions be made to re-organise these alliances?' Despite the intellectual fantasies of critical and post-critical writers, architecture is already a radically anti-disciplinary field, spread across traditional boundaries with connections to economic structures (funding, fees, liability), political forces (codes, civic buildings, urban plans), resource management (HVAC systems, materials use and transportation, site planning), and cultural expression (built form, urban form, memorials). Architects can take this organisational diagram as a primary object of their design practice in order to design, in effect, their participation in the world; a practice that necessarily refuses the accepted boundaries of professional fields, academic disciplines, etc., and instead proposes alliances that serve specific social and political – and environmental – needs or desires.

It is perhaps through a rethinking of 'environmentalism' that architecture can gain social and political relevance. Organising environmentalism as a discussion about changing social conditions, rather than about preserving 'nature' per se, allows for a reading of complexity in architecture that disrupts assumptions about culture/nature divisions and produces new mechanisms for politically relevant practices.[24] If an environmental crisis is a crisis of social and political conditions, and if environmental architecture is the development of new mechanisms for the realisation of new social formations, regardless of the disciplinary boundaries that would traditionally prevent the development of such strategies, then the determinant of architecture's diagram, in any given practice or for any given project, is based on an ethics of environmental action. It is this possibility that seems to justify a continued search for the new and innovative, a contemporanaeity that organises new forms of production rather than adds a theory of disjunctive affect to the old ones – a 'neo-criticality', perhaps, or a 'critical environmentalism' that eclipses both the critical and the post-critical in attempts to generate social relevance for architectural practices.

Notes

1   For a description of the various players in the post-critical landscape, see George Baird, ' "Criticality" and its Discontents', *Harvard Design Magazine*, 21, Fall–Winter 2004, pp. 16–21.

2   See, for example, K. Michael Hays, 'Critical Architecture: Between Culture and Form', *Perspecta*, 21, 1984, pp. 14–29; and Rosalind Krauss, 'Death of a Hermeneutic Phantom: Materialization of the Sign in the Work of Peter Eisenman', in Peter Eisenman (ed.), *Houses of Cards*, New York: Oxford University Press, 1987, pp. 166–184.

3   '*N* for Negri: Antonio Negri in Conversation with Carles Guerra', *Grey Room*, 11, Spring 2003, pp. 86–109, p. 94. It should be clear that I am identifying militancy as a tactic to achieve goals; in no way does this use of militancy imply or condone other goals that are currently associated with the term.

4   '*N* for Negri', p. 102.

5   Robert Somol and Sarah Whiting, 'Notes Around the Doppler Effect and Other Moods of Modernism', in Michael Osman, Adam Ruedig, Matthew Seidel, and Lisa Tilney (eds), *Mining Autonomy*, a special issue of *Perspecta*, 33, 2002, pp. 72–77, p. 75.

6   Michael Speaks, 'Design Intelligence, Part 1: Introduction', *A+U: Architecture and Urbanism*, December 2002, pp. 10–18, p. 17.

7   Somol and Whiting, 'Doppler Effect', p. 75.

8   Gilles Deleuze and Felix Guattari, *A Thousand Plateaus*, Minneapolis: University of Minnesota Press, 1987, p. 142; see also Somol and Whiting, 'Doppler Effect', p. 75.

9   Somol and Whiting, 'Doppler Effect', p. 77.

10   Ibid., p. 75.

11   Ibid.

12   Gilles Deleuze, *Foucault*, Minneapolis: University of Minnesota Press, 1986, p. 57.

13   Brian Massumi, 'Sensing the Virtual, Building the Insensible', in 'Hypersurface Architecture' special issue of *Architectural Design*, 133, 1998, pp. 16–25, p. 20.

14   Ibid., p. 22.

15   Ibid., p. 20.

16   Rosalind Krauss, 'Death of a Hermeneutic Phantom: Materialization of the Sign in the Work of Peter Eisenman', in Peter Eisenman (ed.), *Houses of Cards*, New York: Oxford University Press, 1987, pp. 166–184, p. 168, written in 1977.

17   Gilles Deleuze and Felix Guattari, *What is Philosophy?*, New York: Columbia University Press, 1994, p. 108. They continue: 'the creation of concepts [such as the diagram] in itself calls for a future form, a new earth and a people that does not yet exist.'

18   Felix Guattari, *The Three Ecologies*, New Brunswick: Athlone Press, 2000.

19   Deleuze, *Foucault*, p. 37.

20   Paul Patton, *Deleuze and the Political*, New York: Routledge, 2000, p. 7.

21   See Reinhold Martin, 'Critical of What? Toward a Utopian Realism', *Harvard Design Magazine*, 22, Spring/Summer 2005, pp. 104–109.

22   In 1975, Gandelsonas defined an autonomous architecture as one that 'transcends history and culture; an architecture which is a force in itself, a language that speaks about itself and does not communicate ideas other than its own'. See Mario Gandelsonas, 'Neo-Functionalism', *Oppositions*, 5, 1975, p. 8. See also Daniel Barber, 'Is it Simple to be an Anti-humanist in Architecture?', *thresholds*, 30, pp. 3–9.

23   See Sylvia Lavin, 'The Temporary Contemporary', in Jeffrey Kipnis *et al.* (eds), *Mood River*, Columbus, OH: Wexner Center for the Arts, 2002.

24   See David Harvey, *Justice, Nature and the Geography of Difference*, Oxford: Basil Blackwell, 1996, p. 147.

Architecture's Critical Context

The Athens activist experiment[1]

Maria Theodorou

Introduction

This chapter presents the historical background and the conditions in which architectural activities focused on the city of Athens were envisaged and implemented in the form of a four-year project, running from 2000 to 2004. These events, only two of which will be presented here, aimed at testing architecture's capacity to 'function' in a critical mode, where critical meant both 'interrogative' and 'in crisis', and indicated a state in which architecture acknowledged its full entanglement with contemporary social, cultural, economic and political conditions. Architecture's critical task, in the case of the Athens activist experiment, stretched beyond the confines of the discipline: to acknowledge its historical background, to understand emerging conditions, and to point out the potential of localities and act upon cultural stereotypes. This was, in fact, an activist plan whose framework was shaped by a critical context, that is, by a context in crisis.

A critical context

The circumstances of the four-year architectural events project cannot be dissociated from the crisis of identity that Greece has experienced since the 1990s, a crisis due – among other factors – to the disruption of a mono-cultural society by an influx of immigrants. During these years, reverberations of the Soviet Union's collapse were felt as a massive wave of immigrants from Eastern-European countries flooded Greek territory. Athens, whose population was 3.5 million, was the destination of 500,000 Albanians in 1992–3 alone. The case, however, was not unprecedented.

History: immigrants/refugees and Athens-building

Two previous instances of massive immigration contributed to the shaping of Athens in the course of its modern history. The first was in 1922–8, when its population rose from 453,000 to 802,000 due to a massive wave of refugees from Asia Minor. The second, in 1950–60, was due to internal migration when Greeks from devastated post-war rural areas moved to the capital in search of a better future. In both cases however, the immigrants were Greek or, in the Asia Minor case, Greek 'brothers' and Christian orthodox.

The 1920s refugees were settled in the outskirts of the city, either in pre-fabricated houses in refugee quarters, or at a later date in modern blocks built in the context of the 'refugee housing state programme'. The presence of modern buildings at the time was an alien entity in the village-like appearance of Athens and thus refugees and their dwellings were set apart, in terms of location, form and culture.

The situation was different in the 1950s. Then the rural Greek immigrants' presence worsened the housing shortages in Athens, but provided cheap labour and contributed to a proliferation of *antiparochi*, i.e. transactions between small land-owners and developers in the form of a part-exchange scheme in which land was exchanged for flat(s). The *antiparochi* were the state's way of passing the housing problem into private hands and the success of the system created a boom in the build-ing industry. Up until the mid-1960s, apartment blocks continued to spread rapidly and turned the city into a continuous 'cement carpet', but nevertheless most Greeks had privately solved their housing problem and modern architecture established its pres-ence and acquired popularity in public and private projects. However, post-1960s living conditions in the city centre deteriorated; in the 1980s, urban growth almost stopped and the affluent moved out to the Athenian suburbs. Since then, small developers have continued to exploit city lots, architecture commissions has been restricted mainly to private house designs and reinforced concrete construction has prevailed.

In the 1990s, building techniques were still based on human labour although its cost had increased. At this moment, the new immigrants arrived. Cheap labour was again available and a new building boom started, accelerated by emerging new conditions. In 1999, the stock market collapsed after one-and-a-half years of frantic expansion. Given the high interest rates in Greece, bank deposits were a safe option for investment, but by 1998 middle-class Greeks had been lured to gamble. In the midst of massive hysteria, they withdrew their bank deposits to buy stocks that promised quick returns and big profits. The experienced and the lucky ones pulled out before the collapse and invested most of their earnings in housing. The increased demand raised real-estate prices to an unprecedented high. Following the collapse, real-estate investment was once again the only secure option, given that bank interest rates had lowered in the context of European integration. Building activity in Athens was speeded up and facilitated by the availability of cheap immigrant labour. However, in the 1990s, the impact of the new immigrants was not restricted to Athens-building; their presence touched upon the unquestioned nineteenth-century ideology of Greek nation-building based on a mono-cultural society.

The 1990s dislocations: from nation-building to nation-branding

Unlike the refugees of the 1920s and the internal immigrants of the 1960s, the 1990s newcomers were different in terms of both nationality and religion. They came to work and settle until conditions in their countries improved, or to use Greece as an intermediary station en route to other Western countries. Greeks (both the people and state apparatus) were largely unprepared for the 'problem'. The immigrants were mainly illegal and the available state processes insufficient. Unsuccessful attempts to 'accommodate the strangers' first drew from the stock of ancient Greek hospitality (*philoxenia*) rules; the immigrants, however, were *xenoi* but not 'guests'. The second attempt was assimilation: to 'adopt' them as 'godsons' by baptism or by just Christianising their names. Neither worked. In the meantime, the immigrants populated abandoned areas in the city centre and transformed not only the city but also the mindset of its inhabitants. Athenians were forced to reassess their set ideas about 'Greekness'.

If the suffix '-scape' indicates a state of continuous transformation,[2] Athens became 'Athenscape' and the minds of Greeks, mindscapes. As the traces of the immigrants' physical presence altered familiar places, the city acquired a 'forensic' quality: its story had to be reconstructed according to the 'evidence' of a new-found inhabitation.[3] In the city-centre market area, in streets named after the ancient Greeks who invented the barbarian as their other, the ghost of excluded barbarism had returned with a force and demanded a second thought. A way of approaching new configurations of the city was to invest the strangers (Albanians, Pakistanis, Nigerians, Chinese, Russian, Polish, etc.) and the evidence of their presence with the appeal of the exotic. The city centre became an unknown and interesting place. The new metro inaugurated at the beginning of 2000 and the unification of archaeological sites project facilitated the movement of the locals back to the centre.

Unlike the 1920s refugees' alien settlements, the 1990s immigrants inhabited the basement and lower stories of existing apartment blocks and the wealthy locals renovated the upper flats that had privileged views onto the acropolis. The *polykatoikia* in Athens centre acquired a vertical ethnic code but hardly a model of social co-existence.[4] Athens was relieved to declare that it had become, for the first time in its history, multicultural. Multiculturalism was and still serves as a strategy to neutralise difference. Everyone has the right to be different as long as s/he partakes in the common denominator of culture.[5] Such an approach collapses when the other declares a radical difference: in today's multicultural schools there are still students and parents demanding that top students who are Albanian should not carry the Greek flag in school parades.

In the 1990s, as Greeks were still busy pondering 'Greekness' in relation to their new-found 'guests', two other events occurred. In 2001, European integration reached a culmination in monetary union. This demanded a reassessment of the peculiar relation that the modern Greek nation-state had established to the rest of Europe; as Stathis Gourgouris puts it:

> The task of Neohellenism as a national imaginary became [...] to proclaim itself simultaneously both father of western culture and mortal enemy [...] Neohellenism experienced itself as both superior and inferior to western culture, being both xenophobic and xenomanic.
>
> (Stathis Gourgouris, *Dream Nation: Enlightenment, Colonization and the Institution of Modern Greece*, Stanford: Stanford University Press, 1996, p. 275)

With European integration underway, this 150-year-old attitude collapsed overnight. Europe could not longer be experienced as the outside. Greeks felt European and proved themselves to be so by a quick adaptation to the introduction of the euro.

In the meantime, Athens had won the bid for the 2004 Olympics. The games were advertised as a 'coming home'. Was this return a repetition of the nineteenth-century romantic interpretation of Athens? Was Athens ready to reconsider its relation with its past? Could the collective national memory forged in the nation-state-building of the nineteenth century still hold in contemporary conditions? Moreover, as the city embarked on its preparations and massive changes were underway mainly in the urban infrastructure, the Greeks were determined to put behind them years of national lamentation and to forget for good the painful experiences of civil war that had divided its people.[6] The nineteenth-century nation-building, a conscious effort of Greek intellectuals supported and never questioned by the people, was now turned into the twenty-first century euphoric race for nation-branding. The nineteenth-century imagery that remained unchallenged was mixed up with images of Mediterranean hedonism to provide the stock of stereotypes on which the branding approach was based.

Architectural events for the new Greek culture of pleasure

Towards the end of the 1990s, a culture of pleasure formed and the wish to enjoy the city as the locus of leisure ripened.[7] Time had come for Athenians to settle their relationship with Athens. As argued elsewhere, Athenians disavowed Athens; they hallucinated the city as their torturer and voluntarily adopted the role of the victim, as if the city were inflicted upon them.[8] This relation was coming to an end. The new infrastructure (metro, tram, ring-road) alleviated the traffic and the city was changing every day to such a degree that its inhabitants had to rediscover every location that was transformed for the Olympics.

Architectural culture, however, was non-existent; and transformation was happening in the absence of major public architectural building projects for reasons that are too complex to be presented here and necessitate a detailed analysis elsewhere. Intense building activity in the public sector was in the hands of contractors. Architects were aware of both their relative weakness in a complicated implementation process whereby projects were assigned to them by subcontractors and – still more – of their inability to demand an uncompromised implementation of projects when they were assigned to them directly. In the midst of feverish building activity, architecture deliberately, or as result of ignorance, was either disregarded or seen with mistrust by the public, politicians and decision-makers. This was, however, a moment of critical context in which established attitudes were on the move. In the absence of an architectural culture, and in the need to create one in order to transform the attitude towards architecture, the author conceived a number of architecture events to be implemented in the form of an activist experiment of the reforming rather than the transgressive kind.[9]

Activism is related to the desire and demand for change and seizes every opportunity available to achieve its aim. If architectural events breached disciplinary limits to reach out and shape the current cultural context, it was expected that a shift in architecture's reception could be achieved. The event's aim was to make statement-acts in which architecture is not a self-enclosed discipline but a cultural practice that induces critical thinking; it enhances understanding of both historical background and current conditions, and draws attention to the importance of acts that could break down and reassemble long-held assumptions. Such operations could assist people in Greece to comprehend and navigate their current critical state of transformation.

Only two events that dealt with locality will be presented here. Given the Greek nation-state investment in the historicity of places, the experiment put forward was not an attempt to revive past memories embedded in location, but to activate and make location effective in the current critical context. The events thus constituted 'the points of entry' into a critical discussion.

Rem Koolhaas in the Athens Byzantine and Christian Museum: church/state politics

The Rem Koolhaas lecture delivered at the Byzantine and Christian Museum in Athens in September 2001 was an attempt to both draw attention to and disentangle the architecture of the place from the institutional role and the cultural politics of Byzantium and Christianity in contemporary Greek culture. The event coincided with a mass mobilisation incited by the Greek Church in response to the government's decision to no longer list religion on identity cards. This was a practice initiated during the Nazi occupation and consolidated in the civil war. According to the Church, the identity card stands for Greek Orthodox identity and card alteration threatens its very fundamentals. The protest included a petition carrying 3,008,901 signatures and demanded a referendum that was declared unconstitutional by the president.[10] Nevertheless, the mobilisation indicated the Church's determination to continue the long tradition of Orthodox Church intervention in state affairs and to foreclose the forthcoming Church/State separation.

The names of Koolhaas and Byzantium/Christianity have clear-cut values for an Athenian audience. The majority of those who admire Koolhaas' work have not

visited the Byzantine museum, despite its recent extension designed by a Greek architect. On the other hand, the traditional friends of the museum would never choose to
attend a Koolhaas lecture – the museum's programme always involves topics related
to its collections – a kind of unconscious self-censoring rather than a deliberate choice.
Although a State institution, the museum's subject matter relates to the Church
and its programme reflects the reluctance to disturb the Church/State entanglement.
At the moment of the Koolhaas event, the building and its content were in
undisturbed coincidence.

The choice of Koolhaas as a speaker relates to his reputation as an architect
with a critical stance towards architecture's context. Moreover, his buildings are 'large
envelopes for unprogrammed but differentiated activities […] [He designs] something
meaningless in which the meaning of activities will evolve'.[11] This is in sharp contrast
with the absolute predictability of programme and building in the case of the Byzantine
museum. Koolhaas is also a global star architect and this, in itself, turned the event
into a lifestyle happening. Some 1,500 architects, friends of the museum and other
Greeks who visited it only in their school years attended the lecture in the delightful
open courtyard of the museum. Sarcophagi and other Byzantine fragments were used
as seats and the museum since then – due to its broad-minded director – has become
an open structure hosting a variety of events. The building and its programme under-
went a productive dissociation and the locality was detached from its unquestionable
historical and cultural determination. The event coincided with a critical historical
moment in which Greek and Orthodox identity could stand apart for the first time since
the constitution of the modern Greek nation-state.

Ephemeral structures in the city of Athens: in the absence of location the political surfaces

Athens is considered a landscape of history. However, it was with the foundation of
the new nation-state in the nineteenth century, in the context of other emerging
nation-states in Europe, that the landscape was invented as a repository of identity.
Geography, geology and archaeology used the notion of landscape to support national
claims. Layers of history became a testament to Greek identity and the material proof
of a direct connection between modern and ancient Greeks. As a repository of national
identity, the landscape of history was sacred and state protected: Greek identity had to
be consolidated and preserved uncontaminated. Building restrictions applied by the
archaeological service created isolated nuclei of ancient ruins within Greek cities but
also within the Greek territory as a whole. New construction kept the prescribed distance and did not lay claim to any continuity or relation with the past. The past and the
present never coincided deliberately and were actually in sharp opposition. Implementation of architecture competitions, the most prominent example being Bernard
Tschumi's New Acropolis Museum, have had to, in one way or another, deal with
layers of history in the building site.

The Ephemeral Structures in the City of Athens International Architecture Competition (jury chairman, E. Zenghelis), addressed the issue of locality and history, by asking the participants to design not for a specific location but 'in the name of Athens' and without adopting the branding approach by using existing stereotypes. The competition programme, side-stepping the traditional dichotomy between site-specific and generic architecture, brought forth the 'symptoms' of the city by introducing the concept of the parasite and the ephemeral, and asked the participants to consider the political in relation to the city's contemporary conditions. The structures were to be guests of the surface, leaving intact embedded memories and traces of the past. The challenge for architects was to shape the experience of emerging conditions within contemporary Athens.

The competition's 466 entries from 46 countries presented an array of beautiful and celebratory projects. The difficulty of formulating architecture's contemporary relation to the political, where the political is defined as the moment in which a crisis dislocates social constructions, was evident. Only two out of the 466 projects touched on the political and presented the city in a state of emergency.[12] The first one employed barricades but redirected any associations with revolt by turning them into barricades for cultural events (see figure below). Apart from the fact that the project was a direct copy of the 1961 Christo and Jeanne-Claude Paris barrel project,[13] the reference to Paris, May 1968, was straightforward but divested of its political fervour. It represents therefore a clear case of 'recuperation': barricades, a symbol of protest and political radicalism, were recuperated into a mainstream cultural activity.[14] The second project is similar; it had as its starting point the 1922 refugee's settlement within the Athens Royal theatre at Kontzia Square. With no further reference to the

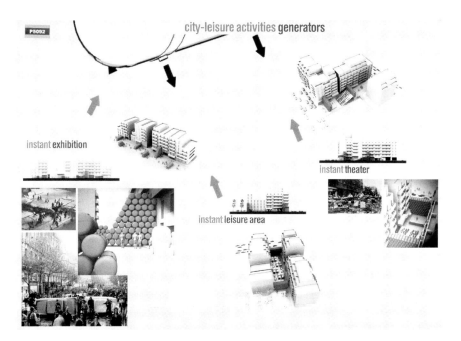

Lacoste Arnaud and Vincon Jerome, 'Barricades: City Leisure Activities Generators' (2002), entry for *Ephemeral Structures in the City of Athens: International Architecture Competition*, Athens. Photograph: Maria Theodorou (2002).

current state of Athens immigrants, the project proposed the occasional occupation of public buildings (parliament, libraries) as a cultural rather than political event.

The competition produced an architecture that celebrated the cultural and indicated the post-critical condition of contemporary architecture. The competing architects were not willing or prepared to think architecture's relation and possible impact onto the changing context, however visible these changes were in the city of Athens. The competition's results called for a critical discussion on architecture's relation to the political – intended as the rupture of existing conditions. The immigrants' catalytic presence in Athens, and in Greece in general, asked for a rethinking of the fragile construction of modern Greek identity, compromised between classical antiquity mythology and conservative Christian Orthodox dogma, and called for a reconsideration of the never contested identification of locality with the stereotypes of national identity. It was an untenable exercise for the architects to design 'in the name of Athens' but it might have been different had they attempted to give shape to Athens' critical context rather than its cultural stereotypes.

Notes

1   'Architecture and Activism' is an ongoing research project that started in September 2005, with a Fulbright visiting fellowship at the School of Architecture at Princeton. The research had, as a point of departure, the work produced in Greece in the last four years of my professional career as Head of the Architecture Network.

2   On the suffix '-scape', see also Arjun Appadurai, *Modernity at Large: Cultural Dimensions of Globalization*, Minneapolis: University of Minnesota Press, 1996, p. 33.

3   Maria Theodorou, 'Athens 2000 A.C.: Forensic Spacescape', *Archis*, July 2000, pp. 68–77.

4   Thomas Maloutas and Nikos Karadimitriou, 'Vertical Social Differentiation in Athens: Alternative or Complement to Community Segregation?', *International Journal of Urban and Regional Research*, 25, 4, December 2001, pp. 699–716.

5   As Slavoj Žižek has pointed out in a number of texts, today's form of multiculturalism comprises a culture that tends to view every culture as a particular difference except itself, and to tolerate everything except criticism (Slavoj Žižek and Glyn Daly (eds), *Conversations with Žižek*, Cambridge: Polity, 2004, p. 20).

6   Athens was the battlefield of the civil war in December 1944. However, such an architectural history of the city's past still remains unwritten, so that painful memories remain undisturbed. An interesting argument was put forward recently by Akes Gavrielides in *H Atherapeuti Nekrophilia tou rizospastikou patriotismou*, Athina: Futura, 2006, where he claims that the victim mentality – adopted as a national idiom by modern Greeks – is a cover for the trauma of civil war.

7   Nikos Sevastakis argues that the civil war took away from thousands of people a 'banal' normal life. It was after the fall of the military junta in 1974 that Greeks gradually discovered normal life pleasures and fully exploited these in the 1990s. Painful memories of loss were substituted with the pleasure of forgetfulness and the enjoyment of the present moment (Nikos Sevastakis, *Koinitope Chora*, Athina: Savvalas, 2004, pp. 49–50). Antonis Karakousis also discusses the formation of this society of pleasure in *Meteore Chora*, Athina: Hestia, 2006.

8   Maria Theodorou, 'Masoch and the Greek City', *Archis*, July 2001, pp. 41–2.

9   On the distinction between reforming and transgressive activism, see Tim Jordan, *Activism! Direct Action, Hacktivism and the Future of Society*, London: Reaktion Books, 2002. In 2000, there was an opening in institutional structures that allowed for reforming activist experiments. The events were included in the Ministry of Culture programme and supported by architectural agents such as the Association of Greek Architects, the Hellenic Institute of Architecture, various schools of architecture etc.

10 On the issue of identity cards and Church mobilisation, see Thanos Lipovats, 'H Koinonia Politon uper tou Xoresmou Orthodoxes Ekklesias kai Kratous', *Sugxrona Themata*, 73, 2000, pp. 12–13; Richard Glogg, *A Concise History of Greece*, 2nd edn, Cambridge: Cambridge University Press, 1992, p. 234.

11 Lian Hurst Mann, '"Spectres of Marx": Contemporary Practices in Critical Realism', in Thomas A. Dutton and Lian Hurst Mann (eds), *Reconstructing Architecture: Critical Discourses and Social Practices*, Minneapolis, London: University of Minnesota Press, 1996, p. 291.

12 'Project P5092' and 'Project P5070', in Maria Theodorou (ed.), *Revelation*, a special issue of *The Athens DOES Series*, vol. 3, Athens: Hellenic Culture Organisation publications, 2003, p. 335 and p. 313, respectively.

13 Christo and Jeanne-Claude, 'Mur provisoire de barils de pétrole, rue Visconti', collage, Paris, 1961, in Jacob Baal-Teshuva, *Christo et Jeanne-Claude*, Köln: Taschen, 1995, p. 20.

14 On recuperation, see Sadie Plant, *The Most Radical Gesture: The Situationist International in a Postmodern Age*, London: Routledge, 1992, passim.

Criticism in/and/of Crisis

The Australian context

Naomi Stead

This chapter is about architectural criticism, journal publishing, and architectural discourse in the Australian context. It takes as its object of enquiry the production, publication, and reception of the author's own essay, 'Three Complaints about Architectural Criticism', commissioned for the commercial journal *Architecture Australia* in 2003.[1] This essay can be seen as a justification and an apology, an argument and a polemic, about the role and significance of architectural criticism for architectural practice in Australia. That context, with all of its constraints and particularities, provides a specific case from which some larger conclusions can perhaps be drawn.

In contemporary architectural discourse, in Australia as elsewhere, the desire to think and to practise critically – to be critical – seems virtually universal, even if the specific meaning or means to achieve this often remain unclear. In particular, the prefix 'critical' appears to have taken on a talismanic character. Employed as a kind of charm, it both pre-empts and wards off a whole range of accusations: of commodification, of irrelevance, of empty formal experimentation, of the submission to spectacle and fashion, and so on. John Whiteman has argued that criticism, and a specifically critical sensibility, is both ubiquitous within and characteristic of our age. Following Immanuel Kant's pronouncement that 'our age is, in every sense of the word, the age of criticism, and everything must submit to it', Whiteman argues that criticism has become a 'way of life' in modern Western societies.

> Truth is what can stand up in the howling gales of criticism. Our age is one of deep suspicion in which everything must be questioned if it is to be substantiated. Truth for us is an unmasking, a laying bare ... We cannot accept the world as it is immediately given to us through 'ordinary' words and images, and instead look for justification behind the veil of deception.[2]

Miriam Gusevich notes that the origins of the word 'criticism', as derived from the Greek 'krinein', are 'to separate, to cut into' and 'to judge, or discern'. Gusevich also states that 'It is also related to a discerning decision, a decisive point, a crisis (kriosis)'.[3] This provides an appropriate entry point into the Australian architectural scene, where there is a widespread belief that architectural criticism is presently, and indeed perpetually, in a state of crisis. Local commentators commonly complain that architectural criticism here is 'not critical enough', and that it is characterised by mild, politely descriptive, aesthetic or formalist approaches. Springing from this are a whole string of further assumptions – that critics are not sufficiently objective, that they are biased by their own connections within the small and close-knit architectural community, that they are complicit with the commercial bias of the journals, that they are timid and afraid of litigation, and that for all of these reasons architectural criticism is as sycophantic as it is irrelevant and ineffectual. But rather than blithely going along with the idea that criticism is in a state of crisis, it will be more interesting here to consider the assumptions and beliefs that these assertions are based upon, and thus examine whether the crisis actually exists.

It is perhaps revealing that the most comprehensive and significant text on architectural criticism remains Wayne Attoe's *Architecture and Critical Imagination*, published in 1978.[4] The fact that this text has not been superseded in nearly three decades is cause for consideration. Perhaps it could be said that the 'theoretical turn' in architectural discourse, which took firm hold in the years after the publication of this book, served to turn attention away from the specific and distinct activity of written architectural criticism. This movement could be seen to have rolled critique and architectural practice together, and thus collapsed the specific and separate utility of written architectural critique. If that is the case, then it is only now that the hegemony of 'criticality' or autonomous and inherently 'critical architecture' is being challenged, that written architectural criticism might be thoroughly re-examined and re-valued.[5] But whatever the explanation, Attoe's book remains a highly useful, if slightly under-theorised, reference point.

This is not to say that there has been no literature on criticism in the intervening years – far from it. A body of literature has attempted to place architectural criticism within a larger theoretical framework, with notable contributions by Miriam Gusevich, and Pattabi Raman and Richard Coyne.[6] The work of Peter Collins has also consistently placed architectural criticism within a larger understanding of judgement in architecture.[7] Other authors, such as Richard Bohn, have concentrated on specific aspects of writing criticism such as the choice of vocabulary,[8] or on the choice of criteria for judging architecture such as Reyner Banham's 'functional considerations'.[9] In recent years there have been several valuable contributions published in the journal *Architectural Record*, and these are distinguished by their emphasis on the practical problems and challenges of writing architectural criticism, especially for a popular audience, and in the mainstream press.[10] There has been some examination of the role of specific journals in bringing together architectural history and theory with practice, with a particular focus on *Oppositions*.[11] There has also been a small but significant subgenre of writing about the role of photography in published architectural criticism.[12] Much of this writing has originated from within the United States or United Kingdom but, within Australia, Paul Hogben has undertaken research into questions of complicity, bias, and 'objectivity' that surround writing in commercial architectural journals.[13] The journal *Architecture Australia* has also taken a lead, especially in recent years under the editorship of Justine Clark, in drawing theoretical discourse and practice together through an intellectual but engaged architectural criticism, and through encouraging a self-reflexive examination of the journal itself as a discursive 'frame'. This brings us back to the object of this chapter, namely the author's own essay, 'Three Complaints about Architectural Criticism'.

This essay, which started with the notional title 'Why Architects Need Critics', was a wide-ranging, journalistic discussion of the milieu of architectural criticism, discourse, and journal publishing in Australia. But the nature of the forum in which it was published, and the rather startling reception that it met on publication, is also relevant here. Within the local scene there is a clear polarisation between academic and journalistic modes of criticism, with the former as long scholarly papers in low-circulation theoretical journals, and the latter as short and accessible articles in high-circulation, glossy commercial magazines. *Architecture Australia* (for which, I should state in the interests of disclosure, I am a contributing editor) is one of the latter. It is also the official publication of the Royal Australian Institute of Architects. It is a commercial, professional journal, primarily aimed at architects, but also with a significant lay readership. It reputedly has the largest circulation of the local architectural journals, however it has sometimes (in the past) been regarded as a rather staid publication, constrained by its association with the Institute, and the attendant responsibility to be the official journal of record in Australian architecture. By comparison, and in crude terms, it is perhaps not as glamorous a magazine as *Monument*, and perhaps not as edgy or eclectic as *Architectural Review Australia*. It is not as theoretically inclined or polemical as the now defunct and sorely missed *Transition*, and neither does it have the scholarly pretensions of the small local academic journals *Architectural Theory Review* or *Fabrications*.

In all of this, *Architecture Australia* emerges as a respectable, quality publication with a measured and generally decorous critical tone. This is not to say that there are no flashes of critical and rhetorical colour, and there have been moments in the journal's century-long history when it has been truly radical. But in the main, *Architecture Australia* represents the mainstream and the establishment. All of this makes the reception of my own essay, 'Three Complaints about Architectural Criticism', all the more interesting. It is worthwhile, then, to re-present some of the argument of that essay here.

Three complaints about architectural criticism

Architectural criticism depends upon architectural practice – this statement is so obvious as to seem silly. The reverse idea, however, that architectural practice also 'depends upon' architectural criticism, is more contentious. The common impulse would be to say that no, architectural criticism is a kind of ancillary activity that takes place outside the margins of true architectural practice, it is always supplementary and therefore subordinate – or even redundant. Yet could it be that works of criticism are sometimes more significant than the works criticised, and even that 'marginal' or 'bad' buildings could give rise to more telling insights than 'good' ones? In the end we must, I would argue, recognise that architectural criticism is useful in itself, in that it contributes significantly to a lively and thoughtful architectural culture. It is a tangible way in which the history and theory of architecture can be rigorously located in current architectural practice, and it is a central and invaluable tool in architectural education – in the basic teaching of design, as well as in the production of reflexive, informed, and discerning professional graduates.

Of course, a practising critic such as myself would naturally believe that criticism is a valuable and worthwhile activity, that critics are not the embittered parasitical nitpickers that we are sometimes made out to be, and that criticism itself can be a productive and creative practice, which is literary but also specifically architectural. More than this, I would like to think that architecture and architectural criticism are bound in a reciprocal and mutually constructive relationship, where each contributes in its own way to the other. But why this perception of constant crisis? And what is it based upon? One obvious answer might lie in Australia's famed 'cultural cringe', with its conviction that everything important, including 'real' architectural criticism, is always done elsewhere. But without delving further into such nationalist anxieties, it is possible to identify three principal attitudes about the purported crisis of architectural criticism in Australia. The first of these is that criticism here is 'not critical enough'.

Architectural criticism as 'not critical enough'

There is a pervasive belief that criticism is only ever rigorous and true if it is negative. In fact, as I have already noted, the etymological origins of the word 'criticism' relate more to discernment, disinterested judgement, and the ability to make distinctions, than to actual fault-finding. Nevertheless, in its everyday usage, the word has become synonymous with negativity, with pulling things apart; and there remains a common belief that even the most insightful and incisive criticism does not count as adequately 'critical' if it comes to an ultimately positive, or even an equivocal conclusion. There is a curious masochism, or at least a deep sense of suspicion, to this sensibility that insists on recasting critical praise as obsequiousness. Perhaps, in some ways, this is a good thing – it is true that things are almost always more complex, and possibly more politically and economically grubby, than they first appear, so a certain scepticism is surely healthy. But it is also rather sad that enthusiasm or praise is read as a sign of naivety or weakness on the part of the critic. It also attests to a kind of readerly bloodlust, a belief that critics should be fearless – either lambs sent naively to the slaughter or willing martyrs to the cause.

Architects seem happy to see their colleagues publicly lambasted: the 'outrage' page in the United Kingdom's *Architectural Review* is often cited as an example of criticism that is appropriately 'strong'. Sure enough, it can be very entertaining to read the rhetorical demolition of a bad building. Likewise, for the critic there is undoubtedly a certain frisson in nastiness, and a righteous satisfaction in condemning bad work. When it comes to their own buildings, however, architects remain astonishingly sensitive and precious, and given to vicious counter-attack.

Architectural criticism almost always happens after the fact, when the building (good or otherwise) is already a fait accompli. This leaves the critic in a difficult position – in the interests of being productive, there seems little point in railing against something that is already done and finished. Of course, bad work can be exposed and discussed as a warning of what should be avoided in the future, just as good work should be emulated. There is also a strong argument that architectural criticism should concern itself with unbuilt schemes, with drawings and ideas and competitions, because it is there that it has the potential to make a direct effect on the design outcome. Architectural criticism also has a role in educating the public about the built environment, which should lead to better architecture through a better-informed client base.

Architectural criticism as ineffectual and irrelevant

The second of the complaints that are levelled against architectural criticism in Australia today seems to ring – rather depressingly – true. This is the idea that criticism is both ineffectual and irrelevant: that the problems of the built environment are so overwhelming and dire, that the vast majority of buildings constructed are so bad, and indeed so actively harmful, that if criticism restricts itself to dilettante commentary on a few notable, largely inner-urban projects, and passes over the worst excesses of the built environment in silence, then it is akin to re-arranging the deckchairs on the Titanic.

But this raises the idea that criticism itself is a kind of honorific activity – that even to be lambasted is a kind of praise, a recognition that the work in question is worthy of note. Likewise, if a work is ignored by the critics, this is an implicit snub, a form of approbation. Embedded within this is the notion of architecture defined in opposition to building. A building only qualifies as 'architecture', and therefore becomes open to serious critical evaluation, if it embodies a sufficient level of quality. The act of architectural criticism carries a judgement of value and worth by definition.

In spite of all this, one need only travel to the outer suburbs of any Australian city to see that architecture is not winning the battle for quality, whether measured according to commodity, firmness, or delight. In the face of such pressing problems, architectural practice itself is marginalised enough, and criticism can be seen to compound this, especially when enacted on solely aesthetic grounds.

But there is a hypocrisy here – on the one hand architectural criticism, particularly in conjunction with the commercial journals, is condemned for its apparent fixation on heroic form and grand gestures, yet on the other hand few people are actually interested in reading about visually or formally bland buildings. Likewise, architects may complain about the prevalence of eye-goggling glamour photography in the magazines, but most still insist on having their own buildings photographed in their best light and from their best angle. Of course there is nothing wrong with this, but if the journals are in fact constrained by an ultimately commercial imperative, then architects (and critics) would do well to examine their own commercial 'bias', especially the exploitation of journals as a form of cheap publicity. And this brings us neatly to the third common complaint about architectural criticism in Australia – that it is not objective enough.

Architectural criticism as 'not objective enough'

The traditional view is that the critic stands in objective judgement of the work, evaluates and assesses it, weighs it against a set of criteria either stated or unstated, and pronounces it good or bad. This conception is predicated on the possibility of absolute value in architecture – the possibility that if a sufficiently authoritative and expert critic could be found, they could make a true and final judgement of a building, and of where it sits on the grand, a-historical scale that is the architectural canon. This criticism would, in turn, be written in a 'universal' voice, as a series of incontrovertible statements. The idea of critical objectivity also extends to the notion that the critic her or himself must be sufficiently 'distant' from the work, preferably being an expert but disinterested bystander. This is partly why academics are commonly seen as particularly suitable critics – because they are ostensibly less enmeshed within the complex webs of friendship, alliance, and commercial rivalry that condition the architectural profession.

These webs of complicity extend to the forums in which criticism is published. In order to be truly critically autonomous, so the logic goes, such a forum must be independent of any implicit or explicit obligation – to audience, architects, advertisers, patrons, or whomever – because any such relationship will result in self-censorship. Accordingly, the commercial journals are argued to perpetuate an architectural 'star-system', a kind of nepotistic 'boys club', where the self-promotion of the architect matters more than the quality of the work. In such a conception, the only winners are the 'favoured circle' of big-name 'starchitects', and architecture degenerates into fashion and commodity fetish. Many aspects of this attitude are questionable, but clearly they all stem from an idea that criticism is only true if it is objective. But this in turn is problematic; the unswerving belief that objectivity is necessary, and that the role of criticism is impartial judgement, should be open and subject to question.

No one approaches architecture with a clean slate: the critic and layperson alike come with a whole array of preconceptions and prejudices – that is, pre-judgements. I would argue that such prejudices are not only inevitable, but they are vital to the interest and value of a given critic's position and voice. The important distinction is less between objective and subjective critics, and more between critics who are explicit about and aware of their biases, and a less reflexive critical practice that leaves its criteria and its assumptions unstated.

Evaluation is not the only, or even the most important, purpose of criticism; critics also interpret, they articulate and identify the significance of architecture. Criticism is also a translation – it relocates and reconstructs the architectural object through language, and in so doing it re-creates that object anew. And this brings us, finally, to the relationship between the practice of architecture and the practice of architectural criticism.

What is good criticism?

It sometimes seems that architects regard critics as blood-sucking ghouls with no talent of their own who take out their frustrated architectural ambitions on the efforts of those who are actually out there doing it. But the fact is that the skills and talents required to be a good architect and those required to be a good architectural critic, while they have a degree of overlap, are quite different. And this provides a hint as to the possibilities of the relationship that might arise between the architect and the critic – a good critic can teach the architect things about their own building, things that they haven't realised, haven't noticed, and perhaps most significantly, haven't intended.

Of the best critics writing in Australia today, some are architects and some are academics; there is no monopoly or franchise on the skill, and few if any of these figures have received formal training in criticism. But their work has significant commonalities. The best critics are informed, they have a body of knowledge – whether about architectural practice, history, theory, or some other thing – and they bring this knowledge to bear upon a work of architecture. In this way they read the work as an exemplar of larger issues, identifying and locating these in the architectural object, while also placing it within a broader physical and intellectual context. The critical process thus simultaneously spirals inwards and expands outwards from the work.

'Three Complaints about Architectural Criticism' was published in the November/December 2003 issue of *Architecture Australia*. By the time the next issue of the magazine was released two months later, it was clear that the essay had created something of a stir. While it may not seem significant on the face of it, by the journal's own standards, three letters to the editor, an unsolicited review in response, two editorials, and anecdotal reports of widespread discussion was an almost unprecedented response. While not all of this was in agreement with the specific content of the essay, all the correspondents concurred that the issues it raised were pertinent, and that there was, indeed, a state of crisis in Australian architectural criticism. But the very unanimity of this response is enough to arouse questions. The essay had set out to articulate some commonly held, but rather under-examined and even lazy assumptions or 'complaints', in order to set them up for a more rigorous discussion and interrogation. What it received was an affirmation of these same complacent assumptions, and the sense that at last, someone had said what everyone was thinking. But this raises the rather curious and paradoxical idea that the crisis in Australian architectural criticism is not at all based in the three complaints rehearsed here, but rather in the comfortable and continuing belief in the crisis itself.

In light of all this, it remains to be seen whether architectural criticism in Australia is actually in crisis, and if so, why this is the case, and what might be done about it. But it is my suspicion that there is in fact no crisis, or at least that the level of crisis at present is the same as it ever was, or even that this so-called 'crisis' is in fact a productive and necessary tension, one that reflects the larger, historically unstable equilibrium between theory and practice, the academy and the profession, architectural discourse and architectural materialisation. Architecture will always need interlocutors to speak of and for it, to analyse and describe, and evaluate it. These interlocutors are architects, certainly, but they are also critics, and both have a crucial role to play in architectural culture.

Notes

1   Naomi Stead, 'Three Complaints about Architectural Criticism', *Architecture Australia*, 92, 2003, pp. 50–2. Discussed here with thanks to Justine Clark, who commissioned the essay, and publisher ArchitectureMedia.

2   John Whiteman, 'Criticism, Representation and Experience in Contemporary Architecture: Architecture and Drawing in an Age of Criticism', *Harvard Architecture Review*, 6, 1987, p. 138.

3   Miriam Gusevich, 'The Architecture of Criticism: a Question of Autonomy', in Andrea Kahn (ed.), *Drawing Building Text*, New York: Princeton Architectural Press, 1991, p. 23, note 20.

4   Wayne Attoe, *Architecture and Critical Imagination*, Chichester: Wiley and Sons, 1978.

5   This is the general argument in a paper co-authored by the author and John Macarthur, 'The Judge is Not an Operator: Criticality, Historiography and Architectural Criticism', *OASE*, 69, 2006, pp. 116–38.

6   Gusevich, 'The Architecture of Criticism', pp. 8–24; Pattabi Raman and Richard Coyne, 'The Production of Architectural Criticism', *Architecture Theory Review*, 5, 2000, pp. 83–103.

7   See Peter Collins, 'The Philosophy of Architectural Criticism', *Architecture: The AIA Journal*, 49, 1968, pp. 46–9; Peter Collins, *Architectural Judgement*, London: Faber, 1971.

8   Richard Bohn, 'Vocabulary: a Critical Discussion of Architectural Criticism, with the View that its Vocabulary isn't Much Help to Professional or Public Understanding', *Architecture Plus*, 2, 1974, pp. 70–1.

9   Reyner Banham, 'Convenient Benches and Handy Hooks: Functional Considerations in the Criticism of the Art of Architecture', in Marcus Whiffen (ed.), *The History, Theory, and Criticism of Architecture: Papers from the 1964 AIA –ACSA Teacher Seminar*, Cambridge, MA: MIT Press, 1965, pp. 91–105.

10 See Suzanne Stephens, 'Assessing the State of Architectural Criticism in Today's Press', *Architectural Record*, 186, March 1998, pp. 64–9; Andrea Oppenheimer Dean, 'Listening to Critics: the Stage is Set', *Architectural Record*, 187, January 1999, pp. 68–70, p. 73.

11 See, for example, Joan Ockman, 'Resurrecting the Avant-Garde: the History and Program of Oppositions', in Beatriz Colomina (ed.), *Architectureproduction*, New York: Princeton Architectural Press, 1988, pp. 181–99; Mitchell Schwarzer, 'History and Theory in Architectural Periodicals: Assembling Oppositions', *Journal of the Society of Architectural Historians*, 58, 1999, pp. 342–8.

12 See Thomas Schumacher, 'Over-Exposure: on Photography and Architecture', *Harvard Design Magazine*, Fall 1998, pp. 4–7; James Russell, 'Fading Photographs', *Harvard Design Magazine*, Fall 1998, pp. 44–9.

13 Paul Hogben, 'Maintaining an Image of Objectivity: Reflections on an Institutional Anxiety', *Architecture Theory Review*, 6, 2001, pp. 63–75.

Architecture-Writing

Introduction

Architecture-Writing

Jane Rendell

The idea for the 'Critical Architecture' conference came from my own dissatisfaction with the current state of architectural criticism.[1] Whether in academic journals or publications connected with professional practice, very few critics seem willing to consider the purposes and possibilities of architectural criticism, or to reflect upon their choice of subject matter and modes of interpretation and operation. The level of self-reflectivity in architectural criticism lags behind architectural history and theory, and certain practices of architectural design. If one compares the level of intellectual debate concerning architectural criticism to discussions in other disciplines, namely art and literature, this sense of stagnation is reinforced.[2] To date, in architecture, although there has been some exploration of the relation between criticism, history, and theory, there has been, to my knowledge, none of the relation between criticism and critical practice.[3]

Art criticism was a hot topic in the British art journal *Art Monthly* in 2003. Essays and letters debated the purpose and appropriate modes of art criticism in terms of ethics, aesthetics and politics. One particular strand of the discussion focused on art writing, providing inspiration for the 'Architecture-Writing' session of the 'Critical Architecture' conference.[4] When, in April 2002, I was invited by Alex Coles to chair a session at a conference at Tate Britain called 'The All New Art Writing', I was keen to raise concerns that focused on space and subjectivity in contemporary art writing, asking critics to consider the positions they occupied not only in connection to art works but also in relation to writing itself. However, post-conference, and in the pages of *Art Monthly*, the debate was constructed along adversarial lines, sticking to binary rather than discursive models: art writing rather than the non-expressive theoretical models of academic criticism, political critique rather the formalism of art writing. My contribution was to say:

> It is worth pointing out that the term art writing is not new, it has been around in so-called academic circles for some time now. Art writing is not about restating a case for formalism, but it does explore differing writing

modes [. . .] the very form of the writing itself is taken to be integral to the way in which a critic positions him/herself. Feminist critics, such as Griselda Pollock, Mieke Bal, Rosalind Krauss and others, have been examining critical distance, questions of intimacy and the relationships critics construct with artists, art works and places for producing and viewing art. The personal and the autobiographical enter the debate, not in order to assert an ego criticism, but as part of an on-going political exploration of subjectivity.

(Jane Rendell, 'Art Writing', *Art Monthly*, 272,
December 2003–January 2004, p. 15)

The points I introduced at 'The All New Art Writing' conference are I think still pertinent to the current debate. They require that we look outside art journalism to other modes of writing in order to develop an art criticism that is self-reflective and creative, as well as politically aware.

The possibilities opened up for criticism by art writing engage closely with debates around the relationship between theory and critical practice in the visual and spatial arts. But what happens when such ideas are taken into architectural criticism? Are such concepts and creative modes of production derived from elsewhere seen to be as relevant to architecture as those generated within the discipline itself? At many points during the 'Critical Architecture' conference we returned to questions concerning disciplinary specificity and this particular line of enquiry runs through many of the chapters in this collection. For some, interdisciplinary debate is a distraction: critical enquiry and architectural production are relevant only when they emerge out of architecture itself.[5] For others, including myself, 'travelling concepts' are indispensable,[6] they allow us to challenge assumptions internal to disciplines and to re-think, in this instance, what architecture is, what it might be and how we might think, write and make buildings critically. This is not to ignore the particularity of the context in which architectural criticism is located – the architectural profession – but to return to it, having been transformed through ideas experienced elsewhere.

I choose 'Architecture-Writing' as a title for the theme of my conference strand and for this section of the book in reference to my research into art writing. Interestingly Katja Grillner, who has also contributed a chapter to *Critical Architecture*, has linked these two words in the opposite way, as 'Writing Architecture'.[7] What difference does it make if one word comes before another, or if a preposition, for example, 'for', 'with', 'to', is inserted between the two terms?[8] And what of the hyphen? This small line that brings architecture and writing into close proximity allows us to think of one in relation to the other, but it also creates a compound or hybrid form. I focus here on this seemingly insignificant point of conjunction, on such a tiny detail as the hyphen, to demonstrate the importance of the decisions we make in designing the position of words – writing constructs as well as reflects meaning.

To date, criticism has operated through the medium of writing, but there is no reason why it cannot take new forms – those of art, film or even architecture. Each medium has an architectonics – a series of procedures for the material organisation, structure and construction of space. In writing we might think of the patterning of words on a page or the design of a page itself – its edges, boundaries, thresholds, surfaces and the relation of one page to another – as the distribution of objects in space. So it is possible to consider criticism as a form of architecture, and it is also desirable, because in so doing, in thinking one in terms of another, we are able to see more clearly what the differences between the two might be, and what is at stake in the binary and often hierarchical definition of those differences. Literary critic Mary Ann Caws makes use of the term 'architexture', and it is one which I think describes beautifully a possibility for architecture-writing:

> The use of the term 'architexture' is meant quite simply to call attention to the surface texture of the construction made by reading. As architecture involves etymologically both the concept of origin and that of the building process, architexture would involve both construction and material texture, would concentrate upon their interplay. As architexture situates the text in the world of other texts. The architexture of a particular work refers to the structure of the connecting passage, bridge, or corridor between elements as it relates to the material of the text or to that stretching between two texts [...].
>
> (Mary Ann Caws, *A Metapoetics of the Passage: Architextures in Surrealism and After*, Hanover and London: University Press of New England, 1981, p. xiv)

Here, in this section of *Critical Architecture*, the first three chapters explore respectively the place of writing, theory and criticism as forms of critical practice, as what we might call practice-led or practice-based research. While Rolf Hughes discusses the prose poem as a hybrid genre that combines critical and creative writing practices, in relation to her own work as an artist, Laura Ruggeri explores the potential of metaphor as a place of spatial transformation, rather than a solely literary or semiotic device. And choosing active criticism over critical action, Paul Shepheard sets out his own proposition for architectural criticism: 'to write about material action by being embedded in it.'

The next three chapters turn to film and photography, as not only subjects, but also modes of architectural criticism. In 'Film as Spatial Critique', film-maker Patrick Keiller suggests that 'film space can offer an implicit critique of actual space', and that researching as well as making films can act as a form of architectural criticism. Igea Troiani considers the potential of the documentary as a filmic genre for developing architectural criticism, one utilised in her own practice as an architectural historian involved in the production of films. By emphasising the importance of conversation as a research tool, the documentary, Troiani argues, places emphasis on the role of collaboration in architectural design. Robin Wilson explores the work of art-architecture collaborative, Warren and Mosely, in order to examine how the architectural photograph plays a critical role in architectural journalism.

Finally, the last three chapters in the section explore the role of memory and writing in relation to architectural criticism. Katja Grillner takes up Walter

Benjamin's comments on the experience of architecture as one of distraction not concentration, and proceeds to demonstrate, by journeying through Haga Park in Stockholm, distracted by her childhood memories, how architectural criticism can operate 'out-of-focus'. Artist Sharon Kivland also examines the role of memory in the rewriting of place in relation to two of her art works, 'Memoirs' and 'Cela aura déjà eu lieu' ('It will have happened already'). In her chapter, she explores memory in relation to the psychoanalytic terms 'repetition', 'resistance', 'recollection' and 'reminiscence'. Finally, also drawing on themes of repetition and reminiscence, my own chapter reworks a series of childhood memories of spaces, following the trajectory of a specific piece of writing from criticism, where the memories evoked provided a critique of an art work, to a work of my own composed of two scenes of writing, one in a window, the other in a book. We might conclude here, with Virginia Woolf, that the writing of a memory is the making of a scene:

> These scenes, by the way, are not altogether a literary device – a means of summing up and making a knot out of innumerable little threads. Innumerable threads there were; still, if I stopped to disentangle, I could collect a number. But whatever the reason may be, I find that scene making is my natural way of marking the past. A scene always comes to the top; arranged, representative. This confirms me in my instinctive notion – it is irrational; it will not stand argument – that we are sealed vessels afloat upon what it is convenient to call reality; at some moments, without a reason, without an effort; the sealing matter cracks; in floods reality; that is a scene – for they would not survive entire so many ruinous years unless they were made of something permanent; that is a proof of their 'reality'.
>
> (Virginia Woolf, *Moments of Being*, edited with an introduction and notes by Jeanne Schulkind, London: The Hogarth Press, 1985, p. 142)

The nine chapters in 'Architecture-Writing' suggest that the objects and subjects, as well as the practices of architectural criticism, may come from beyond architecture and might include art, film, writing and philosophy. 'Architecture-Writing' expects that in order to reflect upon the specificity of our own modes of operation as architectural critics, we draw on knowledge gleaned both from within architecture but also from beyond it, recognising that the new understandings produced have relevance both to architecture but also to other subjects and disciplines. Finally, if we consider the modes in which we practise criticism to define and produce critical positions, then the 'architectonics' of criticism – the structure, processes and materials of the media employed – should be considered integral to the construction of architectural criticism. 'Architecture-Writing' shows that criticism is itself a material practice, which focuses on the interrogation and configuration of the changing relationship between a critic, architecture and writing.

Notes

1   For a summary of the 'Critical Architecture' conference content, see www.bartlett.
     ucl.ac.uk/architecture/events/conferences/conferences.html.

2   See, for example, Gavin Butt (ed.) *After Criticism: New Responses to Art and Perfor-
     mance*, Oxford: Blackwell Publishing, 2005.

3   See Kate Nesbitt (ed.) *Theorizing a New Agenda for Architecture: an Anthology of
     Architectural Theory 1965–1995*, New York: Princeton Architectural Press, 1996, p.
     16; Michael K. Hays (ed.) *Architecture Theory Since 1968*, Cambridge, MA: MIT
     Press, 2000, p. v. See also Neil Leach (ed.) *Rethinking Architecture*, London: Rout-
     ledge, 1997; Iain Borden and Jane Rendell (eds) *InterSections: Architectural History
     and Critical Theory*, London: Routledge, 2000.

4   See Alex Coles, 'The Bathroom Critic', *Art Monthly*, 263, February 2003, pp. 7–10;
     Michael Archer, 'Crisis what Crisis?', *Art Monthly*, March 2003, 264, pp. 1–4;
     Rasheed Araeen, letter in response to 'Crisis what Crisis?', *Art Monthly,* April 2003,
     265, pp. 12–13; Matthew Arnat, 'The Middle Distance', response to Michael Archer,
     Art Monthly, April 2003, 265, p. 43; Peter Suchin, 'The Critic Never Sleeps', *Art
     Monthly,* May 2003, 266, p. 41; Michael Archer, 'Critical Task', letter in response to
     'The Critic Never Sleeps', *Art Monthly*, June 2003, 267, p. 9; Rasheed Araeen,
     'Opportunism', letter in response to 'Critical Task', *Art Monthly*, July–August 2003,
     268, p. 14; J.J. Charlesworth, 'The Dysfunction of Criticism', *Art Monthly*, September
     2003, 269, pp. 1–4. The debate then turned to the role of the artist/curator, but has
     recently reverted to discussions of criticism in the form of artist Dave Beech's attack
     on critic Julian Stalleybrass. See Dave Beech, 'Art's Debunkers', *Art Monthly,* Febru-
     ary 2005, 283, pp. 2–4. See also Sarah James, 'The Ethics of Aesthetics', *Art
     Monthly,* March 2005, 284, pp. 7–10.

5   A variation on this position is the one that argues that architecture is itself interdisci-
     plinary and so has no need to engage with other disciplines. For an expanded discus-
     sion of many of these issues, see Jane Rendell, 'Architectural Research and
     Disciplinarity', *ARQ (Architecture Research Quarterly)*, 8, 2, 2004, pp. 141–7.

6   For an extended discussion, see Jane Rendell, 'Travelling the Distance/Encountering
     the Other', in David Blamey (ed.), *Here, There, Elsewhere: Dialogues on Location and
     Mobility*, London: Open Editions, 2002, pp. 43–54; Jane Rendell, 'Writing in Place of
     Speaking', in Sharon Kivland and Lesley Sanderson (eds), *Transmission: Speaking and
     Listening,* vol. 1, Sheffield Hallam University and Site Gallery, 2002, pp. 15–29.

7   See www.akad.se/progwri.htm (AKAD: The Academy for Practice-based Research in
     Architecture and Design), in particular the workshops: 'Writing Architecture' (June
     2004 to January 2005, KTH Royal Institute of Technology, Stockholm). See also Katja
     Grillner 'The Halt at the Door of the Boot-Shop', in Katja Grillner *et al.* (eds), *01.AKAD*,
     Stockholm: AKAD and AxlBooks, 2005; Katja Grillner, 'Writing and Landscape –
     Setting Scenes for Critical Reflection', in Jonathan Hill (ed.), *Opposites Attract:
     Research by Design*, a special issue of *The Journal of Architecture*, 8, 2, Summer
     2003, pp. 239–49. See also the chapter by Rolf Hughes in *Critical Architecture*; Rolf
     Hughes, 'The Poetics of Practice-Based Research', in Hilde Heynen (ed.), *Unthinkable
     Doctorates?*, a special issue of *The Journal of Architecture*, 11, 3, 2006, pp. 283–301.

8   The role of the preposition is a personal fascination. For me, prepositions indicate the
     importance of 'position' and 'relation' in the spatial encounter between the critic and
     the art or architectural work. Michel Serres, for example, writes of the angelic qual-
     ities of prepositions in terms of their role as messengers and their transformational
     qualities. See Michel Serres, *Angels: a Modern Myth*, Paris: Flammarion Press, 1995,
     pp. 140–7.

The DROWNING METHOD

On giving an account in practice-based research[1]

Rolf Hughes

> The search for the voice in language, this is what is called thought.
>> (Giorgio Agamben, quoted in Mladen Dolar, *A Voice and Nothing More*,
>> Cambridge, MA: MIT Press, 2006, p. 11)

> It has rightly been said that all great works of literature found a genre or dissolve one – that they are, in other words, special cases.
>> (Walter Benjamin, 'The Image of Proust', *Illuminations*, edited by Hannah Arendt, translated by Harry Zohn, New London: Fontana Press, 1992, p. 197)

> la battaglia delli diversi pensieri . . .
> The battle of diverse thoughts –
> The actual twisting
> Of many and diverse thoughts
> What form should that take?
>> (Louis Zukofsky ' "Mantis", An Interpretation' [1934], *New Directions*,
>> New York: New Directions Publishing Corp., 1936)

According to Gilles Deleuze and Felix Guattari, Friedrich Nietzsche laid down the task of philosophy when he wrote:

> [Philosophers] must no longer accept concepts as a gift, nor merely purify and polish them, but first *make* and *create* them, present them and make them convincing. Hitherto one has generally trusted one's concepts as if they were a wonderful dowry from some sort of wonderland.

But this trust, Deleuze and Guattari write, should now be replaced by distrust – above all, philosophers should be distrustful of those concepts they did not create themselves.[2] The development of practice-based research in the creative disciplines has created an urgent need for new writing practices that challenge conventions of objectivity and judgement in research writing, and investigate through a close engagement with *genre* and *style* related questions of *voice* and *subjectivity*, *point-of-view* and *per-*

spective, *gender* and *embodiment*, as well as the indivisibility of *meaning* and *material-ity*. This chapter accordingly explores how elements of literary, critical and philosophi-cal genres of inquiry can contribute to more insightful analyses, resonant descriptions and reflective accounts of design practice.

When we distinguish between 'creative' writing (stories, poems, novels, plays, monologues, aphorisms, etc.) and 'critical' writing (essays, theoretical articles, reviews, scientific papers, academic dissertations, monographs, research reports etc.), we are left with an inconvenient heap of 'in-between' genres – philosophy, certain historical, religious or meditative texts, the lyrical essay and various experimental generic hybrids – that do not sit easily in one category or the other and thereby under-mine the impulse to distinguish between 'creative' and 'critical' writing.[3] The increas-ing hybridisation of professional and disciplinary practices and identities suggests that when giving an account of such cross-pollinated activities, we will need to hybridise the genres of writing as well. Those now staking a claim for their practice to be regarded as a form of research – among others, artists, designers and architects – are ideally situated to extend the *forms* of critical writing, its generic assumptions and epistemic implications. Such issues resonate far beyond art and design research itself at a time when the epistemological foundations of knowledge have been shown to be, at best, provisional and mutable.

Did philosophy begin with a burp, a belch, a hiccup? The idea is supported by possibly the most famous outbreak of hiccups in history – those that afflicted Aristophanes in Plato's *Symposium* at the precise moment when it was his turn to deliver a speech in praise of love, an attack so violent that, we are told, 'making a speech was totally out of the question'.[4] The question implies a set of questions about the relation between the body, the voice, the word and – eventually – the written text. According to Simon Goldhill, the development of the prose of philosophy and science was inseparable from the vigorously contested issue of 'giving an account', or *logon didonai*, in the classical city of Plato and Socrates. Each was based on an unresolved tension between authority and persuasiveness – the seemingly irreconcilable impulses of disclosure and dissimulation.[5] Thus, Goldhill claims, at the same time as Plato is designing a formal model of philosophic argumentation – effectively setting up philo-sophy as *the* authoritative model for understanding the world – he is also 'brilliantly adopting and adapting the persuasive, dramatic power of the dialogue format and its lures of narrative and characterization'. Socrates – 'the authority figure who claims and disclaims [his own] authority' – is central to this project:

> Central to the paradoxical fascination of Plato is the strategic choice not to represent his own voice but always to remain concealed within and behind the conversation of the bare-footed wandering gadfly, questioning and teasing whomever he happens to meet.
>
> (Goldhill, 'Philosophy and Science', p. 109)

With Aristotle's treatises on logic, however, argument becomes its own master – 'Argument's truth or authority does not depend on an ability to persuade an audience, but on its own rules,' Goldhill writes.[6] Debate – the clamour of competing voices – becomes silenced by the authority of philosophic argument. And with the arrival of prose comes a new sense of humankind as a responsible and knowing agent, making prose 'the medium of the intellectual, cultural and social revolution of the Greek enlightenment'.[7]

The theological dimension to this struggle between voice and Word (in all its abstract, disembodied authority) can be found in Saint Augustine's interpretation of St John's Gospel, specifically his analogy of John the Baptist as *voice* as opposed to Christ, who remains Word, *verbum, logos*:

> The voice precedes the Word and it makes possible its understanding [...] What is the voice, what is the word? Examine what happens in you and form your own questions and answers. This voice which merely resonates and offers no sense, this sound which comes from the mouth of someone screaming, not speaking, we call it the voice, not the word [...] But the word, if it is to earn its name, has to be endowed with sense and by offering the sound to the ear it offers at the same time something else to the intellect.
>
> (St. Augustine, *Confessions*, quoted in Dolar,
> *A Voice and Nothing More*, p. 16)

This marks an early separation of medium and message, mediator and meaning, poetry and sense. Augustine writes of the necessity of the voice (John the Baptist) diminishing, even being effaced, as the Word (Christ) grows.[8] In this dichotomy of embodied voice and disembodied signifier, we see why Western philosophy has long shunned detailed investigation of the implications of its own *materiality* – in other words, the acknowledgement that its history is largely a history of *written texts*. Berel Lang writes:

> The assumption [...] is that the act of writing has nothing – at least nothing *essential* – to do with the act of philosophy; that philosophy as spoken, 'oral' philosophy, would have the same character that written or 'literary' philosophy does, and that the two of them would be identical to philosophy as it might be thought but not yet expressed, or even to philosophy in its hidden truth before it had been thought at all.
>
> (Berel Lang, *The Anatomy of Philosophical Style*, Oxford:
> Basil Blackwell Ltd, 1990, p. 11)

Syntax and *language*, as well as the materiality of *manuscripts* and *books*, affect *what* is written as much as individual authorial *style* – for all its residues of the author's voice.[9] In contrast, several theorists of practice-based research, among them Jenny Wolmark and Eleanor Gates-Stuart, advocate that we consider research not as a codified form of academic inquiry but rather as 'a cultural practice that is generated by and through the intersection with other cultural practices'. This acknowledges that all experience is *embodied* and that knowledge is therefore *situated*: 'Situated knowledge is no longer decontextualized and removed from the social and cultural relations in which it is embedded.'[10] This clarifies the potential contribution of strategies, methods and concepts from other discursive regimes, such as literature, to forms of practice that cannot be satisfactorily articulated within the formal properties of reason alone. I therefore propose an account of writing for practice-based research (one informed by exploratory or so-called 'creative' writing) that is not antagonistic to the practical (or 'tacit') knowledge of artists, architects and designers, but rather an integral tool during such investigations. One important aspect of this concerns the capacity of literary and philosophical writing to influence and extend our way of seeing the world.[11]

A good reader acquires the ability to discern the parameters of a representation and the play of interpretative possibilities in a manner analogous to that involved in the appreciation of a work of art. The reader acquires *judgement* – a 'way of seeing' comparable to the Aristotelian notion of *phronesis* (practical wisdom). Like *phronesis*, this involves a skilled performance, acquired through repetitive practice but only after exposure to a range of ambiguous concepts and the repertoire of strategies employed for their resolution.[12] As in *phronesis*, the development of a given level of skill creates the conditions for still more skilled performances in the future. Just as practical wisdom becomes second nature to the *phronimos*, so good judgement – an essential attribute of a successful designer and researcher alike – becomes second nature to the person who can reason in a way that is both relevant and yet innovative.

Art and design researchers can learn from *dialogical* forms such as the paradoxical literary genre of the prose poem, or the staging of perspectives in Ludwig Wittgenstein's *Philosophical Investigations,* a form which borders on the literary and aphoristic, staging on the page an internalised, seemingly irreconcilable philosophical dialogue.[13] Both examples are compelling and complex forms for modelling argument. Critical language in particular has much to learn from the capacity of the prose poem to innovate, its subversive neither/nor status (neither poetry nor prose, prose nor poetry) and its ability to transform the way we see the world by substituting alternative, 'unthinkable' or 'animal' logics, staging shifting points of view, changing perspectives, empathetic as well as analytical forms of understanding, appeals to embodiment, the sensory, the comical, the absurd, in short – experiential knowledge.

So what exactly is a prose poem? Michael Benedikt answers as follows:

> The best working definition that we can give at this point – that perhaps *ought* to be given at this point, when we ourselves are in the midst of such a widespread exploration of the form – is that it is a genre of poetry, self-consciously written in prose, and characterized by the intense use of virtually all the devices of poetry, which includes the intense use of devices of verse. The sole exception to access to the possibilities, rather than the set priorities of verse is, we would say, the line break.
>
> (Michael Benedikt, *The Prose Poem: an International Collection*,
> New York: Dell Publishing, 1976, pp. 46–7)

For Jonathan Monroe, the prose poem is 'a genre that does not want to be itself'. The pairing of the words 'prose' and 'poem' suggests a synthetic utopian third term (neither poetry nor prose but something *other* altogether), but it also implies (Monroe continues) the continuing irresolution of the two opposing terms that constitute it, thereby focusing our attention on the desire for a resolution of existing contradictions and antagonistic relations.[14] It is thus a paradigmatic example of what Fredric Jameson has called the 'symbolic enactment of the social within the formal and the aesthetic'.[15] In Nikki Santilli's account, the prose poem variously designates 'the literary space of battle' – it is a genre 'founded on subversion' in which 'a network of different discourses [Mikhail Bakhtin's dialogism] appropriates a recognisable genre and subverts it in each text', thereby exposing 'the extent to which our understanding of language is driven by our recognition of types of discourse'.[16] It is interesting in this respect to note that what would conventionally be classified as a critical work, albeit an unconventional one, namely Roland Barthes' *L'Empire des Signes*, has also been claimed as a prose poem, one that expresses the ideology of genre and the impossibility of translating its use-value from one culture, or historical epoch, to another.[17] In short, what characterises the various accounts of the prose poem genre, as well as writings about it, is the element of 'struggle, formalized by paradox'.[18] At the same time, Benedikt rightly emphasises that:

> Most prose poets – particularly the crucial, founding figures such as Baudelaire, Rimbaud, Mallarmé, and Valéry – were considered to be among the major poets in verse; and that many of the pioneering writers in the form 'discovered' prose poetry towards the ends of their careers, when their command of poetry and their sense of its possibilities were presumably at their most practiced and acute. Surely, if one is to derive definitions from the perspectives of poets, rather than from critical stipulations imposed from without, one also ought to define the prose poem in terms of the feelings of those writing it, the substantial stature of its poets, and their importance to poetry generally.
>
> (Benedikt, *The Prose Poem*, pp. 47–8)

What interests me here is the possibility of a *hybrid genre*, a *monstrous* fusion of creative and critical strategies, one that exhibits simultaneously a *love* and *distrust* of language and seeks not to embellish what can be said more simply, but to find the most direct, straightforward way of saying something complex. For, crucially, if we lose our capacity to be surprised, to be taken aback, to be astonished (with all the reversals of expectations this implies), we have also lost the means of escaping the monotonous repetition of our disciplinary and discursive heritage. It is our capacity for *astonishment* that brings about change in the dawning of an aspect. We can find astonishment in philosophy, of course, but art – and, specifically, poetry – is particularly attuned to catching us off guard:

> To defend poetry means to defend a fundamental gift of human nature, that is, our capacity [...] to experience astonishment and to stop still in that astonishment for an extended moment or two.
>
> (Adam Zagajewski, *Another Beauty*, translated by Clare Cavanagh, New York: Farrar, Straus and Giroux, 1998, p. 116)[19]

Now is the moment to pause this discussion for an extended moment or two, to dwell on (or in) the following text:

Air Trance 16

If the motion of wind were to be slowed, as weather is slowed briefly when an animal is born, we would notice a man building and destroying his own house. If we speak to a man through a dense rain, our speech is menaced by the DROWNING METHOD, and we appear to him to be people that are angry and shouting. If my father is the man we are looking at, he will shout back at me, protecting the house with his hand, and his voice will blend with whatever weather he has decided to create in the sky between us to form a small, hard animal, which, once inside me, will take slow, measured, strategic bites. The animal's eating project will produce in others the impression that I am kneeling, lying, or fading in an area of total rain, taking shelter behind my upraised hand. Since they will be standing above me, the people will need to request special powers of vision, which will be immediately granted, in order that I appear in slow, original colours, viewed from any possible perspective, chewing with great care at my own body while the house gets smashed behind me.

(Ben Marcus, 'Air Trance 16', in *The Age of Wire and String*, New York: Alfred A. Knopf, 1995)

'Air Trance 16' is not a *typical* prose poem. No such thing exists – the prose poem form invents itself unceasingly. But let us at least note a number of characteristics of the prose poem on display here – for example, the greater *compression of information* than is typically found in narrative fiction – due in part to a general indifference to *transitional expressions* (i.e. to 'logical' causality).[20] Prose poems typically open abruptly, with a *statement*, *proposition*, *question* or *fragment* that establishes setting, mood, attitude, personality, circumstance (and thereby, in short, 'situates' the reader). Details may not be connected in any familiar way – rather, disconnection, the eruption of the unexpected combined with an absence of rules, typically recur. There is conventional grammar in the passage, but grammatical rules are also frequently violated – the threat of dissolution is never far away as the prose poem thrives in the borderland between coherence and incoherence, structure and freedom, audience and marginality. Finally, although a prose poem may be highly visual, as here, it rarely neglects to order its images or events into a *sequence*; things happen, the centre does not hold, the conclusion slams shut one door even as several others fly open in different directions (or the house collapses altogether).

So while I may not 'understand' this passage on a first reading (assuming that understanding and meaning are part of my reading agenda), I do feel curiously *moved* by it, and, importantly, this motivates me to look closer. I might then notice the *visual* imagery and the active dramatic terms that are used ('menaced', 'angry', 'shouting', 'smashed'), which yet co-exist with a strong sense of *time* being slowed, almost to the point of stasis, almost as if it were a *tableau* being described. And yet there is nonetheless narrative development – a conflict, a crisis and a resolution are depicted, corresponding to Aristotle's proposed beginning, middle and end in *The Poetics*. So we have a formal tension between two contrary motions – that of narrative, development, 'progress', on the one hand, and that of stasis on the other. If (still at the general level) we seek clarification by asking the type of questions that are useful to ask of fiction (and of criticism too, for that matter) – such as: *who is speaking? To whom? At what distance? And with what motivations?* – we get stuck at the very first question since there is no single identifiable 'voice' to help us to establish perspectives in the text – there is a movement from the first person plural ('we'), to the third person ('him'), to a more specified third person ('my father'), to the first person ('I'); in other words, from the general to the specific, or from the collective voice of the crowd to an individual voice, of which the gender, age, nationality, background, the humanity even, remain unspecified. Such perspectival morphing is accompanied by shifts in perspective ('[…] we would notice […] we appear to him to be […] he will shout back at me […] the animal's eating project will produce in others the impression that I am kneeling, lying, or fading […] they will be standing above me […] I appear in slow, original colours, viewed from any possible perspective […]' etc.), and these are accompanied, in turn, by changes in agency (or authority) – from the indeterminate ('[…] as weather is slowed briefly when an animal is born […] the people will need to request special powers of vision, which will be immediately granted […]' etc.), rendered by the use of the passive tense (another formal contrast to the aforementioned dramatic, dynamic verbs), to the highly specific ('[…] a man building and destroying his own house […] a small, hard animal, which, once inside me, will take slow, measured, strategic bites […]' etc.). It should now be clear that logic here is being interrogated at the level of *grammar* – that 'Air Trance 16' can be read as a Wittgensteinian language game, one that constructs its edifice of meaning in the liminal zone between sense and non-sense. Even the prominence of the conditional at the head of the first three sentences ('*If* the motion […] *If* we speak […] *If* my father […]', *my italics*), with its invitation to *play* (to say, in effect, 'let's pretend'), is reminiscent of Wittgenstein's recurring rhetorical gambits ('Consider this […] Imagine the following […]' etc.). Such invitations are inclusive, dialogic and connective – they acknowledge the reader's role in the game of making sense. Jerry McGuire discusses this in terms of the balance struck between 'eccentricity' and 'communicative pleasure' via the '(verbal) commonplace':

> We love it when our words connect us, so much so that we're willing to sacrifice much valuable eccentricity – of meaning, of feeling, of perception […]. Every poet strikes his or her own balance between eccentricity and the (verbal) commonplace.
>
> (Jerry McGuire, review of *Small Boat* by Lesle Lewis, in Brian Clements (ed.), *Sentence: a Journal of Prose Poetics* 2, Dallas: Firewheel Editions, 2004, p. 201)

We might further discuss the repetitive and ritualistic aspects of the piece (the title hints at a form of industrial production, or at least implies the existence of 'Air Trance

1–15' – and, conceivably, 'Air Trance 17–18' – while the unending construction and deconstruction of the home, the 'special powers of vision' which are routinely requested and 'immediately granted', the presence of the body as simultaneously source of knowledge and punishment, implied parasite (metaphorically, on the father) and parasitic host (for both the 'small, hard animal' and, subsequently, the unoriginal self), as well as the cyclical destruction of the house with which the piece ends, all suggests that we are within the realm of ritual, a place where normal rules do not apply, but where rules, inscrutable as they may be, are nonetheless sacrosanct. Some readers may choose instead to focus on the relationship(s) of the father to others in the text – the paterfamilias, or dreadful Old Testament *auctor vitae* with his remorse-less drive towards destruction, violence and, it seems (we are denied access to the father's motivations), authority for authority's sake. Others still might examine the treatment of *space* in the work, the problematisation of boundaries separating *inside* and *outside*, spectator and observed. Whatever our critical lens, it is clear the *hybrid* principle is at work in this mode of discourse – 'DROWNING METHOD', for example, clearly belongs to the reference work, scholarly citation, the orthodoxies of footnotes and encyclopaedic cross-reference. At the same time, each discursive practice, by being radically de-contextualised, is subjected to the corrosive, de-familiarising effect of a form of (literary) sampling, (grammatical) manipulation and (narrative/logical) sequencing. This, I suggest, is one site where literary and philosophical writing meet. The hiccups are cured, the Word effaced; the reader rubs up against the grain of the voice(s).

Prose poems thus radically de-familiarise prevailing ideological conventions and codes, and are often associated with (as Bakhtin celebrates in the novel) 'the eter-nally living element of unofficial language and unofficial thought'.[21] Moreover, the appropriation and re-contextualisation of a broad range of discursive practices creates a fundamentally unsettling hybrid textuality – to the extent of destabilising the terms by which meaning, conventionally, *means*. Both critical and imaginative faculties are called into action; the reader *experiences* the point being made, which becomes all the more compelling as a result.

> 564. Now when the aspect dawns, can I separate a visual experience from a thought-experience? – If you separate them the dawning of the aspect seems to vanish.

> 565. I think it could also be put this way: *Astonishment* is essential to a change of aspect. And astonishment is thinking.
> (Ludwig Wittgenstein, *Last Writings on the Philosophy of Psychology*, vol. 1, edited by G.H. von Wright and Heikki Nyman, translated by C.G. Luckhardt, §129)[22]

Can we create conditions favourable to astonishment? If so, how might such con-ditions be represented in literature, architecture and research? The question is for another time, but we might note Wittgenstein's emphasis on knowledge as something

– startlingly – *animal* in *On Certainty*, which illustrates his aim to 'dissolve' philosophical metaphysical problems on the basis of alternative representations:

> I want to regard man here as an animal; as a primitive being to which one grants instinct but not ratiocination. As a creature in a primitive state. Any logic good enough for a primitive means of communication needs no apology from us. Language did not emerge from some kind of ratiocination.
>
> (Ludwig Wittgenstein, *On Certainty*, edited by G.E.M. Anscombe and G.H. von Wright, translated by Denis Paul and G.E.M. Anscombe, Oxford: Basil Blackwell Ltd, 1979, p. 62e, §475)

When we compare these alternative representations, we gain insight into what we might call the 'grammar' of concepts.[23] Hence the value of 'impure' or hybrid genres, and of experiential and sensory knowledge. Metaphor, like *form* (as Jacques Derrida argues in *Writing and Difference*), is never innocent, but rather orients research and fixes results.[24] If writing in practice-based art and design research is to be a tool of discovery or a performance of inquiry, rather than a ritualised repetition of established generic conventions, metaphor and form may appropriately be architectonic, disruptive, dialogic, polyphonic, animal, monstrous even – in short, structured according to a different logic of argumentation, one which unsettles generic conventions and the author's implied authority alike. As research is, above all, concerned with *difference* – a state of affairs, a situation, or our relationship to a particular concept, or family of concepts, is changed through undertaking, understanding, or applying research – metaphor can subvert cultural and epistemic assumptions, unravel expected results, become, in Gregory Bateson's phrase, *the difference that makes the difference*. Metaphor repeatedly breaks into the temple of stable meaning – that ideological construct based on an implied consensus – and rearranges the furniture, changing the ceremony in the process. We can replace conventional distinctions between the creative and critical (or perhaps design-led research and research-led design) by a conscious redrafting of generic and disciplinary boundaries. Literature can thus not only forge practical conceptual and reflective tools for designers, writers and researchers, but also remind us to seek greater imaginative and intellectual freedom while making ever-greater demands on the tools and materials of our professions, so that we may persuasively communicate such freedom with others.

Notes

1   This chapter was originally presented as part of the 'Architecture-Writing' session of the *Critical Architecture* conference at the Bartlett School of Architecture, University College London, 26–27 November 2004. I would like to thank Dr Jane Rendell for encouraging me to develop the text further. I also gratefully acknowledge the financial support of the Swedish Research Council, which allowed me to attend this conference.

2   Friedrich Nietzsche, *The Will to Power*, translated by Walter Kaufman and R.J.

Hollingdale, New York: Vintage, 1968, p. 409. Cited in Gilles Deleuze and Felix Guattari, *What is Philosophy?*, translated by Hugh Tomlinson and Graham Burchell, New York: Columbia University Press, 1994, pp. 5–6.

3   Prominent examples of such unclassifiable works include Lucretius' *On the Nature of Things*, Michel de Montaigne's *Essays*, St Augustine's *Confessions*, Rousseau's *Confessions*, Rochefoucauld's *Maxims*, Laurence Sterne's *Tristram Shandy*, Milan Kundera's *The Unbearable Lightness of Being*, Roland Barthes' *S/Z* or *A Lover's Discourse*. John D'Agata goes so far as to claim 'The poem and the essay are more intimately related than any two genres, because they're both ways of pursuing problems, or maybe trying to solve problems' (quoted by David Shields in 'Reality Hunger: a Manifesto', in Heidi Julavits, Ed Park and Vendela Vida (eds), *The Believer*, vol. 4, no. 2, San Francisco: McSweeney's Publishing, March 2006, pp. 27–8). Problem-solving, however, is a significantly more limited zone of activity than identifying and recombining the *grammar of concepts*, an area this chapter seeks to explore.

4   Plato, *Complete Works*, edited by John M. Cooper, Indianapolis/Cambridge: Hackett, 1997, 185c–e. Quoted by Dolar in *A Voice and Nothing More*, p. 25. Dolar highlights the 'unintentional intrusion of an uncontrolled voice, which changed the order of speakers in the highly structured dramaturgy of the dialogue' and remarks:

> This involuntary voice rising from the body's entrails can be read as Plato's version of mana: the condensation of a senseless sound and the elusive highest meaning, something which can ultimately decide the sense of the whole. This precultural, non-cultural voice can be seen as the zero-point of signification, the incidence of meaning, itself not meaning anything, the point around which other – meaningful – voices can be ordered, as if the hiccups stood at the very focus of the structure.
>
> (Dolar, *A Voice and Nothing More*, pp. 25–6)

Another reading is possible by which the hiccups stand – rather like Cordelia's obstinate and wise silence in Shakespeare's *King Lear* when confronted by her father's insistence that she state her love for him *competitively* against the claims of her sisters ('Which of you shall we say doth love us most?') – for the response of tacit knowledge, in this case, a non-verbal acknowledgement of the insufficiency of language to articulate love – which makes the passage even more promising when applied to the limits of practice-based research representation. See Rolf Hughes, 'The Performance of Uncertainty: Oppositional Metaphor and the Adversarial Tradition', in Rolf Hughes and John Monks (eds), *The Book of Models: Ceremonies, Metaphor, Performance*, Milton Keynes: Open University, 1998, reprinted 2003.

5   Simon Goldhill, 'Philosophy and Science: the Authority of Argument', *The Invention of Prose*, Oxford: Oxford University Press, 2002, p. 109.

6   Ibid., p. 110.

7   Ibid.

8   'The voice gradually loses its function as the soul progresses to Christ. So Christ has to increase and John the Baptist has to be obliterated' (Augustine, *Confessions*. Quoted by Dolar in *A Voice and Nothing More*, p. 16).

9   Lang comments: 'All that counts philosophically in this view of the history of philosophy – past or future – is the "what" which is asserted there, not the "how" by means of which the "what" puts in an appearance.' See Berel Lang, *The Anatomy of Philosophical Style*, Oxford: Basil Blackwell Ltd, 1990, p. 11.

10 See Jenny Wolmark and Eleanor Gates-Stuart (2002) 'Research as Cultural Practice', in *Working Papers in Art and Design*. Online, available at: www.herts.ac.uk/artdes1/research/papers/wpades/vol2/wolmark.html (accessed 12 September 2006). See also Jane Rendell, 'Architectural Research and Disciplinarity', *Architectural*

Review Quarterly, 8, 4, 2004, pp. 141–7; Jane Rendell, 'Architecture-Writing', in Jane Rendell (ed.), *Critical Architecture,* a special issue of *The Journal of Architecture,* 10, 3, 2005, pp. 255–64.

11   See Rolf Hughes, 'The Poetics of Practice-Based Research Writing', in Hilde Heynen (ed.), *Unthinkable Doctorates?,* a special issue of *The Journal of Architecture,* 11, 3, 2006, pp. 283–301.

12   Kuhn's analysis of the role of 'exemplars' in effective scientific problem-solving illustrates the centrality of reliable judgement, acquired through practice, to scientific inquiry and research. See Thomas Kuhn, *The Structure of Scientific Revolutions,* Chicago: University of Chicago Press, 1962.

13   Ludwig Wittgenstein, *Philosophical Investigations,* Oxford: Basil Blackwell Ltd, 1953.

14   Jonathan Monroe, 'Introduction: the Prose Poem as Dialogical Genre', in *A Poverty of Objects: the Prose Poem and the Politics of Genre,* Ithaca and London: Cornell University Press, 1987, p. 15.

15   Fredric Jameson, *The Political Unconscious: Narrative as a Socially Symbolic Act,* Ithaca: Cornell University Press, 1981. Quoted by Jonathan Monroe, *A Poverty of Objects,* pp. 18–19.

16   Nikki Santilli, 'Introduction', *Such Rare Citings: the Prose Poem in English Literature,* Madison: Fairleigh Dickinson University Press, 2002, pp. 13–25.

17   The claim is made by Thomas O'Beebee in *The Ideology of Genre: a Comparative Study of Generic Instability,* Philadelphia: Pennsylvania State University Press, 1994, p. 125. Cited by Santilli in *Such Rare Citings,* p. 15.

18   Santilli, *Such Rare Citings,* p. 14.

19   Cited in Jan Zwicky, *Wisdom and Metaphor,* Kentville, Nova Scotia: Gaspereau Press, 2003, p. 108.

20   This discussion of characteristics of the genre is indebted to Barry Silesky's 'Structure in Prose Poems?', in Brian Clements (ed.), *Sentence: a Journal of Prose Poetics,* 2, Dallas: Firewheel Editions, 2004, pp. 121–6.

21   From Bakhtin's account of the novel, in Mikhail Bakhtin, 'Epic and Novel: Toward a Methodology for the Study of the Novel', *The Dialogical Imagination: Four Essays by M.M. Bakhtin,* edited by Michael Holquist, translated by Caryl Emerson and Michael Holquist, Austin, Texas: University of Texas Press, 1981, p. 20.

22   There is, of course, a danger in romanticising the appeal of 'astonishment' in Wittgenstein's work or elsewhere. There is, presumably, no virtue in cultivating naivety simply to increase one's capacity for astonishment. As Paul Bernays remarks, 'Wondering is heuristically fruitful only where it is the expression of an instinct of research.' See Paul Bernays, 'Comments on Ludwig Wittgenstein's Remarks on the Foundations of Mathematics'. Online, available at: www.phil.cmu.edu/projects/bernays/Pdf/wittgenstein.pdf (accessed 12 June 2006).

23   See Allan Janik, 'From Logic to Animality or How Wittgenstein Used Otto Weininger', in *NÓMADAS, 4 Revista Crítica de Ciencias Sociales y Jurídicas* (2001). Online, available at: www.ucm.es/info/nomadas/4/index.html (accessed 12 June 2006). See also my own discussion of Franz Kafka's 'Leopards in the Temple', in Hughes, 'The Poetics of Practice-Based Research Writing'.

24   *Form* fascinates when one no longer has the force to understand force from within itself. That is, to create [...]. Criticism has not always known this, but understands it now, and thus is in the process of thinking itself in its own concept, system and method.

(Jacques Derrida, 'Force and Signification', in Jacques Derrida, *Writing and Difference,* translated by Alan Bass, London: Routledge, 1978, reprinted 1981, pp. 4–5)

The Poetics of Urban Inscription

From metaphorical cognition to counter-representation

Laura Ruggeri

The debate generated by the 'Critical Architecture' conference calls for an expanded and reconfigured notion of poetics that can account for hybrid forms of inscription where the materiality of writing is understood in the broader sense of 'leaving a mark', as an all-surface, all-terrain, spatialised writing that extends far beyond the limits of the page, as suggested by its etymology.[1] Such poetics should reassess the importance of the metaphorical and productive imagination in the continuum of theory and practice. To imagine is to create images, it is to display relations between ideas, and between ideas and things. The inherently figurative aspect of metaphor enables us to see the image as an instance of emerging meaning and calls into question the artificial distinction of theory and practice.

The relationship between discursive and iconic representations of the city and spatial practices is a driving force in my work; in particular the question of how to move from representations of space that are the product of capitalist relations of production and reproduction to counter-representations of space that are both generated by, and generating of, an imaginative, critical and political experience of space. In this chapter I explore the critical role played by metaphor, as a form of cross-domain mapping – conceptual and empirical – in my spatial practice, focusing in particular on two projects, 'Abstract Tours' and 'Hong Kong Inscriptions'.

The term 'metaphor' here will not simply refer to a subset of language, but rather to the transference principle that encompasses all thought and perception by projecting and carrying over meaning from one sphere to another. I will draw on this transference principle and on theories of embodiment and metaphorical cognition to argue for a shift from fetishised, abstract representations of space to critical spatial practices that are reflective (uncover and question the ideas that underpin practice), and reflexive (consider the socio-political role played by the practitioner and his/her forms of expression).

I am reluctant to define my practice as 'art', believing that such a definition, by creating a set of expectations, modes of fruition and audience, limits the field of possibilities. At a time when art and aesthetic processes seem to creep into the interstices created by the shrinking space of political debate and action, rejecting the definition might help to reposition a critical practice within the political, and restore a social dimension to the debate on the future of the city and the role played by architecture. As long as the tactics of architects camouflaged as artists result in little else than a circumvention of social responsibility, I remain sceptical of the benefits of eschewing the socio-political arena for an elitist art forum.

The refusal to label my spatial practice as art also offers the opportunity to engage in what used to be called 'semiotic guerrilla actions',[2] where the agents behind the subversion of signs remain elusive, and their identity undeclared. Once a spatial intervention is not defined as art (or architecture), it becomes an anomaly, and as such invites a wider range of readings, interpretations and speculations about the agents, their motives and objectives. Abandoning the definition not only means engaging in 'the production of restless objects and spaces that provoke us, that refuse to give up their meanings easily',[3] as advocated by Jane Rendell, but also calls into question the alleged freedom of the artist who 'doesn't need cultural permission to carry out certain corrective tasks in relation to society' as Liam Gillick maintains.[4] I find the prospect of a society where only artists are granted such permission while other unauthorised groups face incrimination for carrying out similar tasks a rather worrying one.

Metaphors at work

Until recently my use of metaphors has been generous, mainly intuitive, and I have paused only occasionally to reflect on the fresh insights they offer. I have assumed that if metaphors are as pervasive in everyday language and thought as George Lakoff and Mark Johnson maintain, then you, the reader, will probably have had the same experience.[5] But on a closer look I noticed that metaphor had played a major role in my conceptual and creative process. More interestingly, I realised how metaphors seemed to travel back and forth between my theoretical writing and practice. Like honey bees, they acted as a sort of cross-pollination agent, ensuring a constant exchange.

It is not surprising that in order to discuss metaphor I resort to using a metaphor, that of the honey bee. It seems that there is no non-metaphorical standpoint from which one can look upon metaphor. The word 'metaphor' itself is metaphorical, borrowed as it is from an order other than that of language, from the realm of movement. *Metaphora*[6] as its Greek etymology suggests, is a kind of change, namely change with respect to location. The moment we connect the spatial order of movement and the linguistic order, we are in the presence of metaphor. Indeed, all language operates in terms of the 'logic' of metaphor. But it is important to note that the metaphor-event exposes the linguistic order as provisional and discloses the tracing of the empirical on language. If metaphor, as Johnson and Lakoff suggest, is a cognitive process reflected in language and rooted in the physical world whereby schemata are formed during our early engagement with the physical world of surfaces, distances and forces – then metaphor is necessarily anthropomorphic.[7] As reflected anthropomorphism, it challenges the mind–body dichotomy that feminist theorists such as Rosi Braidotti, Elizabeth Grosz and Donna Haraway, among others, have tirelessly contested when arguing for a process-based knowledge based on 'corporeality' and bodily practices.[8]

Whenever the metaphor-event occurs, explicit metaphors are superimposed upon a perceived world, which is itself a product of earlier or unwitting metaphors. As observed by Paul Ricoeur, linguistic imagination generates and regenerates meaning through the living power of metaphoricity.[9] Metaphor expands reality and enhances language's dynamism. Metaphor operates on a principle of substitution and, as such, is not based on the similarity or resemblance between objects. Signifiers are always arbitrary and metaphor pushes this arbitrariness to the limit: as words are robbed of their usual context and linked to new referents, new linkages and semiotic assemblages become possible through the interpretative cooperation of those who are connected through a different desire, a relationship of 'reciprocal presupposition' with one another. Metaphor enables different modalities of interaction – connections, disjunctions and conjunctions – between various semiotic flows (of both material and semiotic signs) according to the processes of deterritorialisation and reterritorialisation that permeate them.[10] Theory and practice are both deterritorialised and reterritorialised by metaphor.

Metaphors not only reveal their empirical origins while transcending them, they effectively impinge on the empirical world to the extent that researchers in the field of metaphor theory now speak of a pragmatics of metaphor. Donald Schön suggests that truly generative metaphors are akin to frame restructuring: to a new way of seeing.[11] He offers the example of squatters' settlements which, when described using two different metaphors, as either 'a disease' or 'a natural community', become framed by different and conflicting research directions and social policies. Here we see how descriptions based on metaphors can lead to difficulties in problem-solving. A metaphorical statement, then, not only has the power to 're-describe' reality, it implicitly prescribes a course of action. 'Seeing-as' – the practice entailed in metaphorising – is both a model of understanding and a model for action.

'Abstract Tours': walking the metaphor in Berlin

If metaphor's power to reorganise our perception of things develops from the transposition of an entire realm, then a project I realised in Berlin in 1997, 'Abstract Tours', can be read as a general metaphor where the geometric, abstract realm of architecture and urban planning was transposed into the realm of tourism. The project stemmed from my literal and clumsy translation of the German word *stadtrundgang* (sight-seeing tour) into 'round tour of the city'. I thought about the possibility of round, as well as square, triangular and hexagonal tours, at which point geometrical abstraction found its way into my project.

As an 'Abstract Tours' agent operating from a Portakabin placed in Schloß-platz, I offered tours based on geometric figures which participants were invited to

Laura Ruggeri, 'Abstract Tours' (1997), Berlin, Germany. Photograph: Laura Ruggeri (1997).

draw on a map of Berlin with the help of Perspex stencils (see figure above). The superimposition of geometric figures (Euclidean abstraction) on a map (cartographic abstraction) aimed to invert the conceptual abstractions that inform the configuration of spatial practices, such as architecture and city planning, the design of routes, the schematic grid of property lines and, ultimately, the construction/destruction of the Berlin Wall and the corporate reshaping of the German capital.

As in the situationist practice of *détournement*, 'Abstract Tours' entailed the capture of a code, not its imitation. It aimed to invert rather than duplicate. By following abstract lines on the ground and hence going through a process of de-familiarisation and disorientation, participants could enrich their experience of the environment by overriding their habitual functional, relational or historical perception of the city. The geometric routes established unfamiliar links, connecting places that had been fragmented, separated by the abstract production of space. Points, lines and areas established a different syntax of sites, based on chance. In order to follow a geo-metric route, you had to trespass, jump over fences or ask strangers if you could pass through their apartments.

These unguided tours, in fragmenting totalising representations of the city, opened up a plurality of perspectives, which in turn produced provisional, transient and partial perceptions and representations. Once these representations were assembled, the spaces of the city were incorporated into something closer to a fictional narrative than an objective record.[12] By re-describing the city, they invented it.

The *dérives* encouraged by 'Abstract Tours' functioned as an immaterial architecture of landscape. Walking became a primary act in the symbolic trans-formation of the territory, an instrument of knowledge. If we think of knowledge as process-based, rooted in 'corporeality' and bodily practices, knowledge and practice become mutually interactive. Indeed, Grosz maintains that a new paradigm for representing the city necessitates a shake-up in the relational representation of the body:

> There is a two-way linkage which could be defined as an interface, perhaps even a co-building. What I am suggesting is a model of the relations between bodies and cities which sees them, not as megalithic total entities, distinct identities, but as assemblages or collections of parts, capable of crossing the thresholds between substances to form linkages, machines, provisional and often temporary sub- or microgroupings.
>
> (Elizabeth Grosz, 'Bodies–Cities', in Beatriz Colomina (ed.), *Sexuality and Space*, Princeton: Princeton Architectural Press, 1992, p. 248)

Grosz's words offer the delineation of new theoretical spaces and spatial metaphors for viewing and representing the city; bodies and the urban meet at an interface in transitory, fleeting moments of connection, establishing provisional linkages that jettison the possibility of any mastery over the urban spectacle from one fixed viewpoint. The border between self and city becomes fluid in the metaphor of the 'abstract tourist' whose experience of place demystifies both the evacuation of time from certain areas of the city (Potsdamer Platz is just paradigmatic of a more general trend) and its fossilisation in other areas where, as the product of selection and exclusion, history becomes something to contemplate in districts that have been historically preserved.

A metaphor is not limited to suspending natural reality – in opening up the imaginative side of meaning, it also provides a dimension of reality that does not coincide with what ordinary language envisages. Both abstraction and tourism rely on fragmentation; space is fashioned to serve as a means of production and a product to be consumed. Sight and seeing, which in the Western tradition epitomise intelligibility,[13] construct a type of space that legitimises only certain practices and procedures, and thus becomes the domain of specialists (urban planners, architects and other agents of abstraction) and tourists.

Rethinking the relationship between space and language in terms of metaphors might, however, suggest other possible forms of critical engagement with both. Not only are spatialisation metaphors pervasive in the language we use and our conceptual system,[14] but space, like language, also 'asserts', 'negates' and 'denies'. Starting out as a linguistic metaphor, 'Abstract Tours' revealed the obscenity of abstract space 'on the ground' – what occurs behind the façade – restoring a material and critical dimension to the otherwise fetishistic experience of tourism.[15]

'Hong Kong Inscriptions'

'Hong Kong Inscriptions' (see figure on page 108), an ongoing project of mine, proposes spatial explorations based on metaphors that are taken from official discursive practices and representations of the city – such as those peddled by the Hong Kong

Laura Ruggeri, 'Hong
Kong Inscriptions'
(2006), Hong Kong.
Photograph: Laura
Ruggeri (2006).

Tourism Board – or those provided by people who visit my website.[16] Unlike 'Abstract Tours', where I recognised the role of metaphor after producing the project, and only then did it become central to my critical discussion of that project, 'Hong Kong Inscriptions' is a project that stems from my research on metaphor and its potential use for a critique of space. 'Hong Kong Inscriptions' as a collaborative platform has only recently been launched and as such is still a work-in-progress, so at this stage I can only offer an account of its theoretical premises and a few examples of early contributions to the website and spatial explorations that have been planned but not yet carried out.

I intend to pursue the elaboration of a political and materialist semiology, one that stresses the functional connections between theoretical critique, spatial practice and political intervention, via the concept of metaphor. The formulation of such a semiology is based on Felix Guattari's assertion that 'semiotic fluxes are just as real as the material ones, and in a sense the material fluxes are just as semiotic as the semiotic machines'.[17]

Writing the city can become a socialised practice, a practice that links the materiality of the city to the virtuality of cyberspace, bringing the performative dimension of texts centre-stage. Choosing the Internet as one of the sites of inscription – those who visit my website are invited to supply metaphors of Hong Kong as images and texts – means using one of the 'deterritorialising machines' made available to us by the 'schizophrenic' tendency of the capitalist mode of production. Semiological inversion, social creativity and counter-representation have mostly been reterritorialised and defused by capital, but have by no means lost their effectiveness for political use. Original metaphors can produce new, unpredictable assemblages of material and semiotic signs, and even worn-out metaphors (once they have been re-appropriated for a different use) are effective.

The project takes a look at the metaphors used by those who are authorised to represent and/or promote the city. One metaphor that I intend to wrench away from its promotional context is the 'city as a shop' metaphor used by the Hong Kong Tourism Board (HKTB) in the context of an annual shopping festival.[18] One of the slogans created by the HKTB is the metonymic 'put the city in the bag', visually underpinned by an image of a giant, pink shopping bag wrapped around the historic landmark Tsim Sha Tsui Clock Tower. As the entire city is promoted as a shopper's paradise, I propose a 'sourcing' expedition, one that takes participants from Hong Kong's glitzy shopping malls to a workers' hell in Guangdong province, just across the border, where rural migrants work 14 hours a day for US$100 a month.

Another slogan favoured by the Hong Kong Tourism Board is 'Hong Kong: The City That Never Sleeps', which uses the metaphor of the city as a happy insomniac. In January 2006 I organised a nocturnal expedition through the streets of Kowloon, an experience that enabled me to debunk the myth of the 24-hour city of leisure and tell a different story, one of bodies worn out by overtime and night shifts. Ironically, the HKTB became a victim of its untimely use of metaphors when, at the beginning of 2003, it used the advertising slogan 'Hong Kong will take your breath away' in a worldwide campaign to lure tourists. It took on a sinister meaning when Severe Acute Respiratory Syndrome (SARS) hit Hong Kong three months later. But even without SARS, the appalling levels of air pollution made it easier for people to grasp the slogan's literal meaning rather than its metaphorical one.

Personal stories can proliferate and inundate sites, adding noise to or subverting master narratives. 'Hong Kong is a broken-heart', one of the metaphors provided by a contributor to the website, encourages the pasting of 'break-up notices' in the exact location where they occur, inscribing personal dramas in a public place.[19] Hong Kong space has been likened by Ackbar Abbas to a 'magnetic tape' that can be erased and reused, leaving no traces of previous use.[20] Property speculation means that buildings in Hong Kong, however new or monumental, face imminent demolition.

When subjected to market forces, the 'magnetic tape' metaphor of urban space conjures up its original, recording function. Another contribution to the website suggested that the whispered grievances of the inhabitants of sites that have been effaced from the urban palimpsest could be recorded and played back during the Hungry Ghost Festival, thus disturbing the peace of developers.[21]

As a practitioner, political activist and writer whose work deals with urban space, I have long been engaged in both the production and deconstruction of urban representations. This is an inherently metaphorical process that constructs meaning by transferring or deferring it from one realm of experience into another. Not only do representations and metaphors become the form in which (partial) knowledge and experience of the urban environment is conveyed but also, as cognitive tools, they produce fresh perceptions and insights. By selecting and creating linkages, one produces not only 'models of' understanding, but also 'models for' understanding and enabling action. Representation is an inescapably ideological and political exercise: by revealing only specific aspects of reality and focusing our attention on certain aspects instead of others, representations have the power to limit the courses of action we follow and frame problems in such a way that we are only able to conceive certain solutions.

'Abstract Tours' and 'Hong Kong Inscriptions' suggest that deconstructing and re-appropriating representation should be socialised through the practice of both virtual and embodied inscription. Inscribing the body in space ultimately means subverting the prescribing and proscribing order that characterises our built environment and re-inscribing desire through actions of political and poetic imagination.

Notes

1   Words for 'write' in most Indo-European languages originally meant 'carve, scratch, draw' (cf. Latin *scribere*, Greek *graphein*); a few originally meant 'paint'. For the physical origin of writing, see Florian Coulmas, *The Writing Systems of the World*, Oxford: Basil Blackwell Ltd, 1989.

2   The idea of semiotic guerrilla warfare gained wide currency in Italy at the time when I was studying semiotics with Umberto Eco at the University of Bologna, thanks in particular to the seminars led by Paolo Fabbri in the early 1980s and its adoption by the creative sections of the radical political movement commonly known as the '77 Movement' in Italy.

3   Jane Rendell, *Art and Architecture: a Place Between*, London: I.B. Tauris, 2006, p. xiii.

4   Liam Gillick offers a seductive definition of art, but experience taught me caution in using the term, as the potential afforded by it is matched by the limits it sets. See www.moma.org/exhibitions/2002/projects/projects79/79_current.html.

5   George Lakoff and Mark Johnson, *Metaphors We Live By*, Chicago: University of Chicago Press, 1980.

6   From the Greek *meta*- 'over, across' and *phorein* 'to carry', 'to bear', *metaphora* literally means 'carrying over', 'transfer'.

7   Lakoff and Johnson, *Metaphors We Live By*.

8   See for example, Rosi Braidotti, *Nomadic Subjects: Embodiment and Sexual Difference in Contemporary Feminist Theory*, New York: Columbia University Press,

1994; Elizabeth Grosz, *Volatile Bodies: Toward a Corporeal Feminism*, Sidney: Allen and Unwin, 1994; Donna Haraway, *Simians, Cyborgs, and Women: the Reinvention of Nature*, London: Routledge, 1991.

9   Paul Ricoeur, *The Rule of Metaphor*, London: Routledge, 2003, pp. 255–359.

10 The concepts of 'deterritorialisation' and 'reterritorialisation' are used in the sense elaborated by Gilles Deleuze and Felix Guattari. See Gilles Deleuze and Felix Guattari, *Anti-Oedipus,* vol. 1 of *Capitalism and Schizophrenia* [1972–80], translated by Robert Hurley, Mark Seem and Helen R. Lane, London: The Athlone Press, 1984; originally published as *L'Anti-Oedipe*, Paris: Les Editions de Minuit, 1972.

11 Donald A. Schön, 'Generative Metaphor: a Perspective on Problem-Setting in Social Policy', in Andrew Ortony (ed.), *Metaphor and Thought*, Cambridge: Cambridge University Press, 1993, pp. 137–61.

12 The closing exhibition, held in the Künstlerhaus Bethanien, included all the particip-ants, who had documented their urban explorations by taking photographs, making videos, audio-recordings, collecting found objects, keeping logbooks etc. The polyphony of voices and redistribution of representational authority raised both polit-ical and epistemological questions about 'who' is authorised to represent the city.

13 Henri Lefebvre, *The Production of Space*, Oxford: Blackwell, 1991, p. 76.

14 For a systematic analysis of orientational and spatialisation metaphors, see Lakoff and Johnson, *Metaphors We Live By*, pp. 14–21.

15 As a form of space production and consumption, tourism is the symptom of an abstract production and transformation of space that, by privileging the visual and spectacular, fragments space according to the logic of capital.

16 After 'following the metaphor' on the ground, participants are invited to submit a doc-umentation of their walks mainly in the form of photographs and texts that will be uploaded to my website, www.spacing.org.

17 Felix Guattari, 'Towards a Micro-Politics of Desire', in *Molecular Revolution: Psychia-try and Politics*, Harmondsworth: Penguin, 1984, p. 96.

18 Contestants from 15 countries engaged in shopping expeditions where they had to spend HK$3,000 in local shops from 6pm to 10pm. The contestant judged to have made the best buys and bargains was then named 'Shopper of the Year' and won a round-trip ticket to Hong Kong.

19 The practice of airing grievances by displaying placards or hanging banners is quite common in Hong Kong. For a more permanent inscription, look no further than Tseng Tso-choi who calls himself the 'King of Kowloon'. The unemployed 78-year-old thinks he is the rightful heir to a large part of the territory. For more than 40 years he has shared his conviction with Hong Kong residents via his trademark black-paint inscrip-tions. His graffiti (known to include slogans insulting the Queen of England) appear on walls, posts and electricity boxes throughout Hong Kong.

20 Ackbar Abbas, *Hong Kong: Culture and the Politics of Disappearance*, Minneapolis: University of Minnesota Press, 1997, p. 76.

21 The Hungry Ghost festival that falls on the seventh month of the lunar calendar is taken very seriously by the Chinese. It is believed that, during this month, the gates of hell are open and the hungry ghosts wander to seek food on Earth and revenge upon those who wronged them in their previous lives.

Critical Action and Active Criticism

Paul Shepheard

The Ruddy Duck is an American species of stiff tail duck that was imported into England to decorate ornamental duck ponds. It escaped – of course – and is now thriving in the wild. Ruddy Ducks are closely related to a rare European species, the White Headed Duck – so narrowly speciated, in fact, that the two can interbreed. The reaction of the biodiversity lobby has been to institute a programme to kill every Ruddy Duck in the country. They say it is not a native species, ignoring the realities of duck nationhood, which are not at all like our own. They don't say, though they might as well: we have to destroy the world in order to save it.

Could this action be construed as a work of architecture, involving as it does the manipulation of the material world to better suit us humans? The critical impasse is certainly familiar, confusing the ideal of a better world with the consequence of material action, which makes the world not a better place, but a different place. It is such a simple confection, that distinction, that one almost prefers the comfort of the confusion: surely the whole point of criticism is to make things better?

The genocide of the ducks is a critical action. It pursues an ideal. It is justified by a tautology – themed 'conservation' – constructed in opposition to the previous tautology of technological expansion, whose enthusiasm for exotica brought the ducks here in the first place. But another kind of criticism could be written from inside the event: it would describe the capture and the escape of the ducks, the infectious character of hybridisation and the ever-changing character of the biomass in a way that made the description itself the action. I'd call it an active criticism – and I'd say it was a more interesting proposition for the critic to engage in than analysis in service of an ideal. But then you may say: what use is a criticism that simply describes? And isn't anything destined to change the world – for better or different – being idealistic?

Perhaps the implicit idealism of criticism springs from the ambiguity of language itself. The simple possibility of translation, which implies a perpetually feasible, other version of what has just been written, and which serves us so well in our interminable human arguments about what to do next, is a problem in architectural criticism. Try as we might to construct unimpeachable tautologies, or measuring frames to judge our actions, there is a mismatch between the criticism and its subject, the material world, in which ambiguity disappears, and the simplest saw cut is effortlessly conclusive. We can chase certainty by emphasising history and typology, as the context-fond Frettonites do. We can employ the power of slogans, as the Koolhaasians do. We can even manipulate the numbers of the bottom line and call it the 'real world'; but, in the face of emergent nature it is all abstraction, as futile as the ethnic cleansing of the duck nation.

So what would an untranslatable, material literature that could do the job of active criticism be like? Painting could be such a thing, inescapably wound up with contexts and narratives as it is, but intensely local and partial at the same time. The contortions that painting has gone through to retrieve its non-representational capacities from the real world have already been mirrored in literature, from consciousness streams to minimalism – I think of the example of Gertrude Stein's beautiful *Tender Buttons*, which were an explicit attempt to write as Picasso painted. Concrete poetry is something else, sculpture by other means, concerned with internal architectonic correspondences and organisations: what I am looking for here is a critical literature that is active in the world around it. Stein's effort was to trap the impressions and associations that mediate the seeing of an object – is this the ether that pre-quantum scientists used to describe as the forces of attraction? And was that itself a naive metaphor for what became in quantum physics the influence of the observer?

Pieces of writing can be materially active, as all art is, traversing one's thoughts and sparking possibilities of further action. In spite of this, critical theory tends to come with its aspirations predetermined as part of the discourse, and with its tactics of oppositions, its undergrounds and its challenges to the mainstream, it hobbles itself. What more could we hope for in a critical writing that acted from inside its subjects, spurring their trajectories, wobbling their orbits and sharing in their evolutionary opportunism? And what would be the difference between this literature and the persuasive polemics that accompany the release of every new architectural event – those little spats between traditionalists and modernists, or between contextualists and iconographists, those emphasis wars that keep that real world turning?

If they were actual wars, it might be clearer. War is not the natural state of humans, but a sort of human skit on the dynamics of the natural state of the world itself – the driving holocaust of emergencies and extinctions that is the material history of the world. But what of the writing that is embedded in the fog, which happens inside the turmoil of the events themselves, as though writing about material action was writing about wild life events? What is that like? Can you imagine a critical writing that is without discrimination, because it can only see itself? That has no future, because each unfolding moment changes everything? That makes no assumptions, because survival crowds everything else out?

The neutrality this proposition requires might look like quiescence. Worse still, the partiality it paradoxically requires might seem like ignorance – so much so that anyone attempting to do it risks being accused of having no values. Indeed, there is something of a backlash going on against the kind of relativism I am espousing. *How can you build a society without values?* it says. And when I say *But I value everything*, it says, *How can you determine action without discrimination?*

I have no answer to that, except to say that action is action and determines itself. The material world is, as it has always been, the wild world, and this is the world an active criticism might be able to describe. After centuries of ring fencing and the worst kind of discrimination, the gift of this moment is to be returned to complexity, inside a dynamic of many simultaneous singular actions, unstable, unpredictable and peculiar: without balance, future or commonality. I think freedom is no longer a question of busting fences, but of choosing where to stand in the tumultuous roar of the emerging world. Why should one give up the possibilities of all that for the simple pleasure of being right?

Film as Spatial Critique

Patrick Keiller

Before films were distributed on video, it was difficult to explore their spaces unless one had access to specialised equipment – an 'analytical' projector or an editing table. The continual and often rapid succession of images that generally constitutes the experience of watching a film is not very conducive to accurate recollection, especially of anything peripheral to a narrative, and it is difficult to draw or make notes in the darkness of a cinema. Perhaps this is why, with a few significant exceptions, architects' theoretical engagement with film was delayed until recent decades. With the introduction of domestic video recorders, and the refinement of the possibility to pause and search, cinema became more accessible for architectural exploration.[1]

Since the 1970s, architects have explored cinema as a source of spatial concepts applicable to architecture, but the excitement that accompanied this discovery seems to have passed. In retrospect, it seems to me – as an architect diverted into making films – that film has a more general significance for architecture as a means of developing a critique, temporal and otherwise, of actual architectural and urban space. What initially attracted – and continues to attract – me to the medium is that it offers the possibility, albeit constrained, to experience non-existent spaces, and in particular to experience spatial qualities seldom, not yet or no longer encountered in ordinary experience. These spaces may be non-existent either because they have not yet been produced, or because they no longer exist. 'Spaces that have not yet been produced' might exist physically, but not experientially or socially: as Henri Lefebvre writes, 'the space which contains the realized preconditions of another life is the same one as prohibits what those preconditions make possible.'[2] Perhaps this prohibition is sometimes suspended within a film, and if so, this might explain the seemingly *utopian* quality of so much film space. Similarly, 'spaces that no longer exist' may still exist physically, but not socially, or they may no longer exist at all. Films can represent physically imaginary spaces, or proposals for spaces to be realised in the future, but for me the medium's allure has always derived from its capacity to imaginatively transform already-existing space, and from the possibility it offers to experience spaces of the past to somewhat similar effect.

I would like to suggest that film space can offer an implicit critique of actual space, so that looking at and researching films can constitute a kind of architectural criticism. I would also suggest that one can make films (and I suppose I would claim to have done so) that set out to criticise architectural space rather than simply depict it (which, given the marked differences between film space and actual architecture, is much more difficult). Lastly, I would suggest that film[3] from the past that depicts urban and other architectural space of its time can offer an implicit critique of similar spaces of the present, and can inform our understanding of the ways in which urban and other landscapes change in time.

A few years ago I embarked on a project to explore urban space as it appears in films made before the mid-1900s.[4] The following paragraphs set out the context for this exploration, and identify coincident periods of transition in the histories of architecture, urban space and film.

Carrington Street, Nottingham in 2003, with inset from *Tram Rides Through Nottingham, Carrington Street*, Mitchell & Kenyon, 1902.

Until the mid-1900s, most films were between one and three minutes long, and consisted of one or very few unedited takes. The Lumière company's films, for example, are typically 48–52 feet long and last about a minute. They were made by exposing a complete roll of film, usually without stopping. Most early films were actualities, not fiction, and many were street scenes or views of other topographical subjects, some of them photographed from moving vehicles and boats. Cinematographers would sometimes pause if there was a lull in the ambient action, if the view was blocked, or for other reasons, but other kinds of editing are unusual. The reconstruction of time and space by joining individual shots together was an aspect of filmmaking that began to dominate only after about 1907.

Tom Gunning has called this early cinema 'the cinema of attractions',[5] a reference to Sergei Eisenstein's 'montage of attractions', conceived as a new model for theatre. Eisenstein took the term from the fairground, where his favourite attraction was the roller coaster, the Russian for which translates as 'the American mountains'. There is an early Biograph film, *A Ride on a Switchback*, which was made by mounting a camera not on a roller coaster, as early films sometimes were, but on a railway engine. A switchback was a railway engineers' device for negotiating steep gradients with a siding and a set of points, entering by one branch and backing out into the other, so as to avoid the construction of a hairpin bend. Biograph's film was photographed in mountains near Fort Lee, New Jersey, which one might imagine were the (or at least some) American mountains. Films photographed from the front of railway engines were known as 'phantom rides', presumably because of the sensation of disembodied consciousness they offer. Views from other moving vehicles – trams and, later, cars – are sometimes also called phantom rides, but the term seems to have been most specific to the view from the front of a locomotive, which was then seldom encountered in ordinary experience, even by an engine driver.

As Gunning writes, after 1907 'the cinema of attractions does not disappear with the dominance of narrative, but rather goes underground, both into certain avant-garde practices and as a component of narrative films'.[6] There is a story that Andy Warhol's *Kiss* (1963) was prompted by an archive viewing of Edison's *Kiss of May Irvin and John C. Rice* (1896), and whether or not it was, the formal evolution of Warhol's films – from the 100-foot rolls of *Sleep* (1963) and *Kiss* (1963) to the 1200-foot rolls of the two-screen *The Chelsea Girls* (1966) – strikingly resembles that of early film.[7] In narrative cinema, phantom rides appear in *films noirs*, often at the beginning of a film or in title sequences, as in Fritz Lang's *Human Desire* (1954), Mike Hodges' *Get Carter* (1971) and the car shots in Jacques Tourneur's *Out of the Past* (1947), Edgar G. Ulmer's *Detour* (1945) – looking backwards – and Robert Aldrich's *Kiss Me Deadly* (1955). Since the 1960s, the cinema of attractions has emerged from underground, in films and installations by a wide variety of artists and other filmmakers, most of them outside the mainstream of Western cinema. Whether in the gallery or in what used to be called art cinema, there is a tendency towards some of the forms of early film.

Both early films and these more recent examples differ from what became the dominant form in the way they represent space on a screen. In films constructed as montage, space is assembled in time, as an implied continuity of fragments. In most early films, space is represented within a single frame, either static or moving. Early films are also less likely to direct the viewer's attention to a single subject in the frame: one's eye can more easily wander in their spaces and, because of this, they invite (or even require) repeated viewing. Moving-camera films often create a striking illusion of three-dimensionality, which early film-makers sometimes referred to explicitly as 'the stereoscopic effect'.

Between the mid-1900s and the outbreak of the First World War, the spaces and spatial experiences characteristic of industrialised economies appear to have undergone significant transformation. These transitions have been described in a variety of ways: for example, in his afterword to the English translation of Henri Lefebvre's definitive *La Production de l'éspace*, first published in 1974, but in English only in 1991, the geographer David Harvey quoted a passage of Lefebvre's opening chapter:

Lister Gate, Nottingham in 2003, with inset from *Tram Rides Through Nottingham, Lister Gate*, Mitchell & Kenyon, 1902.

The fact is that around 1910 a certain space was shattered. It was the space of common sense, of knowledge (*savoir*), of social practice, of political power, a space thitherto enshrined in everyday discourse, just as in abstract thought, as the environment of and channel for communications; the space, too, of classical perspective and geometry, developed from the Renaissance onwards on the basis of the Greek tradition (Euclid, logic) and bodied forth in Western art and philosophy, as in the form of the city and the town [...] Euclidean and perspectivist space have disappeared as systems of reference, along with other former 'commonplaces' such as the town, history, paternity, the tonal system in music, traditional morality, and so forth. This was truly a crucial moment.

(Henri Lefebvre, *The Production of Space*, p. 25)

This passage, quoted by Harvey in his *The Condition of Postmodernity*, followed mention of 'the incredible confusions and oppositions across a spectrum of possible reactions to the growing sense of crisis in the experience of time and space, that had been gathering since 1848 and seemed to come to a head just before the First World War' and 'that 1910–14 is roughly the period that many historians of modernism (beginning with Virginia Woolf and D.H. Lawrence) point to as crucial in the evolution of modernist thinking'.[8] For Harvey, the crisis was one 'of technological innovation, of capitalist dynamics across space [and] cultural production'. He notes the slightly different emphasis of Stephen Kern who, in *The Culture of Time and Space 1880–1918*, offered 'generalizations about the essential cultural developments of the period'.[9] Other writers have dealt with these in detail: for John Berger, 'The Moment of Cubism' was the period between 1907 and 1914, and during the period 1900–14 'the developments which converged at the beginning of the twentieth century in Europe changed the meaning of time and space'.[10] Berger listed these as:

An interlocking world system of imperialism; opposed to it, a socialist inter-national; the founding of modern physics, physiology and sociology; the increasing use of electricity, the invention of radio and the cinema; the beginnings of mass production; the publishing of mass-circulation news-papers; the new structural possibilities offered by the availability of steel and aluminium; the rapid development of the chemical industries and the production of synthetic materials; the appearance of the motor car and the aeroplane.

(John Berger, *The Moment of Cubism and other Essays*, London: Weidenfeld and Nicholson, 1969, p. 5)

More recent writing (including that of Kern and Harvey) has stressed the role of telecommunications; others mention emigration, both within and away from Europe.[11] Some of these developments suggest comparisons with the present.

At about the same time, architectural theorists began to develop new con-cepts of architectural space. For Reyner Banham, in *Theory and Design in the First Machine Age*, 'a series of revolutionary gestures around 1910, largely connected with the Cubist and Futurist movements, were the main point of departure for the develop-ment of Modern architecture'.[12] Banham's narrative is that of evolving concepts of space, specifically 'the change-over from the Lippsian idea of space, as *felt volume* [my emphasis] [...] to the later concept of space as a three-dimensional continuum, capable of metrical subdivision, without sacrifice of its continuity'.[13] The idea of space as volume enclosed by solid surfaces (characteristic of early modern architects such as C.F.A. Voysey or H.P. Berlage, and of Ildefons Cerdà's Barcelona) began to give way to concepts in which the solidity of matter was less certain, just as the early modernist city, with its bicycles and electric trams, would give way to the city of the motor car. By 1929, Laszlo Moholy-Nagy was able to formulate the minimum definition – 'space is the relation between the position of bodies'[14] – which for Banham confirmed 'the whole revolution in architectural theory that had been going on since 1908'.[15] One of Moholy-Nagy's earlier spatial expositions was his 1921–2 proposal for a film, *Dynamic of the Metropolis*, which somewhat anticipates Dziga Vertov's 1929 *Man with a Movie Camera. Dynamic of the Metropolis* was never realised, but by 1929 Moholy-Nagy had made *Berliner Stilleben* (1926) and perhaps also *Marseille Vieux Port* (1929), so that the 'minimum definition' of modernist space was put forward by a theorist who was also an experienced film-maker.

Banham saw the distinction between Lipps's and Moholy-Nagy's spatial concepts as sequential, but the idea of space as 'felt volume' only slightly pre-dated the subsequent, more abstract formulation – it appears that the word 'space' (*raum*) was not used in Lipps's (or any other architectural) sense before about 1900[16] – and Lipps's concept never really went away. The distinction between the two spatial concepts is very like that between Gunning's two kinds of cinema, and the spatiality of the early films – their depiction of architectural space within a single frame, their uninterrupted, lengthy spatio-temporal continuities (the tram rides especially) and the 'stereoscopic effect' – is easy to identify with Lipps's formulation. Banham's *Theory and Design* was published in 1960, before the revival of urbanism in architectural theory in the mid-1970s, since when architects and others have attempted to revive this early modernist space, just as film-makers have revived some of the forms of early cinema. Both Lipps's space and the 'cinema of attractions' might be seen as early modernist forms that were eclipsed in the late 1900s, as part of a wider cultural transformation, but have since re-emerged, usually in opposition to the mainstream architectures and cinemas of Western and other capitalist cultures.

In *The Condition of Postmodernity*, Harvey also quoted the famous passage from Walter Benjamin's 'The Work of Art in the Age of Mechanical Reproduction':

> Our taverns and our metropolitan streets, our offices and furnished rooms, our railroad stations and our factories appeared to have us locked up hopelessly. Then came the film and burst this prison-world asunder by the dynamite of the tenth of a second, so that now, in the midst of its far-flung ruins and debris, we calmly and adventurously go travelling.
>
> (Walter Benjamin, 'The Work of Art in the Age of Mechanical Reproduction' [1936], in *Illuminations*, edited by Hannah Arendt and translated by Harry Zohn, London: Fontana, 1973, pp. 219–53, p. 238)

Benjamin's 'now' refers to film as it had evolved after the mid-1900s – his essay, published in 1936, mentions nothing earlier than the films of Abel Gance, Vertov and Joris Ivens – but it is not entirely clear at what date 'came the film and burst this prison-world asunder'. If the development of cinema was a significant factor in the transformation of urban and other space during the 1900s, one wonders whether this was the development of cinema per se, or the development of cinema with editing, narrative and close-up as it was undertaken after the middle of the decade. The fragmentation Benjamin describes can be identified in post-1910 experience as a breaking up of space into individual shots, in which case 'the dynamite of the tenth of a second' is the interval between the end of one shot and the beginning of the next, rather than the medium's primary fragmentation of continuous duration into the discontinuous individual frames of a single shot. But the essay also famously stresses 'the incomparable significance of Atget, who, around 1900, took photographs of deserted Paris streets',[17] and it might seem to us (over 70 years later) that in some ways one could 'calmly and adventurously go travelling' (even) more easily in the early 1900s than in the period of Gance and Vertov.

Whatever the date of the films that Benjamin had in mind, something happened to the medium in the mid-1900s. The change that Gunning identified seems to have followed a distinct lull in output, during or soon after which many of the pioneers ceased production. After the mid-1900s, films are generally longer but with shorter shots, close-ups and, increasingly, fiction and studio sets, few of them show very much of ordinary landscapes. When they do, the shots are usually so short as to permit relatively little exploration, even when examined frame-by-frame. In contrast, the brief, continuous or near-continuous films of spatial subjects made by the Lumière and Biograph companies and their contemporaries before about 1903 accumulate an extensive document of ordinary, everyday spaces of their period: the spaces that Lefebvre and others suggest were radically transformed soon afterwards. In enabling us to see so much of this landscape, these early films are truly extraordinary, as they offer the most extensive views of the landscape of another time at or just before the moment of that landscape's transformation, a transformation brought about (at least in part) by the development of the very medium in which the opportunity to explore these long-lost spaces was constructed.

What do these films mean for us? On looking at them, what struck me first was a contrast between their often familiar-looking landscapes and the unfamiliarity of the society glimpsed in them. In the last 100 years, the material and other circumstances of the UK's population have altered enormously,[18] but much of the urban fabric of the 1900s survives, often – like so much of the built environment – in a surprisingly dilapidated condition. In terms of life expectancy, physical health, income, mobility etc., we are far better off than our predecessors of 100 years ago: developed economies experience unprecedented levels of consumption and GDP per head, but in other respects – especially when measured in terms of social, cultural and environmental assets – wealth has not increased anything like as much. In some ways, in some places, it has probably decreased.[19] In emphasising this, the films might be thought subversive.

Walking in the streets of UK towns and cities today, the decline of what Lefebvre described as 'the environment of and channel for communications [...] in the form of the city and the town' is easily recognised. One often detects a sense of absence, even in the centre of London. The spatial qualities suggested by many early films are very like some of those that attract tourists to less advanced or (some) socialist economies – to places where artisanal production or its past products survive, where domesticity is still found in city centres, and where there are fewer cars, or at least less traffic engineering. In advanced economies, such environmental qualities are typically achieved or retained through socialist (as in, say, Barcelona) or social democratic (as in the Netherlands) politics.

In this context, Lefebvre's shattered 'space of common sense' suggests both the spatial concepts of Lipps and the urban design of Camillo Sitte. In 1903, Lipps 'argued that our bodies unconsciously empathised with architectural form'[20] and Sitte,

> rooted in the craftworker tradition of late nineteenth-century Vienna [...] sought to construct spaces that would make the city's people feel 'secure and happy' [...]. He therefore set out to create [...] spaces – plazas and squares – that would promote the preservation and even re-creation of a sense of community.[21]

(Harvey, *The Condition of Postmodernity*, p. 276)

Such ideas re-emerged in the postmodern urbanism of the 1970s, for which early films might initially seem to offer some support, with their depiction of what to us appear 'traditional' urban spaces in which we might imagine we could be 'secure and happy', spaces that 'would promote the preservation and even re-creation of a sense of community'. Sitte's polemic, however, was not in favour of the actually existing spaces of the 1900s – the spaces that appear in the films – but against them, 'abhorring the narrow and technical functionalism that seemed to attach to the lust for commercial profit', and seeking 'to overcome fragmentation and provide a "community life-outlook" ',[22] rather as we might today. Also, though Sitte is popular with present-day urban designers, his desire for spaces that he believed would promote 'community' was not unproblematic. As Harvey writes:

> many of the Viennese artisans whom Sitte championed [...] were later to mass in the squares, piazzas and living spaces that Sitte wanted to create, in order to express their virulent opposition to internationalism, turning to anti-semitism [...] and the place-specific myths of Nazism.
>
> (Harvey, *The Condition of Postmodernity*, p. 277)

The spaces of UK cities in the early 1900s were subject to transformations at least as sudden as any we experience today,[23] but there were few cars until later in the decade.[24] Early films depict a space in which there are electricity and telecommunications, but not much oil, so that the transformations of circa 1910 can be seen in terms of the coming of the oil economy and the motor car, which since the mid-1970s has been so widely cast in opposition to conventional formulations of dwelling, and to certain kinds of urban space and architecture. Here again, pre-1907 films might seem to offer a polemic – for streets without cars, for architecture, for public transport, and for a less centralised, less dematerialised economy. They might even resemble science fiction: a future in which the costs of distant labour, and of energy, and hence transport, have increased, so that production becomes more local. At the same time, we can assume that, as images, the films bestow an illusory coherence on their subjects. The spaces that appear in the films were dynamic, subject to tensions as unsettling as (and sometimes surprisingly similar to) any we experience today. Architecture is increasingly seen as a process structured in time: in films, we can explore some of the spaces of the past, in order to better imagine the spaces of the future.

Notes

1   For more on the implications of electronic media for experience of moving images, see Laura Mulvey, *Death 24x a Second: Stillness and the Moving Image*, London: Reaktion, 2005.

2   Henri Lefebvre, *The Production of Space*, translated by Donald Nicholson-Smith, Oxford: Blackwell, 1991, pp. 189–90.

3   By 'film', I mean film footage in which architecture and landscape are visible, rather than particular films about architecture and landscape. After about 1920, such footage is perhaps more widely encountered in feature narratives, especially after 1945, when location cinematography began to become more common.

4   *The City of the Future*, a research project based at the Royal College of Art, London, see vads.ahds.ac.uk/collections/CF.html (accessed 18 October 2006).

5   Tom Gunning, 'The Cinema of Attractions: Early Film, its Spectator and the Avant-Garde', in Thomas Elsaesser and Adam Barker (eds), *Early Cinema: Space, Frame, Narrative*, London: British Film Institute, 1990, pp. 56–62.

6   Gunning, 'The Cinema of Attractions', p. 57.

7   See Tony Rayns, 'Death at Work: Evolution and Entropy in Factory Films', in Michael O'Pray (ed.), *Andy Warhol Film Factory*, London: British Film Institute, 1989, p. 164.

8   David Harvey, *The Condition of Postmodernity*, Oxford: Blackwell, 1990, p. 266.

9   Stephen Kern, *The Culture of Time and Space 1880–1918*, Cambridge, MA: Harvard University Press, 1983, p. 5.

10   John Berger, *The Moment of Cubism and Other Essays*, London: Weidenfeld and Nicholson, 1969, p. 6.

11   According to Kern, 30 million emigrants left Europe between 1890 and 1914 (Kern, *The Culture of Time and Space*, p. 220).

12   Reyner Banham, *Theory and Design in the First Machine Age*, London: Architectural Press, 1960, p. 14.

13   Ibid., p. 67.

14   Ibid., p. 317.

15   Ibid., p. 311.

16   Ibid., p. 66.

17   Walter Benjamin, 'The Work of Art in the Age of Mechanical Reproduction', p. 228.

18   Average income in employment increased about three times as much as indices of retail prices. The cost of housing has generally increased more than average income.

19   See, for instance, T. Jackson, N. Marks, J. Ralls, S. Stymne, *Sustainable Economic Welfare in the UK 1950–1996*, London: New Economics Foundation, 1997, who report that the UK's Index of Sustainable Economic Welfare (ISEW) peaked in 1976, and has since dropped by 25 per cent to the level of the 1950s, increases in GDP per head etc. having been offset by environmental decline, increased inequality and other factors. Similar patterns have been found in other advanced economies, notably the US.

20   See Kern, *The Culture of Time and Space*, p. 157.

21   See Camillo Sitte, *City Planning According to Artistic Principles*, London: Phaidon, 1965, first published in Vienna in 1889.

22   Harvey, *The Condition of Postmodernity*, p. 276.

23   See, for instance, Georg Simmel, 'The Metropolis and Mental Life' [1903], in *On Individuality and Social Forms*, Chicago: University of Chicago Press, 1971, pp. 324–9.

24   Among over 50 urban actuality films from the years 1895–1903, I have encountered only one in which cars appear: *Busy London – Traffic Passing in Front of the Bank of England and Mansion House*, Walturdaw, 1903, in which there are two cars, among a multitude of horse drawn vehicles and pedestrians. In contrast, the surviving incomplete print of Cecil Hepworth's *City of Westminster*, 1909, begins with a 90-second moving-camera view photographed by Gaston Quiribet from a car that drives from the north end of Whitehall, up the east side of Trafalgar Square into St Martin's Lane. The traffic includes cars, horse buses, horse-drawn carts and vans, bicycles, hackney cabs, motor taxis, a steam lorry, and many people crossing the road between them. After the mid-1900s, such shots are rare.

Architectural History, Friendship and Filmed Conversations

Igea Troiani

My own perspective on architectural friendships in history was first revealed in my doctoral thesis titled 'The Politics of Friends in Modern Architecture 1949–1987'.[1] By focusing on writing modern architectural history through a series of political friendships, the dissertation represents my interest in the intersection of criticism and architectural writing, read here as 'Critical Architecture'. Taking inspiration from philosophy and architectural theory, my thesis is the translation of two critical propositions into architectural history. One is the late Jacques Derrida's 1997 book, *Politics of Friendship*.[2] The other is Beatriz Colomina's 1999 essay, 'Collaborations: the Private Life of Modern Architecture'.[3] *Politics of Friendship* is an historical examination into the workings of political collaborations, an examination of *how* things happen through powerful friendships based on likeness. Colomina's essay complements Derrida's text. In it, she contends that there appears to be a shift away from documenting *what* to writing about *how*; as she defines it, 'the practice of architecture' or 'architecture as collaboration'.[4] She writes:

> Architects themselves have started to tell us private stories about their desperate attempts to get jobs, about their pathological experiences with clients [...]. And we pay more attention than when they were trying to dictate to us what their work meant.
>
> (Colomina, 'Collaborations', p. 468)

My method of bringing friendships to the fore of architectural history writing by focusing on conversations with architects has more recently been tested in an alternative critical architecture-writing project. After my thesis, I began a separate second project on the work of the relatively unknown Australian architect, Stuart McIntosh. I met McIntosh for the first time in August 2003 and over a year studied his archive. Through our conversations I became aware of an event he had experienced, one associated with his winning, in 1963, a prestigious national design competition for the Great Hall (see figure on page 126), a 1,250-seat auditorium at the University of Queensland, and his subsequent appointment and then dismissal as architect for the project.

It was because of McIntosh's agreement to be involved that I elected to test the boundaries of writing architectural history by side-stepping into documentary film-making. I collaborated with a young film-maker, Shaun Charles, to produce a 20-minute independent film titled *Building Mayne Hall*, some stills from which are shown in this chapter[5] (see figures on pages 126 and 127). This change of medium allowed me to focus on filmed conversations with interviewees who were all privy to events – McIntosh, James Birrell and James Maccormick. In *Building Mayne Hall*, the architects talk publicly about the private politics of the design process, so intersecting, for me, with Colomina's work. The film is concerned with *how* architects obtain commissions and gain professional success. It does so by piecing together excerpts from the filmed conversations, some of which follow.

McIntosh, filmed in his home study (see figure on page 126), relays a discussion before he moved from Melbourne to Brisbane to take up the commission with his University client group, a body who had not been involved in the judging:

> Just before I came, a friend of mine who was a lecturer at Melbourne University said, 'Watch 'em. They're dishonest and they're vicious', and I just laughed. When I came here, I found them very hostile [...]. At any meeting, I was treated rudely [...] They left me in no doubt they didn't like me and they didn't like my building.
>
> (Stuart McIntosh, *Building Mayne Hall*, filmed in his residence on 21 June 2004)

Birrell, who was University Architect from 1961–1966, is filmed in his apartment sitting in front of a painting (see figure on page 126), explaining the advice he gave to McIntosh at the time:

> Do it *their* way. [But] there was no negotiation possible.
>
> (Birrell, *Building Mayne Hall*, filmed in his residence on 21 May 2004)

McIntosh was dismissed as architect for the project in 1965. Six years later, a second architect, his neighbour Robin Gibson, was appointed outright to design the Great Hall, renamed Mayne Hall during that period. In our only unrecorded conversation on the project, Gibson relays his fond memories of the procurement of Mayne Hall, a building he produced in collaboration with the newly appointed, in 1970, Vice Chancellor Zelman Cowen.[6] For Gibson, building Mayne Hall was as much a story of his friendship with Cowen as the production of his first major building. While I interviewed Cowen, it was as an audio discussion, since he declined to be filmed, and I was unable to use the material because it was unclear.[7] The documentary concludes: 'Robin Gibson did not respond to offers of the makers of this documentary to participate in it' (see figure on page 127).

Maccormick, the University Architect appointed after Birrell, was filmed in his studio, his computer in the background (see figure on page 127). He explains:

> As soon as that first introduction took place [...] Cowen [...] took a shine to Gibson and said, 'Okay, I want him to be my architect for Mayne Hall'.

The Great Hall, the University of Queensland,
in *Building Mayne Hall,* produced by HAPPENinc.,
research/narration/script by Igea Troiani,
film/editing/music by Shaun Charles.

Stuart McIntosh, filmed in his residence on 3 September 2004,
in *Building Mayne Hall,* produced by HAPPENinc.,
research/narration/script by Igea Troiani,
film/editing/music by Shaun Charles.

James Birrell, filmed in his residence on 21 May 2004,
in *Building Mayne Hall,* produced by HAPPENinc.,
research/narration/script by Igea Troiani,
film/editing/music by Shaun Charles.

Photograph of image of Robin Gibson,
in *Building Mayne Hall*, produced by HAPPENinc.,
research/narration/script by Igea Troiani,
film/editing/music by Shaun Charles.

James MacCormick, filmed in his residence on 3
September 2004,
in *Building Mayne Hall*, produced by HAPPENinc.,
research/narration/script by Igea Troiani,
film/editing/music by Shaun Charles.

The James and Mary Emelia Mayne Centre, previously
Mayne Hall
in *Building Mayne Hall*, produced by HAPPENinc.,
research/narration/script by Igea Troiani,
film/editing/music by Shaun Charles.

Zelman is saying, 'I *like* Gibson'. [...] To what extent they talked about design, as they may well have done over dinner at the Cowen's quite independently of me, [...] I have no idea. [...] That's all good stuff. A close relationship between a patron and the artist is the way it should be. [...] Stuart McIntosh's competition entry was never mentioned. [...] Maybe they were too embarrassed to mention it.

(Maccormick, *Building Mayne Hall,* filmed in his residence on 3 September 2004)

My research shows that McIntosh's failure to procure the building had a detrimental effect on him. He was unable to work for several years immediately after his dismissal, but did return to practice. Conversely, Gibson benefited from having befriended Cowen. His success in building Mayne Hall (see figure on page 127) allowed him to obtain other prominent commissions and contributed to his receipt of many architectural accolades.

While textual writing is the conventional medium for historical representation, documentary film is an alternative method. By incorporating those 'previously marginal details of how things actually happen in architectural practice', to quote Colomina, recorded through conversations, the documentary form allows me to write architectural history from a critical perspective and to focus on friendships in architectural production.[8]

Notes

1   Igea Troiani, 'The Politics of Friends in Modern Architecture 1949–1987', unpublished doctoral thesis, Queensland University of Technology, 2004.
2   Jacques Derrida, *Politics of Friendship*, London, New York: Verso, 1997.
3   Beatriz Colomina, 'Collaborations: the Private Life of Modern Architecture', *Journal of the Society of Architectural Historians,* 58, 3, September 1999, pp. 462–71.
4   Colomina, 'Collaborations', p. 462.
5   *Building Mayne Hall*, research/narration/script by Igea Troiani, film/editing/music by Shaun Charles, produced by HAPPENinc, 2004.
6   My conversation with Robin Gibson took place at his office premises at 130 Mary Street, Brisbane, on 31 March 2004. Cowen was Vice-Chancellor at the University of Queensland from 1970–1977.
7   On 2 July 2004, I interviewed Zelman Cowen in his Treasury Place office in East Melbourne. Cowen agreed to have the interview tape-recorded but declined to be filmed. At this interview, Cowen read from Zelman Cowen, 'Architects and Architecture', a lecture delivered at the 50th Anniversary of the Royal Australian Institute of Architects (New South Wales Chapter, Sydney) on 13 July 1979, referring also to his friendship with Gibson: 'The Senate of the University of Queensland agreed to commission Robin Gibson to produce a design [...]. So began a strong and continuing friendship between Robin Gibson and me.'
8   Colomina, 'Collaborations', p. 462.

Image, Text, Architecture

The presence that 'WAS HERE'

Robin Wilson

This photo–text chapter has as its starting point an article I produced for *The Architects' Journal* in 2002.[1] The article discussed the work of the artist and architect collaboration Sophie Warren and Jonathan Mosley, focusing in particular on their newly completed house in the Redcliff area of Bristol. My intention is not to revisit my own work of journalism. Rather, I will draw attention to an aspect of the article that is seemingly an accident of reproduction and outside the intent of any specific agent as such.

These observations are part of a much wider research project into the documentation of architecture in architectural photography and journalism, in which I explore how the architectural media functions through adherence to generic formulae, professional and institutional codes of representation. This wider project draws on the work of Fredric Jameson and Louis Marin on the unconscious and meta-discursive processes of utopian literature, through which I seek to account for such 'accidents' as I will outline below, as ruptures, blind spots in the discourse of the architectural media, wherein the critical limits and the vested interests of the architectural profession are inscribed.[2]

The Architects' Journal article was a product of collaboration between myself, the photographer Nigel Green (an artist and photographer, with whom I had worked previously), and Warren and Mosley. I thus make no claims as to the document's 'neutrality' or 'critical distance', as such. I wrote about this project (the Redcliff house) because I was intrigued by the practice of Warren and Mosley. I understood the article to take the form of a proposition through the re-presentation of Warren and Mosley's work. If the article achieves 'criticality' in any direct sense, it would do so through the way it recounts aspects of Warren and Mosley's own strategies and concerns, by portraying a kind of approach to the integration of art and architectural practice that I felt to be under-represented in the journal. What I aim to describe here, however, is what we might call a reflexive indication of the critical limits of the institutional frame into which the work of Warren and Mosley had been placed.

The title page of the article comprises a photograph showing the front and side elevations of the house, with a small amount of textual information, including the

Bristol fashion

Sophie Warren and Jonathan Mosley's new house in a Bristol
suburb builds on themes from their earlier artist/architect
collaborations to make a subtle but functional domestic design

By Robin Wilson. Photographs by Nigel Green

Title page to 'Bristol
Fashion', *The
Architects' Journal*,
216, 16, 31 October
2002.

title of the article: 'Bristol Fashion' (see figure above). This title was provided by the
editors of the journal and without consultation with myself, the photographer or
Warren and Mosley.[3]

The image of the completed house affects a certain degree of divergence
from the norms of architectural photography. While, as usual, a large or medium-
format camera has been used, and attention paid to the correction of perspectives,
Green's image is otherwise quite abnormal. Whereas most architectural photographs

will position the architectural object centrally, dominating the composition, in this image the principal object of design – the house's front elevation – is displaced to the left-hand third of the mid-ground, leaving a large, empty foreground of irregular road surface, with the remaining two-thirds of the mid-ground comprising the whitewashed wall of the building's side elevation and its adjacent empty plot. In so doing, Green has included an unusual degree of contextual information.

Writing of her experience of the standard or generic use of architectural photography whilst working as an editor, Janet Abrams describes architecture in terms of a 'specimen', lifted from 'its earthbound anchorage and into a new and commanding prominence'.[4] Yet, in Green's image of the house, other 'specimens' might attract our attention: an abject lamppost stands a lonely sentinel on the limit between mid- and foreground, and a fringe of resurgent weed growth has colonised the margins of the empty site. The faint, green glow of cellulose is, moreover, one of the few indications that this is a colour image, not monotone. For, unlike the well-lit, blue-sky imagery of the industry norm, here the sky above the house is almost as pallid as the whitewash, and there is no play of shadow to increase the drama of the built form.

Journals tend to resist divergence from the norms of architectural photography or any reflection on the level of 'truth' photography offers, for to do so would be to question the basis of a journal's claim to critical objectivity. It is perhaps not surprising, therefore, that the title of the article, 'Bristol Fashion', would seem to comprise an attempt to re-centre the object, to bring back design from the edge of the photograph into its usual position of centrality and dominance. The title also seems to attempt to counteract the sense of absence in the image with the more secure signifier of the place name, Bristol. The anonymity of the scene is thus immediately reclaimed on behalf of a regional identity, or more precisely, a regional cliché – 'ship-shape and Bristol fashion' – an allusion to the city's maritime history. The title thus seems to affirm the 'emptiness' of the image and the building's blank surfaces, but as cleanliness, efficiency and economy, well presented and well scrubbed like a well-run ship.

Reading through the article, one would have cause to return to this image. My article informs the reader that a text intervention appears on the side elevation of the house. The words 'WAS HERE' have been written in black lettering, and then washed over a few times with the same white paint that covers the rest of the elevation.

The 'WAS HERE' text was the culmination of a series of works that responded to the process of the house's design and construction (see figures on pages 132). The lack of a pronoun or proper name begs the question, who or what was here? We might deduce that the text refers to some past presence eradicated by the architectural process itself, that the text relates to the history of the site and that this new house replaced another building. But, equally, the text confronts us with its own imminent absence, the possibility of the disappearance of the blank façade by future development, for we view it across an empty plot, a negative space against the house's positive presence.

**Sophie Warren and
Jonathan Mosley,
'Understanding the
Measure of Things'
R-type colour (2002),
Bristol.**

**Sophie Warren and
Jonathan Mosley,
'WAS HERE' Black
and white emulsion
(2002), Bristol.**

However, in a cursory glance at the title page, or even in a more prolonged observation, it is unlikely that a reader would register this typographic/graffiti presence the first time around. In reproduction, the 'WAS HERE' text has become considerably more faint than in the real. Its presence only becomes apparent on the page through a sustained looking, through an attentive search of that 'blank' surface. Indeed, when spotted, the text seems to emerge there as if from the page beneath.

The whitewashed wall becomes like a blank page, from which the text emerges, only visible under the scrutiny of a *direct* gaze. The text seems engrained in the materiality of the page and yet is also consistent with the perspective of the architectural object in space. Once found, the 'WAS HERE' text establishes or opens up a space between the architectural object and the page, between image and language. It seems to unleash a deconstructive force within the journal, as if it were some form of reflexive intervention, encouraging a reader's conscious awareness of the difference between the real and the printed sign, between the physical site in Bristol and its photographic representation.

The 'displacement' of the front façade to the left-hand-side of *The Architects' Journal* title page photograph was clearly the photographer's response to the position of the text intervention, and the pallor of the image resulted from attempting to adjust the aperture to register the text's fragile tonal values. But whereas the photography responds to the presence of the text, the journal's titles and captioning do not. The 'WAS HERE' text is thus registered visually in the journal, not directly, but only through an adjustment to the compositional norms of architectural photography.

But this repressed element of the title page also seems to return, visible under the scrutiny of the direct gaze of the reader of the journal, a ghost presence that oscillates between presence and absence. The 'WAS HERE' text, once transferred to the media context, provides a moment of disturbance or rupture in the assumption of referential truth within the architectural journal. It does this, not through a direct critique of the journal's 'assumptions' as to the status of its representation, but through the way it demonstrates the materiality of the representation's support, the journal page and the act of viewing that page.

This typographic effect emerges in the gap between affirmation and negation, between the editorial decision to include Warren and Mosley and the process by which the nature of editorial language excludes the more challenging aspects of their work through the manner of its presentation, through the way it is 'framed' discursively. Thus editorial practice forges an absence from the presence it invites into the journal; it simultaneously assimilates and expels, displays, and obscures. A kind of differential play between approval and disapproval takes place upon page 22 of *The Architects' Journal*, between an intellectual acknowledgement of Warren and Mosley's practice on one perhaps personal level of editorial practice (commissioning) and the exercising or perpetuation of a repression at another more institutional level of editorial practice (presentation).

Marin has written extensively on the phenomena of written texts inscribed within the iconic spaces of history painting of the European tradition – such presences as a motto, signature or other instructional, textual element surreptitiously included on an empty surface of the painted scene. Marin has defined the effect of such superimpositions of the linguistic sign into iconic space as productive of a 'site of [...] confusion that is "properly" u-topic'.[5] For, as Marin continues, such instances of duality mark a moment of reflexivity or 'opacity' on the mimetic surface, creating a rupture in the 'visual cohesion and narrative coherence' of the representation, and drawing attention to what is involved in the painting's construction.[6] This affects, Marin suggests, 'a *state of crisis*' within the representation, 'concerning the formal and structural conditions of the possibility of the sign'.[7]

The inclusion of Warren and Mosley's work in *The Architects' Journal* similarly forces a site of 'crisis' to emerge, wherein the limits of the frame of representation (the limits of editorial discourse) are inscribed. On the title page of the Warren and Mosley article, the discursive frame fragments, as the page is expressed both in its glossy materiality and as an iconic surface, as the limits between textual space (a text about architecture) and architectural space (where a text is written on architecture) blur. This blurring takes place before our eyes, as an effect upon the page, in the fugitive play of the 'WAS HERE' text, between emergence and disappearance. As a potential indication of the 'formal and structural conditions of the sign', could it be that the 'WAS HERE' text, transferred to the site of its media dissemination, acts to question our very ability to represent architecture in the first place?

Notes

1   Robin Wilson, 'Bristol Fashion', *The Architects' Journal*, 216, 16, 31 October 2002, pp. 22–7.
2   See for example, Robin Wilson, 'At the Limits of Genre: Architectural Photography and Utopic Criticism', in Jane Rendell (ed.), *Critical Architecture*, a special issue of *The Journal of Architecture*, 10, 3, pp. 265–73.
3   It should be noted that since the redesign of *The Architects' Journal* in 2005 by the art editor Sarah Douglas and the design practice APFEL ('A Practice For Everyday Life'), this popular newspaper style of titling has largely been phased out.
4   Janet Abrams, 'Available for Viewing', in Martin Craiger-Smith (ed.), *Sitework: Architectural Photography Since Early Modernism*, London: The Photographers' Gallery, 1991, pp. 77–81, p. 78.
5   Louis Marin, 'Topic and Figures of Enunciation', in Stephen Melville and Bill Readings (eds), *Vision and Textuality*, London: Macmillan, 1995, pp. 195–214, p. 206.
6   Marin, 'Topic and Figures', p. 206.
7   Louis Marin, 'The Order of Words and the Order of Things in Painting', *Visible Language*, 23, 2/3, 1989, pp. 188–203, p. 201.

Fluttering Butterflies, a Dusty Road, and a Muddy Stone

Criticality in distraction (Haga Park, Stockholm, 2004)[1]

Katja Grillner

Haga Park, spring 1977: Bus 515 – the Pelouse – the Copper tents. In the last week of school, Adolf Fredrik Music School and its annex school, Little Adolf Fredrik, make an excursion to Haga Park. We take bus 515 from Odenplan and are let off at Haga North. Doris is our teacher. Each class has an assigned area for picnicking on the Pelouse.[2] There are probably around 50 classes, from primary all the way up to upper secondary school. Surrounding us, a swarm of older (adult) children walk in clusters from the gates (Haga North) towards the tents. We are small. Doris places us rather far down the slope, under the trees to the right. What are we eating and drinking? Cake and lemonade? A faint recollection of some kind of performance, or is it just singing – crinolines and the 'fluttering butterfly' song?[3] We are singing it too. Is this me, today, just imagining? Perhaps, but it is not far-fetched to imagine that, in 1977, students from the music classes would have jumped at the opportunity to act out a Bellman Haga.[4] Was it in fact the very reason for us being there? Let's say it was. I further connect the Pelouse at this time with the oval-shaped wine bottles of Perle Rosé. Didn't its label have an Arcadian motif? Many years of these excursions (should be six) are floating in the Hagafolder I store in my mind. The impressions assemble around three spaces: the dusty road (arrival – departure – crowd), the huge sea of grass (the Pelouse) with all the older children out there, ourselves on the shore under the trees, and – when we are old enough to explore on our own – the ruin.

'Buildings,' Walter Benjamin wrote in 1936, 'are appropriated in a twofold manner: by use and by perceptions – or rather by touch and sight. Such appropriation cannot be understood in terms of the attentive concentration of a tourist before a famous building.'[5] In Haga Park, autumn 2004, I find many reasons to reflect on this proposition. Could I be a tourist here? The park does not easily present itself before my eyes. I find myself in it (on the path, by the water, on the edge of the woods, breathing damp autumn air). Wherever I rest my eyes, my body is set in motion before me. Or if the weather was nicer, if it was spring or summer, I could have had a picnic, watching the sky, the clouds, the treetops, or the pages of my book.

But, on the other hand, Haga Park is very well-suited to the attention of tourists at a number of well-chosen spots. It is one of the finest examples of eighteenth-century landscape gardens in Sweden.[6] There are the views, the vistas that open up in a carefully composed manner (over the Pelouse, towards the Copper tents, from the lake-shore pathway towards Gustav III's pavilion and further on to the Temple of Echo, and from the top of the steep precipice where the whole of Lake Brunnsviken spreads out before you with the pavilion in the foreground). And there are the pavilions, the *fabriques*, delicately placed in the park (the Turkish pavilion, the Chinese temple, the Temple of Echo, the Copper tents, and Gustav III's pavilion). Haga is a pleasure park, one intended to be enjoyed as a world of fancy. The eighteenth-century visitor could busy herself, happily browsing for pretty views, contemplating them as painted scenes (for real). The next minute she could step into the frame and live out the reality of its imagined situation. Appropriation by perception and by use, in Benjamin's words, a useful fiction.

It is now 212 years since this fairytale world at Haga was laid fallow by the 1792 assassination of the king, Gustav III. For the aristocratic subjects the landscape park addressed, the imagination had played an active role in the everyday experience of the park. For the gardeners as well as the 'live ornaments' exhibited for view in the park, the everyday experience of the park was naturally different, but not necessarily without fancy. In this chapter I attempt to capture in writing an account of Haga Park today, as experienced by use and by perception. I use myself – my own memories, impressions and activities – as the primary source of this account. Going back in time, my experience disintegrates into a multitude. The 1970s: the annual school excursion. We take bus 515 from Odenplan. The Haga Park is in the country. The ruins are very adventurous (they bring to mind 'The Famous Five'). The 1980s: sports classes at the Matteus' School take me out jogging over Norrtull, the Haga Airport Bus terminal, the Copper tents, the allotment gardens, and back again. In between: family excursions, sometimes to Haga, sometimes to Bergianska. Late 1980s, early 1990s: some romance. More, and longer, jogging rounds. Summer picnics. I find Caspar David Friedrich through my camera lens.

Following a path into the woods from the meadow just by the little park café, one is readily alone among the fallen leafs. These woods are light and the ground is wet. It goes up-hill. Bare grey granite cliffs and lonesome pine trees at the end of the path promise a view. This point of view is marked in Fredrik Magnus Piper's *Haga Plan* from 1786 and the painter Elias Martin painted this very view in the late 1790s.[7] Deep down from the edge of the cliff runs the lake-shore pathway. People pass by, running or walking. You cannot see them. You can see Gustav III's pavilion, the Temple of Echo, the roof of the tree-tops and Lake Brunnsviken; on the other shore, Bergianska Botanical Gardens and the Museum of Natural History and, further away, Hjorthagen and the Värta gas and electricity plants. I did not (I think) find this place until some time in the late 1980s (1988?). I am carrying my camera around, hunting for images. It is probably quite late in the autumn, bright sun, crisp air. The lonesome pine tree is twisting its branches in an exquisite, tortured manner.

It is Caspar David Friedrich. This I know when I stand there as an 18-year-old. I do not know of Elias Martin. Neither do I know of Fredrik Magnus Piper. But I know that my euphoria, my beating heart, and everything that belongs to the experience of the romantic sublime, is slightly wrong, a bit embarrassing. I have studied; I am a confirmed post-modernist. What can I possibly do? The view is, however hard you try to brace yourself, rather sublime. Returning now, in 2004, the same thing happens. I can't help it. I love great prospects.

Elias Martin's view (2004). Image: Katja Grillner.

This site is built from its natural topography – the precipice at one end, the pleasant slope towards the other. The light woods add to the drama by softly wrapping around the experiencing subject, separating her from the main path while walking up to the edge. There are many paths and they are vague. The fallen leaves smudge out the edges. The inclination seems to pull the feet upward. And then, when you get there, what is there to do? (–) In the 'ahh' – the romantic sigh – we trace a repressed desire to drift on. Climbing over the edge we simply glide out and over – as much now as then.

Benjamin's thesis on appropriation by use and by perception has fascinating implications for architectural representation. Even though we all live and operate within buildings of different kinds, and thereby subject ourselves to these modes of appropriation daily, they are remarkably difficult to grasp. Architectural photography tends to capture the object or an objectified spatiality. Architectural drawings tend to capture material facts (the exact location of the wall, the extension of the floor). Architectural writing tends to describe visual, sometimes tactile, qualities. The text may be flavoured with experiential exclamations and metaphors to fully capture an architectural idea – always under full concentration. Architectural criticism thereby falls into the habit of a tourist's (even though professional) mode of contemplation. Useless – according to Benjamin. To change focus and to turn to a close-up study of architectural usage does not necessarily bring about a fuller understanding of architecture. Rather, Benjamin points us to a fundamental distractedness of architectural experience.[8]

But to contemplate the appropriation of buildings and other designed spatial structures through the distracted experience of use is a difficult challenge for a writing architect. The task seems even more complicated when faced with the everyday appropriation of a park. The typical functionality of a park is unspecific – walking (alone or together), picnicking, playing ball-games, running, sun-bathing, adventure, love.

Almost all the surfaces of the park prove useful for a number of these activities. The park programme is, in general, vague, as is its functionality. The challenge is to capture the material reality of the Haga Park (its woods, its paths, its lake, its rocks) that glimpses through, that is a mere background to a multitude of ongoing everyday practices. Writing architecture (here, landscape) means then to write a background. The lens of the text, to borrow a photographic notion, must be adjusted, refocused on the walking, the playing, the love-making and so forth. This is what is going on. We simply have to make a detour in order to catch a glimpse of the park (incidentally).

Side-walk, facades, at a right angle. Pacing out against the pattern of the concrete slabs. Norrtull Street widens in the last block. Norrtull. Short of breath. Green light. Four zebra crossings. Under the junction crossing the car park. Haga Terminal, then tennis courts to the right. Lake Brunnsviken and Wenner-Gren Centre in the right corner of the eye. Big tree in front of large meadow, left. Asphalt road turns to fine gravelled pathway, wide. A short uphill slope. (Anna – who else? Selina perhaps, and Therese? They are already walking. Should stop too. Not very cool to run.) Picking up pace alone. Fine, fine gravel, water glimmering through the shrubs in the right corner of the eye. A steep bushy slope up the hill to the left. Short downhill slope. Sunny meadow left, right. Short uphill slope. Coffee house right. (Was it open then?) Ice-cream stand left. Down-hill for a while. Second wind. Precipice left. Lake right. The Pelouse in view. Opening. Copper tents left. Lake right and now the steep rocks on the other shore. Now it comes, the long up-hill slope. Linden tree avenue up to the Copper tents. Glimpses of the Pelouse between the tree trunks. In the woods to the right there is a ruin. Stitch right-side. Must walk. Keep running. Pebble in hand. Finally, the crackling sound from the course gravel surface. Copper tents right. Pelouse left. Keep leftish now. Long down-hill slope. Passing the allotment gardens (?) right. Not much left. Wooden houses. Into the beech woods. The gates. Asphalt parked cars. Back to Matteus' School. Score a good time.

The year is 1984 – the sports class, jogging round at Haga. The description is void of most of the thoughts that would have floated in my mind on this occasion – streams of thoughts that tend to make us blind to our surroundings, or that stubbornly hook on to particular sites without having anything at all to do with them in reality – distracted encounters. To reconstruct and to put perceptions into words is remarkably difficult. To excavate a blurry image from one's memory and to try hard to focus it demands great caution. As soon as you imagine the focus to be just right, when you think you 'know' how it was, this new image will be stored together with your 'original' memory. If you have been careless, you may very well have forged your own memory. In this text, I try to extract a pre-professional Haga from myself. I am uncertain, what is it that I find?

My body holds a particular knowledge of the topography of this park. Is that important? In my mind there are visual flows registered, remembering rhythms between clearings and closures. More precisely: the pressure on the left shoulder of the bushy slope, the attraction of the glimmering water through shrubs and under-wood, the unavoidable left turn of the head, and chin up, by the Pelouse, the relief as the gravel crackles on the terrace of the Copper tents. At the same time, my thoughts are everywhere else. Then? I cannot remember anything but the small anxiety caused by my lazy classmates as they took the first left as soon as our teacher was out of sight. Better then to run alone.

There is a Haga Park that follows me around. A remembered place that I store in my mind, it is a place that expands, evolves, even disappears in part over time. In this sense it is unique, as unique as any other person's particular place perceptions. We bring all these places along through life, and yet they are impossible to fix with certainty. We do not know what it is we remember. In *The Remembered Film*, Victor Burgin discusses the impact of filmic scenes – settings, landscapes, spaces – on our memories and imagination.[9] How memories of filmic landscapes float into those of our real-life experiences and merge, seamlessly sometimes. There are a number of ways for a critic to approach Haga Park from the outside (of first-hand place experience). There are maps, there are plans, there are letters and lists, there are books, there are drawings, there are experts and charts. But, as they enter the mind of the critic, these sources also form a place of their own. They merge in various ways through the work of the imagination into an ephemeral Haga Park, whether experienced in real-life or not. Attached to *this* park are memories of archives and dry air, a snotty professor and a book that disappeared. Not even this park can be fixed. There is no outside.

This text, then, seeks to explore the inside from within. It is suggestive of a mode of critical writing that allows for, at once, a distracted experiential engagement with a particular place, and a critical engagement with that same distraction. It makes use of personal recollections in order to investigate with a specific kind of ephemeral precision what it may be that we can say that we know about a place, or the experience of being in (acting in) a place, the effects of habit and of use on the way we see, hear, smell, taste, and feel our spatial surroundings, how we remember the places we have lived. Memory may serve as a bridge for the critical imagination to embark on work elsewhere.[10] Allowing at once both distant examination and immersive experience, it offers a critical method to complicate and distract our desire to make a neat little parcel of every critical endeavour. Not even the tourist's attention escapes distraction. (At the Parthenon in 1987 I hear, I see, my sister laughing. A butterfly has landed and refuses to leave my otherwise unassuming white sunhat. We both end up with tears in our eyes.)

I cannot recall how we get there. It is a cloudy day, 1980 (perhaps). The ruin is located in the woods beside the Pelouse. We run around the roofless rooms. I do not remember what it is we are playing. Hide and seek? It is difficult to hide. Several occasions blend into one. At one point I know that I imagine the Middle Ages; wonder what it was like to live here (this thought floats up in my memory and it did happen precisely there). But I also know, even then, that the Middle Ages do not belong here. In 1786 the first stone was laid in the ground. In the ruin I think about the soldiers, and all the stone they hauled. Our teacher must have told us.

Late autumn, 2004, I turn onto a path from the Copper tents to find my way back to the ruin. When was I last here? On my way there I find a huge boulder and stray rocks on the edge of the woods, balancing on the downward slope to the Pelouse – a picturesque arrangement? Perhaps. But the ruin is not picturesque. A ten metre strip of trees and brushwood away, I stand in a clear-felled forest. The ruin is a gaping wound. It has more in common with the E4 and its noise barriers than with the rest of Haga Park. (The buzzing noise from the E4 accompanies you around the park. There is a brief pause when the E18 takes over the noise production. It is remarkably brief.)

I am not alone. My phone rings. I balance on a muddy stone. I could slip. I am looking for an opening in the foundation that I observed from the other side of the ditch as I arrived. Now it's gone (but it's captured on film). (Hi. – Ok. I'll buy the groceries. – I'm in Haga. – Bye.) I feel safe with my phone. I wonder: do people live here? There are rooms but no roofs. It's cold and damp. Close to the city. (I just encountered a provisional hut – Winnie the Pooh, an Eeyore-style house – up on the ridge behind the Copper tents.) I climb the high foundation wall (around three metres high). My phone rings again. A green safety railing bars my way. (Hi. – Good. – No in Haga. – What, err. – No, no, not there. By the ruin. Another memory.) Was that railing here when I was little? I do not recognise it. On the other hand, I do not recall anything of the ruin's outward appearance (to arrive at or to leave the ruin). The design of the railing could very well be from the 1930s. I find another way up onto the wall. The height of the walls strikes me. Inside it is almost five metres down to the ground (the floor of the roofless rooms). This is not the way it was. When I ran around these rooms I did not (as I remember) give a thought to the height. In 1980 I was 152 centimetres tall.[11] I do not climb down today. There is only one way out. I am alone.

While writing this text I made three excursions to Haga. I brought a video camera along, casually recording while walking and biking around selected locations. Playing the films at home I was surprised to see how many trivial details I recognised – specific tree trunks, tiny bumps in the road, puddles of water – not from the particular visits that autumn – but from 28 years of recurring visits. At the same time as this discovery confirms that in some way I really do 'know' this park, the images stored in my memory are still floating about, getting mixed up. A number of times in this text I mention the allotment gardens lining the road running south from the Copper tents. But were they really allotment gardens? Looking at an aerial photograph from 1963, it rather looks like tiny patches of arable land. Today the same road is lined with a sloping meadow (a new Pelouse) that hides the E4 (from view).

I never crossed that meadow (the new Pelouse). On my last visit I take bus 515 from Odenplan. I plan to get off at Haga North, just as we did back then. But going on a highway bus makes me nervous. I do not want to end up in Solna. It cannot be more than one stop from Haga Forum, I conclude, and get off at the linen-weaver's cottage. I find myself in a huge concave excavation of the road-side earthwork. I thought I would find the sculpture face-vases here.[12] Where are they? I know I have seen them several times from the airport bus. They must be higher up, on the other side of the embankment. Beginning to stride up, I realise that I got off the bus too early. I get excited. I would never have come here otherwise. (Why is there a bus-stop here, after all?) I am on the other side of that noise-barrier meadow. I have to try to get down to the regular road. (I am heading for the ruin.) It is not sunny. Drizzling fog and it is cold. Most of the leaves have fallen. The ground is yellow.

I don't walk down. There is a path running north. Recently planted shrubs turn into a consistent pine forest. Dry grass and tiny aspen brushwood. The air is as dry as the ground. Roaring cars below. The pine forest ends abruptly. A perfectly straight line divides the forest. Small withering oak trees, birches and other mixed species of deciduous trees. It is here I encounter the hut, Eeyore's House (Winnie the Pooh). There are no signs of anyone living here now. Neither is there any official information about a possible 'hut-project'. It is surrounded by sticks covering the ground. The still-green surface of the Pelouse glimpses through the trees on my right. Blue Copper tents ahead. When did they become blue? In my memory they are pale, sun-bleached: green, red, and yellow. Or perhaps one of them was blue?

I should not have gone alone. The Temple of Echo echoes. I have never tried it before. It echoes my feet. It echoes my words. But not in the middle. It is mute.

Acknowledgements

The research for this chapter has been supported by the Swedish Research Council through AKAD (www.akad.se). I wish to thank my colleagues in AKAD and in the Spatial Imagination in Design research cluster (www.spatialimagination.org) – in particular Jane Rendell – for providing challenging and inspiring input to this research.

Notes

1   This chapter was published in Swedish in 2005 in an earlier version. I wish to thank Christina Engfors of the Swedish Museum of Architecture for the invitation to write that text. See Katja Grillner, 'Kritik och Förströelse (vi befinner oss i Hagaparken, Stockholm)', in Christina Engfors (ed.), *Varje dags arkitektur – Arkitekturmuseets Årsbok 2004*, Stockholm: Arkitekturmuseet, 2005, pp. 38–56. Since its first presentation at the 'Critical Architecture' conference in 2004, this project has generated several independent but deeply inter-related offsprings. See, for example, the installation 'Out of Focus (In Distraction)', *Spatial Imagination*, London: Domo Baal Gallery, 2006, and the associated catalogue essay by Katja Grillner, 'Out of Focus (In Distraction)', in Peg Rawes and Jane Rendell (eds), *Spatial Imagination*, London: The Bartlett School of Architecture, UCL, 2006, pp. 10–11; as well as Katja Grillner, 'In the Corner of Perception – Spatial Experience in Distraction', *Architectural Research Quarterly*, 9, 3/4, pp. 245–54.

2   'Pelouse' comes from the French *pelouse* – a meadow. At Haga, the concave meadow sloping down towards Lake Brunnsviken has, since it was designed by

Fredrik Magnus Piper in 1787, been referred to as the Pelouse (= *äng* or *gräsplan* in Swedish).

3   The song 'Fjäril'n vingad syns på Haga' ['The Fluttering Butterfly is Sighted at Haga'] by Carl-Michael Bellman (1740–95).

4   The poet Carl-Michael Bellman's songs were praised in both popular and courtly culture at the time, and they continue to be sung widely in Sweden today, and to be frequently re-interpreted by contemporary musicians and singer-songwriters. The songs portray a pastoral lifestyle, combining high and low, mythology and the every-day, happiness and melancholy.

5   Walter Benjamin, 'The Work of Art in the Age of Mechanical Reproduction' (1936), *Illuminations*, edited by Hannah Arendt and translated by Harry Zohn, London: Fontana, 1973, pp. 217–51, p. 236.

6   The Haga Park project was initiated in 1771 when the king, Gustav III, bought the southern part of the park. In 1787 he bought the larger northern estate of Brahelund that enabled the creation of a large-scale landscape park. Gustav III had by then engaged the landscape designer Fredrik Magnus Piper as superintendent of the royal parks and gardens. Piper had been trained in 'state-of-the-art' landscape gardening in England and France by order of the king. For further garden historical information, see for example Magnus Olausson, *Den Engelska parken i Sverige under gustaviansk tid*, Stockholm: Piper Press, 1993. For an English reference, see the Scandinavian section in John Dixon Hunt's *The Picturesque Garden in Europe*, London: Thames and Hudson, 2002, pp. 142–51; Torbjörn Andersson's essay on Haga Park 'Haga – The History and Restoration of a Park', in Karin Lindegren (ed.), *Fredrik Magnus Piper and the Landscape Garden*, Katrineholm: Kungliga Konstakademin, 1981, pp. 56–71.

7   Fredrik Magnus Piper's plan of Haga Park and Elias Martin's wash-drawing from the late 1790s are both reproduced in Hunt, *The Picturesque Garden in Europe*, pp. 145–6.

8   For an extended discussion, see Grillner, 'In the Corner of Perception – Spatial Experience in Distraction'.

9   Victor Burgin, *The Remembered Film*, London: Reaktion Books, 2004.

10   In the installation 'Out of Focus (In Distraction)', three Haga Park settings from this chapter were presented (the Temple of Echo, the Ruin, and Eeyore's House) by still images and sound distributed through light boxes in the gallery stairwell. In relation to this chapter, the installation took a bridging step towards such an 'elsewhere' – a place, perhaps, in-between autobiographical recollection and fictional construction.

11   Passport for Katja Maria Grillner, issued by the Swedish Police Authority, Stockholm, Henry Isaksson, 13 November 1980.

12   Integrated sculpture and pedestrian bridge at Haga North by Sivert Lindblom, 1993.

Memoirs

It will have happened already

Sharon Kivland

Sharon Kivland, from the series, *Lieux imaginaires* (2002–6).

When at last I finished writing the paper I would give at 'Critical Architecture', I was called away from my desk. I had not saved what I had written and returned to find my application had quit unexpectedly. On restarting my computer, I found an empty document. I had to reconstruct from memory what I think I wrote, though I knew it was not what I had written. Perhaps this is what underlay the two works I described. Without text, without images (or only two anyway), with only six books remaining from the first work, 'Memoirs' (though there may be others in circulation or even on bookshelves somewhere in the world), and a book that might not be published due to a budget cut or change of local government in the *mairie* of the town where I made the second work, 'Cela aura déjà eu lieu' ('It will have happened already'), what real chance do I have to prove events happened, with certain effects? How am I to remember them?

A film is present in both works, directly and indirectly. I first saw Alain Resnais' *L'Année dernière à Marienbad* (1961) in 1975. Hardly a year has gone by in which I have not seen the film at least once, but each time I fall asleep at precisely the same point. I went to Marienbad in 1994, then again in 1996. It is, of course, really Máriánské Láznê, and it was not at all the location of the film. I have forgotten the origin of my compulsion, yet out of habit I fall asleep anyway. Robbe-Grillet knew of Resnais' work, recognizing an echo of his own slowness of attitude, creating a work between an opera and a statue. Both of them, he felt, constructed the mental spaces of time and memory, without any excessive insistence on relation of cause-and-effect or the time-sequence in narrative.

One might say, despite my tendency to fall asleep, to lose documents, to be incapable of taking a decent light reading, that I started here and returned here, in a film that refuses to obey the rules of narrative with resolution. Of the first work, enough time has passed for it to enter the past. Indeed, it may have almost disappeared: I have my last six copies, at least, the last in my possession. Like Marienbad, the place no longer exists, for the purpose it was intended anyway. In a way, the same is true of the location of the second work. Both are real places, however, and real places do tend to get in the way of thought. While something about memory and architecture underlies both, the memories are not mine and there is no guarantee of their truth.

The first work, 'Memoirs', is a collection of small books, rather like old school exercise books, held in a paper slipcase, made in response to St Edwards Hospital, in Cheddleton, near Leek, Staffordshire, UK. Built as the North Staffordshire Asylum over 100 years ago, it closed in 2001, to be re-developed as luxury flats. My work was commissioned shortly before its closure, as part of a larger project initiated by Staffordshire University, called *Making History*. I do not attempt to provide a historical record of the hospital or to make any intervention in the lives of those who were patients there. In initial meetings with the staff of the hospital, the extent of their loss, their trauma, became clear; the long-term patients were too heavily medicated to demonstrate any reaction. Although both parties were obviously held in the spell of the institution, it was the staff who found themselves without a compass upon the closure of the hospital.

Each of the four books relates to a particular location in the hospital and each suggests certain kinds of behaviour in these spaces. Book I, 'Repetition', is dependent on memory, the memory of June Haycock, who carefully mapped out the entire hospital. For Sigmund Freud, repetition is the incessant exposure to horrible or upsetting events and circumstances, the compulsion to repeat an act when its origins are forgotten. Unless one remembers the past, if events are suppressed, something is returned in one's actions.

Book II is called 'Resistance', a term Freud first uses for the unwillingness to bring repressed memories to conscious recognition, which describes all the barriers to the progress of the work of a psychoanalytic treatment and which is inherent in the process of analysis. In Seminar 2, Jacques Lacan speaks of an irreducible residue of resistance that cannot be overcome, 'which may be what is essential'.[1] In *Écrits,* he remarks, 'When the patient's resistance opposes suggestion, it is only a desire to maintain the subject's desire.'[2] What could be more desirable than the flowers, the dresses that Evelyn Mountford draws? However, from the fabric of the page something less attractive emerges.

Book III is called 'Reminiscence', and while the analytic process may not aim at reliving past experience, at feeling the same emotions of the past, it still happens. In reminiscing, stories are embellished, made better or worse, and so occupy a register of the imaginary. Memories are evoked, to be sure, and while this book demonstrates intense emotional effects, it is no more than a fiction. For all that, it has a certain optimism and a certain truth, and the style of writing echoes quite faithfully the slippery connections of psychotic speech, in which everything and nothing makes sense.

The last book, IV, is 'Recollection', closer to the symbolic process of the assumption of one's history. The images show the stores and archives, the cataloguing of illness that cannot be revealed. The centre pages unfold, yet show only the white blankness of bed linen. The drawings are by Michael Garside, who draws what he sees on television. During the production of the book, his drawing ceased, and he became very anxious as a result. He told me through the blur of medication that he no longer felt very well. His only ability to describe the world abandoned him and he was in great pain. The records are also abandoned, now destroyed; there is no longer any need to retain them as the hospital gives way to new development.

The books have never been for sale. They were circulated through the Mental Health services, and unlike many works of art, elicited a large response. Though I would not claim this myself, it appeared that for those who wrote to the project organizers, I had described their experience of working in mental health. Yet what did I know of it? Had I only 'bent down and picked up what is to be found', transcribing what was to be seen and what was said, reading from later to earlier? I called the work 'Memoirs', and in French, '*mémoire'* has a number of meanings. It is the faculty of conserving and recalling what has happened and what is associated with those events of the past; it is the mental function of representation of the past; it is what a person may leave behind for the future. It is also the reminder of a bill outstanding. In his discussions on memory, Freud moves to the speculation that all memories are screen memories: 'It may indeed be questioned whether we have any memories at all *from* our childhood: memories *relating* to our childhood may be all that we possess.'[3]

With this in mind, I took up the strange process of recollection at the Chateau de Morsang. It is a work in four parts: a gold and blue invitation card, an opening event at which a choir rehearsed for a performance it had already given, a photograph and a wall text and some sumptuous gold silk curtains, a postcard that would circulate in three ways, and then, at last, a small book. If you were there on the opening night, you would have received a postcard two weeks later and seen yourself in the audience. This is what the lovely card said:

This is an invitation to a project in several parts. It is a work that takes various forms, including that of recollection. Without you, it will come to nothing, for your presence is essential to its resolution. There is this invita-tion, which you may have just received in the post and are now reading. If you know me, then what I have written, what I am writing, will be familiar. There will be a photograph, which while set in the present – though not the present where you are reading my invitation – is constructed in the past. There will be a rehearsal for a concert that has already taken place. There will be a second photograph taken in the same place as the first, and this will become a postcard, circulating after the event it documents. Of course I worry if I am making sense, if my confusion of tenses, defying diachronic time, is sensible. It is how one thinks and dreams, though, in leaps back and forth. The title of the work, all its parts, is in the tense called the future ante-rior, sometimes called the future perfect. Something will have been.

There will be an audience. Perhaps my invitation will prompt you to be part of it. I do hope so. It will not be audience to a concert, though there will be some lovely music at a near distance. Rather, it will become, as audience, the subject of a postcard, as it fills the empty chairs carefully arranged in rows to form a scene that duplicates that of the photograph behind what will appear to be a stage. It is not really a stage, yet there will be a performance, off-stage, out of clear view. It will not be the first time the choir has sung together, but it will be the first time it has performed in this way. Yesterday I left a message for the musical director. Today he left a message for me. We have not yet spoken though we know each other's voices. The performance of the choir will not be the object of the audience.

I do not think I have ever seen the park outside. The shutters have always been closed. I will open them when I take my first photograph. My sense of time is imprecise. Events recede and lose their proper order. It is not merely a matter of subjective feeling. Neither is it simply a question of following the supposed sequence of events, for no events have taken place yet and I am writing them into existence. Time – and memory – both act in reverse and in anticipation. What takes place in the present touches and shapes the past, and the past reaches out and finds an image at last. Events that may or may not have occurred are rewritten. What happens now, what will happen, will affect what has already happened. I am waiting for the return of a hundred metres of gold silk, which will become the elegant curtains of all the doors of the salon where you may anticipate being when you receive this invitation and decide to accept it. It will seem as if the curtains have always been there, because look, in the photograph I have yet to take, there they are (but their colour is not as I remember it).

There is then more than one event, more than one moment. There is a certain repetition, rather than matters moving along, being neatly resolved. I heard about this place long before I saw it and my passage there has been marked by delay, hesitation, before reaching any conclusion. I did not remember the existence of the doors through which you will enter, if you choose to attend, for I have always entered by another door. What will happen determines what is happening now. I am imagining how the salon will look and so will attempt to make it appear as I imagine it to be. In thinking about retroaction and anticipation, I am looking forward to a 'moment of concluding'. The words are not mine, but those of the psychoanalyst Jacques Lacan, writing about the logical time of the unconscious. What you are reading, well, they are not quite my words either, for they will have passed through a translator. When I read them, I will not be able to tell if they are as I am writing them now.

I almost forgot to tell you. There will be another text. If you are here, on the night of the opening, it will be behind you, as you sit waiting, though you are welcome to visit at any time (it will not be the same, of course). You may be reading this now as you wait, facing a stage on which nothing is to be performed except the recording of your presence. I must add, there will be another part, a third chapter to the story I have started to tell you, in a small book. I hope I have explained enough here, enough to engage you at least. I am inviting you to a séance.

The gold texts on the apple-green panels of the *boiseries* of the Chateau read:

He had accepted the invitation he had received in the post a week ago, though it had seemed rather enigmatic. Usually he had a resistance to this sort of thing, particularly as he was not terribly interested in what he considered to be the exclusive games of contemporary art. He did not like to be manipulated; yet something about the phrasing on the invitation card, combined with an image he could not entirely decipher, had succeeded in capturing his attention. He knew nothing about the artist and could not imagine why she appeared to have singled him out for this event, though he realized this was probably no more than a projection on his part. He had not visited the chateau before, yet remembered passing it several months ago, having mistaken his route (he had been on his way to a sale of old photographs, of which he was a keen, if amateur, collector). At the time, he had wondered casually about the use of the elegant, if slightly rundown, building. Perhaps it was the reproduction on the card that had drawn him. It was strangely familiar, yet he could not say where he might have seen it. The scene enclosed in the oval mirror might have been that of a room he had known as a child, though its location evaded him. He did, however, remember a mirror above a marble fireplace and the disturbing sensation of heat as he imagined he admired the faded *boiseries*, the ornate ceiling. The chandeliers, he noted with disapproval, were modern. He felt himself to be the object of an external regard. He noticed the large photograph hung at the end of the room, behind a small stage where a camera on a tripod was standing. Although the woman in front of him was obscuring his view, he felt that the photograph had something of the same quality as that on the card. It appeared to be of the room in which he was now seated. For lack of anything else to do, he turned and began reading, with difficulty, a text on the wall climbing into the reflection. It was discomforting to read about himself. He stopped reading.

When she had received the invitation to the exhibition of her friend, she had been pleased to accept, despite her reluctance to leave the city. She knew a little about the intentions of the work, and indeed, shared an interest in the concepts of psychoanalysis that she believed to form the background to the work. She understood that the work should be approached through Freud's idea of 'deferred action', the way in which the past is no more than a set of memories constantly reworked according to the events of the present. She knew that these events were not important, in psychoanalysis, as real events, rather that their interest lay in the way in which they were recounted. She felt rather nervous on behalf of her friend, wanting the work to be well received. She had to prevent herself from approaching those other guests who were looking bemused or even irritated, initiating charming conversations in which she might guide them towards an explanation of the work that would engage them. It was clear that some were uncertain as to what they were supposed to be doing or seeing. She wondered how she might set an example, having always considered herself to be a viewer with perfect behaviour (if occasionally flawed in her interpretation). The large photograph of the room in which she now stood looked much as she had imagined it when it had been described to her earlier in the year. It was slightly smaller than she had hoped, and she tried to suppress the vague sentiment of disappointment she so often felt in the presence of works of art, unless they were of the most classical nature. There were some discrepancies between the photograph and its subject. The way the area in front of it had been arranged, including a camera on a tripod, prevented her from examining it closely in any detail. It was as though she had arrived with a memory of the salon, a memory that now proved to be incorrect or false. A man who was seated behind her suddenly moved, and this drew her attention to a text on the wall behind her. At the end of reading it, she read that she had stopped reading. Following what she felt to be her instructions, she stopped reading.

These texts are now collected in a small book, the cover of which reproduces the invitation card. The postcard and a photograph that is not the postcard, mirror each other, at the beginning and at the end. Some of the photographs are of the chateau; some are not, and yet they might be. The centre image is a photograph in a mirror. This book is not for sale either, and has circulated to those who were there at the opening event, to those who came later and asked what there was to see, and to those who have never been there. The unconscious does not obey the rules of narrative, yet nonetheless narratives emerge as the unconscious finds pathways into speech. And at this moment, I stopped reading.

Notes

1   Jacques Lacan, *The Seminar Book II: The Ego in Freud's Theory and in the Technique of Psychoanalysis, 1954–5,* translated by Sylvana Tomaselli, notes by John Forrester, Cambridge: Cambridge University Press, 1988, p. 321.

2   Jacques Lacan, *Écrits: A Selection,* translated by Alan Sheridan, London: Tavistock, 1977, p. 271.

3   Sigmund Freud, 'Screen Memories' [1899], *The Standard Edition of the Complete Psychological Works of Sigmund Freud,* Volume 3, edited by James Strachey and Anna Freud, London: The Hogarth Press and the Institute of Psycho-analysis, 1953–74, p. 322.

Sharon Kivland, Postcard. *Cela aura déjà eu lieu* [*It will have happened already*] Chateau de Marsang (2005).

Site-Writing

Enigma and embellishment

Jane Rendell

With a background in architectural design, followed by research in architectural history, and then a period teaching public art and writing art criticism, my research has tended to focus on interdisciplinary meeting points – between feminist theory and architectural history, conceptual art practice and architectural design, art criticism and autobiographical writing – through individual and collaborative research projects.[1] Recently I have begun to recognize how these different sites of interdisciplinary exchange follow a spatial pattern – I move outside the discipline in which I am located to a new one from which I can review the mechanisms of operation of my former discipline, before returning in order to suggest alternative modes of enquiry. Although my aim is constant, I seek to make manifest the position of the writing subject and her choice of objects of study and subject matters, processes of intellectual enquiry and creative production; my methods have transformed from the more dogmatic and literal attempt to produce a feminist Marxist architectural history to more lateral and metaphoric texts.[2]

My current work explores the position of the author, not only in relation to theoretical ideas, art objects and architectural spaces, but also to the site of writing itself. This interest has evolved into a number of writings (at first site-specific writings, now site-writings) that investigate the limits of criticism, that ask what it is possible for a critic to say about an artist or architect, a work, the site of a work and the critic herself and for the writing to still 'count' as criticism.[3] This chapter outlines some conceptual concerns that frame my argument for the spatialization of criticism as a form of critical spatial practice, before discussing one piece of site-writing that has transformed over time in relation to specific sites.[4]

The enigmatic message

Where I am makes a difference to *who* I can be and *what* I can know. In postmodern feminism, new ways of knowing and being have been discussed in spatial terms, developing conceptual and critical tools such as 'situated knowledge' and 'standpoint theory' to examine the inter-relations between location, identity and knowledge.[5] The work of Rosi Braidotti exemplifies this beautifully; for her, the figure of the 'nomadic subject' describes not only a spatial state of movement, but also an epistemological condition, a kind of knowingness (or unknowingness) that refuses fixity.[6]

However, despite advances in feminist thought concerning subjectivity and positionality, criticism is often still positioned as an activity that takes place at a distance from the work. Even in current discussions in art criticism concerning relational aesthetics[7] and dialogic practice,[8] the critic remains located 'outside' the work. I am interested in how art criticism can investigate the spatial and often changing positions we occupy as critics materially, conceptually, emotionally and ideologically. I suggest that the position a critic occupies needs to be made explicit through the process of writing criticism. Along with Hal Foster, who has examined critical distance in terms of identification,[9] and Isobel Armstrong, who has explored the differences between close and distant reading, distinguishing between what she calls a criticism of affect and one of analysis,[10] I would argue that such a project involves rethinking some of the key terms of criticism, specifically judgement, discrimination and distance.

By repositioning the engagement between the critic and art work as a site, 'site-writing' starts to investigate the spatiality of the critic's relation to a work, adopting and adapting both Howard Caygill's notion of immanent critique where the criteria for making judgements are discovered or invented through the course of criticism,[11] and strategic critique where the critic may make a discriminate judgement at a moment of externality where the work 'exceeds itself' and 'abuts on experience',[12] as well as Mieke Bal's exploration of the critic's 'close engagement' with art.[13] Rather than write *about* the work, I am interested in how the critic constructs his or her writing in relation *to* and in dialogue *with* the work. The focus on the preposition here allows a direct connection to be made between the positional *and* the relational.[14]

Theoretical explorations in literary criticism of the different subject positions authors can occupy in relation to the text, multiple 'I's',[15] for example, as well as 'you' and 's/he',[16] are relevant here, as are the writings of post-colonial critics who have woven the autobiographical into the critical in their texts, combining poetic practice with theoretical analysis to articulate hybrid voices.[17] A 'voice' in criticism can be objective *and* subjective, distant *and* intimate. From the close-up to the glance, from the caress to the accidental brush, such an approach to the writing of criticism can draw on spaces as they are remembered, dreamed and imagined, as well as observed, in order to take into account the critic's position in relation to a work and challenge criticism as a form of knowledge with a singular and static point of view located in the here and now.

'Site-writing' is what happens when discussions concerning site-specificity extend to involve art criticism, and the spatial qualities of the writing become as important in conveying meaning as the content of the criticism.[18] My suggestion is that this kind of criticism, or critical spatial writing, in operating as a mode of practice in its own right, questions the terms of reference that relate the critic to the work positioned 'under' critique. This is an active writing that constructs as well as traces the sites of relation between critic and work.

In visual and spatial culture, feminists have drawn extensively on psychoanalytic theory to further develop relationships between the spatial politics of internal psychical figures and external cultural geographies.[19] The field of psychoanalysis explores these various thresholds and boundaries between private and public, inner and outer, subject and object, personal and social in terms of a complex understanding of the relationship between 'internal' and 'external' space. Steve Pile has described it like this:

> While inner life is distinct, there is continuous exchange between the internal and external, but this 'dialectic' is itself interacting with the transactions between 'introjection' and 'projection'.
>
> (Steve Pile, *The Body and The City*, London: Routledge, 1999, p. 91)[20]

The psychic processes of introjection and projection, as well as identification, provide a rich set of conceptual tools for exploring the complex relationships made between subjects and others, and between people, objects and spaces. Psychoanalyst Jessica Benjamin has suggested that once we start to think in terms of relationships between subjects, or subjectivity, we have no choice but to consider these intraphysic mechanisms of relation, most importantly identifications: 'Once subjectivity is embraced, we have entered into a realm of knowledge based on identifications, hence knowing that is intrapsychically filtered.'[21] Feminist theorist Diane Fuss states that identification is 'a question of *relation*, of self to other, subject to object, inside to outside';[22] it is, she says, 'the psychical mechanism that produces self-recognition'.[23] While she outlines how identification involves the interrelationship of two processes, each working in different directions – introjection, the internalization of certain aspects of the other through self-representation; and projection, the externalization of unwanted parts of the self onto the other – visual theorist Kaja Silverman has explored identification in terms of cannibalistic or idiopathic identification where one attempts to absorb and interiorize the other as the self, and heteropathic identification where 'the subject identifies at a distance' and in the process of identification goes outside his/herself.[24]

If criticism can be defined by the purpose of providing a commentary (for some a judgement, for others a discriminating point of view, for others yet a response or perhaps even a point of departure) on a cultural work – art, literature, film and architecture – then criticism always has an other in mind. If so, the central task of criticism might be considered as: how does one make a relationship with an other? It is this question that is at the heart of psychoanalysis. As Benjamin writes:

> An intersubjective theory of the self is one that poses the question of how and whether the self can actually achieve a relationship to an outside other without, through identification, assimilating or being assimilated by it.
>
> (Jessica Benjamin, *Shadow of the Other: Intersubjectivity and Gender in Psychoanalysis*, London: Routledge, 1998, p. 80)

In thinking more carefully about the position of the other in criticism and psychoanalysis, the work of Jean Laplanche is illuminating. A psychoanalyst who trained with Jacques Lacan, Laplanche has examined the points at which he argues Sigmund Freud went astray. This most famously includes Freud's controversial abandonment of the seduction theory, and his turn to the child's fantasy to explain seduction, thus at some level avoiding thinking-through the complex interplay of inner and outer worlds between the child and what Laplanche calls 'the concrete other'.[25] Laplanche argues that this early scene of seduction is of key importance to psychoanalysis as it works to de-centre the position of the subject in its articulation of the formation and role of the unconscious. For Laplanche, it is the embedding of the alterity of the mother in the child that places an other in the subject. This other is also an other to the mother – as it comes from her unconscious. Thus the message imparted to the subject by the other (for Laplanche, the mother or concrete other) is an enigma both to the receiver but also to the sender of the message: the 'messages are enigmatic because [...] [they] are strange to themselves'.[26]

Laplanche does not confine his discussion of the enigmatic message to the psychoanalytic setting; he suggests that transference occurs not first in the psychoanalysis to be applied in culture, but the other way around, 'maybe transference is already, "in itself", outside the clinic'.[27] Yet, when he does talk of the cultural message it is in psychoanalytic terms – as an enigma:

> If one accepts that fundamental dimension of transference is the relation to the enigma of the other, perhaps the principle site of transference, 'ordinary' transference, before, beyond or after analysis, would be the multiple relation to the cultural, to creation or, more precisely to the cultural message. A relation which is multiple, and should be conceived with discrimination, but always starting from the relation to the enigma. There are at least three types of such a relation to be described: from the position of the producer, from that of the recipient, and from that of the recipient-analyst.
>
> (Laplanche, *Essays on Otherness,* London: Routledge, 1999, p. 222)

For Laplanche, then, the critic or recipient–analyst is involved in a two-way dynamic with the enigmatic message: s/he is, 'caught between two stools: the enigma which is addressed to him, but also the enigma of the one he addresses, his public'.[28]

This is a very different position from the one that, following Freud, draws on psychoanalysis to 'psychoanalyse' an artist or a work.[29] It is possible then to use psychoanalytic theory not to 'explain' the intention of an artist or to unravel the 'unconscious' aspects of a work, but to turn the relationship around the other way. Indeed, Laplanche notes André Green's suggestion that: 'In applied psychoanalysis [...] the analyst is the analysand of the text.'[30] In drawing parallels with the analytic process, but this time following Lacan, an approach, taken up in the collection of essays *In the Place of an Object,* edited by Sharon Kivland and Marc du Ry, proposes that for the viewer, the work of art occupies the place of the analyst or the lost object. In an interview in this volume, Danuza Machado states:

> A work of art has a special quality that doesn't have to do with cultural factors, or moral or political positions. It is something that provokes in the viewer a turning point like the psychoanalytic act.
>
> (Alex Potts and Danuza Machado, 'A Little Object', Sharon Kivland and Marc du Ry (eds), 'In the Place of an Object', special issue of the *Journal of the Centre for Freudian Analysis and Research*, London: Aldgate Press, 2000, pp. 3–11, p. 3)

With respect to art criticism, this position in itself produces a turning point and makes it possible to imagine that the critic occupies the position of the analysand rather than the analyst, and responds to the artwork as one would to the comments of the analyst, through free association and story-telling. However, to complicate matters further it has also been proposed, by psychoanalyst Ignes Sodré, in a conversation with the writer A.S. Byatt, that it is the analyst, not the analysand, who operates as story-teller: 'The analyst as "story-teller" offers the patient different versions of himself.'[31]

I would want to go further, though, and argue that the critic occupies both the position of analyst and analysand, and works through critical analysis and interpretation, as well as associative states such as story-telling, remembering and imagining. I combine such modes in my writing to create what I have called the 'critical imagination', using an analytic mode to outline the structure and form of my response, and memories – sometimes real, sometimes fictional – to create the content-filled detail.[32]

Literary critic Mary Jacobus has described 'the scene of reading' in terms of the relation, perhaps a correspondence, that exists between the inner world of the reader and the world contained in the book.[33] Taking up this insightful observation, I suggest that criticism involves a movement between inside and outside: works take critics outside themselves offering new geographies, new possibilities, but they can also return the critics to their own interior, to their own biographies. This double movement suspends what we might call judgement or discrimination in criticism and, instead, through what I call the practice of 'site-writing', traces and constructs a series of interlocking places, which relate critic, work and site.

To Miss the Desert[34]

'To Miss the Desert', an essay I wrote for Gavin Wade in relation to a work he curated for *Art and Sacred Spaces* – Nathan Coley's 'Black Tent' – positioned personal memories of architectural spaces in relation to more professional descriptions. Wade had read a piece of mine, where I questioned whether it was possible to write architecture, rather than write about architecture, and so he approached me and asked me to 'write a tabernacle'.[35] 'Black Tent' had developed out of Coley's interest in sanctuaries in general, but particularly the evocative and precise description of the construction of the tabernacle given in the Bible.

Consisting of a flexible structure – a number of steel-framed panels with black fabric stretched across them – 'Black Tent' moved to a number of sites in Portsmouth, including two in Portsmouth Cathedral, reconfiguring itself for each location. The essay I wrote related in both form and content to the artwork. Structured into five sections, each one composed around a different spatial condition, such as 'in the middle' and 'around the edge', my text explored the relationship between specific locations and generic conditions. This interest paralleled two aspects of the siting of Coley's work – the particular position of the work in relation to each site and the differing configuration of the panels of the piece depending on where 'Black Tent' was located. My central spatial motifs were the secular sanctuaries of home and refuge. I decided to investigate the changing position of the subject in relation to material details of architecture and psychic spatial experiences of security and fear, safety and danger. The narrative I composed was spatial, like the squares, it had two sides, two voices.

The first voice remembered a childhood spent settling into various nomadic cultures and countries in the Middle East. The second voice was drawn from the architectural design of contemporary sanctuaries, specifically a series of community buildings for different 'minority' groups. These included ethnic communities, gay and lesbian organizations, single mothers with young children and people in long-term mental-healthcare being moved from large-scale institutions into 'care in the community' programmes. The texts were taken from design proposals and drawings, construction details and specifications that I had, when working as an architectural designer, been closely involved in producing. The two voices were pitched against one another to create a dynamic between personal and public sanctuary. One voice used memory to conjure up spaces of safety; the other adopted a professional tone to describe various sanctuaries at different scales and stages of the design process.

The following extract is taken from 'To Miss the Desert':

Around the Edge
The bathroom has a floor of polished marble, black, interwoven with white veins. Perched on the toilet, with her feet dangling off the ground, she traces the white lines with her gaze. She keeps alert for cockroaches, at any time one might crawl through the cracks around the edge of the room and into the blackness.

14 Floor Finishes
1. Location G6
Lay new flooring 300 mm × 300 mm terracotta unglazed tiles with sandstone colour groat 10 mm wide joints.
All tiles to be laid out from centre line.
Finished floor level to match G5.

All the floors are marble, smooth and cool, laid out in careful grids, except for the big golden rug next to the sofa. She likes to follow its intricate patterns with her feet, like paths around a secret garden. But if you dance around the edge of the squares, you mustn't be silly enough to fall in, who knows what could lie in wait for you in an enchanted garden?

The proposal is for the building to be single storey with a pitched roof located at the north end of the site. The eaves height is 2 m along the perimeter walls rising to a ridge height of 5 m. There are a few windows along the perimeter walls facing north and east but the rooms are mainly lit by roof lights so that the new building does not over-look adjacent property.

Along one edge of her garden are a number of small rooms. These are home to Gullum and Kareem. Gullum is tall and fair skinned, with light hair and green eyes. Kareem, is shorter, stockier, with darker skin, hair and eyes. They have fought each other in the past, and they will fight again, when the Soviets come to Kabul, and then again, when her own people search the Hindu Kush to wipe out all evil. But for now, there is no fighting, once the sun has gone down, they sit and eat together.

The café will seat up to 30 people and has a door to an outside area. It may be possible to create a garden area with a paved terrace adjacent to the building for both the café and the crèche. This entrance could be made wheelchair accessible by sloping the garden area from the street to the edge of the paving to eliminate the level difference.

He is a man with property and wives. Inside the walls of his house are sunlit orchards with trees full of dark purple fruit. A group of women dressed in different shades of red watch them arrive. Some have covered their faces, but she can still see the pink nail varnish on their toes. Then, as her family draws closer, the women disappear.

14 Floor Finishes
2. Location 1.5 and G5
Forbo Nairn lino sheeting 1.5 mm to be laid on 6 mm wbp ply sub floor.
Ply and lino to run under appliances and around kitchen units. Colour tba by client.
Aluminium threshold at junction with G2, G6 and 1.1.

They sit upstairs, in a long veranda overlooking the garden, the only furniture is a carpet laid out in a line down the middle of the room. Important men from the village, all in turbans, sit cross-legged around the edges of the carpet and eat from the dishes laid out between them. Her mother, her sister and herself are the only women. As they walk back down through the dark house to leave, she sees a pair of eyes watching her. The eyes belong to a girl, a girl with the hands of a woman, a woman who glints with silver. Later she learns that this is Kareem's youngest wife, once a nomad, who carries her wealth in the jewels on her fingers.

An Embellishment: Purdah[36]

For *Spatial Imagination in Design* (2006) an exhibition at the domoBaal Gallery, London, I made a work called 'An Embellishment: Purdah'. I selected twelve short extracts from 'To Miss the Desert' and rewrote them as 'scenes', laid out in the catalogue as a grid three squares wide by four high, to match the twelve panes of glass in the west-facing window of the gallery looking onto the street. Here I repeatedly wrote the word 'purdah' in black kohl in the script of Afghanistan's official languages – Dari and Pashto (see figures on pages 158–9).

In the Middle East, the term 'purdah' describes the cultural practice of separating and hiding women, through clothing and architecture – veils, screens and walls – from the public gaze. The particular manifestation of this gendering of space varies depending on location. In Afghanistan, for example, under the Taliban, when in public, women were required to wear a burqa, in this case a loose garment, usually sky-blue, that covered them from head to foot. Only their eyes could be seen, the rims outlined with black kohl (perhaps only in a Westerner's imagination) looking out through the window of an embroidered screen.

By day or by night, from inside the gallery or from outside on the street, the work changed according to the viewer's position – transparent/opaque, concealing/revealing – this embellishment or decorative covering invited the viewer to imagine beyond the places s/he could see.

Nathan Coley's 'Black Tent' offered me an enigmatic message. I replied with my own in the form of an essay, a piece of criticism, 'To Miss the Desert'. In selecting and reconfiguring 'scenes' from the essay into two complementary parts – one a text in a book and the other in a window – 'An Embellishment: Purdah' was a response to the site of a gallery. But it is also the case that the two textual components of this work are responses to one another. While 'Black Tent' uses black squares to mark the edges of newly created sanctuaries, and 'To Miss the Desert' is structured according to spatial conditions, such as 'Around the Edge', 'An Embellishment: Purdah' responds to the specific quality of the window as an edge, articulating the interface between inside and outside, between one and another.

In re-writing the word 'purdah' across the glass, this embellishment of the window surface is an act of repetition and, as Sharon Kivland has pointed out in the previous chapter:

> Repetition, for Freud, is the incessant exposure to horrible or upsetting events and circumstances, the compulsion to repeat an act when its origins are forgotten. Unless one remembers the past, if events are suppressed, something is returned in one's actions.
>
> (Sharon Kivland, 'Memoirs', in Jane Rendell *et al.* (eds),
> *Critical Architecture*, London: Routledge, 2007)

Her mother tells her another story, this time of her own life before she was born. She taught the Sheik's sister's daughter English, so she was allowed to go inside the hareem. Inside, under their burqas, she saw that the women wore make-up and perfume. For her labours, the sheik offered her a gift. She asked for a gold leaf burqa, the costume only the wives of the sheik can wear.

Her mother's labour is not easy; she refuses to come out. She walks the dunes along the creek, back and forth, past the apartment block where she lives, but still she waits inside, for a night and a day. The chance of infection is high. There is no glass in the hospital windows. A caesarian section might kill them both, one for sure if she was carrying a son.

Fortunately there is a woman who is willing to take a chance. On the second night of her labour, the hospital is almost empty, everyone who can has gone, to feast, to break their fast. A nurse runs a drip to encourage her out. But she holds her ground. The nurse turns the drip up. Still she refuses to budge. The drip is turned up again, faster, and again.

For her labours, the sheik sends her mother a gift along with his apologies. Sorry, he said, so sorry it isn't a boy. For a boy I would have sent you a watch, but here, with my condolences, is a gift for the girl, a gold coffee pot on a gold chain. She is a hajia, born on the eve of the haj: she will never have to make the journey to the east, to Mecca.

Surrounding her house is a moat of flints with furrows running through it at regular intervals like a ploughed field. When you run up and down these slopes, you can loose your footing and slip, and that is when you know the sharp-looking stones really can cut your knees. Still it is safer here, than beyond the walls in the waste-ground of dry bushes and stinging insects, where hyenas cry in the night.

The hallway cuts the house in half, and ties it together, with rooms leading off on both sides. The tiled floor is hard and shiny, at night she comes here to catch insects. Many creatures skulk across it, ants and spiders, and some more sinister whose names she doesn't yet know. Trapped under her glass jar with its smooth edge that meets the marble without making gaps, she is safe to watch them.

Inside her house all the floors are marble, smooth and cool, laid out in careful grids, except for the big golden rug. In the evening, when the sun is in the west, the rug glows. At this time of day, she likes to follow the intricate patterns with her feet, like paths around a secret garden. But if you dance around the edge of the squares, you musn't fall in, who knows what lies waiting in the enchanted garden?

Around the edge of the garden are the homes of two men, one tall and fair skinned, with light hair and green eyes; the other shorter, stockier, with darker skin, hair and eyes. They have fought each other in the past, and will again when the Soviets come to Kabul, and again, when her own people search the Hindu Kush to wipe out all evil. But for now, there is no fighting, once the sun has gone down, they sit and eat together.

He is a man with property: land and wives. Inside the walls of his house are sunlit orchards full of dark purple fruit. Among the trees his wives sit. Dressed in shades of red, some of the women have covered their faces, others have painted their toenails pink. From a distance, the women watch them arrive, disappearing inside as they draw closer.

The guests are taken upstairs to an empty veranda overlooking the garden. The only furniture here is a carpet laid out in a long line down the middle of the room. Men sit cross-legged in turbans around the edge of the carpet and eat from the dishes laid out in front of them. They are invited to sit down – the only women – her mother, her sister and herself.

After the meal, as they walk through the dark house to leave, she sees a pair of eyes watching her from behind a screen. The eyes belong to a girl her own age but whose hands glint with silver like a woman. Later she learns that this is his youngest wife, once a nomad, who carries her wealth in the jewels on her fingers.

Her own dress is set with tiny mirrors and a handsome square of embroidery at the front. It is hard work to get on, with no fastenings and a fabric so thin it could rip. In this dress she feels just like all the other Afghan girls. Except that they wear their dresses a bit softer, sometimes black. She wonders whether it is to match the black around the edge of their eyes.

Jane Rendell, 'An Embellishment', in Peg Rawes and Jane Rendell (eds) *Spatial Imagination*, London: The Bartlett School of Architecture, UCL, 2005, pp. 34–5, p. 35. Designed by Penelope Haralambidou.

35

Jane Rendell, 'An Embellishment: Purdah', in *Spatial Imagination*, London: The Domo Baal Gallery, 2006.

Yet, in taking the form of an embellishment, repetition, as a form of remembering, can also be linked to reminiscence. Kivland continues: 'And while the analytic process may not aim at reliving past experience, at feeling the same emotions of the past, this still happens. In reminiscing, stories are embellished, made better or worse, and so occupy a register of the imaginary.'[37] The playing out of these reminiscences is an articulation of the critical imagination. Like an enigma, 'An Embellishment: Purdah' offers a message that appears to require deciphering, yet the work recognizes that cultural position and linguistic difference determine specific understandings of images and words. This 'site-writing' positions itself in relation to thresholds, transforming itself in response to the demands of changing sites, configuring and reconfiguring the relationship between criticism and practice, work and text, one and another.

Notes

1   See for example Jane Rendell, *Art and Architecture: a Place Between*, London: I.B. Tauris, 2006; Jane Rendell, *The Pursuit of Pleasure: Gender, Space and Architecture in Regency London*, London: Athlone Press, 2002. See also Jane Rendell, 'Critical Spatial Practice', in Judith Rugg (ed.), *New Curating Practices*, Bristol: Intellect Books, forthcoming, for an account of my collaborative work.

2   Compare for example Jane Rendell, *The Pursuit of Pleasure*, to Jane Rendell, 'Travelling the Distance/Encountering the Other', in David Blamey (ed.), *Here, There, Elsewhere: Dialogues on Location and Mobility,* London: Open Editions, 2002, pp. 43–54; Jane Rendell, 'Writing in place of speaking', in Sharon Kivland and Lesley Sanderson (eds), *Transmission: Speaking and Listening*, vol. 1, Sheffield Hallam University and Site Gallery, 2002, pp. 15–29.

3   For a more detailed account of the conceptual framework that underpins my practice of 'site-writing' and relates it to four pieces of criticism, see Jane Rendell, 'Architecture-Writing', in Jane Rendell (ed.), *Critical Architecture,* a special issue of *The Journal of Architecture*, 10, 3, June 2005, pp. 255–64.

4   For an account of another piece of 'site-writing', which transformed over three sites, see Jane Rendell, 'Site-Writing', in Sharon Kivland, Jaspar Joseph-Lester and Emma Cocker (eds), *Transmission: Speaking and Listening*, vol. 4, Sheffield Hallam University and Site Gallery, 2005, pp. 169–76.

5   For example, Donna Haraway's 'situated knowledges', Jane Flax's 'standpoint theory' and Elsbeth Probyn's notion of 'locality' all use 'position' to negotiate such ongoing theoretical disputes as the essentialism/constructionism debate. See Jane Flax, *Thinking Fragments: Psychoanalysis, Feminism and Postmodernism in the Contemporary West*, Berkeley: University of California Press, 1991, p. 232; Donna Haraway, 'Situated Knowledges: the Science Question in Feminism and the Privilege of Partial Knowledge', *Feminist Studies*, 14, 3, Fall 1988, pp. 575–603, especially pp. 583–8; Elsbeth Probyn 'Travels in the Postmodern: Making Sense of the Local', in Linda Nicholson (ed.), *Feminism/Postmodernism,* London: Routledge, 1990, pp. 176–89, p. 178. See also Seyla Benhabib's articulation of 'feminism as situated criticism' in *Situating the Self: Gender, Community and Postmodernism in Contemporary Ethics*, Cambridge: Polity Press, 1992, pp. 225–8; and bell hooks' discussion of the margin in *Yearnings: Race, Gender, and Cultural Politics,* London: Turnaround Press, 1989.

6   See Rosi Braidotti, *Nomadic Subjects*, New York: Columbia University Press, 1994.

7   See for example Nicholas Bourriaud, *Relational Aesthetics*, translated by Simon Pleasance and Fronza Woods, Paris: Les Presses du Réel, 2002.

8   See for example Grant H. Kester, *Conversation Pieces: Community and Communication in Modern Art*, Berkeley: University of California Press, 2004.

9   See Hal Foster, *The Return of the Real: The Avant-Garde at the End of the Century*, Cambridge, MA: MIT Press, 2001, pp. 223–6.

10   See Isobel Armstrong, *The Radical Aesthetic*, Oxford: Blackwell Publishers, 2000, p. 87.

11   Howard Caygill, *Walter Benjamin: the Colour of Experience*, London: Routledge, 1998, p. 34 and p. 79.

12   Caygill, *Walter Benjamin*, p. 64.

13   See Mieke Bal, *Louise Bourgeois' Spider: the Architecture of Art–Writing*, London and Chicago: University of Chicago Press, 2001, p. xi. See also Norman Bryson, 'Introduction: Art and Intersubjectivity', in Mieke Bal, *Looking In: the Art of Viewing*, Amsterdam: G+B International, 2001, pp. 1–39, p. 12.

14   The significance Trinh T. Minh-ha assigns to the shift from speaking 'about' to speaking 'to' has also been stressed by Irit Rogoff, who underscores how, instead of taking power relationships to produce spatial locations, it is possible for a change in position to advance a change in relation. See Irit Rogoff's discussion of Trinh T. Minh-ha's assertion in Irit Rogoff, 'Studying Visual Culture', Nicholas Mirzoeff (ed.), *The Visual Culture Reader*, London: Routledge, 1998, pp. 14–26, p. 18.

15   See Italo Calvino, *Literature Machine*, London: Vintage, 1997, p. 15.

16   See Roland Barthes, *The Grain of the Voice: Interviews 1962–80*, translated by Linda Coverdale, Berkeley and Los Angeles: University of California Press, 1991, pp. 215–16.

17   See Gloria Anzaldua, *Borderlands/La Frontera: the New Mestiza*, San Francisco: Lute Books, 1999; Hélene Cixous, 'Sorties', translated by Betsy Wing in Susan Sellers (ed.), *The Hélene Cixous Reader*, London: Routledge, 1994.

18   On art and site-specificity, see for example, Alex Coles (ed.), *Site Specificity: the Ethnographic Turn*, London: Black Dog Publishing, 2000; Nick Kaye, *Site-Specific Art: Performance, Place and Documentation*, London: Routledge, 2000; Miwon Kwon, *One Place After Another: Site Specific Art and Locational Identity*, Cambridge, MA: MIT Press, 2002.

19   See for example Susan Stanford Friedman, *Mappings: Feminism and the Cultural Geographies Of Encounter*, Princeton: Princeton University Press, 1998; Diane Fuss, *Identification Papers*, London: Routledge, 1995; Elizabeth Grosz, *Volatile Bodies: Toward a Corporeal Feminism*, Bloomington and Indianapolis: Indiana University Press, 1994; Irit Rogoff, *Terra Infirma*, London: Routledge, 2000; Kaja Silverman, *The Threshold of the Visible World*, London: Routledge, 1996.

20   See also Grosz, *Volatile Bodies*, pp. 27–61.

21   Jessica Benjamin, *Shadow of the Other: Intersubjectivity and Gender in Psychoanalysis*, London: Routledge, 1998, p. 25.

22   Fuss, *Identification Papers*, p. 3.

23   Fuss, *Identification Papers*, p. 2.

24   Silverman, *The Threshold of the Visible World*, pp. 23–4.

25   Cathy Caruth, 'An Interview with Jean Laplanche', www3.iath.virginia.edu/pmc/text-only/issue.101/11.2caruth.txt (accessed 3 May 2006). Laplanche notes that Freud uses the terms *der Andere* and *das Andere* to distinguish the other person and the other thing. See 'The Kent Seminar, 1 May 1990', in John Fletcher and Martin Stanton (eds), *Jean Laplanche: Seduction, Translation and the Drives*, London: The Institute of Contemporary Arts, 1992, pp. 21–40, p. 25.

26   Cathy Caruth, 'An interview with Jean Laplanche'.

27   Jean Laplanche, *Essays on Otherness,* London: Routledge, 1999, p. 222. See also
      Jean Laplanche, *New Foundations for Psychoanalysis*, translated by David Macey,
      Oxford: Basil Blackwell Ltd, 1989, pp. 152–4.

28   Laplanche, *Essays on Otherness,* p. 224.

29   See for example Sigmund Freud, 'Delusions and Dreams in Jensen's "Gradiva" (1907
      [1906])', *The Penguin Freud Library: Art and Literature,* vol. 4, translated from the
      German under the editorship of James Strachey, London: Penguin Books, 1990, pp.
      27–118; Sigmund Freud, 'Leonardo da Vinci and a Memory of His Childhood (1910)',
      The Penguin Freud Library: Art and Literature, vol. 4, pp. 143–231.

30   Laplanche, *Essays on Otherness,* p. 222.

31   Rebeccca Swift (ed.), *A.S. Byatt and Ignes Sodré, Imagining Characters: Six Conver-
      sations about Women Writers*, London: Chatto and Windus, 1995, p. 245.

32   See Peg Rawes and Jane Rendell (eds), *Spatial Imagination*, London: The Bartlett
      School of Architecture, UCL, 2005. See also www.spatialimagination.org.uk
      (accessed 13 October 2006).

33   Mary Jacobus, *Psychoanalysis and the Scene of Reading*, Oxford: Oxford University
      Press, 1999, p. 18.

34   Jane Rendell, 'To Miss the Desert', in Gavin Wade (ed.), *Nathan Coley: 'Black Tent'*,
      Portsmouth: Art and Sacred Places, 2003.

35   Jane Rendell, 'Writing in Place of Speaking', pp. 15–29.

36   See Jane Rendell, 'An Embellishment: Purdah', in *Spatial Imagination*, London: The
      domoBaal Gallery, 2006, with an associated catalogue essay, Jane Rendell, 'An
      Embellishment', in Rawes and Rendell (eds), *Spatial Imagination*, pp. 34–5.

37   Sharon Kivland, 'Memoirs'.

Criticism by Design

Introduction

Criticism by design

Jonathan Hill

Critical architecture

Associated with words not drawings or buildings, and the writer not the designer, architectural criticism is widely known and understood. But it is assumed that few architects are critical. This assumption is itself open to criticism, however. First, because it relies on a limited understanding of what is architectural. Second, because it caricatures who and what is critical. To consider both issues, the history of the architect is a useful point of departure.

Drawing the architect

Before the fifteenth century, the status of the architect was low due to association with manual labour and dispersed authorship. Of little importance to building, the drawing was understood to be no more than a flat surface and the shapes upon it were but tokens of three-dimensional objects. The Italian Renaissance introduced a fundamental change in perception, establishing the principle that the drawing truthfully depicts the three-dimensional world, and is a window to that world, which places the viewer outside and in command of the view. For the first time, the drawing became essential to architectural practice.

The command of drawing unlocked the status of the architect. Interdependent, the drawing and the architect affirm the same idea: architecture results not from the accumulated knowledge of a team of anonymous craftsman working together on a construction site, but from the artistic creation of an individual architect in command of drawing who designs a building as a whole at a remove from construction. Thus, the architectural drawing depends on two related but distinct concepts. One indicates that drawing is an intellectual, artistic activity distant from the grubby materiality of building. The other claims that the drawing is the truthful representation of the building, indicating the mastery of architects over building production.

The histories of the architect and the drawing are interwoven with those of design. The term 'design' comes from the Italian *disegno*, meaning drawing, suggesting both the drawing of a line on paper and the drawing forth of an idea. Dependent on the assumption that ideas are superior to matter and, thus, that intellectual labour is superior to manual labour,[1] *disegno* enabled architecture, painting and sculpture – the three visual arts – to be identified as liberal arts concerned with ideas, a position they had rarely been accorded previously. *Disegno* is concerned with the idea of architecture, not the matter of building. Leon Battista Alberti notably states that: 'It is quite possible to project whole forms in the mind without recourse to the material.'[2]

Alongside the traditional practice of building, architects acquired new means to practise architecture: drawing and writing. To affirm their status as exponents of intellectual and artistic labour, architects began increasingly to theorise architecture in drawings and books. Sebastiano Serlio[3] and Andrea Palladio[4] are notable early exponents of this tradition, Le Corbusier[5] and Rem Koolhaas[6] more recent ones.

Often, a design does not get built, and an architect must be persuasive to see that it does. Sometimes a building is not the best way to explore an architectural idea. Consequently, architects, especially influential ones, tend to talk, write and draw a lot as well as build. The relations between the drawing, text and building are multidirectional. Drawing may lead to building. But writing may also lead to drawing, or building to writing and drawing, for example. If everyone reading this introduction were to list all the architectural works that have influenced them, some would be drawings, some would be texts and others would be buildings either visited or described in drawings and texts. Studying the history of architecture since the Italian Renaissance, it is evident that researching, testing and questioning the limits of architecture occurs through drawing and writing as well as building. As drawings, books and buildings are architecture, they are also potential sites for critical architecture, independently or together.

Ideas and appliances

The history of design from the fifteenth century to the twenty-first is not seamless, however, and a significant departure occurred in the eighteenth century, when the meaning of both design and ideas changed somewhat.

Opposed to utility, the classification of the fine arts – notably poetry, music, painting, sculpture and architecture – is primarily an invention of that century. Associated with utility, the design disciplines that proliferated due to industrialisation, such as product design, are defined as applied arts at best. In the Renaissance, a form was synonymous with an idea.[7] But, especially since the nineteenth-century codification of formal type, a form is less about ideas and more about production.[8] Painters and sculptors discarded design once it became associated with collective authorship and industrial production. Among the fine arts, which include the three original visual arts, only in architecture is the term 'design' regularly referred to today. Many people associate design with the newer design disciplines, which affects how architectural design is understood. But in the discourse of architects, the older meaning of design – drawing ideas – and the newer meaning of design – drawing appliances – are both in evidence. Critical architecture fits the first concept of design more than the second one. The architectural profession is especially compatible with the newer concept of design, and is a significant hindrance to critical architecture. Since the nineteenth century, architects and non-architects alike assume that it is natural for the architect to be a professional and that there is no alternative. To the apparent benefit of practitioners, consumers and the state, the professions reflect the desire to manage capitalism's excesses and reduce the threat of economic and social disorder. Professionals are neither expected nor paid to generate ideas, whether critical or not. Focusing on technical competence and acquiescence to commercial and regulatory forces, the architectural profession wants neither architecture nor architects to be critical. To be critical, therefore, the architect must be critical of the profession.

For architects, from the fifteenth century to the twenty-first, design can potentially draw forth an idea. In the Italian Renaissance an idea was understood as universal and superior to matter. But in his *Essay Concerning Human Understanding* (1690), John Locke argues that ideas are dependent upon experience,[9] undermining the distrust of the senses in Renaissance theory.[10] In 1757, David Hume adds that: 'Beauty is no quality in things themselves: it exists merely in the mind which contemplates them; and each mind perceives a different beauty.'[11] Consequently, perception is subjective and changeable. Any change in the weather, the time of the day or the position or mood of the viewer can affect perception, so that even an object seemingly as solid as a building may not seem the same from one moment to the next. Focusing attention on subjectivity transformed the visual arts, its objects, authors and viewers. No longer was architecture a cohesive body of knowledge dependent on universal proportions. Since the eighteenth century, design may draw forth an idea that is provisional and dependent on experience at conception, production and reception, which may overlap. However, all recent architecture does not fit this model; early twentieth-century functionalists made claims to universality, for example.[12]

Criticism by use

With regard to critical architecture, design as it was first understood has a number of failings. First, it suggests that creativity is a one-way street and fails to recognise the creativity of the user and others involved in the conception and production of architecture. Second, it assumes that as ideas emanate from the architect to the user, so does the critical. Third, it promotes the superiority of the intellect and denigrates the manual, material and experiential. The original meaning of design, as the drawing of a line and the drawing forth of an idea, remains valuable to architectural practice and research as long as its limitations are acknowledged and tempered by the eighteenth-century understanding of ideas as provisional and dependent on experience.

A principal purpose of the drawing is to describe an object that contains and sub-divides geometric space, rendering the user either abstract or absent. But the user's experience is essential to architecture. To use a building is also to make it, either by physical transformation, using it in ways not previously imagined, or in conceiving it anew. Just as each reader makes a book anew, each user makes a building anew.[13] And, as books and buildings are remade and re-imagined by readers and users, so too is the critical. Whether a building is critical depends on the user as much as the architect; both draw forth ideas. Architects do not have a monopoly over architecture. And neither do they have a monopoly over critical architecture.

The nine chapters in 'Criticism by Design' question the continuing relevance of design to architects' practice and consider its potential to engage experiences as well as forms and ideas. The reader will identify many connections between the chapters, which are ordered here into three groups. Its opposition to weather has historically defined architecture, but in the first two chapters, Jonathan Hill and Philippe Rahm propose the weather and climate – internal and external – as means to develop an understanding of design that acknowledges its own limits and places the evolving experiences of users as architecture's focus.[14] The interaction between peoples and places, and the means by which they can develop and promote specific models of community and design, is the subject of the chapters by Igor Marjanovic, Katarina Bonnevier and Ben Nicholson. From diverse sources, the final group, with chapters by Stephen Cairns, Tim Anstey, Penelope Haralambidou and Victoria Watson, brings the discussion back to where it began to re-assess the potential of the drawing to consider actions, allegories and ideas.

Notes

1   Plato, *Timaeus, Critias, Cleitophon, Menexenus, Epistles,* translated by R.G. Bury, Cambridge, MA: Harvard University Press, 1929, p. 121.

2   Leon Battista Alberti, *On the Art of Building in Ten Books*, translated by Joseph Rykwert, Neil Leach and Robert Tavernor, Cambridge, MA and London: MIT Press, 1988, p. 7. First published as *De Re Aedificatoria, c.*1450, translated by James Leoni, as *Ten Books on Architecture*, 1726.

3   Sebastiano Serlio, *Sebastiano Serlio on Architecture*, vol. 1, books I–V of *Tutte l'opere d' architettura et prospectiva*, 1537–51, translated by Vaughan Hart and Peter Hicks, New Haven and London: Yale University Press, 1996.

4   Andrea Palladio, *The Four Books on Architecture*, translated by Robert Tavernor and Richard Schofield, Cambridge, MA: MIT Press, 1997. First published as *Quattro Libri dell' Archittetura* in 1570.

5   Le Corbusier, *Towards a New Architecture*, translated by Frederick Etchells, London: Rodker, 1927. First published as *Vers une architecture* in 1923.

6   Rem Koolhaas, *Delirious New York: a Retroactive Manifesto for Manhattan*, [1978], Rotterdam: 010, 1994.

7   The Renaissance was named in recognition of the revival and reinterpretation of Classical antiquity, notably Plato's claim that all the things we perceive in the material world are modelled on the ideal 'forms' of a divine geometry (Plato, *Timaeus*, p. 121).

8   Alberto Pérez-Gómez, *Architecture and the Crisis of Modern Science*, Cambridge, MA: MIT Press, 1983, pp. 302–11.

9   John Locke, *Essay Concerning Human Understanding*, [1690] edited by Peter H. Nidditch, Oxford: Clarendon Press, 1975.

10 Marsilio Ficino, 'Letter to Giovanni Cavalcanti', quoted in Albert Hofstadter and Richard Kuhns (eds), *Philosophies of Art and Beauty*, Chicago: University of Chicago Press, 1964, p. 204.

11 David Hume, 'Of the Standard of Taste', in *Selected Essays*, edited by Stephen Copley and Andrew Edgar, Oxford: Oxford University Press, 1993, pp. 133–54, pp. 136–7.

12 Le Corbusier, *Towards a New Architecture*, p. 10, p. 241.

13 Roland Barthes, 'The Death of the Author', in *Image–Music–Text*, translated by Stephen Heath, London: Flamingo, 1977, pp. 142–8.

14 Weather is a local variation in a wider climate.

Centuries of Ambiguity

Sublime and beautiful weather at the Farnsworth House

Jonathan Hill

The ambiguous object

Ambiguity is a quality rarely attributed to the critical. More often it is assumed that if an idea travels directly from the artist to the viewer and from the architect to the user, then so does the critical. In art since the early twentieth century, shock is often the agent of the critical and the artist its author. Shock may help to promote new architectural ideas and spaces. But it wears off quickly and is comparatively ineffective as most buildings are experienced not once but many times when they are not the focus of attention. As the user's experience depends on complex juxtapositions of many moments and many conditions, whether a building is critical may depend not on instantaneous shock but enduring ambiguity, the ability to appear ever-changing, resist resolution and remain open to interpretation.

Modernist architecture is widely described as didactic and determinist. But Manfredo Tafuri offers an alternative interpretation:

> What joins together the entire Modern Movement is [...] the concept of architecture as ambiguous object [...]. The observer becomes more and more the user who gives meanings to the object or to the series.
>
> (Manfredo Tafuri, *Theories and History of Architecture*, translated by Giorgio Verrecchia, London: Granada, 1980, p. 84)

Tafuri identifies the origins of the ambiguous object in the design and appreciation of picturesque gardens, which developed alongside the increasing value given to personal opinions and experiences in the eighteenth century: 'Architecture, from absolute object, becomes in the landscaped context, relative value: it becomes a medium for the description of an edifying play.'[1] Contrary to Tafuri's claim, the ambiguous object does not apply to the entire Modern Movement because there are many modernisms, not one; functionalism intends no ambiguity, for example. But he correctly assumes that the origins of modernism's ambiguous objects are found in the ideas and architectures of the eighteenth century.[2] For example, fascination for the illusions of parallax –

the perceived differences in an object's position when seen from different locations – in the eighteenth-century picturesque were important to the development of modernist architecture and the promotion of a discontinuous and temporal conception of space.[3]

To connect modernism to the picturesque, Caroline Constant selects the Barcelona Pavilion (1929–30), designed by Ludwig Mies van der Rohe:

> The term 'pavilion' was first associated with garden structures for temporary shelter in the late seventeenth century, such buildings provided the architectural leitmotif of the English landscape garden, which emerged in the following century as a vehicle of the new sensibility.
>
> (Caroline Constant, 'The Barcelona Pavilion as Landscape Garden: Modernity and the Picturesque', *AA Files*, no. 20, Autumn 1990, pp. 46–54, p. 46)[4]

Fusing building and garden into one, the 1929 Pavilion extended the idea – crucial to the eighteenth century – that associates nature with human nature and personal liberty.[5] To encourage and punctuate journeys, surfaces of onyx, travertine and alpine marble were combined with other elements animated by the wind: two large flags, water in the two pools and water lilies in the larger pool.[6] As the eighteenth century progressed, immediate and intuitive experience was favoured to the extent that narratives became less evident in the picturesque garden, as is the case in the Pavilion.[7] The pleasure of perception is the purpose of the eighteenth-century picturesque garden and the twentieth-century modernist Pavilion.[8]

The Farnsworth House

As a display of modernism and nationalism, the German Pavilion at the 1929 Barcelona Universal Exposition was didactic. Abstraction, multiple vistas and the absence of an everyday function made it appear ambiguous, which its many and varied assessments confirm.[9] But its demolition in 1930 and reconstruction as a museum display in 1986 prevented the Pavilion's status as an ambiguous object from being tested by regular use.[10]

The focus of this chapter is another building that exposes both the didacticism and ambiguity of modernist architecture. In 1951 Mies completed a weekend house for Dr Edith Farnsworth at Plano, Illinois. A typical mid-west town built around a railway line and station, Plano is an untypical weekend base for prosperous Chicago residents, who tend towards the shores of Lake Michigan to the east. Consisting of one principal room glazed on four sides, the Farnsworth House is designed for a single occupant.[11] But the two bathrooms in the central core indicate that guests are expected, either during the day or also overnight,[12] and the long kitchen confirms that the house is intended for entertaining as well as retreat.[13] As social events in 1950s America often focused on family life and a single person was unlikely to be invited,

Ludwig Mies van der Rohe, Farnsworth House (1951), Plano, Illinois, view from the north. Photograph: Yeoryia Manolopoulou (2004).

some critics focus on the personality and gender of the original owner. Alice T. Friedman gives particular importance to Mies' comment that the addition of a guest bathroom prevented visitors from 'seeing Edith's nightgown on the back of the bathroom door'.[14] But rather than the suppression of a specific gender, a wider disinterest is implied, which invites no personal design expression other than that of the architect.

In other projects – such as the Barcelona Pavilion and the Tugendhat House, Brno (1930) – Mies-designed furniture accompanies the building. Mies intended that the Farnsworth House would also contain only his furniture. But architect and client fell out before the house was furnished. Farnsworth, who claimed that she found the house uncomfortable but still lived there for twenty years, placed her objects and furniture around the house. Photographs suggest that they added little to the design. Peter Palumbo, a great admirer of Mies and the house's second owner in 1970, included furniture designed by the architect and, in 1972, employed Mies' grandson Dirk Lohan to supervise the renovation. In the 1997 visitor guide, which he commissioned from Mies' biographer Franz Schulze, Palumbo perches uneasily on the edge of a Mies daybed. A valued memento, a signed photograph from Margaret Thatcher thanking Palumbo for his support, was displayed in a bathroom. In 2003, Palumbo sold the Farnsworth House. Owned by the National Trust for Historic Preservation and managed by the Landmarks Preservation Council of Illinois, it is now an historical monument open to the public for hourly visits.

To the question, 'is the owner expected to express his or her identity in the Farnsworth House?', the answer is no. For early modernist architects, discomfort with comfort was a recurring theme and domesticity was dismissed as bourgeois. The early modernist house was rarely designed as a home, as László Moholy-Nagy's criticism of people 'who look for the essence of architecture in the meaning of the conception of shelter' indicates.[15] Mies curated the Weissenhofsiedlung, a Stuttgart housing development built as part of *Die Wohnung* (*The Dwelling*), the 1927 exhibition arranged by the Deutsche Werkbund. In an accompanying poster, a large red 'X' obliterates a photograph of an interior full of the daily clutter of domestic life.[16] The Farnsworth House typifies Mies' disinterest in designing a home abundant in the possessions, memories and traces of its occupants.[17] Like many a Mies building, the Farnsworth House does not readily absorb everyday objects because it is already complete. What does it accommodate, therefore? And how does it relate to the picturesque?

A picture of nature

In the grand house of an eighteenth-century land-owning family, paintings, furniture and heirlooms accumulated. Adjacent, the picturesque garden housed pleasures rather than furnishings. Family and guests visited a garden pavilion occasionally, to start or conclude an extensive dinner, for example. Maintaining another house in Plano as his principal weekend residence, Palumbo often visited the Farnsworth House in a similar manner; sometimes his stays were longer. On my visit with two friends, the Farnsworth House immediately brought to mind favourite pleasures: a steak, a smoke, a glass of wine. When the house was empty, and before surveillance cameras were installed, its terraces were known as a favourite picnic site. Rather than accommodate objects, the Farnsworth House accommodates pleasures.

The appreciation of nature is one such pleasure. Parallel with the north bank of the Fox River and next to a black sugar maple – one of the most venerable in the area but now sadly dying after a lightning strike – the Farnsworth House is sited in meadow and deciduous woodland. But left untouched and maintained as found, the landscape is untypical of the picturesque; it is not cultivated, or craggy or made for wandering.[18] Fritz Neumeyer identifies Bauhaus teacher Siegfried Ebeling as an important influence on Mies. In *The Space as Membrane*, published in 1926,[19] Ebeling conceives of architecture as a protective membrane between interior and exterior similar to the bark of a tree.[20] Viewing nature from a sealed glass enclosure is a familiar theme in modernist architecture. As early as 1915, Le Corbusier proposed a universal 'neutralising wall' to isolate inside from outside, maintaining the internal temperature at a constant 18°C, wherever a building's location.[21] According to Mies:

> Nature, too, shall live its own life. We must beware not to disrupt it with the color of our houses and interior fittings. Yet we should not attempt to bring nature, houses, and human beings together into a higher unity. If you view nature through the glass walls of the Farnsworth House, it gains a more profound significance than if viewed from outside. This way more is said about nature – it becomes a part of a larger whole.
>
> (Mies van der Rohe, in Christian Norberg-Schulz, 'A Talk with Mies van der Rohe', in Neumeyer, *The Artless Word*, p. 339)[22]

The height and detailing of the structure confirm the conceptual and physical detachment of architecture from nature. Twelve steel H-columns raise the floor and roof planes above the meadow; a black service stack is hidden in the shadow. Welded, ground smooth, then primed and finished in three coats of white paint, the structure seems to be cut from a single material without detail and weight:

> This approach is first seen in the X-crossing of his Barcelona Chair, whose appearance Adrian Gale has compared with those curviform eighteenth-century chairs whose legs and rails are fluidly shaped, and invisibly jointed, to convey an impression of the whole frame having been carved from a single block of wood.
>
> (Maritz Vandenburg, *Farnsworth House: Ludwig Mies van der Rohe*, London: Phaidon, 2003, p. 21)

In 1937 a commission from Helen and Stanley Resor for a vacation house straddling the Snake River near Jackson Hole, Wyoming, first brought Mies to the United States.[23] In 1939 he produced two drawings showing the dramatic views up and down the river. The drawing looking south combines a black-and-white photograph of a rugged landscape with two riders, a 1928 Paul Klee painting owned by the Resors, *Colorful Meal*, wood veneer representing a wall, and ink lines demarcating a column and window frame, insubstantial in comparison to the other fragments of the drawing.[24] In the designs for the Resor House, and in Mies' statement on the Farnsworth House, architecture and nature are kept apart. Their relationship is visual alone; nature is reduced to a picture. Such an attitude is quite different to the picturesque. Thomas Whately, author of the respected *Observations on Modern Gardening*, published in 1770, states that 'Gardening [...] is as superior to landskip painting, as a reality is to a representation', adding that paintings are 'studies, not models' for gardens.[25] The picturesque garden is not experienced like the painting, which absorbs the viewer at a distance.[26] Instead, the visitor is immersed and active within the garden. Vision is considered not in isolation but in relation to the other senses.

The Fox River House

Viewing nature through the windows of the Resor House, there is a clear distinction between the safe and comforting interior and the landscape beyond. At the Farnsworth House, the soft browns of timber and travertine affirm Mies' request not to disrupt nature 'with the color of our houses and interior fittings'. Nature is seen on all sides; the view is a panorama rather than a single picture. But rather than commanding, the interior feels exposed and vulnerable.

Mies' statement – 'If you view nature through the glass walls of the Farnsworth House, it gains a more profound significance than if viewed from outside' – suggests a disinterest in the complete sensual experience of nature and an emphasis on the visual that is cited by many historians of Mies and confirmed in projects such as the

Ludwig Mies van der Rohe, Farnsworth House (1951), Plano, Illinois, view from across the Fox River. Photograph: Yeoryia Manolopoulou (2004).

Resor House.[27] But since the Farnsworth House was first occupied, nature has regularly intervened to challenge this statement and emphasise the vulnerability of the interior. In winter, the under-floor heating is insufficient, while excessive condensation collects on the single-glazed walls and stains adjacent surfaces.[28] With delicate silk curtains and the foliage of the maple tree the principal protection from the sun, the Farnsworth House is often uncomfortable in summer. Aided by an electric fan in the floor, some cross-ventilation is possible when the entry doors to the west and hopper windows to the east are open and the wind is blowing in the right direction.[29] Given the size of the kitchen, principal room and terraces, the Farnsworth House can comfortably accommodate between one and twenty people. In winter, such a crowd may be an asset, providing extra warmth, while in summer it interrupts airflow and makes the internal temperature even more uncomfortable. Attempting to defend the design, Schulze notes that domestic air-conditioning was unusual in the 1940s and people in the mid-west 'were long accustomed to enduring summer heat in their homes'.[30] But they did not live in a glass house.

At first the meadow grass was left long and uncut but, in combination with the river, it caused mosquitoes to proliferate in summer.[31] In the 1947 model exhibited at the Museum of Modern Art in New York, a mosquito screen is shown around the upper terrace. But Mies was not pleased with the idea and it was not in place in early 1951.[32] Farnsworth added a screen later that year after her relationship with Mies worsened.[33] As enquiries suggested a maximum flood of 0.9 m above the meadow, the upper terrace was placed at 1.6 m. For much of the year the undercroft is shadowy and barren, while in autumn the wind forms eddies and mounds of leaves. At other times the eddies are watery and a greater threat. In 1954 the Fox River flood peaked at 2.8 m above the meadow and 1.2 m above the internal floor, ruining carpets and furniture. Fortunately the central core, faced in primavera wood-veneer, survived. In 1996 the river rose 0.3 m higher still, cracking two of the glass walls and destroying the wood-veneer, carpets, furniture and fittings. In 1997 a second renovation by Lohan was commissioned, which allows the wood-veneer panels to be dismantled and stored high within the house. Floods above the internal floor-level are now a common occurrence. Myron Goldsmith, who worked on the Farnsworth House in Mies' office, claims responsibility for not placing the floor above the flood 'because it was finally my responsibility'.[34] But Maritz Vandenburg describes the high floods 'partly as a result of the outward expansion and paving over of Chicago's environs, the volume of water run-off increased and flood-levels began to rise dramatically in the 1950s'.[35]

A difficult beauty

Farnsworth made clear her criticism of her architect and her house. In 1951 she and Mies sued each other, principally over money. The case was finally settled out of court in 1956 with Farnsworth paying Mies less than he demanded. Citing the house's constructional and environmental failings, she claimed that Mies had falsely represented himself as 'a skilled, proficient and experienced architect'.[36] Sixty-five at the completion of the Farnsworth House, and the architect of many buildings in Europe and the United States, Mies was indeed an experienced architect. He failed to predict the rising flood. But it is likely that he would have understood that the Farnsworth House would suffer from condensation, glare, overheating in summer, cold in winter[37] and that the absence of a hearth to the fireplace would have 'the unhappy effect of creating a wild circulation of ash throughout the interior'.[38] Maybe he considered these environmental 'failings' to be acceptable or even necessary to the experience of the Farnsworth House, contradicting his statement that architecture and nature should be kept apart.[39] Certainly, many architects have said one thing and done another. The pink suede Barcelona chairs Mies intended for the interior counter his request that architecture's colours should not disrupt nature, and would have made 'the house look like a Helena Rubenstein studio', as Farnsworth remarks.[40]

Praised by Walter Gropius and other architects, the traditional Japanese house is a precedent for the modernist open plan.[41] A flexible and flowing spatial organisation is cited as their principal similarity.[42] Another important but less recognised similarity is the low level of thermal and sound insulation that their open internal volumes and delicate elevations provide. In the traditional Japanese house, windows are faced in opaque rice paper, oiled to become waterproof. Paper accentuates senses other than the visual but on the glass walls of the Farnsworth House condensation may have a similar effect and can be made, adjusted and erased by the user. In the traditional Japanese house partial heating is provided by the stove, while the traditional Korean house, which was less well-known to early-twentieth-century modernists but has similar spatial qualities and papered windows, uses under-floor heating as insufficient as in the Farnsworth House. On life in the traditional Japanese house, Arthur Drexler remarks that 'Winter was held to offer an experience of difficult but rewarding beauty'.[43] These words are as applicable to the Farnsworth House except that a 'difficult but rewarding beauty' is found not in winter alone. In summer opaque and porous paper provides a cooler environment than clear and solid glass.

The sublime and beautiful

Is beauty the only appropriate term, however? Recalling the evening she first discussed the house with Mies, Farnsworth concludes that 'the effect was tremendous, like a storm, a flood, or other act of God'.[44] Whether she is referring to the house or its architect is uncertain, but Farnsworth describes an experience distinct from beauty. Romanticism, which developed towards the end of the eighteenth century, did not represent a decisive departure from the late picturesque. But it equated self-exploration with the exploration of wild landscapes rather than gardens, focusing further attention on weather as a means to fully appreciate the qualities of a place and a person. An influence on the picturesque and romanticism, Edmund Burke's *Philosophical Enquiry into the Origin of our Ideas of the Sublime and Beautiful* was first published in 1757.[45] His description of the sublime was not new; Joseph Addison's 'The Pleasures of the Imagination', published in 1712, was but one influence. Burke's achievement was to compile the sublime and the beautiful into a system that provides a coherent argument for the sublime. While the sublime is magnificent, the beautiful is pleasant. The sublime is evoked by a desolate and expansive landscape subject to the uncertain drama of natural forces. The pleasure of the sublime is first threatening and then reassuring as comprehension increases and fear diminishes:

> Whatever is fitted in any sort to excite the ideas of pain, and danger, that is to say, whatever is in any sort terrible, or is conversant about terrible objects, or operates in a manner analogous to terror, is a source of the sublime; that is, it is productive of the strongest emotion which the mind is capable of feeling [...]. When danger or pain presses too nearly, they are incapable of giving any delight, and are simply terrible; but at certain distances, and certain modifications, they may be, and they are delightful, as we everyday experience.
>
> (Edmund Burke, *Philosophical Enquiry into the Origin of our Ideas of the Sublime and Beautiful* [1757], Oxford: Oxford University Press, 1998, p. 36)

From Burke developed the principle that the arts, including architecture, should attempt to evoke not natural forms but experiences found in nature. The Farnsworth House's vulnerable interior heightens awareness of nature's sublime effects. In Palumbo's recollection of 'an electric storm of Wagnerian proportions illuminating the night sky and shaking the foundations of the house to their very core', the experience of nature is sublime.[46] But when the Fox River becomes a roaring torrent and bursts its banks, nature is less contrite, putting the sublime in such danger that a safe distance may be replaced by the sheer proximity of terror.[47]

The Farnsworth House does not keep nature and architecture apart. The environmental conditions outside so temper and intrude on those inside that the relationship between nature and architecture is by no means visual alone. Within its vulnerable interior, the full effects of weather and weathering are amplified and experienced, from the pleasant beauty of sunlight to the painful beauty of cold and condensation, from the majestic sublime of thunder and lightning to the fearful flood when immediate danger overcomes the sublime. But we do not know if this was Mies' intention.

On reflection

Its opposition to weather, which represents a physical and psychological threat, has historically defined architecture and continues to do so even though, since the eighteenth century, weather is also understood as just another resource to be manipulated. David Sibley notes that 'Nature has a long historical association with the other'.[48] Banister Fletcher writes that 'Architecture [...] must have had a simple origin in the primitive efforts of mankind to provide protection against inclement weather, wild beasts and human enemies'.[49] In an early demonstration of linear perspective, made between 1413 and 1425, Filippo Brunelleschi depicted the square around the baptistery in Florence. But, rather than draw the sky, he silvered part of a wooden panel so that it was seen in reflection, and a different sky was always present.[50] Brunelleschi's demonstration seems to confirm the opinion that weather is outside architecture and outside architectural representation. But an alternative interpretation indicates the importance of weather to architecture and its potential to expand ambiguity and uncertainty in architecture, which was recognised occasionally in the Italian Renaissance. Leonardo da Vinci's fascination for the effects of weather is wonderfully expressed in the title of his painting *A Town Over-whelmed by a Deluge*, *c.*1515. Leonardo credits Sandro Botticelli for noticing that 'various inventions are to be seen' in a building stain[51] and identifies similar potential in weather: 'I have in the past seen in clouds and walls stains which have inspired me to beautiful inventions of many things.'[52] Attention given to the effects of weather and weathering is, however, an architectural tradition developed principally from the picturesque, sublime and romanticism.

Today the assumption that weather and architecture are distinct is unconvincing. First, because the terms 'architecture' and 'weather' are imprecise intellectual constructs through which we comprehend and create our world. Second, because very little weather is only natural. The Farnsworth House indicates that architecture and nature are two inter-related elements of a complex system. Critical awareness of the weather, its causes and effects, is a valuable basis for architecture because, in all stages of building, it recognises the co-existence of architecture with its immediate and wider environments, leading to action against climate change, for example. And one of weather's greatest assets to critical architecture is its potential to expand and extend ambiguity.

Notes

1   Tafuri, *Theories and History of Architecture*, p. 82.

2   The understanding that ideas are provisional and dependent on experience at concep-
    tion and reception is discussed in the introduction to 'Criticism by Design'. Henry-
    Russell Hitchcock and Nikolaus Pevsner relate the eighteenth-century picturesque to
    twentieth-century modernism. See Henry-Russell Hitchcock, *Modern Architecture:
    Romanticism and Regeneration*, [1929] New York: Hacker Art Books, 1970, p. 220;
    Nikolaus Pevsner, 'Twentieth-Century Picturesque: an Answer to Basil Taylor's
    Broadcast', *Architectural Review*, 115, 688, April 1954, pp. 227–9, p. 229.

3   The claim that modernist architecture is specific to the twentieth century means that
    the influence of the picturesque is often ignored. Sigfried Giedion, *Space, Time and
    Architecture: the Growth of a New Tradition*, [1941] Cambridge, MA: Harvard Univer-
    sity Press, 1956, pp. 14, 432–43.

4   With reference to *The Compact Edition of the Oxford English Dictionary*, Oxford:
    Oxford University Press, 1971, p. 572.

5   Liberty, however, was limited to the learned and prosperous. In the eighteenth
    century, picturesque gardens proliferated in conjunction with parliamentary land
    enclosures, which transformed open land into regular fields defined by hedges and
    walls, creating larger estates. Looking out as well as in, the picturesque garden
    enforces clear power relations between those who own the landscape and those
    who work it, and between a landscape of pleasure and one of production.

6   In the 1986 reconstruction of the Pavilion, neither the flags nor the water lilies are
    present. For the possible reasons for this absence, refer to Jonathan Hill, *Actions of
    Architecture: Architects and Creative Users*, London and New York: Routledge, 2003,
    pp. 160–1.

7   Thomas Whately distinguishes between the emblematic, which requires careful
    analysis and understanding, and the expressive, which emphasises immediate and
    intuitive experience, and which he favours (Thomas Whately, 'From *"Observations on
    Modern Gardening"*' [1770], in John Dixon Hunt and Peter Willis (eds), *The Genius of
    the Place: the English Landscape Garden 1620–1820*, London: Elek, 1975, p. 38).

8   Jonathan Hill, *Immaterial Architecture*, Abingdon and New York: Routledge, 2006,
    pp. 135–7.

9   Robin Evans, 'Mies van der Rohe's Paradoxical Symmetries', in *Translations from
    Drawing to Building and Other Essays*, London: Architectural Association, 1997, p.
    268; Manfredo Tafuri, *Architecture and Utopia: Design and Capitalist Development*,
    translated by Barbara Luigia La Penta, Cambridge, MA: MIT Press, 1976, p. 148.

10 Ignasi de Solà Morales, Christian Cirici and Fernando Ramos, *Mies van der Rohe:
    Barcelona Pavilion*, translated by Graham Thomson, Barcelona: Editorial Gustavo Gili,
    1993.

11 'Interview with Ludwig Mies van der Rohe', *Listener*, 15 October 1959, p. 620.

12 The alternatives are to share the double bed, sleep on the sofa or a mattress on the
    floor.

13 Alice T. Friedman, *Women and the Making of the Modern House: a Social and Archi-
    tectural History*, New York: Harry N. Abrams, 1998, p. 134.

14 Mies, as reported to Alice T. Friedman in April 1988 by Myron Goldsmith, Mies' asso-
    ciate on the Farnsworth House (Friedman, *Women and the Making of the Modern
    House,* p. 143).

15 László Moholy-Nagy, *The New Vision 1928*, 4th revised edition [1947]; *Abstract of an
    Artist*, translated by Daphne M. Hoffmann, New York: George Wittenborn, 1947, p. 59.

16 Willi Baumeister, *Die Wohnung Werkbund Ausstellung*, Stuttgart, 1927. See
    Friedman, *Women and the Making of the Modern House*, pp. 143–4.

17   The comfortably bourgeois character of Mies' Chicago home is worth noting, however.

18   A dramatically craggy landscape is more often a feature of the late-eighteenth-century picturesque rather than the early picturesque, which favoured a softer landscape.

19   Published in German as *Der Raum Als Membran*.

20   Fritz Neumeyer, *The Artless Word: Mies van der Rohe on the Building Art*, Cambridge, MA and London: MIT Press, 1991, p. 175.

21   First devised for the Villa Schwob, La Chaux de Fonds, 1915 (Reyner Banham, *The Architecture of the Well-tempered Environment*, Chicago: University of Chicago Press, 1984, pp. 156–63).

22   First published in *Baukunst und Werkform*, 11, 11, 1958, pp. 615–18.

23   The house was not built.

24   Ludwig Mies van der Rohe, *Drawings from the Collection of the Museum of Modern Art, New York*, New York: Museum of Modern Art, 1969, figure 18.

25   Whately, quoted in John Dixon Hunt, *The Picturesque Garden in Europe*, London: Thames and Hudson, 2002, p. 62. Whately uses the Old English term 'landskip'. Its original meaning was 'a picture of the land, not the land itself'.

26   Walter Benjamin, 'The Work of Art in the Age of Mechanical Production', in *Illuminations: Essays and Reflections*, edited by Hannah Arendt, translated by Harry Zohn, New York: Schocken Books, 1969, p. 239.

27   Jose Quetglas, 'Fear of Glass: the Barcelona Pavilion', translated by Stan Allen, Beatriz Colomina and Mari Marratt, in Beatriz Colomina (ed.), *Architectureproduction*, New York: Princeton Architectural Press, 1988, pp. 134–5; Manfredo Tafuri and Francesco Dal Co, *Modern Architecture*, vol. 1, translated by Robert Erich Wolf, London: Faber and Faber, 1986, p. 157. Evans, 'Mies van der Rohe's Paradoxical Symmetries', p. 258.

28   Vandenburg, *Farnsworth House*, p. 15. Others included a cost over-run and leaking roof. A 1972 restoration by Dirk Lohan addressed some of the building's environmental problems.

29   Ibid., p. 21.

30   Franz Schulze, *The Farnsworth House,* Plano: Palumbo, 1997, p. 15.

31   Today, the meadow is cut to a lawn to reduce mosquitoes.

32   Schulze, *The Farnsworth House*, p. 17.

33   The screen was designed by an assistant in Mies' office, William Dunlap, with Mies offering advice without Farnsworth's knowledge.

34   Goldsmith, interview with Keith Harrington, CCA, Tape 7: Side 2, quoted in Phyllis Lambert, 'Mies Immersion', in Phyllis Lambert (ed.), *Mies in America*, Montreal: CCA, 2001, p. 508.

35   Vandenburg, *Farnsworth House*, p. 26.

36   Quoted in Friedman, *Women and the Making of the Modern House*, p. 140, from the Kendall County Circuit Court, Yorkville, Illinois, summary of the case proceedings.

37   Another failing was caused by roof insulation placed below the waterproof membrane, common practice at the time of the Farnsworth House's construction. Warm, moist air rising to meet the cold surface of the waterproof membrane caused staining, mould growth and diminished insulation. This failing was one of those addressed in the 1972 restoration.

38   Schulze, *The Farnsworth House*, p. 14. To alleviate the problem, Dirk Lohan added a raised travertine hearth in his 1972 restoration.

39   Elsewhere Mies designed oblique views that confuse the relationship between architecture and nature. At the Haus Lemke, Berlin, 1933, views proceed from interior to garden to interior, and from interior to garden to interior to garden to interior to garden at the Haus Esters, Krefeld, 1930.

40   Edith Farnsworth, 'Memoirs', chapter 13, unpaginated, quoted in Friedman, *Women and the Making of the Modern House,* p. 143.

41   Walter Gropius, *Apollo in the Democracy: the Cultural Obligation of the Architect,* New York: McGraw Hill, 1968, p. 120.

42   However, social cohesion in Japan and Korea, informed by the prevalence of Confucian values, ensures that a social boundary need not necessarily be physical.

43   Arthur Drexler, *The Architecture of Japan,* New York: Museum of Modern Art, 1966, p. 41.

44   Schulze, *The Farnsworth House,* p. 18.

45   Referring to the late-eighteenth-century picturesque, which is more expressive and less allegorical than the early-eighteenth-century picturesque, Uvedale Price claims that the picturesque sits between the beautiful and the sublime and is able to combine the two (Uvedale Price, 'From *"An Essay on the Picturesque"* ', [1794] in Hunt and Willis, *The Genius of the Place,* p. 354).

46   Peter Palumbo, 'Foreword', in Vandenburg, *Farnsworth House,* p. 8.

47   Ibid., p. 8.

48   David Sibley, *Geographies of Exclusion: Society and Difference in the West,* London: Routledge, 1995, p. 26.

49   Banister Fletcher, *A History of Architecture on the Comparative Method,* 7th edition, London: B.T. Batsford, 1924, p. 1.

50   Hubert Damisch, *A Theory of/Cloud/Toward a Theory of Painting,* Stanford: Stanford University Press, 2002, pp. 123–4; Robin Evans, *The Projective Cast: Architecture and its Three Geometries,* Cambridge, MA: MIT Press, 1995, p. 133.

51   Leonardo da Vinci, *Leonardo on Painting: an Anthology of Writings by Leonardo da Vinci,* edited by Martin Kemp, translated by Martin Kemp and Margaret Walker, New Haven and London: Yale University Press, 1989, p. 201.

52   Da Vinci, *Leonardo on Painting,* p. 222.

Immediate Architecture

Philippe Rahm

La qualification n'est que spatiale, situationnelle, en aucun cas analogique.
(The qualification is only spatial, situational, absolutely not analogical.)
(Roland Barthes, 'Littérature Objective', *Essais Critiques*, Paris:
Editions du Seuil, 1964, p. 33)

Architecture itself

Architecture is not the instrument of expression of something beyond architecture. It is not the reflection or representation of something else. The cause of its form is architecture itself, in space and time. In his article on 'objective literature', Roland Barthes recognises in the literary work of Alain Robbe-Grillet a will to remove any possibility of metaphor and analogy and thus to kill 'the singular and total adjective which succeeds in tying all the metaphysical bonds of the object'.[1] Denouncing the 'tyranny of significances', Robbe-Grillet gives the example of those adjectives that, when added to a name, impose a psychological reading of space and reduce the freedom of a sentence. For example, 'village blotti dans la colline' – 'village snuggled up against the hill' in English – gives an affective idea to a physical fact.[2] Our ambition for architecture is of the same order as that of Robbe-Grillet for literature. We refuse meanings beyond architecture in order to guarantee the freedom of architecture as a space and time open to interpretations, to modifications of behaviour, to new fashions of dwelling, to the unexpected, to the unknown. We want architecture 'to be there before being something' as Robbe-Grillet remarks. The 'Hormonorium' that I conceived in the Swiss Pavilion of the *8th Venice Architecture Biennale* in 2002 was of this kind.[3] By working with certain quantifiable and quantified data of the space – an oxygen rate lowered to 14.5 per cent, a light intensity increased to 10,000 lux – it questioned the language of space, the vacuum as a chemical quality, the light as an electromagnetic field, and consequently renewed the elements of architecture from the interior of the discipline.

Function and form follow climate

Relative humidity, variation of temperature, light intensity, and spectrality are the elements that are questioned in the production of our architectural projects, in which the use of the space does not determine the shape of the building. On the contrary, it is the shape that freely produces various practical interpretations and uses. Our projects are the product of an inversion of use and form. Function follows form but also function and form follow climate. The starting point of each design is the problem of building techniques linked to sustainable development. Rather than adapting these techniques to a preconceived architectural project in accordance with symbolism or use, the techniques generate the architectural form. My ambition is to transform a problem of building physics into an architectural question, to the point that this question becomes the efficient cause of the form. This introduces new sensual and physiological relations between the inhabitant and the space according to the constraints of the technical equipment of the building. The problems of the degree of humidity in the air, its regulation within the home, and the distribution of air in space according to its temperature density, define, by their physical and sensory nature, the organisation of the building in plan and section. New typologies of habitat appear, unexpectedly, not based on modern house planning with its divisions between day and night, intimate and public, but emerging from the sensual and physiological results of the treatment of building techniques.

Architecture as a gradual lowering of certain ambient climatological values

As an example, our project for a new museum in Estonia is nothing more than the gradual lowering of certain ambient climatological values such as the degree of humidity, the quantity of UV rays, or the intensity of light. The objective is to satisfy the museum's obligation to preserve the materials of the artworks through time by shielding them from certain natural chemical and physical conditions that bring about their deterioration. The works' preservation necessitates, according to their organic or mineral nature, a specifically determined climate. It follows that the museum is organised as a reduction of the natural climate, progressing rigorously and rhythmically from the exterior towards the interior, from the most humid to the driest, from the brightest to the darkest, from the strongest ultraviolet to the weakest. The plan of the museum is organised as a concentric series of filtering and enveloping glass layers, traversed one after another as one passes from the more corrosive ambient natural milieu to a milieu that is more and more diminished and chemically neutral. The various rooms are located in one or another of these climates according to the chemical requirements for the artworks' preservation.

A new manner of visiting a museum is invented here, in the very physical phenomenon of preservation, in the physiological perception of a climate that

Philippe Rahm
Architects, Estonian
National Museum,
Competition (2005).
Collaborators: Cyrille
Berger, Mustapha
Majid and Marc
Eychenne.

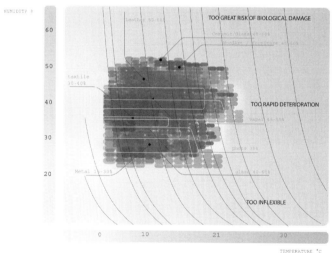

Recommended level of relative humidity for the conservation depending on the material.

Philippe Rahm
Architects, Estonian
National Museum,
Competition (2005).
Collaborators: Cyrille
Berger, Mustapha
Majid and Marc
Eychenne.

Philippe Rahm Architects, Mollier's Houses, urban and architectural design for the area of Vassivière, Limousin, France (2005). Client: SYMIVA; collaborator: Jérôme Jacqmin.

approaches an effacement of time, where chemical degeneration disappears little by little, and in which the visitor begins to sense an architectural form of permanence.

Climates for living in

The project for the Mollier's Houses reveals and characterises an invisible, yet essential, connection between interior space and humidity. It engages closer ties with the lake landscape of Vassivière in Limousin – physical and chemical ties – as it is situated in the material character of the territory itself, in its humidity. Our interest is the lake as a visual landscape but also as a physiological territory of humidity. An occupant of an indoor space produces water vapour, not in a constant manner, but according to his/her primary activity. The presence of water vapour in the air originates naturally from respiration and hot-water usage. Our architecture is designed, and the living spaces are given form, according to the variation of the relative humidity level, from the driest to the most humid, from 20 per cent to 100 per cent relative humidity. By means of the water vapour content, the quality of the architecture takes shape as the real and physical immersion of the inhabitants' bodies in the humid and variable body of the space. Our project establishes a stratification of the levels of humidity within the space and refuses to programme the space functionally according to specific activities. We don't create functional spaces like a kitchen or bedroom with a specific size. We prefer to create spaces that are more or less dry, more or less humid, to be occupied freely, to be appropriated according to the weather and the seasons. The plan of the

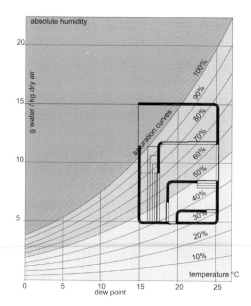

Mollier's graph

Philippe Rahm
Architects, Mollier's
Houses, urban and
architectural design
for the area of
Vassivière, Limousin,
France (2005).
Client: SYMIVA;
collaborator: Jérôme
Jacqmin.

house is a spatial representation of the Mollier diagram – a diagram that shows the physical relation between temperature and relative humidity – creating new programmatic correspondences, in which one space can receive several functions that are assumed to be separate. None of the rooms are specifically determined by a function. They remain free for appropriation according to the level of humidity sought. The dryer part of the house could be used as a sauna or an office. The wetter space could be used as a swimming pool or a living room. A kitchen could also be a bathroom.

Archimedes's Houses

The Archimedes's Houses seek to establish an intrinsic relation between the house and the air by spatially representing the functions of the home (sleeping, resting, bathing, etc.) in the very matter of the air, in its density, its temperature, its movements. The house is organised according to the physiological needs of inhabitants, so as to relate to their bodily activity and their nudity. This vertical architecture is structured around the precise need for heat in each space. It must provide for the thermal comfort of the inhabitant and create spaces in which the interior temperature is adapted to the activity and the clothing of the occupants. Modernity led to uniform, consistent spaces in which the temperature is regulated around 21°C. The aim here is to restore diversity to the relation that the body maintains with space – with its temperature – to allow seasonal movement within the house, migrations from downstairs to upstairs, from cold in the basement of the house to warm at the top of the house, winter and summer, dressed and undressed. For example, the first floor could be used as a living room during the summer and a bedroom during the winter. Today, confronted with the will to economise energy resources, the Swiss construction norm SIA

Philippe Rahm
Architects,
Archimedes's
Houses, urban and
architectural design
for the area of
Vassivière, Limousin,
France (2005).
Client: SYMIVA;
collaborators:
Jérôme Jacqmin,
Irène D'Agostino,
Cyrille Berger and
Alexandra Cammas.

Philippe Rahm
Architects,
Archimedes's
Houses, urban and
architectural design
for the area of
Vassivière, Limousin,
France (2005).
Client: SYMIVA;
collaborators:
Jérôme Jacqmin,
Irène D'Agostino,
Cyrille Berger and
Alexandra Cammas.

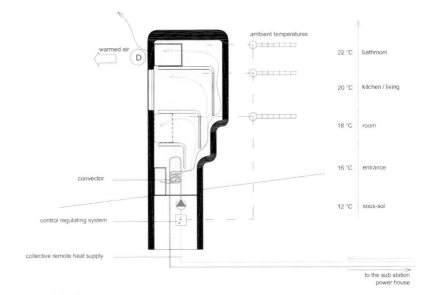

thermal draught heating system

3842 gives the following indicative values for ambient temperature: living rooms 20°C, bedrooms 16° to 18°C, bathrooms 22°C, etc. The sections of the house are therefore designed to follow the form taken by the air in the entire height of the house, in accordance with vertical air movements in relation to temperature, and the functions that are suggested as a result.

Our architecture is, as a consequence, physically climatic. It does not follow any presupposed use or symbolism and is developed solely within its own medium. By not reflecting any programmatic use or symbolic interpretation, it allows new modes of living that spring from the very language of architecture, in space.

House dilation

Our project for Grizedale works on the whole of a natural site. It dilates functions through various places, climates and qualities of light, temperature, and moisture, chosen according to the moments of the day or the seasons. In this situation, architecture removes its outer skin or jacket and it is the environment that then takes on this role, becoming this last skin, filtering the light, containing, or repelling moisture, heating or cooling, according to place and moment. Three sites are selected: in the meadow, at the boundary of field and forest, and in the forest itself. Each site is determined by its specific climatic qualities: the light, temperature, and humidity created by the trees. According to the hour of the day and the time of season, the interior quality of the rooms will vary. Activity in each dilation will relate to the particular and required climate: the heat of the night forest, the warmth of the field in the winter during the day, the freshness of the forest edge in the spring.

Conclusion

Architecture should produce meaning, but from within its own language of space and time. It should not illustrate but produce matter to be illustrated. It should not represent, but present spaces and times, climates, geographies, and physiologies. Our aim is to allow the sudden appearance of original practices of space. In place of functional and symbolic constraints, we substitute a freedom of use and interpretation. This is

Philippe Rahm Architects (Philippe Rahm, Jerome Jacqmin), House Dilation, Artfarm in Ambleside, Cumbria, England, 2006. Client: Grizedale Arts, Adam Sutherland, Director; collaborator: Mustapha Majid.

what fascinates us in the novels of Robbe-Grillet. Avoiding any dogmatism or morality, it is his formidable capacity to realise spaces and times in the moment of reading, to draw within the length of a sentence extraordinary labyrinths where reality is reinvented with each word, where 'the places, the objects, the situations, combine, change, amalgamate, reverse themselves, multiply, under our eyes', as Gerard Genette remarks.[4] It is the continuous present of the 100 minutes of the film *Last Year at Marienbad*;[5] it is the motionless giddiness of hours of reading *In the Labyrinth*.[6] I'm fascinated by this extreme opening of reality, the possibility to discover there, in the present, unexplored dimensions where architecture causes a sudden appearance of times, spaces, and practices within its matter.

Notes

1   Roland Barthes, 'Littérature objective', p. 33.
2   Alain Robbe-Grillet, 'Une voie pour le roman futur', in *Pour un nouveau roman,* Paris: Minuit, 1963, pp. 20–2.
3   Décosterd and Rahm, associés 'Hormonorium', Swiss Pavilion, *8th Venice Architecture Biennale*, Italy, 2002.
4   Gérard Genette, 'Vertige Fixé', *Figures 1*, Paris: Editions du Seuil, 1966, p. 88.
5   *Last Year at Marienbad*, directed by Alain Renais, 1961.
6   Alain Robbe-Grillet, *Dans le labyrinthe*, Paris: Les Editions de Minuit, 1959.

Alvin Boyarsky's Delicatessen

Igor Marjanović

Maybe this happened . . .

Surrounded by a wall of drawings, the collector dives into one of his beloved books. He flips through Peter's monograph, carefully looking at each print. His eyes slowly get tired and he puts the book back on the shelf. He stubs out the cigar, leaves the library and quickly enters the drawing room. As the rays of sun drift through the layers of smoke, they illuminate Zaha's painting on the wall. The room disappears behind yet another wall of books and floors covered with Persian rugs. In the middle of it all is a small coffee table covered with postcards. They remind him of last night's soirée with Rem and Maddy and all the wonderful food, drinks and cigars! He chuckles as he puts the postcards back in their boxes. He leaves the salon and descends into the foyer. He grabs his raincoat and locks the front door behind him.

It is a surprisingly lovely English afternoon. The sky above London is bright and sunny, with some clouds forming in the distance. A relaxed stroll between Oakley Square and Bedford Square should take no more than twenty minutes. As he leaves his home, he closes the unpolished wooden door behind him and sees the green park in front of him. He then turns right towards Eversholt Street. He sees a row of nineteenth-century ter-raced houses, so different from the soaring towers of public housing in the background. He makes a left turn towards Euston Station and walks past the Asian convenience store. What might be a Pakistani or Hindu shop owner waves his hand. He smiles back; he too is an immigrant. The childhood memories of Montreal are mixed with images of Oregon and Chicago. Identity is elusive: a North American, of Eastern European Jewish descent, maybe a Londoner. His backward glance is not melancholic. He never had time for myths.

He turns right on Euston Road, but decides it is too noisy and makes a quick left into Gordon Street. He then sees Wates House, home of the Bartlett. He looks at that strange brick structure, probably designed in some committee meeting, and thinks how different from his two homes it is. It doesn't have a restaurant or a bar. He remembers teaching at the Bartlett while it was still in the old main quad and recalls sharing one of those small offices with Reyner.

It starts to drizzle, he opens his umbrella and walks faster. His steps are small, but frequent and energetic. He turns right on Torrington Place and then makes another quick turn to Gower Street. He feels more energized – he is getting close to his other home. The rain stops. He puts back his umbrella as he gazes at the bookshop window that occupies this busy corner. He likes books very much; he collects them. The street slowly becomes very busy with noisy buses and disoriented tourists occupying the sidewalk lined with seedy hotels and offices. He likes tourists though; they remind him of his postcard collection.

He enters Bedford Square, feeling that uneven, yet beautiful and soft-looking paving. He finally sees his second home in the distance: an elegant townhouse rising behind the tall trees. Suddenly, he pauses for a minute. He notices the strangely familiar tower made of wood and numbers. He is confused, but only for a second. Then he remembers; it is John's installation 'The Collapse of Time' proudly claiming the public space in front of his home. He smiles and enters the building, passing by a group of students chatting on the doorstep. He moves up quickly, passes into the Members' Bar – and finally sees his group; they start talking. He nibbles on snacks while reaching for a glass of wine. Home again! He lights the cigar and the 'conversazione' begins.

He is Alvin Boyarsky.

Peter Eisenman, Charles Jencks and Alvin Boyarsky (1985).

Igor Marjanović

Introduction

This chapter examines Alvin Boyarsky's Architectural Association (AA) as a generator of architectural thinking, building and pedagogy. During his tenure (1971–1990), the AA became one of the most influential design schools in the world. Designers bloomed in the studios Boyarsky seeded, most notably Zaha Hadid, Rem Koolhaas, Bernard Tschumi and others. They became international stars and symbols of design-centred architectural education and practice. The emphasis on design was paired with the blossoming of thinking that surrounded design projects within AA publications, exhibitions, seminars and public lectures. All these discursive events propelled an international dialogue that was conducted in the hallways, studios, the AA bar, as well as at Boyarsky's own family residence. Overlapping these physical conduits of social interaction and architectural discourse was Boyarsky's informal school, a network of designers and educators around the world who engaged in an ongoing dialogue. The conversations that casually began at the AA bar were followed in Boyarsky's salon and then further expanded through decades of official and unofficial records: the AA publications and its chairman's personal correspondence. Within these two houses, we find letters, books and postcards, as well as traces of many meals and meetings where faculty, students, visiting designers, critics, historians and artists engaged in a continuous writing of architecture's future. In this chapter, I propose that Boyarsky created a multiplicity of schools as physical and figurative networks of people, places and ideas. These schools overlapped and complemented each other, ultimately leading to the transformation of 'architectural' practice.

People: the cultural politics of friendship

The first metaphor that I propose in this chapter is the school as an international network of people. The AA network bridged Boyarsky's own social and professional friendships. He studied architecture at McGill University immediately following the Second World War. At Cornell University he studied under Colin Rowe,[1] a prominent member of the 'Texas Rangers'.[2] As they scattered around the world, 'Texas Rangers' such as John Hejduk at Cooper Union and Bernhard Hoesli at ETH Zurich, slowly became important administrators. Boyarsky began his teaching career within this network: he taught at the University of Oregon between 1959 and 1962 alongside 'Texas Ranger' Lee Hodgden. After Oregon, Boyarsky taught at the AA and at the Bartlett, where he shared an office with Reyner Banham. In 1965, he accepted the position of associate dean at the University of Illinois at Chicago-Circle (UIC), where he generated a forum of social life at the school. He entertained Archigram, Rowe, Banham and many others who came to UIC to give lectures or workshops.

This confluence of European and North American networks became particularly visible in the International Institute of Design (IID), a series of summer sessions that Boyarsky organized in London between 1970 and 1972. Students produced urban projects for six weeks full of 'public lectures, razzamatazz, beautiful posters, postcards, street parties'.[3] Boyarsky's goal was to bring together people of diverse backgrounds and establish an ongoing forum, or in Boyarsky's words, 'I had this idea of operating in a comparative way and of providing an alternative to the available education. And so I tried to marry these two ideas into an International School which brought together people from diverse situations.'[4] The success of IID was also evident in its publication machinery, including the *Manhattan Workshop Briefing Document* (1972), designed by Archigram. The publicity surrounding the IID helped Boyarsky to secure a chairmanship at the AA, which in 1971 faced an unprecedented crisis. The AA Council voted to close the school, while the school community rebelled and asked for the creation of a chairman position, a leadership post with great powers. In the international search, Boyarsky was chosen over Kenneth Frampton. Boyarsky's sense of sociability matched well with the culture of the AA and its history of lectures, parties, masked balls and reviews. He was well aware that these events, although costly, would bring enormous and needed publicity to the school, which would in turn ensure the recruitment of wealthy international students able to pay high tuition fees. The technocratic UK government pressured independent schools to join larger universities, cutting state bursaries for students of small independent institutions such as the AA. After a failed merger with Imperial College, the AA was eliminated from the government mandatory bursary list and, as result, very few British students came to the AA. They went to universities where their tuition was subsidized by the state.

Boyarsky's AA was independent from both state power and private capital. Although he rejected government interference, he met with Margaret Thatcher, the UK minister of education, on several occasions in order to resolve the issue of government bursaries. He also rejected interference from the profession under the auspices of RIBA or ARCUK, who wanted to impose a model of architectural education based on corporate practice. Boyarsky wanted the AA to be an ongoing party. Although he moved through many 'clubs', such as the network of 'Texas Rangers' for example, he was more open than that. His parties were open to students; the AA Members Bar was open to non-members. Boyarsky rejected the formality of British establishment, the self-referential, closed, formal and bureaucratic environment of traditional architectural schools and British social clubs. The AA enrolled international students of all races, genders and ages. Although most of them came from the international wealthy classes, these students probably represented the most diverse student body in the world.

Places: the permeable house

The second metaphor I propose is academia as a cross between school and home. In Boyarsky's work, personal intersects with professional, public with private, institutional with domestic. His residence was at 64 Oakley Square,[5] within walking distance from the AA located at 36 Bedford Square. His home often served as an extension of the

AA, a comfortable venue for chairman's dinner parties and discussions about architectural education. Boyarsky's house was an unusually permeable domestic space. He blurred the boundary between his AA office and his home library, between the AA Members Bar and his kitchen table. At both places, he felt at home, in a place 'where one best knows oneself – where "best" means "most", even if not always "happiest".'[6]

A passionate book collector, Boyarsky was equally attached to his own library and to the AA library and its rare book collection: 'I am dying to re-do the library. I have an image of a big, leather-covered table with all the rare books set out around it – the heart of the building.'[7] Writing as if referring to his personal library, Boyarsky transcends the distinction between the two houses. He operates dialectically on the public and private, institutional and individual, work and home. At the AA, Boyarsky worked in the chairman's office, 'with the bust of Wren behind him, the ever-growing pile of publications, the very personal art works made by friends'.[8] At home, he worked at his kitchen table, mailing invitations and calling his friends or, in his own words, 'I used to sit in my bathrobe at the kitchen table in Chicago and call Moscow you know and do things.'[9]

Changes in academic leadership have often been accompanied with the renovation of facilities – such as the case of Hejduk at the Cooper Union – suggesting that institutional transformation could be facilitated by the physical transformation of spaces. These renovations were as much ideological as structural. By 1982, the reorganization of the AA under Boyarsky culminated in the renovation of its facilities based on Rick Mather's design.[10] Like other events at the AA under his leadership, this renovation was widely publicized. A special issue of *The Architectural Review* covered the AA's curriculum, people, events and the renovation itself. The editorial text suggests that the AA was fully identified with its chairman; the beliefs and feelings of Boyarsky became the values of the institution itself: 'Alvin Boyarsky believes that the AA needs to present itself publicly as a refined, intelligent, even glamorous institution.'[11] The renovated 36 Bedford Square provided a backdrop for such glamour. As an appropriated domestic space, it enabled creativity. In his book *How Buildings Learn*, Stewart Brand discusses the use of of old buildings as hubs for creative activity.[12] From the garages of Silicon Valley, where firms like Hewlett-Packard began, to the loft spaces of artistic studios, Brand argues that old buildings provide a sense of simplicity and freedom that enhances their occupants' creativity and ability to experiment and improvise. With its quasi-domestic environment, the many books on the shelves, smells of food, drinks and smoke, the AA was a home of architectural experimentation. It was an antidote to formalized corporate practices of the time and, as such, it was a place where unusual drawings and writings bloomed.

With their similar layouts, 64 Oakley Square and 36 Bedford Square provided an uninterrupted work-space for the chairman. Both were typical London townhouses situated on a square with a park in the middle; both revolved around ideas, exchange, drinks, meals and soirees; both structures facilitated architectural discourse with their layouts. With their interconnected rooms, the houses enabled people to 'bump' into each other, unlike the modern buildings of the 1970s that had long separate corridors with terminal rooms on both sides. Similar to Sir John Soane's house nearby at 13 Lincoln's Inn Fields, the AA was composed of three conjoined townhouses with many interconnected spaces where people could mingle between the gallery, library, bar, etc. With their multiple doors, these rooms enabled social interaction and casual encounters. Robin Evans, himself an AA notable, wrote beautifully about the importance of rooms with multiple doors and how they enable social interaction. In his essay 'Figures, Doors, and Passages', he called for a type of architecture 'that recognizes passion, carnality and sociality. The matrix of connected rooms might well be an integral feature of such buildings.'[13] The location of the AA also enabled networking – it is strategically positioned as a central node in the architectural network of London. Since 1927 it has been located at 36 Bedford Square and surrounded by many firms and architectural institutions.[14] This, coupled with the enjoyable club-like setting of the house itself, helped the AA to bring more people to its events, leading to the increase in membership, so necessary for its financial survival.

The AA's social life was publicized through exhibitions, catalogues and books, all of which quickly became global commodities for prospective and current students. The bookshop at the AA became 'like a delicatessen where you sniff the aromas as you walk by and get interested. We set up the restaurant in the basement, because sitting and talking is an essential thing.'[15] The metaphor of a delicatessen is not a coincidence. Boyarsky ran the AA like a good restaurant, a meeting-place where people would be well-fed, entertained and want to come back to see their friends. The restaurant atmosphere helped to domesticate the AA's institutional spaces. While in Chicago, Boyarsky entertained school's guests either in one of the neighbouring Greek Town restaurants or at home. Unlike the closed social clubs of the time, Boyarsky created an open, inclusive and ongoing party. With the help of affordable jet travel, Boyarsky's parties became an international restaurant of ideas and an extension of traditional classroom spaces. Jack Naughton, Boyarsky's former student from UIC-Circle, called him:

> a good 'chef' for the College [...]. There is no doubt that what he prepared was spicy and not for all tastes. Nevertheless, his ingredients were always fresh – the flavors he strived for complex and sophisticated. Furthermore, one can be sure that when Alvin was in the 'kitchen,' nothing would stick to the bottom of the pan.[16]

Ideas: global exchange

The third metaphor I propose is a school as a place of exchange, rather than a place of production. The AA does not have conventional studio spaces where student work is produced. Instead the AA is a maze of meeting spaces, where faculty and students come together to 'exchange' work, rather than 'produce' it. This exchange takes the form of informal and formal critiques, meetings at the bar, as well as many reviews and exhibitions throughout the school. The elimination of studio space has proved a virtue, but it began out of necessity: large studios with individual student workspaces were unaffordable in a location like Bedford Square. The actual production of work – both student work and faculty work – did and does not take place at the AA. Boyarsky sensed a shift in the modes of artistic production that took place in the 1970s when the Bauhaus-type 'factory' was substituted with a system of isolated studios in 'an era of dispersed production, peripheral sites, and a decentered subject'.[17] Advances in communication and transportation technology facilitated this process of dispersal, enabling Boyarsky to build an international network of collaborators. The 'guests' would fly to London and their work was published and distributed globally through the AA Publications. Conceptually, the international AA diaspora can be read as a transition from late modernism, a new stage that Peter Galison and Caroline Jones described as 'a postmodern architecture of data flows and ethernets; the postmodern production of art takes place not in a factory-modeled studio but in the spectacular and discursive realms of print, film, and photographic media'.[18] The exchange of ideas at the AA took the form of exhibitions and architectural publications that circulated around the world. It also took the form of social encounters within AA's interconnected rooms where one could mingle with many guests and members of the AA community.

Both 64 Oakley Square and 36 Bedford Square are museums. With their walls covered with architectural photographs and drawings, they are homes of the collector, echoing Sir John Soane's house. At 64 Oakley Square, we find the shaky lines of Frank Gehry's sketches, juxtaposed with tight orthographic drawings by Peter Eisenman, sprinkled with OMA's renderings and large black and white photographs of Le Corbusier's buildings, all surrounded by drawings of Hejduk, Tschumi, Peter Cook, Hadid and others. We also find two beautifully crafted wooden boxes with dozens and dozens of vintage postcards. They are mostly late-nineteenth-century and early-twentieth-century postcards of North America depicting slaughterhouses, grain elevators, canals, highways and other imagery associated with industrial progress. While these images are in the box, the walls are reserved for the artistic renderings, suggesting the primacy of formal elegance in Boyarsky's AA. In addition to drawings and postcards, Boyarsky also collected china, rugs, cigars, early aerial photographs and, most importantly, books. A passionate publisher at the AA, he was also an ardent book collector at home. His library is a shrine to a bibliophile's passion; it is filled with monographs and anthologies – many in precious first editions. Hejduk observed that he 'will always remember the way he [Boyarsky] held them gently and with deep reverence [as] something sacred and immortal'.[19] This reverence for books may have been an expression of Boyarsky's own diasporic condition, in which the text operates as a portable homeland.[20] In Boyarsky's AA, 'the People of the Book' were 'Architects of Books' – 'friends' who stopped by to talk, eat and make architecture through writing, drawing and publishing.

Doorways, Books and Encounters: Alvin Boyarsky's Library, 64 Oakley Square, London. Photograph: Igor Marjanovic (2004).

Conclusion

Boyarsky reflects the romantic myth of a great modern educator: an international father figure often called just 'Alvin', like 'Mies' or 'Corb' before him. He was a powerful chairman, a 'dangerous personality' even, as David Dunster has phrased it.[21] Although he decided which potential 'visitors' would be allowed into his houses, at the same time, he opened his 'salons' and 'kitchens' to those *others* who historically have not had access to such 'clubs', such as foreigners and women.[22] His efforts to open up the AA to the working class were less successful. It was a hard fact dictated by the AA's dependence on tuition income. Boyarsky resisted 'professionalisation', accreditation, licensing and other forms of governmental or professional control. He operated the AA independently, both financially and ideologically. In the process, he 'withdrew' to the salons of the AA and his own house where he found a physical and figurative escape from the 'boredom' of contemporary architectural practices. No professional practice courses were taught at the AA and no 'professional' drawings were to be found on any of its walls.

Julienne Hanson has defined a house as 'a domain of knowledge [...] a certain ordering of boundaries, which together constitute a social interface between inhabitants and visitors'.[23] In Boyarsky's case, his home was fully permeable and he made himself at home everywhere. He provided a 'homey' environment for foreigners, domesticating the AA into a space of transit for its 'stars' as they moved to new destinations. He and his family lived a diasporic life, allowing the AA to enter their domestic space. This model of living became the cultural fabric of the school itself. Since they did not have any studios, the students at the AA had to work at home, allowing the AA to enter their homes as well. It must be acknowledged that, while this worked well for the wealthy students, it was more problematic for those living in crowded working-class apartments.

Peter Galison and Caroline Jones remind us that, in an age of diaspora and dispersed production, the work of art becomes 'meaningful only in the dispersed spaces of print and verbal exchange, rather than harkening back to a privileged centre, an isolated studio, or a genial subject'.[24] Boyarsky's AA was not a centre, but a node in an international network. It was a place of exchange filled with chatty people, food, drinks, visionary drawings and texts – all widely publicized through AA Publications. Through its printed media, the AA did not make built architecture; it made an exchange value of architecture. It branded itself through an international exchange of books, projecting AA images and creating a new market for its celebrities. Eventually, this led to the transformation of AA notables from 'theorists' and 'paper architects' to designers who built. The possibility that institutional change can lead to the transformation of practice suggests that broader social and economic change is achievable. This is where Boyarsky's criticism becomes operational, establishing the importance of his work for the contemporary architectural education and practice.

Notes

1   Boyarsky defended his Master's dissertation on *Camillo Sitte* under Colin Rowe's supervision.
2   This group also included John Hejduk, Bernhard Hoesli, Robert Slutzky, John Shaw, Werner Seligmann and others, all of whom were associated with the University of Texas in the 1950s.
3   'Ambience and Alchemy: Alvin Boyarsky Interviewed', *The Architectural Review*, 174, 1040, October 1983, p. 27.
4   From the taped conversation between Alvin Boyarsky and Bill Mount in 1980. Transcript courtesy of the Alvin Boyarsky Memorial Trust, London, UK.

5   Boyarsky purchased the house from architectural historian Robin Middleton in the early 1970s.

6   Nigel Rapport and Andrew Dawson, *Migrants of Identity: Perceptions of Home in a World of Movement*, Oxford: Berg, 1998, p. 9.

7   'Ambience and Alchemy: Alvin Boyarsky Interviewed', p. 29.

8   Kenneth Frampton, condolence letter to Boyarsky family, 10 August 1990.

9   'The Go-Between: Alvin Boyarsky by Alvin Boyarsky', an interview with Alvin Boyarsky by Bill Mount, 1980, not paginated; edited and unpublished transcript, courtesy of the Alvin Boyarsky Memorial Trust.

10   Rick Mather and Alvin Boyarsky first intersected at the University of Oregon, where Mather studied under Boyarsky.

11   'Interior Design: Remodeling the AA interiors', *The Architectural Review*, 174, 1040, October 1983, p. 76.

12   Stewart Brand, *How Buildings Learn,* New York: Penguin Books, 1994, p. 24.

13   Robin Evans, 'Figures, Doors and Passages', in Robin Evans, *Translations from Drawing to Building and Other Essays*, London: Architectural Association Publications, 1997, p. 90. For discussion of how people connect with each other and how spaces enable or disable such connectivity, see Jamie Horwitz, 'Fabricating Pluralism', in Sara Caples and Everardo Jefferson (eds), *The New Mix: Culturally Dynamic Architecture,* a special issue of *Architectural Design,* 75, 5, September/October 2005, pp. 24–31.

14   The Architectural Association has had many different homes before settling down at its current location at 36 Bedford Square: Lyon's Inn Hall (1847–1859), 9 Conduit Street (1859–1891), 56 Great Marlborough Street (1891–1903), 18 Tufton Street (1903–1916), 34–36 Bedford Square (1917–present) and Mount House, Hadley (1939–1945). For more information about the AA's history before 1947, see John Summerson, *Architectural Association: 1847–1947*, London: Pleiades Books Limited, 1947.

15   'Ambience and Alchemy: Alvin Boyarsky Interviewed', p. 29.

16   Jack Naughton, 'Alvin Boyarsky at the Circle', 23 April 1992, p. 11; unpublished essay, courtesy of the Alvin Boyarsky Memorial Trust.

17   Peter Galison and Caroline Jones, 'Factory, Laboratory, Studio: Dispersing Sites of Production', in Peter Galison and Emily Thompson (eds), *The Architecture of Science*, Cambridge: MIT Press, 1999, p. 498.

18   Ibid.

19   John Hejduk, 'A Sense of Spirit', *AA Files*, 20, Autumn 1990, p. 4.

20   For a discussion of Jewish diaspora and its 'mobile homeland', see George Steiner, 'Our Homeland, the Text', *Salmagundi: a Quarterly of the Humanities and Social Sciences,* 66, Skidmore College, Winter 1985, p. 5. Karen Bermann makes an analogy between Ann Frank's house and her diary, where both are sites of refuge, physical and literary. See Karen Bermann, 'The House Behind', in Jennifer Bloomer editor for a special issue of *ANY*, 4, January/February 1994, pp. 16–21.

21   See David Dunster's essay, 'Boyarsky and the AA, Some Thoughts on the London Scene of the 60s and 70s', in Paul Davies and Torsten Schmiedeknecht (eds), *An Architect's Guide to Fame*, Oxford: Architectural Press, 2005, pp. 33–47.

22   In her essay 'Curriculum Vitae' Katerina Rüedi Ray discusses her cultural capital based on her qualifications and their representation through her resume. When talking about her education at the AA in the 1980s, she says that she 'experienced no gender or race discrimination there; the majority of her friends were not British'. See Katerina Rüedi, 'Curriculum Vitae: the Architect's Cultural Capital: Educational Practices and Financial Investments', in Jonathan Hill (ed.), *Occupying Architecture: Between the Architect and the User*, London: Routledge, 1998, p. 35.

23   Julienne Hanson, *Decoding Homes and Houses*, Cambridge: Cambridge University Press, 1998, p. 6.

24   Galison and Jones, 'Factory, Laboratory, Studio', p. 530.

Out of the Salon

With Natalie Barney towards a critically queer architecture[1]

Katarina Bonnevier

In the brief for 'Criticism by Design' we were asked: 'can a design, whether drawn or built, question existing conditions and propose alternatives?' Through interpretation of architecture from a critically queer position, I would like to reply with an affirmative: 'yes.'

Architecture reflects power relations, contributes to categorisations and subordinations of gender and sexuality; simultaneously, the cultural production that surrounds us is not as straight as heteronormativity makes it look. I will be moving within the scene of the Salon to raise questions of opposition and transgression of normative orders.[2]

The literary Salon of Café Copacabana

Inspired by Natalie Barney's famous Salon in Paris of the 1920s the literary Salon at the Copacabana now starts its third season. Every Saturday of the month we present historic and topical cultural and queer feminist themes. At each Salon Copacabana offers a menu composed exclusively for the night.

(From the flyer of the literary Salon at Café Copacabana, autumn 2004; my translation)

Between 2003 and 2004, four seasons of literary Salons were staged at Café Copacabana on Hornstulls strand in Stockholm. They closed for one hour to wipe the floor and prepare for the night. There was always a long line of women who waited in the early dusk for the door to open. For each Salon there was an invited guest and a theme, Lisbeth Stenberg talked about 'Selma Lagerlöf and her women', Eva Borgström presented 'Kristina – the king of all queens' and one night was called 'Suzanne Osten in dialogue with Tiina Rosenberg'. Through the large windows, the bouncing light of a space full of people spread to the street outside. Passers-by spec-

Katarina Bonnevier, 'Prototypical Enactment: Out of the Salon' (2004), Stockholm, Sweden. Photograph: Marie Carlsson (2004).

ulated on what was taking place. My sister Malin and I have often talked about the events as living utopias.

The Café Copacabana is situated close to the water on the western-most part of the south island of Stockholm. On the other side of the sound you can see the industries, the piers and the conference centre of Gröndal. The Café Copacabana, on the street level of a block of apartment buildings, has two shop front windows and, in between the windows, a glazed entrance door. At night, they're nowadays shielded by a metal jalousie.

A Salon is a material container but also an event. In *Feminism and Theatre* Sue-Ellen Case calls the Salon a personal theatre; a place where women shape public discussions.[3] Natalie Barney's Salon of the 1920s was important in the staging of a lesbian lifestyle, which counteracted the invisibility of lesbians in everyday life. Her

Katarina Bonnevier – continued

Katarina Bonnevier – continued

Salon was extravagantly performed through masquerading, cross-dressing and theatrical encounters, it was a disguise that hid, disclosed and even bent reality simultaneously.[4] Barney went beyond creating a scene within Paris; she created another Paris.[5] Sally Munt writes in 'The Lesbian *Flâneur*': 'Lesbian identity is constructed in the temporal and linguistic mobilisation of space.'[6] The individual actor is important but nothing without the collective. And they, we, who perform this scene, are always on the move in, or around the corners of, architecture.

The living room of a private house is often called the salon, but the Salon as an event can exist beyond that room. The Salon is architecture – matter and event. In the case of Café Copacabana the container is not a salon, but a café, until the Salon takes place here. This is what is interesting from an architectural point of view; that an event can transform matter into a Salon. Architecture appears in the event, or the act,

Katarina Bonnevier – continued

Katarina Bonnevier – continued

and generates meaning, showing that architecture plays a part in performativity. The architecture of the literary Salon is on the move in the actions of the social scene. The Salon of matter, 'the theatre Salon', props and backdrops, and the enactments – dialogues, flirts, readings, portrayals, *tableaux vivants* – are woven together by the participants' engagement at a particular moment.

The Salon is a model that can show how the built environment plays a role in the construction of gender and sexuality. This, I think, is key to understanding and creating architecture other/wise, to make it a less-determined, suppler and more apt transformation.

Katarina Bonnevier – continued

Jalousie/jealousy

On Friday 12 November 2004, a firebomb was thrown through the window of the Café Copacabana. The entire place was destroyed. The kitchen melted and smoke entered everywhere. All the work invested in the place and the careful atmosphere that had been created were brutally ruined. Two young men, around 20 years old, were arrested. They had severe burn injuries; one boy's face was completely damaged.

The Café Copacabana had been vandalised twice before. During a period when the threat was heavy, volunteers of AFA (Anti-Fascist Action) patrolled the area. At a literary Salon held at Café Copacabana, the participants were told to watch out for each other and not walk home alone.

Why has Café Copacabana become a target? Café Copacabana has never been promoted as 'homogay'. Their standard advertisement asks the question: 'Who will make the coffee the day after the revolution?'

What makes Café Copacabana so provoking is its overwhelming boundless-ness. It has acted as a queer scene, connected with political feminist activism, which has not prevented the Café Copacabana from also being an everyday hangout. Like a public living room, it is a place of dissonance for 'people like us'. The Café Copacabana is a symbol of a culture that won't stay in place; it refuses binary categories such as 'heterosexual' or 'homosexual', and as such it is part of a 'threatening' movement that challenges the norms of gender and sexuality.

On Monday 29 November 2004, there was a support gala for Café Copaca-bana, to raise money to install a jalousie of metal. 'Jalousie' is a shutter made of angled slats but the term also refers to the feeling of jealousy. Through an etymologi-cal connection, jalousie can be thought of as something that enviously protects against unwanted gazes. More than 700 people joined the party. We were asked to 'Keep the fire burnin' – homogay heterogay unite!'

Two months later, the place re-opened. At first glance it looked like nothing had happened. But the main visible influence of the fire is the metal jalousie, which is pulled down every night after closing time.[7] Hard work had made the destruction dis-appear. Everything was back, the light, the people, the large windows; it felt like they had made a fold in time; a refusal to be ruled by hatred. In a little niche above the toilet door is a memento of the fire; a feminine couple of partly melted miniature figures.

Notes

1 This piece – text and portraits – comes out of a PhD project called *Behind Straight Curtains*, where the Salon acts as a model for a critical practice. The portraits, six out of thirty-four, were created at a 'prototypical enactment' on 17 November 2004, where the model of the Salon, based on the literary Salon of Natalie Barney, was explored in the disguise of an academic seminar. I wish to thank Katja Grillner and Marie Carlsson for their critical involvement.

2 Film and mass culture theorist Alexander Doty uses the terms 'queer' and 'queer-

ness' as 'a range of nonstraight expression in, or in response to, mass culture. This range includes specifically gay, lesbian, and bisexual expressions; but it also includes all other potential (and potentially unclassifiable) nonstraight positions' (Alexander Doty, *Making Things Perfectly Queer: Interpreting Mass Culture*, Minneapolis: University of Minnesota Press, 1997, p. xvi).

3   Sue-Ellen Case, *Feminism and Theatre*, London: Macmillan, 1988, pp. 46–61.

4   Natalie Barney's Salon took place at 20 Rue Jacob, in Paris, on Friday evenings from 4 pm to 8 pm almost every season from October 1909 to 1968 (Jean Chalon, *Chère Natalie Barney*, Paris: Flammarion, 1992). An important guest from an architectural point of view was architect Eileen Gray; see Katarina Bonnevier, 'A Queer Analysis of Eileen Gray's E.1027', Hilde Heyen and Gulsum Baydar (eds), *Negotiating Domesticity: Spatial Productions of Gender in Modern Architecture*, London and New York: Routledge, 2005, pp. 162–80.

5   A particularly revealing article on the impact of Barney's Salon is Amy Wells-Lynn, 'The Intertextual, Sexually-Coded Rue Jacob: a Geocritical Approach to Djuna Barnes, Natalie Barney, and Radclyffe Hall', *South Central Review*, 22, 3, 2005, pp. 78–112.

6   Sally Munt, 'The Lesbian Flâneur', in David Bell and Gill Valentine (eds), *Mapping Desire: Geographies of Sexualities*, London and New York: Routledge, 1995, p. 125.

7   The Café might not be able to keep the jalousie since it was installed without building permission.

Writing About Things and the Doing of Them

Ben Nicholson

Preface

Here is an extract from an imaginary story about the future of a community in rural America. Part fact and mostly fiction, it suggests a plan for reawakening a small town with a large history, in a way that does not fall into the trap of providing vinyl houses and a brand new shopping mall. The narrative is annotated by plans for landscapes and architectural solutions that are driven by ethical principles, arbitrated by the potency of good design. The full text, of which this is an eighth part, was published by Archeworks in 2006,[1] and included a withering attack by the editor on the impotence of propositional writing. Six months have past, and there is a sign of movement, albeit very small. Read on.

Dreaming

The Midwest is littered with the spent shells of utopia. Wherever one looks across the prairie, someone had a dream greater than themselves. Hope against hope, the vision starts, and if its echo lasts long enough in the community's imagination, something remarkable happens. Utopians believe in the betterment of humanity, and forge a way of being that is so permeated with goodwill towards fellow men that the societal organism, the very concept of the city itself, becomes an x–y–z dimensional construct of ethical wherewithal.

Although hard to believe, horses and buggies still ply the dusty roads of Ohio, laden with good sense and family values. In Illinois, Albion was founded in 1818, and the Mormons built Nauvoo in 1839 and, fast-forwarding a little, Illinois architects have successfully carved out visions of utopia, expanding designs conjured up in the drafting studio. Frank Lloyd Wright flees the metropolis of Chicago to set up an Arts and Crafts haven at Taliesin; Mies Van Der Rohe leaves Germany to establish a Modernist utopia in Chicago's South Side, and Archeworks establishes a Can-Do-Topia, a place where ideals are brought to action. These institutions are all committed to their particular vision of built communal life, each having an ethos that serves the city's inner gyroscope, between good and bad, right and wrong and fair and unfair.

To recite names like Chautauqua, Penland, Sundance, Aspen, Cranbrook, Kendall, Interlaken, Brevard and Arrowmont is to murmur a litany of places that at one time or another have been gold standards of otherness. They understood art to be the medium in which the spirit is lived out in practice, they provide safe harbour for creative energy and most still work to bring the poetry out of anonymous souls. In these places, living was never pulled from the pages of a textbook but became a collective desire to pass on a gift in which a full, thoughtful life becomes the added value of being a citizen. Scores of utopian settlements can be added to the above list, almost all of which are now in a state of touristic freeze. Both art colonies and utopian towns are familiar to us, and both represent the place where the imagination longs to be.

Somewhere in North America, someplace needs to be cultivated where all the sensibilities of living can come together in close geographic proximity, in high-focus and articulate relief, so that the quality of life to which we aspire can be seen all the more readily. The dot-on-the-map known as New Harmony, Indiana, can be such a place, if only because it has been thrice moulded as a utopia over 200 years. Somehow it has bucked the touristic model, and continues to be a domain of visionaries bent on cultivating the erotic of the imagination at the intersection of opportunity and circumstance. Here, fiscal capital is exchanged for cultural capital and cultural capital is in league with a capital of the spirit; each trade conducted to nurture a life of thoughtfulness rather than consumption.

In a world where the suburban norm is to wear sweaters in summer and shorts in winter, it seems that all that is left of culture is to do the opposite of what comes naturally. Now is the moment to stand up for something that will necessarily seem out of time, and show that what we consider unproblematic *is* now a problem.[2] A town already used to utopian visions could bear the burden of this collective task, and take the spirit to a place where it is not used to going. One more time, we go to the well and draw up a new heterotopia: its imaginary crafting having an equal responsibility towards ethical civility, as does the untidy actuation of real-time town-life.

And being grounded

A city that has living evidence of its first ground plan gives comfort to the notion of urbanity. A myth of origin, that anchors its layers of history, provides a quality of civic wherewithal that is situated somewhere between the euphoria of nostalgia and an untainted bloodline. The opposite of the slow aging process of a ripening city is utopia: it fast-forwards the emotive loyalties of urbanity, and establishes the whole kit-and-caboodle of an instant city with a bravado that leaves one wondering if you have just been cheated.

Yet, visions of the ideal place have encouraged hope in the worst of times. For cities do not need to be actual to be useful: witness Jerusalem, which touches more people in the imagination than it does on the ground. The New Jerusalem, carefully recorded in the Book of Revelations, is an imaginary city of divine proportions and has inspired generations of dreamers to coax that vision down to Earth.

Idealised cities exist in every culture: Greece had both Atlantis and Troy. Theseus, best known for slaying Minators and nubile hearts, established the city of Athens as a perfect metropolis of good government. It is the mother-of-all-cities in the Western mindset, albeit a situated *Topia* rather than a *Utopia*, a no-place. Less known is his method of building the democratic city, in which he disposed of his adversaries and kept himself as the high judge.[3] Thereafter the pattern is set: someone with the oats hacks out a space in some unwilling virgin territory, and imparts a vision of how things ought to be.

Turning the clock forward to 1814, German Rappites built the town of Harmonie on the banks of the Wabash in Southern Indiana, a stone's throw from Illinois across the river. Here, a finely tuned Utopia was run with the efficiency of a Swabian Mercedes: its inhabitants prepared themselves on Earth to live a life in harmony, primed for the moment when the Chosen are called to heaven in an instant of ecstatic Revelation. The inhabitants of Harmonie were ready for Rapture, but God was not. George Rapp became edgy with waiting, cashed out and sold up to a Welshman called Robert Owen in 1825.

Owen was a tough industrialist who bought New Lanark, Scotland, to consolidate his cotton-spinning empire at the beginning of nineteenth-century Regency Britain. A savvy self-educated businessman with the gift of the gab, he realised that ethically run cotton mills, where human capital and cash capital hold equal sway, would dissolve inequalities and at the same time line his pockets. By providing a dynamic education, shorter working hours and fewer kiddies getting their fingers stuck in the spindles, the new managerial ethic would be good for everybody. Soon the work practice was the envy of the nation, and the system was printed and proselytised to every willing ear, from ladies' sewing circles to the inner halls of government the world over.[4] He was to meet his match in politicians, who would not turn his vision into law, despite Owen's unflagging attempts.

As is inevitable in such circumstances, a clean slate in the middle of nowhere becomes the beckoning magnet for visions that no one is willing to adopt in the real world. Owen bought the town of Harmonie from Rapp and renamed it New Harmony, a place where men and women would live equally according to his secular epistles, in the full spectrum of three-dimensional town-life. He turned the Rappite Church into an Athenaeum, where education and the pursuit of knowledge were the guiding forces of civic life. It lasted all but a year or two, but not for want of trying. The old ways of Owen, that speculated on how creature human beings could be pointed in the right direction for the benefit of the corporation, rubbed up against his new desire to determine how to work together to maximise collective well-being.

His intentions were good and left a remarkable legacy. The town of no more than 1000 inhabitants attracted a Boatload of Knowledge filled with hugely inventive educators, scientists and artists, and spawned nine Owenite Communities over the next 20 years. These individuals went on to advocate such venerable American institutions as the Smithsonian, the United States Geological Survey, the Public Library system and equal voting rights (albeit for whites only). Even its problematic rigidity inspired personalities such as Josiah Warren, who not only patented the continuous sheet printing press that enabled the mass production of newspapers, but also published a text extolling a very different way to form the ideal society.[5] His was a system of 'un-government' in which every man operates for himself with the expectation of practising a wholly ethical code. Just as New Harmony is known as the Cradle for Socialism, it is also the birthplace of the Sovereignty of the Individual, otherwise known as Political Anarchy.

In the 1940s, the vision of human well-being was realigned once more in New Harmony with the presence of Kenneth Owen and his wife Jane Blaffer Owen. Today, 65 years later, Jane Owen works tirelessly to share her vision that both celebrates its fruits and makes time to reside in the quiet of contemplation. Through a diligent life of assembling hauntingly beautiful buildings and garden-scapes, the ethereal spirit and the earthy landscape are brought into each other's realm.

New Harmony is unique in that it is a place where the hiccups of past visions are respected for what they are. Residents and visitors are excused impossible standards of self-righteousness, and instead witness a way of life that considers options to the high-on-the-hog trappings of rank consumerism. Money does flow down the Wabash River into town, but not towards fostering the cult of stuff. Projects have been made and ideas nurtured with the conviction that there has to be some place in the American landscape that considers the work-of-art and the art-of-work to be a biological need that can release the spirit.

But what if it dissolves, like every other utopia seems to have done, and the visions are kept aloft with a keg of imported gold? Does it matter? Surely there is no higher calling than the expenditure of capital pointing towards the unlocking of the human spirit. At a point in history when mechanised production has the opportunity to emancipate essential need, what better way to acknowledge the gift of being on the Earth than to lay down something that is intrinsically unknowable, and that has no practical or useful purpose beyond the acknowledgement of collective well-being?

Some places on Earth are destined to live not only for themselves, but also for the shared imagination of those beyond the immediate confines of that location. Whether it likes it or not (as if it could do much about it) the scratch-on-Earth known as New Harmony is such a place. The pineal gland senses its quality, but our twenty-first-century technologies, set against the dying gasp of the Enlightenment, have not yet found the words to adequately convey the emotion of the place successfully. Language is crafted to articulate desire, but what kind of language needs to be developed to communicate within towns like this? Are words enough? A new hyperlanguage could be developed to engage the full complement of the body's receptors, to trip the entirety of civic experience as lived through the corpus. Words need to reattach themselves to the daily computational goings-on-of-life, words like 'scratching', 'combing', 'padding', 'chewing' and 'brushing one's hand over a head of petals'. The computer, the body and the city come together to make a full and untried language, where all the sensibilities of living are attached in close geographic proximity, in high-focus and articulate relief, so that the quality of life to which we aspire can be shared all the more readily with others.

Prose poetry has an equal responsibility towards good civic conjunction, as does the untidy actuation of real-life town-life. Topia, utopia, heterotopia and dystopia all started with some sort of dream, and without that dream nothing real is likely to happen. It is the stuff of history books to determine what worked and did not work; what got remembered and what deserved to be forgotten. Somewhere between dreaming and being grounded lies a state of happiness: it is up to us to go and find it.

Nature, violence and hubris

In the last 200 years, New Harmony has witnessed all that Mother Nature can muster when she has a very bad-hair day. In 1811 it was near the epicentre of a New Madrid earthquake that reversed the direction of the Mississippi and set church bells ringing in Boston. In 1925, a monster force-five tornado, packing winds of 300 mph, cut a mile-wide swath through the neighbouring hamlet of Griffin, wiping the community clean off the Earth.[6] Only this month, a copycat force-three tornado tore a path through Evansville, a mere 30 miles away. In four out of seven years, the Wabash River rises 20 feet and licks the toes of the town; it is a regular host to the Army Corps of Engineers with their trailers full of woven sandbags. The force of the Wabash is also felt in the horizontal axis: each year its buxom meanders run like a chainsaw through the fertile meadows around town. The river has its eyes on the whole town, ready to carve an ox bow lake down Main Street whenever our dear, somnambulant Mother Nature so desires. God forbid that all three events happen simultaneously; the town would then be at the epicentre of a rushing, whistling, shaking thing of diabolic proportions, a perfect, perfect, perfect storm!

Also lurking beneath the surface of the town's soil is a ley line, a pulse of magnetic energy that travels from Russia to the Bermuda Triangle. Dowsers have a field day with their twitchy sticks; their trip to New Harmony is a veritable homecoming. To add to its intensity, the United States Government is warning that the dreaded bird flu may well travel down our migrational flyways. New Harmony is perched upon the Wabash River Basin flyway, as well as being a few miles from another bird route running down the Ohio River. Washington's hawks of paranoia tell us disease will be with us soon.

For too long, townies have considered themselves to have risen above such irritants as weather and disease, regarding nature as little more than a misbehaving leaf blower. Instead of being in a state of perpetual denial over the force of nature, what would it be to go towards it, to embrace its power and bathe amongst its winds?

If we are happy to go to Great America fairgrounds and sit in a silly Jules Verne machine that burrows towards the centre of the earth, why not elect to make a building or two that are comfortable with being shaken by quakes, blown by the wind and stirred by the eddies of the Wabash? Big Weather forces us to understand our smallness in the order of things, and to reappraise our dealings with nature might encourage us to dump our extreme climbing gear and just start to live a little, and learn to know our place.

The monster quakes, devastating floods and apocalyptic tornadoes are the symptoms of Earth's composite mix of earth, water and air: all that is missing from the natural quadrivium is the element of fire, not something that anyone would want to introduce in quantity, but it is always warming to see from afar. If the DIA Art Foundation can deliberately build a lightning field of metal spikes a kilometre square,[7] what would it be to turn a copper rod into a slender, 100-foot spike, sharpened at the tip to beckon Zeus's crooked finger down from the sky? When the rain drops start and the sky turns a putrid mix of magenta and fetid yellow, a blinding flash announces an ear-splitting crack, leaving a faint perfume of spent ozone hanging on the air: it is Nature's calling card. And if the lightning will not come on its own accord, there is always the bonfire, one of the few things that came to Earth through the back door without the permission of the gods. An annual bonfire is a thrilling, purging thing onto which all manner of yesterdays can be placed with gay abandon, knowing that there is no power on Earth greater than this, for bringing all to naught.

Energy

With such potent fuels available today, it is hard to get a concept of what they are capable of in relationship to what *we* are capable of. It would help to have a squirrel cage fitted out with a human being hooked up to a dynamo and a toaster, just to see how many minutes on the treadmill it would take to toast a bagel. You would think that because motors are rated in horsepower, it would clarify what energy means, but because we have stopped riding horses it is hard to understand the relativity of that equation. You need a paddock of 115 horses to get a grip on knowing why your Honda Civic can hum along at 90 mph day in, day out, and another 340 horses to restrain a Hummer from bounding out over the virgin landscape, but these equations are not believable and they don't really help us to get a feel for the beauty of energy.

When opening up a glossy magazine and reading about British Petroleum (BP) and its drive to introduce itself as being *Beyond Petroleum*, don't you wonder what exactly are they getting at? Do the green and yellow florets heralding clean energy fool anybody? Driving around the environs of New Harmony, you see oil crickets pumping away in stains of oil-soaked earth in the middle of the fields. A little further beyond are extensive coal fields. The terrain around this locale dwells on sucking petroleum, hacking coal and chopping wood; the imagination gets taxed when going much beyond a gallon of gas and a cord of logs for the winter fire.

On Church Street, the main east–west axis, there are a couple of gas stations selling the usual snack paraphernalia associated with the transitory life of the automobile. If BP was serious about going *Beyond Petroleum*, what would it take for them to play out their guarded vision in a town that has been involved with social and cultural experimentation since it was founded? If a major petroleum corporation, such as BP or Exxon, fostered a real commitment to cleaning up the gummy oil fields around the township, it would be a red-letter day. Nice shiny equipment, maintained like a Swiss milking parlour, would draw the oil out of the ground without spilling a drop onto the surrounding earth. New Harmony's oil fields would then become the national standard of good oil manners, visitors would come to see the model of decent practice, a short bicycle ride away from the centre of town.

Back at the imaginary BP gas station, a big 1000-gallon cauldron of crude, with its lip cut at the level of a little kid's nose, sits in a low hunched building. The cauldron is carved out of a single block of stone, and the oil oozes through its Permian walls, filling the room with the diabolic perfume of the ground below. In here, every man, woman and child can dip their pinkie into the elixir, to know first hand what 'crude' really means. A polished brass dipper hangs nearby, and at the appointed hour the scoop is sunk into the oil and ladles out a stream of the precious fluid into a bowl, carved out of a block of coal. The bowl is taken out into the open and all of it burned in some unholy moment, just to know the red-hot value of the sticky stuff and give an opportunity to allay our fears.

To the south-east of town is a line of wooded hills rising to 500 feet, and beneath the ridge, an oil pipeline goes to and from somewhere. The long ridge of hills would be an ideal site to establish a farm of wind turbines, creating the power for the town to no longer depend on fossil fuels. The quiet pulsating voltage would make turning on a light bulb a pleasure, knowing that all is well, ecologically speaking. The resident could actually see the relationship of wind power to light bulbs, and the BP station would have a big meter in the forecourt, showing the wattage harvested and the wattage consumed. A smile of satisfaction would indicate the difference.

Be forewarned that wind turbines are prime candidates in the latest NIMBY (Not In My Back Yard) wars: there are complaints of the relentlessness of their monotonous cycle to the eye, the haunting off-key lament that whines in the sweet night breeze, and the enormous blades cutting up flights of migrating geese as if they were passing through a pastrami slicer. All of the above is paranoid NIMBY speak, little more than the modern version of a fish wife's tale. Living in paradise does have responsibilities, and a line of warbling turbines may be the cross it has to bear. The Dutch turned their creaky old windmills into a rural tourist industry, so public trips up the towers to see exactly what goes on would be sensible: the visit would be a rich component of education within a town committed to its environs being a living classroom.

And sunshine is abundant in New Harmony; it would be a good candidate for solar power, a fitting response to that petal burst of yellow–green energy atop the BP mast. Encouraging people to install panels that could collectively *add* to the electric grid rather than *take* from the grid would be a significant move towards fostering a culture of true individualism rather that succumb to a centralised power structure.

Update

There is nothing more nerve wracking, for a one-man-band writer, than to receive an envelope with the address of a law firm running across its top. Upon opening the letter, I found it was an invitation to join a committee in New Harmony to determine the viability of a turbine to take the town off the grid. After studying the situation, the project was cancelled due to insufficient winds.

Pharmaceutical farm

Straight as an arrow, Church Street is the main entrance from the east. It is an untidy struggle between upright clapboard houses and downright messy businesses: a real-life swirl of mini-storage, old farmsteads, cheap gas stations, a nursing home and bright new McMansions that stretch their lots to capacity. It is an ultra-light industrial corridor with half a conscience; some outfits play the game of Neat and Tidy and others deliberately flaunt it. It portrays the nitty-gritty outskirts of a small mid-western town to a tee; an unholy, unnecessary mess, diametrically opposed to the eye-candy we would expect from such a place.

Every square inch of an urban landscape has the capacity to be cared for. My favourite garden in Chicago is outside a 12-flat apartment block, home to Romanian families from the Old Country. At the front door to the apartment block is a skinny concrete patio with a wooden bench and a scattering of well tended pot-plants. Over the years, the concrete slab has settled in relation to the concrete walkway out front, and a half-inch crack has formed between the two rafts of cement. Each year a resident fills the crack with soil and sows a line of neatly spaced seeds, which then blossom into Chicago's thinnest garden of Impatience. The worst gardening conditions have been turned into the most cared for spot in the concrete jungle: it just takes time, patience and a packet of seeds.

Returning to Church Street, a long, low retirement home stands 100 yards back from the road. Out front, a nondescript swath of grass is mown short and sports a lonely advertisement for the place. The typology of this building is old and noble; long, low, single-storey almshouses can be found in Abingdon, England, harking back to 1446. The difference between the two is that the medieval almshouses have a magnificent walled garden attached to them, in which the resident old-age pensioners can still sit and take in the sun. The gardens were originally physic gardens, full of herbs and flowers, which supplied the raw materials for the monastery apothecary.

Indianapolis is home to one of the largest drug companies in the world: Eli Lilly. What would it take for a business such as this to recreate an apothecary garden, in order to have some place where the relationship between plants and well-being could be made explicit? Some 4000 years ago, Mesopotamian doctors prepared a formula from date pits to be given for a bad headache; the concoction had the same ingredients as aspirin. By demonstrating the relationship of botany to medicine, the opacity of the drug industry might be tempered somewhat by associating the plant which salves the pain. The resident pensioners would also become beneficiaries, and could spend a couple of hours weeding the beds or laying out seedlings for the next year's harvests, as well as chat with visitors.

In nearby fields there is the opportunity to grow rows of plants that could be used in pharmaceuticals, farmed at a different scale to the physic garden, but no less important to the well-being of the town's hinterland, a place that could portray the complex interconnection of body and medicine.

Update

Upon being asked to comment on the kind of plants to grow in such a garden, the residents of the nursing home produced their own list running to 30 flowers and vegetables native to a farmer's garden, such as corn, okra, tomatoes, zinnias and daffs. The project adjusted its direction, but not the intent of the writing. Half-a-year later, with vigorous input from Illinois Institute of Technology and School of the Art Institute Chicago students, the Garden Club of New Harmony and the Enabling Garden of The Chicago Botanic Garden, the story has morphed into a plan, funding and action for a winter building programme to make a low-tech-no-design solution to bring plants back into the hands of farmer families bound in wheelchairs. It opens this summer, 2007.

Endnote

To write about a vision for a small town and then go and live in it, lock, stock and barrel, is to call one's own bluff. Hanging a shingle on a door with the name of a professional business written in red paint is one way out, but waiting for a knock on the door can be time-consuming. Another way of work is to invent the whole procedure and then work towards its implementation: in that way there will be fewer impediments between raw thought and raw action – maybe.

Notes

1   Ben Nicholson, *The Archeworks Papers*, 2006, 1, 3, edited by Stanley Tigerman, Chicago: Archeworks, 2006.
2   Thanks to Dr Peg Birmingham for forming these words.
3   Plutarch, *Parallel Lives*, 24.1, edited and translated by Bernadotte Perrin, Cambridge, MA: Harvard University Press, 1912.
4   Robert Owen, *A New View Of Society* [1813], Harmondsworth: Penguin, 1991.
5   Josiah Warren, *Manifesto* [1841], Berkeley Heights: Oriole Press, 1990.
6   Akin Wallace, *The Forgotten Storm: the Great Tri-State Tornado of 1925*, Guilford: Lyons Press, 2002, p. 111.
7   Walter De Maria, *The Lightning Field*, 1977, Quemado, New Mexico.

Quilting Jakarta

Stephen Cairns

The Renaissance practice of *disegno*, to which contemporary architectural design practice remains indebted, is defined as an intellectualising form of drawing. *Disegno* teaches architects, as Vasari put it, to hold that which 'has been imagined in the intellect and fabricated in the *idea*'.[1] It is a form of tactile thinking calculated to enable architects to simultaneously fabricate and make sense of the world. What, then, are the fortunes of this robust practice today? How might it operate in the flux and fluidity of contemporary urban life?

One approach to these questions would be to elaborate the themes of thinking, fabrication and drawing. In Lacanian psychoanalytic theory, the phrase 'quilting point'[2] describes one of the mechanisms by which we make sense of the world. The quilting point identifies, in the language of Saussurean semiotics, the points at which the fluid surfaces of signifier and signified are connected. The quilting point is where 'floating signifiers' are anchored, enabling them to function as master signifiers around which wider systems of meaning might be generated. 'Everything,' Jacques Lacan suggests, 'radiates out from and is organised around this signifier, similar to these little lines of force that an upholstery button forms on the surface of material.'[3] Quilting, then, halts the slippery play of meaning that Ferdinand de Saussure diagnosed in his semiological theory and generates the stable reference points around which we can construct meaningful worlds.

The quilting mechanism operates retrospectively. Alenka Zupancic offers a useful illustration of what is meant by this: 'suppose you are on your way to the airport when your car gets a flat tyre. Because of this you miss your flight, which is lucky for you, as the plane that you should have been on crashes.'[4] The flat tyre, in this illustration, takes on its meaning retrospectively: 'If the tyre had not gone flat, you would have been dead.'[5] Looking back, it is much more than a flat tyre; it is a life saver. The flat tyre is bestowed with purpose and meaning in excess of its everyday particularity such that it seems to have 'had a purpose', 'was intended', conveying 'the message that you had not yet been destined for death'.[6] In this analysis, sense takes the future anterior form – something 'will have been' – and so must always be anticipated.

Kronologi, 'Gamel Fauzi is heading to his office…' (2003), Jakarta.

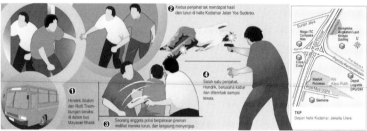

Kronologi, 'Hendrik Silalahi and Rudi Tinambungan are operating inside the bus…' (2003), Jakarta.

'*Motor kumpulan*' (2003), Jakarta.

'*Kronologi* map'
(2005), Stephen
Cairns, Edinburgh,
UK.

Kronologi, 'Tini, who
was doing
homework, was told
by Tito to do the
dishes . . . ' (2003),
Jakarta.

Kronologi, 'In the
village of
Pengarengan, Cecep
Dayat (23), seller of
the motorscooter,
was approached by a
buyer...' (2003),
Jakarta.

More recently, the concept of quilting has been productively elaborated in analyses of (ideological) meaning as it is constituted collectively.[7] Slavoj Žižek, to cite perhaps the best-known example, examines the way in which the famous Marlboro advertisement – 'the picture of the bronzed cowboy, the wide prairie plains' – comes to be quilted into the national imaginary of America.[8] The radical nature of Lacan's insight, Žižek insists, is not merely that meaning is constructed by connecting arbitrarily related signifieds and signifiers, but that, through the quilting process, an inversion takes place such that '"real" Americans start to identify themselves (in their ideological self-experience) with the image created by the Marlboro advertisement'.[9] As Žižek notes, 'America itself is experienced as "Marlboro country".'[10] Quilting points such as these serve to anchor collective cultural life within representational mediums, offering the co-ordinates by which we 'gain our bearings in a social world'.[11] This is not a simple relationship based on an unmediated engagement with the real. Quilting points enable us to insulate ourselves from the trauma of the real by propagating the illusion of fixed meanings.[12] Such illusions are, as Lacan points out, necessary for the proper functioning of the self in society.

If Lacan's quilting point concept is used to elaborate an account of sense-making in the world at large, and it is elaborated to explain the emergence of a national imaginary, then might it also be deployed in relation to more specific analytical contexts such as the city? Might it be applied to the practice of design in such contexts? Can we think of the city being quilted? In a way, Kevin Lynch[13] was calling for a kind of urban quilting in his investigation of cognitive mapping techniques in the context of rapidly expanding cities of post-war North America. This study led him to propose a notational system that privileged those visual markers – edges, nodes, paths and monuments – that he believed enabled people to orient themselves within and navigate through a city whose fabric no longer offered the stability it once seemed to have. The visual instability and fluidity that Lynch diagnosed in North American cities was, of course, quickly surpassed during the later decades of the twentieth century as the process of urbanisation intensified and became a more global phenomenon. Today, it is the mega-cities of Asia, Africa and South America that pose the most profound challenge to the question of orientation and urban sense-making. These 'other' cities, with their irregular and patchy urban fabrics, have offered up a range of emergent practices by which the co-ordinates for collective urban imaginaries are established. By way of illustration, I want to examine one such practice that takes place in the city of Jakarta.

Every evening, other than Saturday, at around 5pm, two young graphic artists arrive at the editorial offices of the *Warta Kota* (City News) newspaper in downtown Jakarta. Each collects a field report on a crime or misdemeanour that has taken place in the city that day. They log onto their computers and begin roughing out the storyboard of their daily *kronologi* (see figures on pages 216 and 217) – an 'information graphic' in the form of a cartoon strip recounting the crime of the day. Having located the scene of the crime with the aid of the Jakarta street directory, they then select an appropriate cast of characters (thieves, victims, car-jackers, suicides, muggers or con-artists etc.) and suitable urban props (cars, motorcycles, bicycles and/or buses etc.)

from the digital image library they have assembled (see figure on page 216) and begin populating their story board. The *kronologi* strips are complete in time for the printing of the first edition of the newspaper at midnight. Their work, located in its regular slot on the front page, is distributed throughout Jakarta in the early hours of dawn.

The library of characters and props that the artists draw upon can be read as a stock of floating signifiers awaiting quilting. Once they are incorporated into the *kronologi* the chaotic trauma of the crime takes on a (retrospective) coherence that makes it understandable in the public realm where it circulates as a generalised signifier of urban fear. Furthermore, when multiple *kronologi* strips are located on a map of the city (see figure on page 217), they take on the look of a unique collective urban image. This is not a cognitive map per se, nor is it the product of an architectural design practice. Yet, the popularity of the *kronologi* with the *Warta Kota* readership is a sign, perhaps, that they are beginning to constitute a set of quilting points around which Jakarta's inhabitants might compose an alternate urban imaginary. In a city that is routinely subjected to drawing and design practices that are conversant with generic principles yet barely attend to the nature of its fabric, the *Warta Kota* graphic designers have invented an in-situ drawing practice. It is a form of drawing that is highly sensitised to the very particular fluidities of that city, to the ways in which its material and semiotic fabrics interact, to the processes by which they are formed, deformed, unformed and reformed. Architectural design practice can learn from this kind of urban quilting.

Notes

1   Giorgio Vasari, cited in Carl Goldstein, *Teaching Art: Academies and Schools from Vasari to Albers*, Cambridge: Cambridge University Press, 1996, p. 14.
2   Jacques Lacan, *The Seminar of Jacques Lacan, Book 3, 1955–1956, The Psychoses*, translated by R. Grigg, London: Routledge, 1993, p. 267.
3   Lacan, *The Seminar of Jacques Lacan*, p. 268.
4   Alenka Zupancic, *Ethics of the Real: Kant, Lacan*, London: Verso, 2000, pp. 209–10.
5   Ibid.
6   Ibid.
7   Paul Eisenstein, *Holocaust Representation and the Hegelian Subject*, Albany: State University of New York Press, 2003; Ernesto Laclau, *On Populist Reason*, London: Verso, 2005; Yannis Stavrakakis, *Lacan and the Political*, London: Routledge, 1999; Slavoj Žižek, *The Sublime Object of Ideology*, London: Verso, 1989.
8   Žižek, *The Sublime Object of Ideology*, p. 96.
9   Ibid.
10   Ibid.
11   Eisenstein, *Holocaust Representation*, p. 44.
12   Ibid., p. 45
13   Kevin Lynch, *The Image of the City*, Cambridge, MA: MIT Press, 1960.

Where is the Project?

Cedric Price on architectural action

Tim Anstey

What is the nature of architectural action? On what kind of field does it operate and through what modes of authorship? The English architect Cedric Price (1934–2003) redefined some of the ground rules concerning such questions.[1] One image, a flow-chart produced by the Price office making a graphic out of the process of creating the project for the 'Fun Palace', serves to examine critical issues that are raised in his architectural production (see figure below).

Developed out of the societal and cultural context in Great Britain during the early 1960s, 'Fun Palace' was to be a building with an open programme providing entertainment to 'everyman' whose form and organisation should be steered, and altered, by that mass will.[2] The project resulted in architectural production that went on for nearly a decade. Given the interdisciplinary nature of the team involved (central figures were theatre producer Joan Littlewood and structural engineer Frank Newby), the form of this production was not limited by the classical tropes of architectural representation. As well as endless internal and official correspondence, the overall output included events, happenings, films, and the lobbying of statutory bodies. Price

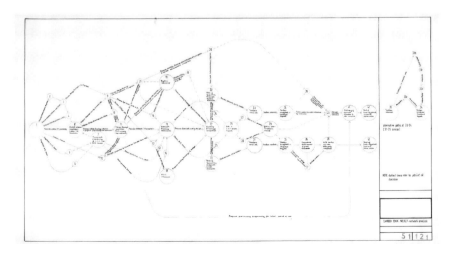

Office of Cedric Price, network analysis representing the decision-making process necessary before the construction of the Fun Palace, graphite and black ink on tracing vellum.

archived even the most transient and ephemeral elements of this production; the flow-chart pictured here is part of that archive.[3]

Given the extreme care with which this diagram is constructed, it must be taken as a telling document. It plots how different fields of institutional authority inter-sect and how procedures for decision-making in one area are conditioned by, at first sight, quite remote theatres of activity and influence; in so doing, it uncovers an almost infinite terrain surrounding acts of construction and effecting their execution (see figures below). This material sheds fascinating light therefore on the landscape of leg-islative, institutional, and contractual relationships that surround architecture. Further, the archives make clear that the 'Fun Palace' authors – the interdisciplinary team behind the project – made an effort to adjust this topography, to bend or revise rules, to lobby decision-makers, to revise categorical boundaries. In a very real sense, then, 'Fun Palace' had an importance outside the realm of its own individual construction. As a completed set of documented manoeuvres and exchanges, rather than as an unre-alised building, it revealed a new kind of ground for thinking about architecture.

Ultimately, that ground has to do with 'context', although the connection might not seem immediately apparent. From its beginnings as a term in architectural discourse, context was used to describe the physical, and often specifically historic, surroundings of a project.[4] It was a term used within an extremely object-based inter-rogation of architecture and in this sense it might have apparently little to do with Price's uncovering of the subliminal forces that condition architectural actions, forces hard to register within the traditional modes of architectural representation and obser-vation that contextualists held dear. Yet it is noteworthy that the discourse on context and Price's questioning of the nature of architectural action developed contemporane-ously, and that both see architectural projects, and by implication architectural actions, as profoundly mortgaged to the conditions that surround them.[5] In this sense they take

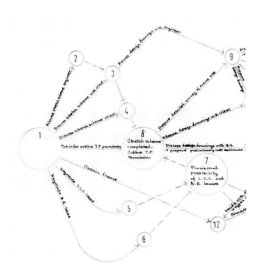

Office of Cedric Price, network analysis, detail.

Office of Cedric Price, network analysis, detail.

similarly critical stances towards modernist dogma; where the champions of context challenged the self-sufficiency of the architectural 'work', Price's interrogation challenged the myth of the modern architect as a self-sufficient author of that work.

Finally, 'Fun Palace' was never built, and other interesting questions about the relationship between authorship and production in architecture result. Where and in what dimension does the project end or start? Where are we to locate its design, the intention of its authors? The archive related to 'Fun Palace', and the drawing with which I started, shows that architectural action, and the intention that produces it, may become manifest not through the composition of 'lines and angles' that define a physical composition solving given problems (societal, formal or technical),[6] but in revealing, and adjusting, the substructures that designate those problems. Yet it remains hard to shift an analysis of the 'Fun Palace' archive away from its significance as the shadow of an unrealised construction. Interpretations of the project are still inclined to anchor it into a developing tradition of architectural history that discusses formal and organisational relationships between buildings (whether real or projected, 'permanent' or 'reconfigurable') in which, for example, 'Fun Palace' can be understood as an ancestor for the Centre Pompidou (see figure below).[7]

This tendency results from an analytical tradition that is highly resilient. The classical definition of the architect as an empowered 'artistic' creator, a model that emerged out of the Renaissance and which was still a dominant trope among architects in the mid-twentieth century, reads architectural intention principally through an analysis of the architectural 'work' – whether built or otherwise.[8] That is to say, the mode in which architects have been characterised as authors impacts on the categories which architectural history chooses in order to understand its subject. Perhaps the most intriguing aspect of Price's work is its potential to criticise this analytical structure. His experiments with multidisciplinary teams, his fascination with ephemera, his early self-delineation as 'anti-architect',[9] can all be seen as part of an attempt to challenge the classical model of the architect as author. And his exploration of the

Office of Cedric Price, anticipated view of the Fun Palace on the banks of the River Lea, photomontage.

intangible forces that condition architecture can be used to question the hegemony of the object-based interpretation that this model produces.

Although Price's career fascinatingly re-inscribed many of the traits that had marked the classical 'author-figure' that he criticised – fascination with his own image, fetishisation of the action of architectural representation – there is no doubt he left that model changed by his own paradoxical example.[10] And his work permitted a shift in perspective that continues to underwrite contemporary projects that cut a critical edge. This change permits actions of architecture to be viewed as things that might take place outside the realm of the formal, and leads ultimately to another idea of the 'context' for architectural action (see figures below).[11]

Alfonso Padro, Philipp Lehmann and Jason Daye, University of East London, School of Architecture and the Visual Arts, Diploma Unit 4 (unit leaders Marianne Mueller and Celine Condorelli), 'City Life', 2001–2, drawing/photograph. This project charts the 'free space' that remains on Waterloo Bridge after subtracting all the regions in which use is controlled by one set of preventative measures or another.

SHoP Architects, Club Lounge for Virgin Atlantic, John F. Kennedy Airport, New York (2003), detail of wall elements. SHoP's work is based in a reassessment of the 'context' of financial, production, contractual and social relations that surround architecture.

Notes

1   For the observations on Cedric Price in this chapter, I am indebted to conversations with Stanley Mathews, Hobart and William Smith Colleges, Geneva, New York, and to the argument he presented in 'Cedric Price as Anti-Architect: The Fun Palace and the Death of the Architect', conference paper given at the SAH year meeting, 6–10 April 2005, Vancouver, Canada. For a thorough reading of the architecture of Cedric Price see Stanley Mathews, *From Agit-prop to Free Space: the Architecture of Cedric Price*, London: Black Dog Publishing, 2006.

2   Fun Palace is described in Cedric Price, *The Square Book*, Chichester: Wiley–Academy, 2003, pp. 53–61.

3   The entire Cedric Price archive is preserved at the Canadian Centre for Architecture, Montreal. The drawing is no. DR1995:0188:246.

4   On the development of the term 'context', see Adrian Forty, *Words and Buildings*, London: Thames and Hudson, pp. 132–5.

5   Key texts in the development of the discourse on context were Aldo Rossi, *L'architet-tura della città*, Padova: Marsilio, 1966 (translated as *The Architecture of the City*, translated by Dianne Ghirardo and Joanne Ockman, Cambridge, MA and London: MIT Press, 1982); Colin Rowe and Fred Koetter, 'Collage City', *Architectural Review*, 158, August 1975, pp. 66–91; revised and expanded as *Collage City*, Cambridge, MA and London: MIT Press, 1978. Rowe and Koetter's vocabulary developed within the Urban Design Studio taught at Cornell University from 1963 onwards and its first theoretical formalisation in print occurred in 1971 (see Forty, *Words and Buildings*, pp. 134–5). Much of Cedric Price's rhetoric that developed during the same period was formally collected in a six-part series for *Architectural Design* between October 1970 and January 1972 (CP Supplements nos 1–5, *Architectural Design*, October 1970–January 1972).

6   The definition of the architect's task as defining the 'lines and angles' that describe a physical composition goes back to Leon Battista Alberti; see Leon Battista Alberti, *On the Art of Building in Ten Books* [1450], translated by Joseph Rykwert, Robert Tavernor, and Neil Leach, Cambridge, MA and London: MIT Press, 1988, I, 1, p. 7.

7   See for example Reyner Banham on the Centre Pompidou, *The Architectural Review*, 161, 693, May 1977, pp. 270–94, p. 277.

8   See Tim Anstey, 'The Ambiguities of *Disegno*', in Jane Rendell (ed.), *Critical Architecture*, a special issue of *Journal of Architecture*, 10, 3, June 2005, pp. 295–306.

9   Price, memorandum (August, 1964), Fun Palace document folio DR1995:0188:526, Cedric Price Archives, Canadian Centre for Architecture, Montreal, cited in Mathews, *From Agit-prop to Free Space*.

10 See Tim Anstey, 'The Ambiguities of *Disegno*', p. 303.

11 This shift is exhibited particularly in the formative phase of the work of Richard Rogers and Norman Foster during the 1960s. The changing idea of what constitutes context is illustrated in the rhetoric of practices such as SHoP Architects in New York:

> Rather than focusing upon a vocabulary of pliant and reconfigurable forms […] our office is researching a procedural agenda, or practice, that is pliant and reconfigurable […]. Here a new definition of context must be used: the context of financial, physical, social, temporal and legislative forces that prepare a thickened membrane within which an architectural intrusion can be inserted.
>
> (SHoP Architects firm profile, quoted from www.dingaling.net/SHoP.htm (accessed 31 August 2006))

The Fall

The allegorical architectural project as a critical method

Penelope Haralambidou

Introduction

According to Angus Fletcher, in the simplest terms allegory says one thing and means another.[1] Deriving from the Greek *allos*, other, and *agoria*, speaking, it signifies a doubleness of intention that requires interpretation. Consequently, Northrop Frye remarks that all commentary is allegorical interpretation and suggests the formal affinities of allegory with criticism.[2] This critical potential of allegory has led commentators to identify the allegorical tradition as a predecessor of psychoanalysis and contemporary literary and critical theory.

Focusing on the role of literary allegory in architectural design and theory, this chapter aims to discuss the allegorical architectural project, an alternative critical practice that employs architectural drawing, the language of describing buildings, to articulate something 'other', *allos*: a critical idiom combining design with text to contemplate on architecture, art, science and politics. The allegorical architectural project, although at times visually and physically inhabited, is often disconnected from the material construction of a building. The imaginative, sometimes poetic bringing together of ideas positions it closer to visual literature and, because of its high dependency on narrative, it can be a bridge between a work of art, painting or sculpture, and a literary text, poem or novel.

Additionally, the allegorical architectural project can be employed to unravel another piece of work, a site or drawing itself by questioning its underlying syntax; allegorical design reveals an analytical inclination and becomes a vehicle for criticism. Architectural drawing, therefore, can be used as a critical method, distancing the architect from the construction site and redefining her as an analyst of spatial phenomena better grasped and investigated through drawing and text.[3] Blurring the distinction between two traditionally divided fields of architectural practice – the building, in terms of the architect as designer and the theoretical/historical text, in terms of the architect as writer – we will study how architectural design can be used as critical theory.

Literary allegory and architecture

The allegorical impulse is a mode of the human intellect linked to the origins of language and representation as the introduction of the 'other', *allos*. Allegory is a structure of thought where meaning is not grasped directly but through metaphor, that often takes the guise of narrative and story-telling. Joel Fineman in 'The Structure of Allegorical Desire' asserts that this other-discourse of allegory accompanies 'the loss of being that comes from re-presenting oneself in language [...] makes the psyche a critical allegory of itself, and [...] justifies psychoanalysis as the allegory of that allegory'.[4]

John MacQueen, in *Allegory*, part of a series entitled *The Critical Idiom*, provides a historical overview of literary allegory, where he recognises its origins as philosophic and theological, closely associated with narrative in the form of myths.[5] Furthermore, MacQueen recognises Plato as the founder of many aspects of the allegorical tradition; many of his dialogues include allegorical narratives, 'which serve to image truths beyond the reach of the discursive intellect'.[6] Allegorical parables populate the Old and New Testament and allegory flourished as the prevalent literary mode during the Middle Ages. In her *Castles of the Mind: a Study of Medieval Architectural Allegory*, Christiania Whitehead studies the potential offered by architecture for allegorical representation and analyses how writers in the Middle Ages turned to the trope of the textual building, or 'scriptural architecture', to describe different themes from ecclesiastical truths to romantic love.[7] Furthermore, Dante Alighieri, author of perhaps the most famous medieval allegory, the *Divine Comedy*, offers the first theory of literary allegory.

The next significant definition of allegory since Dante arrives in the twentieth century with Walter Benjamin's analysis of Baroque allegory, as Bainard Cowan asserts. According to Cowan, Benjamin saw allegory as a literary theory, 'casting it in cultural and ontological terms'.[8] Indeed, in Benjamin's analysis, allegory is primarily an experience; an experience of the world as no longer permanent, but fragmentary and enigmatic: 'transforming things into signs is both what allegory does – its technique – and what it is about – its content.'[9]

Departing from this brief historical overview of literary allegory, this chapter seeks to specify its role in the architectural project. Although allegory exists in the experience of built architecture – for instance, Emile Mâle has shown how a medieval church is a historical allegory written in stone glass and wood – this chapter looks at imaginary projects using drawing to express something 'other' than the construction of a building.[10] Recent examples of projects that can be seen as allegorical include: a series of collaborative projects by Rem Koolhaas, whose pseudo-historical narratives add a fictional dimension to his critical historical analysis in *Delirious New York: a Retroactive Manifesto for Manhattan* (1978); *Temple Island: a Study*, a project by ex-Archigram member Mike Webb featuring poetic drawings critically investigating geometry and representation as the substructure of a fleeting childhood recollection; Ben Nicholson's *Appliance House* (1990), that contemplates on domesticity and the collector and offers a re-evaluation of architectural drawing through collage; and *Actions of Architecture: Architects and Creative Users* (2003), by Jonathan Hill, who uses design to challenge architectural institutions.[11]

Although chronologically close and clearly using allegory to structure and represent spatial ideas, these examples are not directly connected. While the authors are most likely aware of each other's work, they do not form a collective. Their critical use of drawing is fuelled by an individual desire for allegory, which for Fineman 'is implicit in the idea of structure itself and explicit in criticism'; this critical tendency defines and separates these projects from their historical 'paper architecture' predecessors.[12] An in-depth historical tracing of the origins of the allegorical project is beyond the scope of this chapter. However, most of the examples above favour narrative as a vehicle for grasping and developing spatial ideas, a tendency originating at schools of architecture, such as the Architectural Association, Cooper Union and most recently the Bartlett, revealing allegorical design as a practice emerging within architectural education.[13]

The Fall

To illustrate the critical potential of the allegorical architectural project I will present here my use of allegorical narrative in *The Fall,* the design of an imaginary building.[14] Originally an entry to an architectural ideas competition, the design formed the hypothesis and set the parameters for a critical method in my research project entitled *The Blossoming of Perspective: an Investigation of Spatial Representation*.[15]

The research takes as its starting point a reconsideration of architectural representation, which is seen as closely connected with the Renaissance invention of linear perspective and founded on a simplistic geometric model of vision: the monocular visual pyramid. Due to the overpowering simplicity of linear perspective, the 'other' eye and binocular disparity are disregarded aspects of visuality that propose an alternative understanding of vision: a visual schema expanding beyond the flat intersection planes of Cartesian space and best conceptualised as a gas or a fluid in motion.[16] The definition of a projection system able to describe this alternative schema became the main objective of the research and the word 'blossoming' came to suggest the passing from the flat plane into a dispersal of particles.[17]

The allegorical narrative of *The Fall* defined the central hypothesis of the research. It described an imaginary building linking two works of art, Leonardo da Vinci's *The Mona Lisa* (*c.*1503–7), and Marcel Duchamp's assemblage, *Given: 1° the waterfall, 2° the illuminating gas...*, (1946–66), and saw the nude figure in Duchamp's assemblage as a 'fallen' Mona Lisa.[18] One of the riddles connected with Leonardo's portrait is the identity of the sitter. A similar secrecy veils the identity of the female nude in *Given*. In my project, the two enigmatic figures merge, condemned to share the same lost identity. *Lady on a Balcony*, a less-known title for *The Mona Lisa*, suggests that the female figure sits on the balcony of what might be a tower overlooking a mysterious landscape. In *Given*, the female nude observed through the door of a backyard lies submerged in a similar landscape. In the project, the two locations converge at the waterfall on the right side of both images. What we see is the same landscape from two different viewpoints; the change of position, which also causes the undressing of the woman, results from her fall from the balcony to the backyard.

The project's architectural structure occupies the void hidden behind the head in the portrait, the visual shadow of Mona Lisa. It comprises the tower supporting the balcony, which joins to a long corridor traversing the void and leading to the view from the backyard. After the fall, the female figure travels through the corridor and climbs the staircase in the tower to assume the original position, only to fall into the landscape again in a repeated cycle of uninhibited falling and following a long, structured path back. *The Fall* is the design of a composite building, a house for the female protagonist, comprising the linear architecture framing her pedestrian journey, the pictorial garden of the cut-out landscape and the sinuous trajectory of her fall (see figure on page 229).

Therefore, on an allegorical level, the hypothesis of the research suggests that the appearance of the nude in *Given* is the result of Mona Lisa's fall from her balcony into the landscape. During the fall, she undergoes a transformation: she loses her clothes and blossoms into three dimensions. The flat portrait, representing perspective construction, turns into the three-dimensional pornographic, but enigmatic, diorama of *Given*.

Given as allegorical appearance

Given's full title recalls a note by Duchamp:

> Preface
> Given
> 1. the waterfall
> 2. the illuminating gas
> We will determine the conditions for an instant Pause (or allegorical appearance), of a succession of a set of phenomena seeming to necessitate each other according to laws, in order to isolate, the sign of accordance between this Pause (open to all countless eccentricities), on the one hand, and a choice of possibilities legitimised by these laws (and also causing them), on the other.
>
> (Marcel Duchamp, *Duchamp du signe: Ecrits*, edited by Michel Sanouillet and Elmer Peterson, Paris: Flammarion, 1994, pp. 43–4; my translation of the French)

So, *Given* is an 'allegorical appearance', a pornographic image that says one thing and means another. Duchamp's note reads as a mathematical problem or a riddle inviting interpretation, but it is unclear whether the riddle is aimed at the viewer or the author himself. What is the hidden meaning of *Given*?

My interpretation followed Jean-François Lyotard's reading of *Given* as an incarnation and inversion of the rules of linear perspective to expose its hidden assumptions.[19] The analysis of this inverted incarnation of perspective construction proposes an alternative expanded spatiality. Duchamp's term 'blossoming' describes the Bride's desire-driven fall and her passing into the fourth dimension, but is also linked to stereoscopy: a

Penelope Haralambidou, *The Fall*, model, 2004.

spatial representation technique, isolating and revealing binocular depth and allowing an image to 'blossom' in space. Blossoming is a vivid phenomenological effect, combining intellectual and affective attributes, which cannot be directly apprehended through monocular vision nor represented by linear perspective. Consequently in *The Blossoming of Perspective*, I suggested stereo-photogrammetry as *Given*'s central and intentional theme: a creative tool, influencing its intellectual content, guiding its manufacturing process and pointing to an expanded representation technique in architecture. Stereo-photogrammetry is based on binocular vision and describes spatial forms through three-dimensional fields of points, similar to floating gas particles, forming an unveiled, undressed, geometry of vision. This study of *Given* as an inverted incarnation of perspective construction defines an alternative spatiality. As in the 'art of memory', *Given* is a *tableau vivant* or 'allegorical appearance' whose components act like mnemotectonic loci: their spatial arrangement bears a coded account of the geometry of desire, a blossoming of perspective.

The Fall, a project aimed to critically analyse Duchamp's allegorical work, is also an allegory and this chapter will seek to explain its function as a critical method by looking at how it shares allegorical traits found in literature and art.

Allegorical traits

In search of a theoretical background for allegory in architecture, we will look at a selection of allegorical traits: the duplicity of meaning that invites interpretation, the use of figurative elements to denote structural relationships, the reciprocity between visual and verbal, the similarity to a battle – an opposition between two forces – or a journey, and the state of being unfinished.

Double meaning

By saying one thing and meaning another, in all allegories there is a duplicity of meaning. But the link between what is articulated and its interpretation, as well as the intentions of the author, differ. We find an intentional single secondary meaning in most Christian and Medieval parables, ambiguity in Baroque allegories, intentionally diverse multiple meanings when a work invites an open-ended interpretation from the receiver, and a concealed meaning to be deciphered through a series of logical steps in an enigma or riddle. Finally, critical interpretation unearths meanings often not intended by the author.

Duchamp approved all interpretations of his work and was reluctant to give any of his own, describing the artist as a:

> Mediumistic being who, from the labyrinth beyond time and space, seeks his way out to a clearing [...]. All his decisions in the artistic execution of the work rest with pure intuition and cannot be translated into a self-analysis, spoken or written, or even thought out.
>
> (Marcel Duchamp, 'Creative Act', *The Writings of Marcel Duchamp,* edited by Michel Sanouillet and Elmer Peterson, New York: Da Capo, 1989, p. 138)

For Duchamp, the work succeeds if it triggers many interpretations, because it is not the artist alone who performs the creative act: the viewers make their own contribution. It is clear, however, from his description of the artist as a 'mediumistic' being that he sees the work presented as a riddle or an enigma not only to the viewer but also to the author. Therefore, the work of art is an allegory in receiving, interpreting, but also in making.

The architectural allegory of *The Fall* used architectural drawing to analyse *Given* and carried out a critical interpretation of Duchamp's work: a form of art theory performed through architectural design. However, on another level, the main intention of the research was to challenge the underlying syntax of architectural representation and to propose a reconsideration of accepted norms. So the problem set by the allegorical project was: if *Given* is an inverted incarnation of the *Mona Lisa,* which represents the principles of perspective construction influencing architectural drawing, then what are the attributes of this alternative inverted perspective and how does it influence architectural representation?

The Fall allegorically encapsulated a set of ideas, which, although complete and intuitively convincing within the allegorical structure, were accepted as an enigma. The ensuing textual and drawing research aimed to interpret, verify and expand the intuitive links established by the project. Therefore, I would like to suggest here that the importance of the allegorical architectural project, and the construction of the design enigma, is paramount within the boundaries of a research project in visual practices as a method of grasping meaning beyond analytical discourse. This is especially true in a research about architectural representation and drawing – which, for architecture, is what language is to literature – where the difficulty of interrogating the substructure of architectural thinking cannot be faced directly and is easier to deal with through a metaphor or an allegorical narrative.

Figurative geometry

Fletcher describes allegory as 'figurative geometry'. Allegorical narrative operates as a mathematical equation or geometric principle, which instead of abstract numbers and letters uses personages, everyday or sublime objects and sites to signify structural relationships. In this pure structurality of allegory exists a bizarre contradiction. However particular its figurative elements are, the allegory remains abstract as if allegorical themes are emptied of their content by the structure that governs them.[20]

We have seen how the female figure, transforming from the fully dressed smiling lady on a balcony to the unhindered recumbent nude in the bush, personified the allegorical hypothesis of the research. Furthermore, the simple diagram of the tower, the corridor and the trajectory of the fall in the landscape, the elements constituting the figurative geometry of *The Fall*, were reoccurring symbols, drawn repeatedly throughout the study. Appearances of this underlying structure in the form of a diagram for a building exist in numerous sketches, the model featuring in the competition submission and a subsequent hybrid between a drawing and a model done retrospectively. The diagram came to allegorically represent the theme, the transformation of perspective into its blossomed other, but also the research methodology. The curved line of the fall, an unhindered connection between the top of the tower and the bush in the landscape, stands for intuition established through the allegorical design project, while the corridor represents the return to the same point on the tower through the subsequent interpretative textual analysis.

Battle and progress

In *Allegory: the Theory of a Symbolic Mode*, Fletcher defines two broad categories of allegorical narratives: what he calls 'battle', an opposition between two forces, or 'progress', a description of a sequence of events that often takes the form of a journey.[21] Unsurprisingly, therefore, most allegorical projects can be seen to belong to either one, and in most cases, both of these two seemingly simplistic categories. And *The Fall* is no exception.

The figurative structure of *The Fall* embodies a set of binary oppositions and therefore can be seen as a 'battle' between *The Mona Lisa* and her reversal in the nude, or perspective construction and its alternative other. The project stages this dialectical interaction between the linear order of perspective and its other, which in the beginning is only metaphorically defined. This allegorical 'battle' as a research method leads to a gradual understanding of *Given* as a precise drawing and revealed the representational potential of stereoscopy.

Additionally, the project stages a journey: the female figure's traversing of the landscape, first by falling and then by walking back to the top of the tower. In an early note, 'progress' around the imaginary spatial configuration of *The Fall* is also seen as the 'scriptural architecture' of the research:

> Start by looking at the picture, running information on a surface, go behind the picture, fall down in the landscape, study the assemblage, picking up clues placed scattered in time, turn and look towards the door, and build the link back to the top. The text describes a spatial understanding/The architecture is the text and the text is the architecture.
>
> (Note from the sketchbook where *The Fall* was sited and developed, pp. 33–4)[22]

Unfinished

Characteristically many allegories are left unfinished. Edmund Spenser's *The Faerie Queene* (1590), Franz Kafka's *The Trial* (1925) and *The Castle* (1926), and Marcel Duchamp's definitively unfinished *The Large Glass* (1915–) can be seen as examples of incomplete allegories.[23] According to Fletcher, the unfinished form and fragmented nature of these works needs to be understood in dynamic terms: 'all analogies are incomplete, and incompletable, and allegory simply records this analogical relation in a dramatic or narrative form.'[24] Furthermore, Owens sees allegory as 'consistently attracted to the fragmentary, the imperfect, the incomplete'.[25]

Allegorical architectural projects are, by definition, unfinished, since they are never built. However, physical construction of the ideas in the drawings and texts is not the intention of the author, who deliberately sites her project in the realm of the imagination. Often, however, the fragmentary, unfinished and incomplete trait of allegory colours the drawing technique itself.

The drawing practices of Leonardo and Duchamp inspired and influenced the sketching and noting technique I used to design *The Fall* and the rest of the research. According to Theodore Reff, there is a fundamental affinity between the two artists – conviction that art is primarily the record of an intellectual process and that their studies in the form of notes became ends in themselves and could be appreciated as such.[26] Although a set of drawings and a model formed the submission to the architectural ideas competition, representations more accurately describing *The Fall* exist in the form of sketches and notes in the pages of the project's sketchbook. There, ideas and thoughts contradict each other, are repeated or left unfinished, because despite some unavoidable post-rationalisation, the sketchbook reflects the fragmentary nature of the design process. However, the sketchbook is not just a representation of the project, but its site and the medium through which it developed. Its pages reveal the true nature of *The Fall*, not as a finished design proposition but as a research method, where the investigation is conducted through the allegory of the fall (see figure below).

Visual and verbal

Craig Owens, in 'The Allegorical Impulse: Toward a Theory of Postmodernism', notes a reciprocity between visual and verbal in allegory: words are often treated as purely

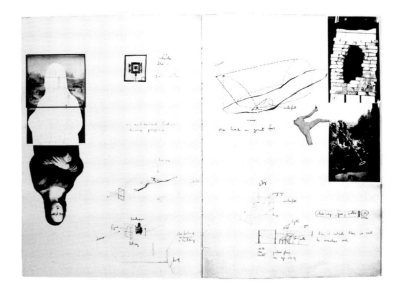

Penelope Haralambidou, *The Fall*, sketchbook, 1998.

visual phenomena, while visual images are offered as a script to be deciphered: 'In allegory the image is a hieroglyph; an allegory is a rebus – writing composed of concrete images.'[27] In the allegorical architectural project drawing and text complement each other in the production of meaning.

The design part of this research is not a separate element that the text accompanies, describes, explains or reacts to, but a drawing-based technique that organises, tests and structures the research itself. This drawing technique I call 'illuminated scribism', a term deriving from Richard Hamilton's interpretation of a note in Duchamp's *White Box,* 1966: 'an "illuminatoresque Scribism" bonds image and word – each shedding light upon and adorning the other.'[28] Hamilton thinks the term is similar to 'pictorial nominalism' and that the fabricated word 'illuminatoresque' means 'illuminated', as in 'illuminated manuscript'.[29]

Although unavoidably guided by aesthetic intentions, the technique is primarily an investigatory method: a series of sketchbooks and free pages with sketches, diagrams, notes, drawings and collages. Even when a page is mainly a constellation of words connected with lines, it is a 'written drawing' rather than just text, and the configuration refers to the structure of the research, the design of both written and drawn parts. Often, the inquiring mode of the notes recedes, they contain no written material, and the pages resemble pictures. Such a page or sketchbook spread displays a single idea and the composition does not only describe the thought process but derives from aesthetic concerns. Therefore the notes, sketches and diagrams shape constellations of ideas which shift between writing and drawing, verbal and pictorial or analytical and synthetic.

Criticism by allegorical design

I attempted to describe here an alternative practice in architecture, where drawing is a critical tool articulating theory rather than the construction of a building. As we have seen, the allegorical architectural project combines design and theory, and its creative and critical traits make it a visual equivalent of literary or critical theory. Rather than a description of a new phenomenon, the chapter provides a new way of looking at the allegorical architectural project and offers novel tools for its evaluation. The introduction of the 'other', through allegory, is a mode of thinking and working in architecture that allows transgression of established modes, and defines the allegorical architectural project as an experimental practice, pointing to ideas impossible to grasp through the profession or in purely discourse-based theoretical investigations.

Notes

1   Angus Fletcher, *Allegory: the Theory of a Symbolic Mode*, Ithaca: Cornell, 1965, p. 2.
2   Northrop Frye, *Anatomy of Criticism: Four Essays*, Harmondsworth: Penguin, 1990, p. 89.

3   Although allegorical projects can be built, this chapter attempts to see drawing and its creative and critical potential as an end in itself and, therefore, discusses projects that hide no intention to materialise in buildings.

4   Joel Fineman, 'The Structure of Allegorical Desire', in Stephen J. Greenblatt (ed.), *Allegory and Representation: Selected Papers from the English Institute, 1979–80*, Baltimore and London: Johns Hopkins University, 1981, p. 47.

5   John MacQueen, *Allegory*, in the series edited by John B. Jump, *The Critical Idiom*, no. 14, London: Methuen, 1976. Examples from the classical world of Greece and Rome include the myth of Demeter and Persephone, an allegorical explanation of sowing and harvesting corn, and inevitably of human mortality, and Orpheus, an allegory of the redemptive powers of the human soul.

6   Examples include a passage from Plato's *Phaedrus,* where the soul is compared to a charioteer driving two steeds, the spiritual and the sensual element in man, and a series of allegories in different styles on the subject of love from Plato's *Symposium.* See MacQueen, *Allegory*, p. 7.

7   Christiania Whitehead, *Castles of the Mind: a Study of Medieval Architectural Allegory*, Cardiff: University of Wales, 2003.

8   Bainard Cowan, 'Walter Benjamin's Theory of Allegory', *New German Critique*, 22, a special issue on Modernism, winter 1981, pp. 109–22, p. 110.

9   Bainard Cowan, 'Walter Benjamin's Theory of Allegory', p. 110.

10 Emile Mâle, *The Gothic Image: Religious Art in France of the Thirteenth Century*, translated by Dora Nussey, London and Glasgow: Collins, 1961. Quoted in McQueen, *Allegory*, p. 40.

11 See, in chronological order: Rem Koolhaas, *Delirious New York: a Retroactive Manifesto for Manhattan*, New York: Oxford University Press, 1972; Michael Webb, *Temple Island: a Study*, London: Architectural Association, 1987; Ben Nicholson, *Appliance House*, Chicago and Cambridge: Chicago Institute for Architecture and Urbanism and MIT, 1990; Jonathan Hill, *Actions of Architecture: Architects and Creative Users*, London and New York: Routledge, 2003.

12 Fineman, 'The Structure of Allegorical Desire', p. 26.

13 Rem Koolhaas, Ben Nicholson and Jonathan Hill have studied at the AA, while Michael Webb's connection to the school is by approximation, through other Archigram members. For over 15 years, Jonathan Hill has been running a successful diploma unit at the Bartlett School of Architecture, UCL, where Ben Nicholson is an external examiner and frequent lecturer alongside Michael Webb.

14 For a critical analysis of other allegorical architectural projects, see Penelope Haralambidou, 'The Allegorical Project: Architecture as Figurative Theory', in Tim Anstey, Katja Grillner and Rolf Hughes (eds), *Architecture and Authorship: Studies in Disciplinary Remediation*, London: Black Dog Publishing, 2007.

15 Professors Phil Tabor and Jonathan Hill at the Bartlett School of Architecture, UCL, supervised my PhD Architectural Design thesis, which was completed in 2003. The original version of *The Fall* was submitted to an international ideas competition organised by Shinkenchiku-sha in March 1998, and received an Honourable Mention.

16 Hubert Damisch presents a similar understanding of the cloud as sign: an oppositional factor to linear perspective with which it interacts dialectically. See Hubert Damisch, *A Theory of /Cloud/: Toward a History of Painting*, Stanford: Stanford University, 2002.

17 The term 'blossoming' belongs to Duchamp; it relates to the Bride and describes her fall, her undressing, the expansion of her desire and her passing to a higher dimension.

18 *Given* is a mixed-media assemblage permanently installed in the Philadelphia Museum of Art and was Duchamp's last major piece, executed in complete secrecy between 1946 to 1966. The viewer enters a dark room with a weathered door and

through two peepholes engages with a concealed pornographic sight: a recumbent faceless female nude, holding a gas lamp and submerged in twigs out in an open landscape bathed in light, where a waterfall silently glitters.

19   Jean-François Lyotard, *Duchamp's TRANS/formers*, translated by Ian McLeod, Venice, CA: Lapis, 1990.

20   Fineman, 'The Structure of Allegorical Desire', pp. 51–2.

21   Homer's two poems reflect these two literary modes: 'Iliad' is the narration of a battle and 'Odyssey' recounts a series of adventures linked by a journey.

22   See also Penelope Haralambidou, The Blossoming of Perspective: an Investigation of Spatial Representation, University of London: unpublished PhD thesis, 2003.

23   Although the claim on Kafka's novels as allegory is often contested, many critics discuss them in allegorical terms, including Fletcher and Bainard Cowan, who states that:

> if new chapters in the history of allegory are to be written, the inquiry ought to start with two German-language Jewish writers: Kafka, of whom Benjamin once commented that his work was like 'the rumour about the true things (a sort of theological whispered intelligence dealing with matters discredited and obsolete)' – and Benjamin himself.
>
> See Fletcher, *Allegory*, pp. 14–5 and Cowan, 'Walter Benjamin's Theory of Allegory', p. 122.

24   Fletcher, *Allegory*, p. 174.

25   Craig Owens, 'The Allegorical Impulse: Toward a Theory of Postmodernism', *October*, 12, 1980, pp. 67–86, p. 70.

26   Theodore Reff, 'Duchamp and Leonardo: L.H.O.O.Q.-Alikes', *Art in America*, 65, January–February 1977, p. 91.

27   Owens, 'The Allegorical Impulse', p. 74.

28   Richard Hamilton, 'An Unknown Object of Four Dimensions', in Marcel Duchamp, *A l'infinitif*, a typotranslation by Richard Hamilton and Ecke Bonk of Marcel Duchamp's *White Box*, translated by Jackie Matisse, Richard Hamilton and Ecke Bonk, Paris: Typosophic Society, 1999, unpaginated.

29   Richard Hamilton, Sarat Maharaj and Mignon Nixon, 'Agendas: Duchamp's Legacy – Richard Hamilton and Sarat Maharaj', lecture, Tate Britain, 7 May 2003 (see www.tate.org.uk/onlineevents/archive/duchamp_legacy.htm (accessed 25 October 2006).

On Drawing Forth, Designs and Ideas

Victoria Watson

Under the conference subject *Criticism by Design* the organisers seemed to be hinting that the notion of 'drawing forth'[1] might be deployed as a conceptual device, a means of opening architecture to new areas of research. Such an opening might, in turn, lead to the emergence of much-needed ideas about what, in relation to contemporary practice, critical architecture is and what critical architecture can do.

This chapter will examine the idea of drawing forth; taking the view that it is, potentially, a valuable critical instrument. But drawing forth can too easily be associated with the idealistic opposition of mind and matter; that is, with the belief that ideas are formed and are stored in the mind and that the architect's role is to act as a kind of shuttle, carrying ideas from the mind, out into the physical world where they are embodied in buildings.[2]

Taken to its extreme, the idealistic understanding of the relationship between ideas and things results in the proposition that there are two worlds: the pure world of ideas and the contingent world of the everyday, of things, of bodies, of feelings, of actions and events. This split haunts architecture's understanding of the relationship between ideas and things, and in so doing it inevitably influences the way architects think about the role of drawing in their activity as designers.

The idealistic understanding of the relation between ideas and buildings is generally believed to have been first formulated for architecture during the Italian Renaissance, when architecture came to be understood, not as a craft, linked to manual labour, but as a liberal art linked to intellectual activity.[3] Leon Battista Alberti's treatise on architecture played a foundational role in this reformulation, and so it seems reasonable to look to Alberti's treatise for clues as to the source of idealistic thinking in architecture;[4] however, I would like to suggest that a careful examination of Alberti's treatise, supported by an experience of the buildings he designed, indicates that it is a mistake to think of Alberti's interest in architecture as evidence of a fundamental idealism.[5]

Drawing in bed

In attempting to understand Alberti's attitude towards ideas and buildings, it should be borne in mind that his research was orientated by a particular set of interests; a visit to Sant' Andrea in Mantua, for example, is quite revealing of the ideas Alberti was concerned to draw forth and to formulate through the work of architecture. A very strong feeling for the *quality* of spatial relationships is evident in the work; it is as if Alberti (and, indeed, other Renaissance architects such as Filippo Brunelleschi, Francesco di Giorgio Martini, Luca Francelli, Antonio da Sangallo the Elder and Antonio da Sangallo the Younger, Luciano Laurana and Donato Bramante) were drawing forth ideas to test the proposition that there might be a harmonious link between imaginary projection and sensual experience.

In his *On The Art of Building*, Alberti suggests there is an inextricable link between building and design; design is what remains if construction is subtracted from building. Alberti states that the 'intention and purpose' of design is to find 'the correct, infallible way of jointing and fitting together those lines and angles which define and enclose the surfaces of the building', and that the 'function' and 'duty' of design is to 'prescribe an appropriate place, exact numbers, a proper scale, and a graceful order for whole buildings and for each of their constituent parts'.[6] For Alberti, design is a matter of structure – a forming, arranging and organising activity conditioned by geometry, that can be carried out in the mind:

> It is quite possible to project whole forms in the mind without any recourse to the material, by designating and determining a fixed orientation and conjunction of the various lines and the angles.
>
> (Leon Battista Alberti, *On the Art of Building in Ten Books*, p. 7)

In effect, for Alberti, the activity of designing is an intellectual pursuit; it is a matter of finding correspondences between immaterial forms projected in the mind, and physical forms projected in space; design is something that Alberti is able to carry out in his head, unassisted by the intermediaries of pencil and paper. But to work things out in one's head requires considerable concentration; such moments of undivided attention, Alberti claimed, often came to him whilst he was lying peacefully in bed.[7] Since Alberti was able to work out his designs in his head, so he was able to regard the physical production of drawings as inessential to design; he regarded drawing as a useful means of testing a design, primarily to check, prior to going through the trouble and expense of construction, if the design was one that he really did like:

> It is the mark of considerable experience to have so thoroughly thought out everything and determined it in the mind beforehand, that in the course of construction, or on completion of the work, one is not forced to admit, 'I wish I had not done this: I would have preferred it done otherwise' [...]. For this reason I will always commend the time-honoured custom, practiced by

the best builders, of preparing not only drawings and sketches but also models of wood or any other material.

(Leon Battista Alberti, 'Profugiorum Ab Aerumna – Libri III', pp. 33–4)

So far as the production of physical drawings is concerned, Alberti's attitude seems to indicate a certain indifference; implying that, although he recommends drawing to others, he himself does not draw. However, towards his mental activities his attitude seems altogether different: it is through the ability to draw forth forms in the mind that the role of the architect is truly confirmed.

I would suggest that Alberti's seemingly indifferent attitude towards drawing conceals a certain anxiety towards the medium. If a design is simply a building stripped of material construction, an assembly in the mind, what then is a drawing? Clearly a drawing is not simply a thing of the mind, for it exists outside of the mind and yet, for all that a drawing is a manufactured thing, the materials of which it is made include abstract, immaterial structures and signs. Alberti's interests in drawing forth were motivated by a desire to discover direct connections between imaginary forms arising in the mind and the embodied sensual experience of measured spatial relationships; in a line of inquiry such as his, there can be no place for the physical drawing, its presence serves only to short-circuit any direct connection there might be between the imaginary form drawn forth in the mind and the spatial qualities drawn forth in the building: the drawing will come to stand as a substitute, representing either the image of the mind or the spatial qualities of the building, perhaps subsuming both in a single, extensive and all-embracing image. I would suggest that it was because he was aware of the potential idealism of his position that Alberti was so parsimonious in the role he attributed to drawing in the production of designs.

In order to demonstrate the logical implications of drawing forth, understood in relation to a world split in two, it is useful to turn to a concrete example of an idealistic philosophy. Arthur Schopenhauer's thought, particularly as represented in *The World as Will and as Idea*, has been selected to serve as the basis of this demonstration. There are three reasons for this choice: first, Schopenhauer's philosophy is said to have exercised a popular appeal, reaching an audience beyond the highly specialised field of professional philosophers, 'to artistic and literary people in search of philosophy that they could believe'.[8] Second, because in his philosophical system Schopenhauer places a high value on all forms of art, including architecture, suggesting that artistic practice enjoys a privileged relationship with the realm of Ideas (which may explain the appeal of his philosophy to artistic and literary people): Schopenhauer believes that, through the contemplation of works of art, Ideas can be redeemed from subjugation to the Will (a formless, evil and purposeless entity that powers the universe) and thus be known in a condition of absolute purity. The third reason for choosing Schopenhauer's system is related to the time of its production; *The World as Will and as Idea* was written between 1814 and 1818, and thus it is not unreasonable to suppose it has some resonance with the emerging sensibilities of the modern world.

A timeless world

In Schopenhauer's thought, the belief that the creative abilities of an artist (or architect) could be attributed to a faculty termed 'genius' is given a novel twist.[9] Schopenhauer assigns the term 'genius' to a special form of knowledge, enjoyed by the human subject and prompted by the surrender of individuality:

> Genius, then, consists, according to our explanation, in the capacity for knowing independently of the principle of sufficient reason, and hence for knowing not individual things but the Ideas of such things, and of being in relation to these things, oneself the correlative of the Idea, and thus no longer an individual, but the pure subject of knowing.
>
> (Arthur Schopenhauer, *The World as Will and as Idea: Abridged in One Volume*, edited by David Berman and translated by Jill Berman, London and Vermont: Everyman, 1995, p. 118)

Genius, then, would seem to consist in the individual's becoming subsumed in a single, extensive and all-embracing relationship with an Idea. For Schopenhauer, the tendency towards genius is by no means restricted to only a few people, but exists in all to a greater or lesser extent, and it is this small semblance of genius in us all that allows the products of art and design to be freely enjoyed:

> Yet this faculty must exist in all human beings in a smaller and different degree; for if not, they would be just as incapable of enjoying works of art as of producing them; they would have no susceptibility for the beautiful or the sublime; indeed, these terms could have no meaning for them. We must therefore assume that there exists in all men this power of knowing the Ideas in things, and consequently of setting aside their personality for the moment, unless indeed there are some men who are capable of no aesthetic pleasure at all.
>
> (Arthur Schopenhauer, *The World as Will and as Idea,* p. 118)

Thus, for Schopenhauer, aesthetic experience is the total embrace of an Idea; it is a condition enjoyed by the human subject in the mode of a somewhat mysterious suppression of individuality – this condition Schopenhauer calls '*contemplation*'. The mode of contemplation consists in two constitutive and inseparable states to which the knowing subject must aspire: first, the knowledge of an object, not as an individual thing but as a Platonic Idea, and second, the 'self-consciousness of the knowing subject, not as an individual but as a pure will-less subject of knowledge'.[10] Here is Schopenhauer describing a person's transfer into the contemplative mode; the emphasis seems to lie in the heightening of perception, the dissolution of boundaries and the formation of an image:

> He ceases to consider the where, the when, the why and the wither of things, and looks simply and solely at the what. He does not allow abstract thought, the concepts of the reason, to take possession of his conscious-

ness, but, instead, gives the whole power of his mind to perception, immerses himself entirely in this, and lets his whole consciousness be filled with the quiet contemplation of the natural object actually present whether a landscape, a tree, a crag, a building, or whatever it may be. He loses himself in this object, forgets his very individuality, his will, and continues to exist only as the pure subject, the clear mirror of the object, so that it is as if the object alone were there without anyone to perceive it, and he can no longer separate the perceiver from the perception, but the two have become one, because the whole consciousness is filled and taken up with one single sensuous picture.

(Arthur Schopenhauer, *The World as Will and as Idea,* p. 102)

In Schopenhauer's terms, the distinction between the artist, whether they be an architect, designer, poet or musician, and the person who is not endowed with the capacity to create is not a distinction between one who is a genius and one who is not. The difference is this: the creative person, whilst being nonetheless absorbed in the contemplative mode, can, at the same time, retain a certain 'presence of mind'.[11] The retention of a presence of mind permits the creative person to represent intuited knowledge in a work that is deliberate and premeditated.

Thus it seems that what the creative person is doing on those miraculous occasions – moments when, at one and the same time, they are lost in a single sensual perception and yet present in mind – is drawing forth Ideas. And yet surely, if the creative person really were engaged with Ideas in a process of drawing forth, then they would no longer be exempt from the powers of the Will, something of their individuality would surely be retained; and we would expect to read in Schopenhauer's description of the transference to and from the world of Ideas more evidence of a struggle. Instead we read of a passive immersion, accompanied by the modest retention of a certain presence of mind; Schopenhauer's creative person serves rather more as a peephole into the world of Ideas than as a provocateur that draws Ideas forth.

'Air Grid'

I turn now to my own design research, which is concerned with an entity called 'Air Grid'. 'Air Grid' is a light-weight, three-dimensional lattice structure made from brightly coloured machine embroidery thread, sewn into a foam-board support and held taut in the grip of fine incisions, sliced into designated members of the support frame. My research into this phenomenon is currently engaged in the feasibility of deploying 'Air Grid' in the manufacture of an architectural apparatus: 'The House of Miniscule Impressions' (see figure on page 242).

In what follows I aim to describe how the phenomenon of the 'Air Grid' came to my attention and to set down the significant moments of its early development. In doing so, I hope that the constellation of events I describe will convey my

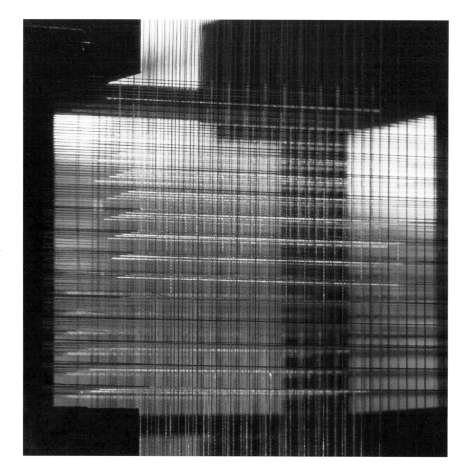

Victoria Watson, *The House of Miniscule Impressions*, detail view.

own understanding of the activity of drawing forth. Notwithstanding the problems of the notion of drawing forth, as exemplified in Schopenhauer's thought, the term does signify the activity of provocation and the presence of a being who provokes, acting as an irritant, persuading ideas to come forth, rather than passively standing by and waiting for them to emerge, like alien beings from another world. In this sense, drawing forth could be regarded as a positive term for summarising the various aggravations, irritations, frustrations, annoyances, accidents and leaps of imagination that have contributed to the development of 'Air Grid'.

The first sketch of a recognisable 'Air Grid' entity appears in a cluster of notes, made as I was reading Henri Lefebvre's *The Production of Space* for the first time (see figure on page 243). The thoughts recorded in the immediate proximity of the sketch show that my engagement with Lefebvre's writing had drawn forth an idea in the form of a question: 'do the qualities of space that emerge in the architecture of Ludwig Mies van der Rohe arise as a consequence of an architect who thinks of space as of a void waiting to be filled?'

For Lefebvre, to think of space as a void waiting to be filled is a grave mistake, most particularly it is a mistake made by architects and by many philosophers.

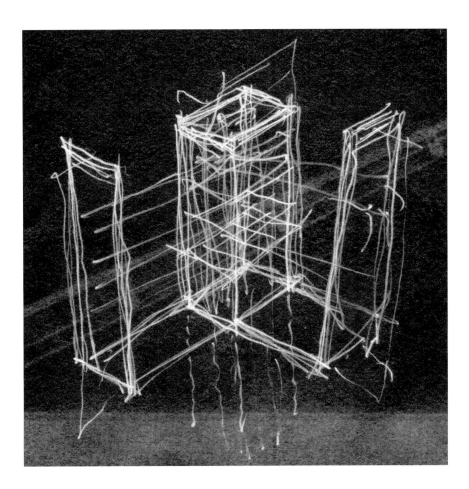

Victoria Watson, sketch: Lefebvre's provocative text seems to have 'drawn forth' an idea.

However, one philosopher who did not mistake space for a void is Gottfried Liebniz. Lefebvre draws on Liebniz's authority to suggest that space be conceived as being necessarily occupied:

> Liebniz maintains that space 'in itself', space as such, is neither 'nothing' or 'something' – and even less the totality of things or the form of their sum; for Liebniz space was, indeed, the indiscernible. In order to discern 'something' therein, axes and an origin must be introduced, and a right and a left, i.e. the direction or orientation of those axes.
>
> (Henri Lefebvre, *The Production of Space*, translated by Donald Nicholson-Smith, Oxford: Basil Blackwell Ltd, 1991, p. 169)

Lefebvre hastens to point out that Liebniz's axes are not those of an observer and a measuring device; they are spatial indicators embedded in space itself, a necessary aspect of a living occupancy that is constitutive of space.

Insofar as space is conceived of as a void waiting to be filled, then the grid can be understood as a perfect device for measuring space and Mies's architecture, marked everywhere with the imprint of the grid, looks as if its author is, indeed, guilty of thinking the constitution of space in terms of a void, a subject and a device that measures. And yet, if this were so, how is it possible to explain the experience of Miesian architecture, which is hardly dry, empty and abstract, as one might expect of a void? Miesian architecture is full of light and air, seeming to radiate a feeling of atmosphere; the void, one imagines to be airless, the experience of being immersed in Miesian space is curiously exhilarating, refreshing, and breathing is easy.

Preoccupied with the presence of the grid in Miesian space, an activity of drawing forth ensued. The aim was to make a grid, in three dimensions, but of negligible materiality. This led to the first experiments with machine thread: appropriately delicate, a filament of machine thread will score a fine line through the air when held taut at either end.

The first problem involved in the drawing forth of a three-dimensional grid made from embroidery thread is that of support. The support has two tasks to perform; first it must serve as an apparatus for measuring and locating points in space, and second it must be able to maintain the shape of the grid. Foam-board is a composite material consisting of a polyurethane core, sandwiched between two layers of thin card. The material is light and rigid but not brittle, and it is easy to punch small, relatively clean, holes through foam-board. Because of its card surface, it is easy to mark setting-out lines on foam-board and the substance is easily cut. The three-dimensional grid is made by drawing thread through a network of holes, pierced through panels of foam-board and held taut in the grasp of a sharp incision cut into the vertical members of the foam-board armature that gives stability to the panels of holes.

The first Miesian work to emerge as a three-dimensional grid made from thread was the 860–880 Lake Shore Drive Apartments, Chicago (1948–51). The cadence of my grid was extrapolated from a 1:500 scale plan and section of Mies's design. The design of the support consisted of two components, the panels of holes – 'hole-panels'; and the frame of vertical and horizontal supporting members – 'stiffeners'. Some, but not all, of the stiffeners are sliced with a rhythm of fine incisions, corresponding to the rhythm of holes on the hole-panels. Because the foam-board yields, the incisions are sufficient to hold the thread taut. Prior to fabrication, an electronic model of the Lake Shore grid and support was produced and this served two practical purposes. First it could be used to generate cutting and hole-punching templates for the hole-panels and stiffeners; second it could be used to generate a coloured ground. The coloured ground was pasted to the inner face of the hole-panels. The intention was to use colour to emulate the aura of the original Miesian work. The Lake Shore model was given a very dark grey, almost black, lining and was sewn in a pale blue thread. The species of thread chosen was 'viscose embroidery' – this was soft, smooth and shiny, with a tendency to blur, or smear, the colour sensation, seeming sometimes to radiate, not blue, but silver or white.

Although the idea that had been drawn forth was conceptually simple, in its material manifestation what was simple (the figure of the grid) was nowhere to be seen. Sometimes the colourful structure would appear to condense a cloud of radiant plasma, at other times to vibrate, as if an invisible force was acting upon the threads, switching them from on to off.

The idea that had been drawn forth quite literally constituted a volume of coloured hatching in the air, a kind of three-dimensional grating of sufficiently fine grain that the human visual system, as it scans back and forth, trying to make sense of what it sees, cannot separate individual images. The effect is like that of a badly tuned television or radio, of unfocused information; vision can make no sense of what passes across its field of sensitivity. But, unlike the effect of a badly tuned instrument, which can be most disturbing to the viewing subject, the experience of watching the 'Air Grid' was both curiously delightful and at the same time annoyingly unsatisfactory: just at the point of stabilising the image, it would slip away. This elusive quality of the 'Air Grid' is provocative, drawing forth the desire to make another one, more stable than the first.

Development of the 'Air Grid' has now reached the point where it is possible to draw forth grids of a size corresponding to the scale of the human body (the Lake Shore model measured only 10 × 13 × 11 inches). As 'Air Grid' slowly emerges as an idea with the capacity to define architectural space, so the ambition to draw from it an architectural proposal becomes increasingly feasible: this is the project referred to as 'The House of Miniscule Impressions'. As the project of drawing 'Air Grid' into an architecture is in its infancy, so it is a project at its most provocative, riddled with aggravations, irritations, frustrations and annoyances, fraught by accidents but fortunately visited from time to time by great leaps of the imagination. It is a project that has arisen from ideas in this world and continues to draw forth ideas of and about this world.

As for the question that prompted the drawing forth of the first 'Air Grid', the answer is no: Mies did not conceive of space as a void waiting to be filled but as a medium teeming with life. The grid presence in Miesian architecture is a constructional grid – unfortunately, it is beyond the scope of this chapter to explore what is meant by this in detail. It is sufficient for now to draw attention to the fact that across the trajectory of Mies's work it is possible to trace a strong desire to fuse the constructional grid with the body of the constructed object; Mies refers to this fusion as the *congruence of thought and thing*.[12] The desire for fusion of this kind is grounded in the same way of thinking about space that sustained Alberti's interest in drawing forth – it is motivated by the belief that the mental ability to perceive beauty can be attained only through experience and practice. Such an attitude to drawing forth is embedded in an understanding of space that is, by definition, absolutely relative, that is, occupied.

Notes

1   The Bartlett School of Architecture, UCL, Conference – Call for Papers: *Critical Architecture*, 'Criticism by Design', November 2004.

2   For a clear statement of what is problematic in this belief, see Adrian Forty, 'Language and Drawing', *Words and Buildings: a Vocabulary of Modern Architecture*, London: Thames and Hudson, 2000, pp. 32–3.

3   For an account of this development and its implications for the role of drawing and writing in the practice of architecture, see Jonathan Hill, 'Jonathan Hill', in Michael

Chadwick (ed.), *Back to School,* a special issue of *Architectural Design,* 74, 5, September/October 2004, pp. 83–6.

4   See, for example, Robin Evans, *The Projective Cast, Architecture and its Three Geometries*, Cambridge, MA and London: MIT Press, 1995, p. 38.

5   In this respect, Erwin Panofsky's entry on 'Alberti' in the section on 'The Renaissance' in his *Idea: a Concept in Art Theory*, is particularly revealing (my emphasis):

> For the same Idea concept which Cicero and Plotinus used to demonstrate the unlimited power of artistic genius and its essential independence from any external experience, serves here *in the case of Alberti* to warn this artistic genius against overvaluing itself and to call it back to the contemplation of nature. 'the idea of beauty which even the most experienced mind can hardly perceive, escapes the inexperienced one' [...]. Alberti believed that the mental ability to perceive beauty could be attained only through experience and practice.
>
> (Erwin Panofsky 'The Renaissance', *Idea: a Concept in Art Theory*, translated by Joseph Peake, Columbia: University of South Carolina Press, 1968, pp. 58–9)

6   Leon Battista Alberti, *On the Art of Building in Ten Books* [1450], translated by Joseph Rykwert, Robert Tavernor and Neil Leach, Cambridge, MA and London: MIT Press, 1988, p. 7.

7   Leon Battista Alberti, *'Profugiorum Ab Aerumna – Libri III'*, Alberti, L.B., *Opere Volgari*, Volume 2, edited by Charles Grayson, Bari, 1966, p. 181.

8   See the entry on Schopenhauer in Bertrand Russell, *History of Western Philosophy and its Connection with Political and Social Circumstances from the Earliest to the Present Day*, London: Routledge, 1961, p. 722.

9   The idea of genius as the creative faculty enjoyed by artists was popularised in Giorgio Vasari's *Lives of the Most Excellent Painters, Sculptors, and Architects*, first published in 1550 with a revised and enlarged edition in 1568. See Giorgio Vasari, *Lives of the Painters, Sculptors, and Architects*, 2 vols, translated by Gaston du C. de Vere, London: Random House, 1996.

10 Arthur Schopenhauer, *The World as Will and as Idea,* p. 119.

11 Ibid., p. 118.

12 Ludwig Mies van der Rohe, 'Where Do We Go From Here?', Fritz Neumeyer, *The Artless Word*, translated by Mark Jarzombek, Cambridge, MA and London: MIT Press, 1991, p. 332.

The Cultural Context of Critical Architecture

Introduction

The cultural context of critical architecture

Murray Fraser

When discussing the idea of a conference on critical architecture, the sheer complexity of the subject was immediately apparent. Nagging away was the issue of whether critical architecture could ever be in any sense reduced to a homogenous and all-embracing category. We of course realised it could not, but equally it seemed wrong to assume there was not some form of linkage between the different understandings of critical architecture. In our eyes, to reject the critical function in architecture would only mirror the worst tendencies of the 'post-critical' position in the United States. The latter is a phenomenon regarded by dismayed outsiders as a sign of a growing detachment of American academics from the wider world; maybe even an existential squeal of anguish in the face of that nation's drift towards neo-conservative policies in global affairs.

It seemed far more useful, instead, to allow room for diversity under the umbrella of critical architecture, accepting that it could vary across the world in terms of regional issues, modes of practice, building types and everyday cultural practices. Perhaps the notion of critical architecture is now even a relative luxury or indulgence in developed Western countries, and more urgently needed elsewhere. To suggest this is not to argue for any essentialist difference between regions of the world, simply to observe that the workings of modernisation and globalisation remain highly uneven and differentiated across the planet, as does the capacity for individual critical action and the expression of oppositional values. We may live increasingly in a space of capitalist flows, but it is equally true that disparate experiences of this global reality are resulting in ever-greater social inequalities. A crucial role for critical architecture surely has to be to explore, express and then attempt to remedy the present imbalances in power and opportunity.

Correspondingly, this section of the book aims to show some of the diversity of culturally specific approaches and possibilities for critical architecture. Broadly speaking, the nine chapters in this section are gathered into three sub-strands. The first strand takes on a more abstract, theoretical tone to ask what kinds of conditions might permit the notion of critical architecture to occur. It starts with Kim Dovey appealing for a genuine sense of criticism to be inserted back into architectural writing. Neatly skewering the follies of 'post-critical' theory, Dovey also picks apart the myths of the modernist avant-garde, showing how formal innovation by itself will always be insufficient to generate critical architecture. For architectural projects to possess a critical facility, they must also, as Dovey argues, rethink social programmes and tackle head-on the hidden workings of power. This is because buildings create meaning not only through their formal aesthetics, but also in the way social space is created and used. So how can this be incorporated into architectural design? In the next chapter, Charles Rice returns to the writings of Walter Benjamin, arguing that a critical function will only come about by looking more at the diffuse workings of the city. This, he says, will displace our concern away from individual buildings and towards an analysis of the variegated urban experiences of modernity.

With a case made for a deeper cultural reading, the next strand shows how critical architecture can operate under very different cultural conditions and with very different protagonists. Beginning with an internalised look at architectural discourse, and set within the relative privilege of bourgeois housing in 1950s Norway, a lyrical description is provided by Elisabeth Tostrup of a pair of dwellings by Arne Korsmo and Christian Norberg Schulz. Seen in its time as an affront to the dominant ethos of Norwegian architecture, Korsmo's house design in particular introduced modernism as a critical approach in Oslo, while at the same time criticising the functionalist separation between workplace and home. Taking an opposing context, Gini Lee writes about the ad-hoc dwellings found in the Australian outback, using post-production theory to argue that these liminal buildings represent an implicit critique of the practices and aesthetics of orthodox architecture. Her images of cannibalised modular structures reveal an inadvertent beauty in otherwise seemingly unthinking designs. An alternative reading of critical possibilities comes in Ana Betancour's account of the street protest movement in Barcelona, triggered by the economic hegemony of the G8 nations and by the misguided military interventions of the coalition in the Middle East, led by the United States and the United Kingdom. Betancour sees a real opportunity for radical practice in art and architecture to immerse itself in political protest, giving the resulting shelters and artworks a sense of urgency that capitalist architecture would otherwise crush out. In terms of the consequences of globalisation, Jianfei Zhu looks at differing scales of operation of architecture in China, as part of that country's march towards economic growth. Zhu notes a curious two-way mediation now taking place: Western architects like Rem Koolhaas are using the experience of China as a tool to criticise practice in Western countries, whereas Western-trained Chinese architects such as Yung Ho Chang and Qingyun Ma are distilling the critical stance of Koolhaas for their own ends, and by doing so, they are creating an architecture of contestation that is finding increasing favour amongst China's emerging middle classes.

The final strand of chapters addresses the actualities of architectural practice. If we accept that architecture is inherently propositional and utopian, and thus always contains at least the potential to express critical values, then how might architects respond to this? There are no easy answers and no set approaches, but clearly a few pointers. Sarah Wigglesworth writes eloquently about the difficulties of being critical in face of client demands and commercial pressures, noting how the project for her house/office in North London – designed with Jeremy Till – offered a chance to question the continuing cultural split between work and domesticity, as well as to thumb a nose at the British architectural mania for cleanliness and minimalist restraint. Instead she argues for design that will accept mess and decay, and that can revel in outré conditions of hairiness, fatness and plurality. Steve McAdam of Fluid Architects follows with an account of 'The Gateway' building on the outskirts of Derby, in central England, where the community was involved in an ambitious regeneration project that blended sport with other recreational activities. On a conceptual level, Alona Nitzan-Shiftan, Ganit Mayslits Kassif and Udi Kassif provide a fascinating account of the motivations behind the 'Neuland' project – an imaginary scheme to build a mirror-image of Tel Aviv on an offshore island, a settlement untainted by the land-grabbing and colonial politics of hardline Zionism. Expressing the feelings of left-wing Israelis outraged by what is being done in their name, the designs for the 'Neuland' project offer a critical take on the Israeli/Palestinian problem, as well as acting as ruminations on urbanity and cultural life that speak to us all. The section ends with my chapter calling for a new phase of critical architecture, one no longer reliant on the disguised (and in the end cynical) tactics of figures like Rem Koolhaas and Bernard Tschumi. What is needed is a return to an open expression of critical values in architecture. Many examples could well be cited from around the world, but here I focus on the Donnybrook housing estate in Bow, designed by Peter Barber. It is a scheme in London's East End that has scandalised many by its open attack on current approaches to mass housing and urban design. If new models for critical architecture are going to emerge in the coming decades, it is surely designers such as Barber who will provide them.

'I Mean to be Critical, But … '

Kim Dovey

When someone begins a statement: 'I don't mean to be critical, but …', then we are forewarned that they do mean to be critical, and they will be. In the practice of architecture, however, the reverse is often the case. Architecture that is meant to be critical becomes incorporated into, and complicit with, a prevailing economic, political and social order: the 'ever-the-same' returns in the guise of the 'critical'. In this chapter I will suggest that critical architectural practices can be seen to operate along two semi-separate dimensions: the 'formal' construction of meaning and the 'spatial' mediation of everyday life. The conceptual oppositions buried here (form/function, representation/action), and the separations between them, are clues to understanding the ways a supposedly 'critical' architecture is neutralised. The illusion of a critical architecture becomes compatible with a specialisation in the production of both symbolic and social capital. I don't mean to be critical, but I want to suggest that a critical architecture may be one that unsettles the architectural field, and one of the tasks of architectural critique may be to expose what might be called a 'critical complicity'.

The ways in which a dominant order appropriates, assimilates, neutralises and marginalises its critics have been well explored by social and architectural theorists operating within a critical theory framework, particularly Walter Benjamin, Theodor Adorno, Frederic Jameson and Manfredo Tafuri.[1] The 'critical architecture' project was originally conceived and pursued in the United States by critics and architects such as Michael Hays and Peter Eisenman; the 1984 paper by Hays entitled 'Critical Architecture' has been seen as seminal, and a brief critique of it will serve as an introduction to the issues I want to raise.[2] Hays defined critical architecture as 'resistant to the self-confirming, conciliatory operations of a dominant culture'.[3] He sketched two extreme positions – the compliant reproduction of dominant values on the one hand, and formalist autonomy on the other – and identified 'critical' architectural practice with a zone of operations between these poles. In practice, however, this formulation of a 'critical architecture' focused on formal critique to the exclusion of social practice; it embodied the promise that an architecture of formal autonomy could resist the dominant order through its very own order of materials, surfaces and forms. 'Critical architecture' was thus confined to the formalist end of the formal/social spectrum, and social engagement in architectural practice was conflated with complicity.

This trajectory of 'criticality' seems to have largely run its course, and many of the products of deconstruction can now be seen as little more than stylistic effects that reframe and reproduce the very social relations they were conceived to resist.[4] Yet the question of a 'critical architecture' remains perhaps the most crucial of the time and has been given a recent twist by the well-publicised attack on it by Michael Speaks.[5] This critique of 'criticality', entitled 'After Theory', can be read as both a call to abandon critical social theory entirely because it stifles innovation, and as a plea to integrate architectural thinking with architectural practice. I will return to this debate later in this chapter; but in order to make sense of it, I want to add a critic from outside this critical theory lineage. Pierre Bourdieu's work on discursive 'fields' of cultural production shows how aesthetic practices camouflage practices of power, how images are appropriated as symbolic capital, and how aesthetic production reproduces social distinction.[6] While there are some parallels between Tafuri and Bourdieu (particularly on the economic role of the avant-garde), Bourdieu's work is widely ignored by most within the 'critical architecture' project. I suggest this is because it unsettles the social 'field' of architectural practice rather than the formal debates within it.

I take a critical architectural practice to mean one that engages broadly with the ways in which architecture is enmeshed in practices of power. It does not necessarily mean architecture steeped in critical social theory, nor one that makes critical statements. Indeed, as my title suggests, the intention to criticise may be the first step to complicity. A definition of a critical architectural practice also depends on how the field of architecture is defined. Are all buildings 'architecture' or (as Nikolaus Pevsner would have it) just those produced by an elite? And is the practice of 'architecture' limited to the imagination and construction of buildings?

At risk of oversimplifying, I think it useful to conceive of the social critique of architecture operating along two closely related yet distinguishable dimensions of representations and spatial practices.[7] The first of these has primarily to do with the ways in which built form constructs social meaning as a form of discourse or text. Largely stemming from the discursive/deconstructive turn in social theory, the key focus here is on the manner in which identities and subjects are produced and reproduced through architecture. Within this framework, a critical architecture often transgresses the codes through which gendered, ethnic, class and other identities are produced and reproduced. A critical architecture may seek to unsettle or disorient its subjects, to transgress the grounded comfort zone of fixed identities and meanings, while engaging with new identity formations. A critical architect will be critical of the thoughtless reproduction of identities and will accept the responsibility of the inevitable production of identities – nations, cities, corporations, communities, families and selves – through architecture. The question is not whether architecture constructs identities and stabilises meanings, but how and in whose interests.

The second dimension involves the ways in which architecture frames spatial practices, actions and events through its spatial programmes. A critical architecture in this regard may pay attention to the structure of social space, the use of boundaries to mediate social encounter and to standardised spatial fields and building types.[8] Questions of identity and subjectivity are approached through a focus on every-day life as mediated by spatial permeability and segregation, by transparency and opacity, and by the desire lines and rhythms of spatial practice. Michel Foucault's insight into the importance of the spatially structured social gaze in the production of normalised sub-jects is crucial here; but no more so than those of Henri Lefebvre, Michel de Certeau and Gilles Deleuze into the role of transgressive spatial practices in reshaping the social world.[9] A critical architecture in this regard will engage creatively with architectural pro-grammes, and will resist the mindless reproduction of socio-spatial practices. It will also resist the idea that because power is invested in programmed boundary control that lib-eration is somehow found in open plans or fractured geometries. Architecture always mediates spatial practices in a semi-coercive manner, it enables and constrains; the question is not whether, but how it does so, and in whose interests.

These two dimensions of architecture – as text and programme – are always connected in constructed buildings which simultaneously construct meanings and mediate spatial flows. Architecture is a multiple 'framing' wherein representations are framed by spatial structures that are, in turn, infused with narrative interpretations. The structure of pathways into and through a building mediates and frames architec-ture as discourse, and meaning in turn is partly produced by the mode of encounter. Represented meanings and spatial practices produce and reproduce each other through architecture. While representations and spatial practices are integrated in the field of everyday life, in the field of architectural critique they tend to be divided. It is this separation of architecture as text from everyday life that has facilitated the appro-priation and neutralisation of 'critical' architecture.

The imperative to integrate meaning and use comes in part from the degree to which meanings are constructed in use – a view with roots in the writings of both Martin Heidegger and Ludwig Wittgenstein. In *Being and Time*, Heidegger distin-guishes between our active engagement with the world (*zuhandenheit*) and our con-templation of it (*vorhandenheit*).[10] While the meanings of works of fine art are based in contemplation, those of architecture have their primacy in everyday life where contem-plation is but one part. The discursively constructed meanings of architecture can neither be reduced to its use nor separated from it. The 'language' of architecture is not added to the spatial programme, but is written through it.

For Wittgenstein, language is a 'game' with meanings of words constructed through the uses to which they are put. To paraphrase him: 'let the use of [buildings] teach you their meaning.'[11] Again, this does not suggest that meaning can be reduced to function, but rather that some primary meanings of architecture stem from what, and who, a building is 'for'. A critical architecture will not separate meaning from action; it may be useful to ask the Deleuzian question – not what architecture 'means', but what it 'does' and how it 'works'.[12] What are the effects of particular semantic and spatial framings, what flows of desire are produced? Such effects may have little to do with the architect's conscious intentions, since the social encounter with architecture is both oblique and contingent; the 'taken for granted' framing by architecture of our collective lives is a key to its potency. As Benjamin puts it, architecture is a social art that 'is consummated by a collectivity in a state of distraction'.[13] Architecture is steeped in habit; it is a production of habitat and of the *habitus* that is defined by Bourdieu as a set of structures, dispositions and rules that frame everyday life and the 'sense of one's place' within it.[14] Bourdieu's work is useful to this issue in part because he links the *habitus* to the discursive *field*; the socially structured practices of everyday life to the production of symbolic capital within institutionally structured fields of power.

I want to step sideways now to illustrate this a little, and to look at architecture as a field of power. For their time, Peter Eisenman's early buildings seemed to be paradigmatic of a 'critical' architectural practice. Many of the reassuring certainties of dwelling, tectonics, function and identity were relentlessly transgressed as he inspired a generation of younger architects with the hope for an architecture that could resist and deconstruct a dominant order. In a recent interview, he is quoted as follows:

> [M]ost of my clients are Republicans [...]. And I have the most rapport with right-leaning political views, because first of all, liberal views have never built anything of any value, because they can't get their act together.
>
> (Peter Eisenman, 'Liberal Views Have Never Built Anything of Value', interview by Robert Locke, 27 July 2004, see www.archinect.com/features/article.php?id=4618_0_23_0_M (accessed 11 March 2006))

Leaving aside the political sentiment, this identification of architectural value with the currently dominant global order gives cause for thought about how a 'critical architecture' has been conceived. Is this the old story of the critical 'young Turk' turning conservative as he reaps the benefits of success, following the oldest of imperatives in getting the job? Or is it more of a desperate attempt to regain the limelight by reframing the field of cultural production? In my view, the persona of Eisenman, his architecture and his career, have been largely produced by the 'fields' of architectural discourse and practice; he has played this field successfully and in a manner that has never threatened broader processes of social reproduction. This is not a new argument; it was most clearly, if rather simply, put by Diane Ghirardo in 1994 when she argued that Eisenman's work creates an illusion of a critical architecture, sustained by staying one step ahead of the audience's capacity to critique it.[15] His work is a sophisticated application of critical social theory, particularly Adorno and Jacques Derrida, yet the alignment of such work with a global empire driven by right-wing politics is cause for concern. This alignment is made possible by the split between text and programme outlined above. The illusion of a 'critical' architecture can be constructed by a reduction of 'architecture' to text protected from criticism by an inaccessible private language. Consider another quotation from the same interview:

> I believe that art and life are two different discourses, and how I want to live is different from how I want to practise architecture. I love living in an

old New England house; my in-laws have a small sea-side house in Connecticut. I had this 1740s farmhouse [...] where I used to live. What I do not want to do is to recreate a 1740s farmhouse; I want the original thing, with the original boards, because you can't get those kinds of wide boards any more, the kind of nails that were made.

(Eisenman, 'Liberal Views Have Never Built Anything of Value')

Here we find the distinction between representations and practices set out clearly; life is reduced to a discourse and separated from architecture as autonomous art. And there is another distinction here that Bourdieu would understand, which is the social capital available to those with the right in-laws and access to seaside houses; the symbolic capital and 'aura' of the rare and authentic original. The anti-essentialism of deconstructivism folds into a new essentialism.

Eisenman has become an easy target, but this issue is not about individuals, it is about fields of power. Daniel Libeskind's 'freedom tower' on the World Trade Center site illustrates this is in a different way. With credentials established by the Holocaust Museum in Berlin, this is a commission that Libeskind is well-qualified to carry out in a critical manner. Instead we find him personifying the freedom-seeking immigrant, wearing the stars and stripes, affirming the dominant ideology of the US as a bastion of freedom and democracy.[16] Perhaps this repetition of the party line, with its simplistic reduction of the 9/11 attack as an assault on Western 'freedom', is the price to be paid by the architects of the new world order – but it can scarcely be called 'critical'. There is a sense that architecture is permitted to be critical at certain moments and in certain places where that criticality helps to both heal social division and legitimate the social order. Libeskind's Holocaust Museum in Berlin and Maya Lin's Vietnam Veterans Memorial in Washington, DC each stand as seminal contributions to a critical architecture of this kind. But they do so by affirming history as a question rather than reducing it to a dominant cipher.

For many critics (and I am among them), the work of Rem Koolhaas comes close to a critical architectural practice; it is one that engages critically with both formal imagery and spatial practice. Much of his programmatic innovation can be construed as an attempt to resist the formularised reproduction of everyday life, and to generate more random social encounter in the interiors of buildings. In my critiques of some of this work, I have suggested that he achieves this with mixed results – the formal magic of architecture produces an illusion of everyday emancipation.[17] Ironically, many of the achievements of Koolhaas come from the degree to which he recognises the limits to autonomy and criticality. Instead of encoding critical comment or opposing the effects of power, his work at times accentuates such effects, rendering architecture more socially transparent.

One could go on deconstructing the Deconstructionists; however, my point is not to target individuals who are often producing good work in a formal sense. It is, rather, to suggest that all this work exists, and all these agents operate, within a field that is structured in a manner that enables a seemingly 'critical' architectural practice to thrive, while at the same time reproducing the very social structures, identities and practices that it purports to challenge.

It is interesting in the case of the 9/11 project to consider the proposal by Michael Sorkin, which was to turn the site of destruction into a memorial and open space while distributing the required floor-space across a series of sites in Lower Manhattan where urban regeneration would be of more social and economic value.[18] This idea, where void rather than solid signifies memory and social value is married to economic value, was never seriously considered because it directly contradicted the ideological agenda in both symbolic and programmatic terms. In his critique of the prospects for a critical architecture, George Baird comments that:

> despite widespread admiration for his critical writings, the substantive theoretical form of Sorkin's 'resistance' is not seen to be centrally embedded in his own design production, as Mies's has been seen to be by Tafuri, or Eisenman's has been seen to be by Hays.
>
> (Baird, 'Criticality', p. 18)

While Sorkin's work is formally engaging, it is not easily reduced to formalist critique and does not fit the prevailing definition of the field of 'critical architecture'. The appropriation by the corporate market of the autonomous form-making of both Mies and Eisenman is not accidental; autonomous formalism is a required condition for the production and renewal of symbolic capital in that field.

This narrow definition of the field is the 'straw-man' deployed by Speaks in his aforementioned essay on 'After Theory', in which he largely conflates theory with critical theory, and declares it finished: 'I would argue that theory is not just irrelevant but was and continues to be an impediment to the development of a culture of innovation in architecture [...] unremitting critique chasing its own tail, without purpose or end.'[19] This notion of the end of 'theory' is mere polemic, since what replaces it in this account is simply a different theory about the opportunities for formal innovation opened up by new technologies and information systems. Yet it does ring true that the trajectory of criticality based on Tafuri's pessimism and Adorno's negative dialectics has largely exhausted its formalist possibilities. Baird has interpreted this turn to what he terms the 'post-critical' in terms of the need for a generation of Eisenman's protégés to move out from under his shadow. Yet, from the broader viewpoint of the field of cultural production, I would suggest that this is a significant move in clearing the field of architecture (in both its theory and practice) for new symbolic capital; it is a correction in a 'meaning market' that has become saturated by images of criticality. The deeper problem with Speaks' critique of criticality is that it suggests an abandonment of critical social theory, while largely preserving the 'field' of critique – a recipe, as Benjamin might put it, for 'more of the same' returning as the 'ever-new'.[20]

These current debates in some ways echo those from long ago between Adorno and Benjamin on aesthetic and social theory.[21] For Adorno, the only hope for art was a retreat into a critical, autonomous and esoteric formalism – an art that resists appropriation by politics, markets and dominant classes. Benjamin, in contrast, saw liberating possibilities for collective aesthetic practices, modes of production and reception. For Adorno criticality is embodied in, and protected by, the 'difficulty' of the work; Benjamin seeks a broader audience and is keen to dispense with the aura of the individual genius. A good deal of what has passed for 'critical architecture' in the Eisenman/Hays trajectory can be seen in the Adorno tradition, one which Terry Eagleton describes as 'offering up the sickness as cure'.[22] There is a certain subversive potential or shock value in such an approach and the deconstructive movement in architecture has exploited and largely exhausted it. The limits of such an approach lie in its autonomous formalism. The framing of everyday life and the representation of identities within it are reduced to text; critical architecture is reduced to architectural criticism. In their pursuit of 'criticality' such buildings can become signifiers of the idea that nothing can be done beyond the production of architecture as criticism. More than the stifling of formal innovation, the deeper problem with such narrow versions of a critical architecture lies in the stifling of programmatic innovation and therefore of social engagement.

In his account of the trajectory of the 'critical architecture' project, Baird points out that 'the museum has continued to be a more receptive venue for critical work than the street'.[23] This stems from the division between art and everyday life that I traced earlier – the critical is contained and neutralised by the gallery. This is not to suggest that unbuilt architecture has no potency; the unbuilt, however, commonly slips into the unbuildable. In order to be classed as 'architecture' there must be some vision for the future of the built environment at stake. This condition is necessary for a debate about critical architecture to begin – a critical architecture must at least plant seeds of desire for a better future. It follows that the image on the screen, the gallery wall or in the magazine is but a means to architecture and not its end; the end is the future that is at stake. One of the ways in which we 'mean to be critical, but...' is that architecture becomes separated from its consequences; the image becomes an end rather than a means. One can critique the image, its antecedents, style, facility and critical social content, but there can be no debate about aesthetic, social or environmental futures if there is no future represented. Architecture is rendered safe for critical attention by reducing social content to representation and by the severing of architectural discourse from any possible future. When the image becomes the end rather than the means, it may become a fabulous piece of 'criticism', but it loses critical potency as 'architecture'.

The issue here is not whether the project has a real site, client community and budget, nor whether it is necessarily buildable, sustainable or affordable. The first question is whether it is understandable as a possible future that could be inhabited; is a future *habitus* evident? The second question is whether it catches the imagination and nourishes the desire for change. This is not to suggest the eradication of forms of aesthetic production that do not represent possible futures. Developments in computer-aided graphics are unleashing a flood of seductive imagery and there is no need to clip these wings of spatial imagination. But does such work come to be seen as 'critical architectural practice' and does this substitution become a form of complicity? The architectural imagination, at its best, produces the desire for a better future; it contains the potency of the possible. The potency of architecture, its politics and its power, lies in keeping the future of the built environment always at stake. In a well-known interview, Foucault was quoted as follows:

> Liberty is a practice [...] it can never be inherent in the structure of things to guarantee freedom. The guarantee of freedom is freedom [...] [architecture] can and does produce positive effects when the liberating intentions of the architect coincide with the real practice of people in the exercise of their freedom.
>
> (Michel Foucault, 'Space, Knowledge and Power', in Neil Leach (ed.),
> *Rethinking Architecture*, London: Routledge, 1997, pp. 371–2)

This suggests that a critical architecture will engage with a third dimension beyond the representations and spatial practices outlined earlier – an engagement with practices of collective action and constructions of collective identity.

The field of architecture has been largely constructed around the identification of architecture as formal innovation – an artistic practice constructed in opposition to all that is 'common'. It is also the framing of everyday life and the invention of a future; and in this regard good architecture is all too uncommon. A critical architecture cannot be practised in opposition to ideas of 'community' – however problematic that concept may be – because that is where collective action takes place, and where collective identities and desired futures are negotiated and constructed. A critical architecture is an unsettling practice, and it may be unsettling for both the architect and the various communities of interest. A critical architecture will destabilise the field of architecture, its boundaries, identity formations and reproductive practices. A partial autonomy of architecture is useful for critical purposes but must remain the subject of critique. The retreat to autonomous practice can entail a conflation and confusion of the freedom of the architect with the broader project of social emancipation. To what degree does the quest for a 'critical architecture' construct a space of 'critical complicity' where innovation can be safely contained; a space where we mean to be critical, but ...?

Notes

1   Some seminal texts here are: Manfredo Tafuri, *Architecture and Utopia*, Cambridge, MA: MIT Press, 1976; Fredrik Jameson, 'Postmodernism, or the Cultural Logic of Late Capitalism', *New Left Review*, 146, 1984, pp. 53–92; Theodore Adorno, *Minima Moralia*, London: New Left Books, 1974; Walter Benjamin, *Reflections*, New York: Harcourt Brace and Yovanovich, 1978; and Hilde Heynen, *Architecture and Modernity*, Cambridge, MA: MIT Press, 1999.
2   George Baird, ' "Criticality" and its Discontents', *Harvard Design Magazine*, 21, 2004, pp. 16–21.
3   C. Michael Hays, 'Critical Architecture', *Perspecta*, 21, 1984, pp. 15–28.
4   See G. Baird, ' "Criticality" and its Discontents'.

5   Michael Speaks, 'After Theory', *Architectural Record*, June 2005, pp. 72–5; see also Baird, ' "Criticality" and its Discontents'.

6   See: Pierre Bourdieu, *Distinction*, London: Routledge, 1984; Pierre Bourdieu, *The Field of Cultural Production*, New York: Columbia University Press, 1993. For architectural interpretations, see Garry Stevens, *The Favoured Circle*, Cambridge, MA: MIT Press, 1998; Kim Dovey, 'The Silent Complicity of Architecture', in Jean Hillier and Emma Rooksby (eds), *Habitus: a Sense of Place*, 2nd edn, London: Ashgate, 2005, pp. 283–96; Katerina Rüedi, 'Curriculum Vitae: the Architect's Cultural Capital', in Jonathan Hill (ed.), *Occupying Architecture*, London: Routledge, 1998, pp. 23–38.

7   For a more detailed version of these two dimensions, see Kim Dovey, *Framing Places: Mediating Power in Built Form*, London: Routledge, 1999, pp. 17–38.

8   The work of Hillier and Hanson is seminal in this regard. See Bill Hillier and Julienne Hanson, *The Social Logic of Space*, Cambridge: Cambridge University Press, 1984; Bill Hillier, *Space is the Machine*, Cambridge: Cambridge University Press, 1996.

9   Michel Foucault, *Discipline and Punish*, New York: Vintage, 1979; Henri Lefebvre, *Writings on Cities*, Oxford: Blackwell, 1996; Michel de Certeau, *The Practice of Everyday Life*, Berkeley: University of California Press, 1984; Gilles Deleuze, *The Fold*, Minneapolis: University of Minnesota Press, 1993.

10 Martin Heidegger, *Being and Time*, New York: Harper and Row, 1962, pp. 97–102.

11 Ludwig Wittgenstein, *Philosophical Investigations*, Oxford: Blackwell, 1967, p. 220.

12 See Gilles Deleuze, *Foucault*, Minneapolis: University of Minnesota Press, 1988, p. 71; Clare Colebrook, *Gilles Deleuze*, London: Routledge, 2002, p. 46.

13 Walter Benjamin, *Illuminations*, New York: Harcourt, Brace and World, 1968, p. 232.

14 Bourdieu's theory of the *habitus* has its roots in architecture, both Panofsky's interpretation of Gothic architecture as a system of thought written in space (which Bourdieu translated) and in his analysis of the Berber house. See Pierre Bourdieu, *Outline of a Theory of Practice*, London: Cambridge University Press, 1977; Dovey, 'Silent Complicity'.

15 Diane Ghirardo, 'Eisenman's Bogus Avant-Garde', *Progressive Architecture*, November 1994, pp. 70–3. See also responses from Eisenman *et al.* in the following issues.

16 Paul Goldberger, *Up from Zero*, New York: Random House, 2004, pp. 8–9, 145.

17 Kim Dovey and Scott Dickson, 'Architecture and Freedom: Programmatic Innovation in the Work of Rem Koolhaas', *Journal of Architectural Education*, 55, 4, 2002, pp. 268–77; Kim Dovey, 'Multiplicities and Complicities: Signifying the Future at Euralille', *Urban Design International*, 3, 3, 1999, pp. 89–99.

18 Goldberger, *Up from Zero*, p. 56; see also Michael Sorkin and Sharon Zukin (eds), *After the World Trade Center*, New York: Routledge, 2002; Daniel Libeskind, *Breaking Ground*, London: John Murray, 2004.

19 Speaks, 'After Theory', p. 74.

20 Graham Gilloch, *Myth and Metropolis*, Cambridge: Polity, 1996, p. 106.

21 See Terry Eagleton, *The Ideology of the Aesthetic,* Oxford: Blackwell, 1990; Martin Jay, *The Dialectical Imagination*, Boston: Little Brown, 1973; Adorno, *Minima Moralia*; Benjamin, *Reflections*.

22 Eagleton, *Ideology of the Aesthetic*, p. 362.

23 Baird, 'Criticality', p. 18.

Critical Post-Critical

Problems of effect, experience and immersion

Charles Rice

To publish an anthology on critical architecture at this time means that it will be received in the context of the recent debate about a post-critical architecture. Yet debates about architectural positions are often short-lived, and the current one already seems a little exhausted; a laissez-faire attitude seems to have descended upon it; or, rather, the post-critical promotes the laissez-faire as an architectural position.[1] There is a need to escape this situation, to think outside of it.

This chapter will deal with some key issues that have been raised by the recent debate, those to do with effects, experience and the built environment as immersive, but it will do so by looking elsewhere for a discussion of them. This 'elsewhere' will be found in aspects of the work of Walter Benjamin, certainly no stranger to architectural theory and, as such, something of an antagonist in a debate whose proponents want to fight theoretical erudition and 'difficulty' as a way of establishing the right 'mood' for architectural practice.[2] In examining Benjamin once again, the presence of the critical will be found within a cluster of concepts and ideas that are supposed to signal its demise.

Before departing from this debate, it is worth signalling its problematic aspects.[3] Reinhold Martin has identified in the context of the debate a conflation between a political critique of architecture, arising particularly in the work of Manfredo Tafuri, and an aesthetic critique that is necessary to the project of autonomy, the key figure in that context being Peter Eisenman. The Tafurian political critique would, as Martin suggests, recognise the impossibility of architectural practice itself being critical (not to mention Tafuri's injunction against operative criticism). Hence there is the emergence of a self-referential project, where aesthetic (self-)critique becomes necessary to the maintenance of autonomy. Exposing the false conflation of these two senses of critique, Martin points out that they are, instead, held within a dialectical tension. Significantly, this is not recognised by Eisenman, who Martin suggests takes the autonomy project as political critique: that, in the continual testing and reinvention of architecture's own techniques, a political critique of the 'external factors' of architecture's production is also being staged.

The desire of the proponents of the post-critical position to kill the father figure of Eisenman, along with Michael Hays as the major interpreter of Tafuri's position in the United States, points to an acceptance and an amplification of Eisenman's conflation. As a result, the post-critical move would seem to be this: by getting rid of the idea that a continual testing and reinvention of architectural techniques must supposedly take place as a critique of 'real conditions', architecture is free to engage with the world again, without any loss of its specificity, or what Robert Somol and Sarah Whiting call the particular expertise of architects.[4] The spirit of the aesthetic critique of the autonomy project is retained (this is what makes architects into architects), while the false identity with a political critique is removed so that architects can stop worrying about the fact that what they perform is a practice engaged with the complex and contradictory world. The post-critical embraces Tafuri's somewhat glib assertion that 'The mass of architects shouldn't worry, they should just do architecture'.[5]

Martin develops a related issue: by what means does one judge the results of such a post-critical practice? Within the autonomous position, any judgement was bound up with self-critique, and was necessary to the maintenance of a position of autonomy. The very title of 'post-critical' suggests a practice beyond reproach, one that is so engaged in the complexity of the contemporary world that to offer a critique of this engagement, or the processes and outcomes that flow from it, begins to look naive, quaintly Marxist, or like a symptom of envy. The maintenance of the specificity of architectural practice seems to occur through the level of engagement with the complex conditions of producing architecture, and the extent to which architecture can reorganise 'multiple economies, ecologies, information systems, and social groups'.[6] But as Martin has shown in his trenchant critical assessment of the entry for the competition for the redevelopment of the World Trade Center site in New York by United Architects – a collection of architects more or less identified with the post-critical position – such an ambitious sense of engagement amounts to no more than a distinctly architectural brand of political naiveté.

This naiveté notwithstanding, a post-critical practice is interested in the generation of effects. Judgement as distanced reflection gives way to experience as environmental immersion. The use of the term 'effects' (and sometimes 'affects')[7] is an attempt to avoid a simple phenomenology of reception, while also offering a reformulated sense of the architect's agency as designer. Effects are said to be a set of (potential) conditions that architects can generate through their designs, even if the exact nature of what those effects would be is left indeterminate (often consciously so). Effects are also considered in terms of the properties and potentials of various materials and their systems that are deployed by architects. Furthermore, an interest in the dynamism of context, and particularly the urban context, allows architects to draw upon the often unacknowledged forces that flow through sites or else that constitute them as fields of interlinked and variable points of intensity. In this way, architecture is said to become a device attuned to those forces and intensities, manifesting and directing them in order to produce effects. For the post-critical position, the way in which effects are considered and deployed across this spectrum comes to define what is specific about architecture as a practice.

But seeking to define the specificity of an architectural practice in this way is still highly problematic. Given the post-critical position's maintenance of the central tenet of autonomy – that one can still identify a discipline and practice called architecture that is distinct from, though related to, the various other practices that form the built environment – the position still entails judgement and, as such, is still related to the critical, a capacity of discernment that is specifically architectural.[8]

In order to explore this issue further, a question may be formulated from outside the terms of the post-critical debate: how is judgement a question literally embedded in the urban conditions of the built environment, yet in a way that is not entirely captured within or exhausted by the discursive history and conventions through which judgement takes place within architecture? This question may be asked in another way. When Benjamin wrote in the 1930s about an 'absent-minded' examination made possible by the relatively new technology of film, he made an analogy with buildings. What significance might the latency of absent-mindedness associated with buildings have for the still-present question of judgement in architecture?

An absent-minded criticality

In the well-known essay, 'The Work of Art in the Age of its Technological Reproducibility', Benjamin writes: 'Buildings have accompanied human existence since primeval times.'[9] In other words, buildings have been around so long that one can sometimes forget they are there. Or rather, one forgets – or at least has no immediate access to – the way in which they might have been consciously designed things; their effects are no longer explainable in terms of design. Architectural historians might fault this argument, but the point Benjamin is making is this: from an urban perspective, buildings are an environment. The metropolis might then be defined as this ubiquity of buildings. Thinking of the relation between buildings and the city in this way enabled Benjamin to formulate a response to the crisis of experience in modernity, the seemingly inevitable shift from a sense of experience as grounded in tradition, place and longevity (*Erfahrung*) – an experience that links judgement to wisdom – to experience as transient, lived in the moment (*Erlebnis*) and, especially in the context of the metropolis, potentially shock-laden.

In the 'Work of Art' essay, the technology of film was the locus of Benjamin's formulations. Where other contemporary critiques of film had focused on it as a degraded form of theatre, and hence part of a modern malaise that was seeing the subsumption of authentic experience by the cheapness of mass entertainment, Benjamin was focused on what was inherent to the medium, and how it performed in relation to this specificity. Examples that Benjamin was interested in included films that engaged directly with the 'hyperstimuli' of the metropolis, not merely taking these as subject matter, but operating in a way that was caught up in the same sense of dynamism as the city itself. Benjamin's theorisation emphasised montage as the crucial aspect of the film's specific materiality, the organising mechanism by which film produced the effects of hyperstimuli for the viewing audience.

Benjamin used the ambient, urban presence of buildings to exemplify the manner in which film had effects for, and indeed affected, an audience. In the 'Work of Art' essay, Benjamin writes:

> Buildings are received in a twofold manner: by use and by perception. Or better: tactilely and optically. Such reception cannot be understood in terms of the concentrated attention of a traveller before a famous building. On the tactile side there is no counterpart to what contemplation is on the optical side. Tactile reception comes about not so much by way of attention as by way of habit. The latter largely determines even the optical reception of architecture, which spontaneously takes the form of casual noticing, rather than attentive observation. As regards architecture, habit determines to a large extent even optical reception. Under certain circumstances, this form of reception shaped by architecture acquires canonical value. *For the tasks which face the human apparatus of perception at historical turning points cannot be performed solely by optical means – that is, by way of contemplation. They are mastered gradually – taking their cue from tactile reception – through habit.*
>
> (Benjamin, 'The Work of Art', p. 268)

Among many points that could be noted in this extract, it is worth emphasising the relationship Benjamin suggests between reception in distraction and effects generated through material qualities. Within Benjamin's argument, this is a relationship in which both film and buildings share, though they do not share it contemporaneously. Film as a medium for the organisation of perception had an immediacy and operativity for Benjamin in the political milieu of Europe in the latter half of the 1930s that buildings, in their seeming a-historicity and ubiquity, did not.

Film, which is 'predisposed' to reception in distraction, allows for a particular critical position to be taken up by the audience as mass:

> art will tackle the most difficult and most important tasks wherever it is able to mobilize the masses. It does so currently in film. *Reception in distraction – the sort of reception which is increasingly noticeable in all areas of art and is a symptom of the profound changes in apperception – finds in film its true training ground.* Film, by virtue of its shock effects, is predisposed to this form of reception. It makes cult value recede into the background, not only because it encourages an evaluating attitude in the audience but also because, at the movies, the evaluating attitude requires no attention. The audience is an examiner, but a distracted one.
>
> (Benjamin, 'The Work of Art', pp. 268–9)

The very ambience of film, an ambience produced in the extent to which the 'cult value' of art recedes, releases a distracted or absent-minded criticality. It is not that film is in this way inherently critical. The danger Benjamin saw was that the organisational potential of film could be exploited for progressive as well as regressive or repressive political ends. What needs to be grasped is that the effects of film, the way they engage perception, are unavoidably political. Understanding this is part of understanding how the deliberate manipulation of its material possibilities relates to a mass, politicised criticality.

In the development of his argument, Benjamin progressively moves away from the everyday experience of buildings. He has no account of how an architectural practice contemporaneous with the sort of film practice he admired might engage in the same issues of an absent-minded criticality. This is perhaps because distracted perception relies on the 'background effect' of buildings in the city, precisely the fact that buildings are mastered through use, over time, rather than being seen as interventions that stand out or impinge upon a series of established environmental conditions. If there is any account of an architectural practice in Benjamin's argument, it is an inherently conservative one, one where a notion of the pre-existing environment is valorised over the new and the disruptive, but where this environment might be able to support new or disruptive instances of engagement.[10]

And so it is perhaps wrong to ask a question that seems most pertinent at this point: what would it mean for architecture as a practice to re-vivify this sense of a distracted perception that seems to be a latent quality of buildings in the context of the city? Looking more closely at the idea of a crisis of experience shows that Benjamin's arguments are, first and foremost, ones to do with reception, which, for architecture as a practice of design, becomes a vexed issue.

Reorganising experience

At the level of philosophical critique, Benjamin was attempting to engage with the crisis of experience by reformulating its Kantian framing. As Howard Caygill suggests vis-à-vis Benjamin's reformulation: 'Space and time, which feature as the givens of transcendental philosophy, become modes of configuration which can be understood speculatively as providing the contours of but one among many possible configurations of experience.'[11] Regarding the way in which Benjamin presented his thoughts in the 1933 essay, 'Poverty and Experience', Caygill suggests further: 'tradition [relating to experience as *Erfahrung*] is but one of a number of possible options for the organisation of space and time. Its destruction raises the possibility not of a single but of a number of possible successors.'[12] In the argument of Benjamin's 'Work of Art' essay, film has the potential to organise the succession from experience based on longevity and a connection to tradition, that which relies on the 'cult value' of art. This might be called the operative value of film.

Important for Benjamin was the drawing of new terms for a configuration of experience from the emergence of, and possibilities for relation between, new material and social organisations. These new organisations would render indistinct the conventional division between a subject and an object of experience; or, rather, would manifest themselves prior to such a division, that division only being one among any number of possible configurations of experience. In this light, one might consider that, for Benjamin, the possibilities for a reconfiguration of experience were to do with reading, which, Caygill emphasises, should be distinguished from a simple perceptual encounter. Where, in a Kantian schema, perception relates to the receptivity of 'raw' material, and then its organisation by the subject, Benjamin's sense of reading involves an engagement with material that is already organised, as it might be in a film. As Caygill suggests:

> experience as reading is not divided between an active 'reader' (subject of experience) and a passive 'read' (object of experience). The 'read' is by no means a passive datum but makes as active a contribution as the 'reader' to the accomplishment of 'perception as reading'.
>
> (Caygill, *Walter Benjamin*, p. 4)

This might be another way of stating the idea of an absent-minded criticality.

So, then, what of buildings and architecture? Perhaps more tentative formulations might now be able to be posed. The city represents the organisation of buildings into a condition that predisposes the urban environment to such an idea of reading. The indistinction between subject and environment is held within the idea of habit, and its relation to distraction. It is broken with the idea of a 'concentrated attention of a traveller before a famous building'.[13] Understood in this urban way, the possibilities for a reconfiguration of experience are not absolute, but rather momentary. Film has the potential to organise an absent-minded criticality for a duration, the duration of a film screening. What Benjamin might have realised, but did not articulate explicitly, is that the existence of the mass as an urban phenomenon has the potential to extend the duration of this absent-minded criticality. The audience, energised and made self-aware as a mass in the movie theatre, might take something of this reorganisation of experience back out into the city streets, returning this heightened apperception to the context where Benjamin saw it to be latent; and, if it is not too long a bow to draw, to precipitate a revolution 'on the streets'.

These kinds of conditions illuminate the present architectural debate in suggestive ways. But if these 'suggestions' are to be taken up architecturally, it must be realised that what one might call this alternative history of an architecture of ambience and effects is freighted with particular conditions of its own. If Benjamin's thinking is useful architecturally in the present circumstance, it is only because criticality is given a value, one related to a kind of environmental reception, and one that relates in no clear way to the agency or identity of the architect as designer. In addition, the historicity of these possibilities Benjamin announced needs to be understood. Regarding film, subsequent historical occurrences only served to develop and reinforce its illusory qualities. In the main, film developed to hold audience members captive, rather than to release a criticality from their absent-mindedness. Indeed, the political potentials of embracing experience as *Erlebnis* have not been borne out. The apperception associated with 'shock effects' has developed together with greater capacities for resistance to such effects, and their uptake in 'auratic' appreciation. As such, it would be naive to think that an architecture interested in ambience and effects could immediately take up these possibilities, whether the explicit links to Benjamin's thinking are made or not.

Given all of this, however, it is still interesting, and indeed critical, to think about how a variety of practices might predispose urban material to the potential of a critical reading. If (or perhaps when) architectural debate gets past its current problems with acknowledging the critical, these questions might begin to show themselves in useful ways.

Notes

1   That the post-critical even represents a 'position' any more is perhaps questionable. In their introduction to a special issue of the journal *Log*, Robert Somol and Sarah Whiting, the major proponents of the post-critical, begin:

> So we hijack this issue, try to give it shape, but unite it neither by thematic nor ideological consistency. At most, it's organized by sensibility and personal affinity. These are the people with whom we hang out, play cards, drink until closing, escape conferences, plot futures, compete with laughter and fight with conviction.

> After they outline what the post-critical might actually involve, they conclude thus: 'For now, we've invited the players, declared the game, and dealt the cards. Nothing left but to let the chips fall where they may' (Robert Somol and Sarah Whiting, 'Okay, Here's the Plan...', *Log*, 5, 2005, pp. 5–7).

2   Somol does call Benjamin to his aid, however, in bearing witness to the end of the journal *Assemblage*:

> experimentation and instrumentality were necessary sacrifices to the critical generation of *Assemblage*; their dreamlike appearance here at the end is but a flashback tinged with regret. Or, as Wally once said: 'Each epoch not only dreams the next, but also, in dreaming, strives toward the moment of waking.'
>   (Robert Somol, 'In the Wake of *Assemblage*', *Assemblage*, 41, 2000, p. 92)

3   Reinhold Martin, 'Critical of What? Toward a Utopian Realism', *Harvard Design Magazine*, 22, Spring/Summer 2005, pp. 104–9.

4   Robert Somol and Sarah Whiting, 'Notes Around the Doppler Effect and Other Moods of Modernism', in Michael Osman, Adam Ruedig, Matthew Seidel and Lisa Tilney (eds), *Mining Autonomy*, a special issue of *Perspecta*, 33, 2002, pp. 72–7.

5   Manfredo Tafuri, 'There is No Criticism, Only History', *Design Book Review*, 9, 1986, p. 11.

6   Somol and Whiting, 'Notes Around the Doppler Effect', p. 77.

7   See Mark Cousins, 'The Aeffect', in Brett Steele (ed.), *Corporate Fields: New Office Environments by the AADRL*, London: Architectural Association, 2005, pp. 146–51.

8   On the 'internal' mechanisms of architectural judgement, or what he calls 'a unique criticality within architecture', see Peter Eisenman, 'Autonomy and the Will to the Critical', *Assemblage*, 41, 2000, pp. 90–1. Eisenman develops his argument as a response to the post-critical position. It is worth, then, comparing this latest version of autonomy with Somol and Whiting's idea of architecture as a deployed expertise. While they want to emphasise 'deployment' as the crucial difference, the reliance on 'expertise' continues to suggest an internal architectural logic.

9   Walter Benjamin, 'The Work of Art in the Age of its Technological Reproducibility

(Third Version)', in *Selected Writings*: vol. 4, edited by Michael Jennings *et al.*, translated by Edmund Jephcott *et al.*, Cambridge, MA: The Belknap Press of Harvard University Press, 1996–2003, p. 268.

10   For a useful discussion of the 'Work of Art' essay in relation to architecture, see Stan Allen, 'Dazed and Confused', *Assemblage*, 27, 1995, pp. 47–54.

11   Howard Caygill, *Walter Benjamin: the Colour of Experience*, London: Routledge, 1998, p. 5.

12   Caygill, *Walter Benjamin*, p. 31.

13   Benjamin, 'The Work of Art', p. 268.

A Critical Architectural Icon and its Contextual Argumentation

Elisabeth Tostrup

The row of three houses that the architects Arne Korsmo and Christian Norberg-Schulz built for their families in Oslo in 1954 was a striking manifestation of international modernism introduced into a society that was engaged in an all-embracing reconstruction programme after the Nazi occupation.[1] It caused great debate. Rumours spread rapidly amongst the small Oslo community of 360 architects. When Korsmo phoned the renowned Oslo architect Frode Rinnan and invited him to visit the new houses, Rinnan at first did not say a word. He just grumbled. Then he said that he might perhaps come if Korsmo provided a proper chair for him to sit in. Ridicule and irony are common expressions of response when confronted by a critical position, in this case acting in defence of fundamental values held by the Norwegian architectural establishment.

In discussing a relatively very small piece of residential architecture, this chapter does so with the conviction that dwelling was – and is – a central issue in modern architecture as well as in modern politics in the Western world. The modernists of the twentieth century had a social programme; they wanted to contribute to a better society for everybody. Housing and dwelling became increasingly important after Norway became an independent nation in 1905, freed from union under the Swedish Kingdom. This coincided with expanding industrialisation and the rapid growth of cities, in which public health programmes demanded light and air in the extensive housing projects that were built. Norwegian architects visited the German *Siedlungen* in the late-1920s, they studied Le Corbusier, and dwelling was a key topic in the 1930 Stockholm Exhibition, the event that is said to mark the breakthrough of functionalism in Scandinavia. Although the Second World War changed the situation drastically, dwelling continued to be a major field of interest in Norwegian architecture until the 1980s.

The relevant issue here, however, is *critical* architecture; in other words, architecture as an instrument of critique. This leads us to ask: a critique of what? Criticism necessarily involves a context; it is relational and implies a negation of values that are different from those that it promotes. Architecture as a means of criticism is not mere words, but involves extensive and expensive material structures erected in order to serve a useful purpose with a certain degree of permanence. The critique must therefore convey positive values and convincingly promote alternatives or improvements to that which is criticised.[2] Since the architects in this case, Korsmo and Norberg-Schulz, wanted to realise their project, both the critique and its context were defined by the framework of values related to the possibilities of building a piece of residential architecture in that particular place at that time. Two kinds of socio-cultural context can therefore be distinguished: first, the state of Norwegian society at the time, its socio-political context and its prevailing/hegemonic form of architecture; second, the international 'modern movement' in architecture, in terms of the ideals of CIAM the two architects adhered to and wished to promote. The first contextual category constituted the values that were being criticised, or the wider framework of the critique; the second provided the features of the critique.[3]

The post-war Norwegian context

In the early 1950s – the project was started in 1952 – Norway was undergoing extensive post-war reconstruction led by the Labour Government, the party that held power from the liberation from the Nazi occupation in the spring of 1945 until the mid-1970s; some 30 years, in fact. There was a great shortage of materials and a great shortage of houses, since a large number of people had lost their homes due to acts of war, and the population was growing rapidly. In Oslo, the capital of around 400,000 inhabitants, strict regulations implied that erecting single-family houses was not to be allowed at all. When built in duplexes or as row houses, the space limit for a family dwelling was 80 m². But most new housing projects were blocks of flats of 60–70 m² in size. Flat roofs were not permitted for housing purposes because of the shortage of asphalt and roofing felt, a factor that supported the use of traditional pitched roofs.

During the Nazi occupation, and even in the few years preceding the war, architectural hegemony in Norway had, as in the other Scandinavian countries, gradually turned away from the clean functionalism of the early-1930s towards a more traditional form of architecture – the 'New Realism' or 'New Empiricism' as presented in the *Architectural Review* in 1947.[4] Amongst a series of publications promoting this view, the large book of *Norwegian Houses* published in 1949 by architects who had all been functionalists in the 1930s aspired to present a comprehensive basis for an architecture that would be able to combine the needs of modern life with nationalist roots and traditional skills, such as in wooden architecture. The prevailing mentality favoured familiar and rather pragmatic tectonic solutions with pitched roofs, timber panel cladding and moderately sized windows. The architect Knut Knutsen, with whom Korsmo had collaborated before the war, now became the 'father figure' for the Norwegian architects who, in the years to follow, adhered to the adaptation and renewal of regional building customs and traditional craftsmanship. Knutsen's own house is an example of this tendency, in which the 'rejection of style' was seen as a major issue.[5]

International modernism

The second kind of context was international modernism in architecture – this being the professional context with which the two architects identified themselves. Both Korsmo and Norberg-Schulz were well acquainted with modernism. Korsmo and his designer wife, Grete, had spent 1949–50 as Fulbright scholars in the United States, where they had met Ludwig Mies van der Rohe, Walter Gropius, Frank Lloyd Wright, Charles and Ray Eames, and other leading figures. They were in fact the very first overnight guests to stay in Edith Farnsworth's famous glasshouse designed by Mies van der Rohe. Norberg-Schulz had been educated under Sigfried Giedion in Zurich, and was later also a Fulbright scholar, visiting Harvard University and Mies van der Rohe in the United States during 1952–3.

When summoned by Giedion in 1950 to form a Norwegian branch of CIAM, Norberg-Schulz urged the 50-year-old Arne Korsmo, who had been a prominent functionalist since the 1930s, to be the leader. Korsmo became the 'father figure' of the group known as PAGON, that included Norberg-Schulz and a handful of other young architects, among them Sverre Fehn (later to become a Pritzker Prize winner).[6] The Danish architect Jørn Utzon, whom Korsmo had befriended in Stockholm during the war and with whom he later toured the United States and Mexico by car, acted as an associate member who took part in several competition projects with Korsmo. The manifesto of PAGON featured in a special issue of the Norwegian architectural journal *Byggekunst* in 1952, and was followed up by a series of other texts and presentations during the following years. Their activity introduced a severe split in Norwegian architecture that was to last for more than 20 years. Thus to Peter Davey, editor of *The Architectural Review*, Norwegian architecture in the 1960s and 1970s still appeared to fall into two camps: that of the followers of Korsmo, with their allegiance to international modernism; and that of Knutsen, with his allegiance to the Arts and Crafts and National Romanticism.[7]

Despite its small size as a domestic project, the piece of critical architecture in question here acted as a key protagonist in this battle for supremacy in the field of post-war Norwegian architecture, in which it came to gain a position of symbolic power, in Pierre Bourdieu's terms. By 1960, modernism had increased its influence greatly, its hegemony being especially visible in Norway through the medium of architectural competitions.[8]

The Norwegian house and its critical dimensions in the mid-1950s

The small row of houses by Korsmo and Norberg-Schulz acted as a negation of prevailing Norwegian architecture by their sheer tectonics, spatial layout and use of materials. The use of a 1.22 m × 1.22 m square grid defined the architectural identity of a complex in which plate-glass panels and white asbestos wallboards were inserted between

Arne Korsmo, The
Korsmo House, Oslo,
Norway, exterior
view. Photograph:
Frode Larsen (2005).

Oregon pine posts. The corresponding steel framework, 3.54 m between centres, constituted the main structural system.[9] A brief look at Norberg-Schulz's own house
showed a consistent spatial arrangement; it was strictly loyal to the grid system, verti-
cally as well as horizontally. Norberg-Schulz was just 29 years old when he moved in
with his Italian wife, Anna Maria. She was used to living in historical Rome and did not
particularly enjoy living on the edge of woods in 'nowhere'. The family sold the house
in the summer of 1956 and moved first to Rome, then back to Norway, where they
settled in a flat in downtown Oslo.[10] Since the Norberg-Schulz house was soon to be
altered by its new owners, and ruined from an architectural point of view, this chapter
will continue its argument based on the Korsmo house.

The Korsmo unit displayed the same structural system, a 1.22 m module
emphasised in its wall proportions, outside as well as inside. The house was 137 m^2 in
area, considerably larger than the typical post-war norm of 80 m^2. This was possible
because the house was defined as a 'live-work' experiment, and so included spaces
for Korsmo and his wife to carry on their professional activities. 'Live-work' is also the
keyword to understand the overall architectural feel, as this idea permeated the entire
house rather than being just confined to a particular room that could be screened off in
order to serve as an office. The couple did not have children, a fact that added to the
notion of mingled uses. The idea of a 'live-work' dwelling was hence the major issue in
Korsmo's presentation of the house in *Byggekunst* in 1955.[11] He stated:

> We have obtained a house that must be paid directly by daily work in the
> square metres that are measured out:
> 1) by my wife in the basement with her experiments and models for the
> goldsmith firm Tostrup [in which she was a partner];

2) metal- and woodwork made by the two of us in the kitchen, and served by an American 'Shop-Smith' machine.

(Arne Korsmo and Christian Norberg-Schulz, 'Tremannsbolig ved to av dem', *Byggekunst*, 37, 7, 1955, pp. 169–89, p. 174)

The first mentioned workshop in the basement, which was actually situated below the ground surface, had a *fenêtre a longueur* above the worktop/bench that runs along the outside wall. In order to improve the spatial qualities of this sunken room, the ground in front was excavated and arranged very precisely in four rather steep tiers, with large wooden cases containing flowering plants and herbs. This stepped garden provided plenty of sunlight and pleasant views for those in the basement workspace.

In the *Byggekunst* article, Korsmo continually praised the 'Shop-Smith' machine and explained how the kitchen – which acted as a second working space – was designed in order to serve both as a workshop with filings and shavings all over the place, and for cooking, eating and doing the laundry. All the walls were covered with mahogany cupboards; even the single window in the room was set into a cupboard in which the front flap could be folded down to function as a table for two or three persons. This table thus sat in front of the window, with the latter appearing rather small, horizontal in aspect, and set into a deep niche.[12] Thus the kitchen with its programmatic flexibility as well as the unconventional solutions for the window, furnishings and materials, was an explicit critique of the prevailing ideal of zoning – whereby all the rooms had to be separated for specific functions, as could be seen in the many plans of standard 1950s Norwegian homes. The design was critical of the prevailing obsession with hygiene and the ideal of the 'professional' full-time housewife locked in her domain, the kitchen. In its own way the house argued in favour of female emancipation, not only by its mixture of uses, but also by the open connection between the kitchen and the nearby living spaces – a device that Korsmo's wife insisted upon because she enjoyed cooking while being in contact with people in the rest of the house at the same time.

Another, third workspace, according to Korsmo's presentation, was the design office on the first floor, which actually could be combined with the master bedroom and a lounge for meeting clients in one continuous space, or could be partitioned off by a sliding door. The beds were to be folded into cupboards to allow space around the drawing tables, and the cupboards were to contain clothes as well as drawings.

Finally, a fourth workspace was provided by the spacious, 7.32 m × 7.32 m living room on the ground floor, which Korsmo said should be:

the frame, the setting for our work, where we could try out models and objects, draw on the chalkboard, use it as an auditorium for lectures with movies and slides, as an exhibition room not only for ourselves but also for our artist friends, and it could provide a small stage.

(Korsmo and Norberg-Schulz, 'Tremannsbolig', p. 176)

Arne Korsmo, The Korsmo House, living room. Photograph: Nils P. Lotherington (2003).

A hundred square cushions, each 600 mm × 600 mm × 80 mm in size, which offered numerous combinations of shape and colours, along with reversible black-and-white wallboards in front of hidden book shelves, provided the main elements of flexible furnishing for this fourth 'live-work' space. Throughout the design, Korsmo regarded spatial considerations to be paramount. Therefore he increased the depth of the roof structure over the living room to eliminate the pillar which otherwise would have needed to be placed in the middle of the space, given the 3.54 m structural module.

This was a striking example of Korsmo's ability to make systemic deviations and adjustments to attain a particular goal, in this case a living room of extraordinary size and qualities. The stairway could be removed to enable a further transformation towards the more theatrical function of the house, with the entrance hall being converted into a stage for the speaker or performer in front of an audience which would be seated below in the living room. The many illustrations made by a painter friend, Gunnar S. Gundersen – some of them published in *Byggekunst* - substantiated the idea of a house that was full of people and activity, as if its real purpose was to serve as a centre for design experimentation and teaching. The couple were in fact central to the post-war Scandinavian design movement; they won two Gold Medals and the Grand Prize at the 1954 Milan Triennale, and Korsmo was in charge of interior design education at the National College of Arts and Crafts.

Flexibility in use and furnishing was just one aspect of an architectural approach that promoted modernity in a way that was meant to be critical of prevailing Norwegian architecture. A further critique in the Korsmo house was materialised in the extensive use of transparent and translucent materials in large glass walls and sky-lights that expressed the modern idea of *transitoriness*. The entire spatial layout, the open spatial continuity within the house as well as between the interior and the outside, also substantiated this critical dimension. Moreover, the use of exquisite types of wood such as mahogany, teak and Oregon pine also represented a critique of the typically staid Norwegian use of pine and conventional jointing techniques.

Finally, a decided Japanese touch to the interior, which was present in several architectural features, gave a sense of alienation from familiar Norwegian traditions. Though they represented subtle transformations, the modularised facades, the many sliding doors, the elaborate design of built-in cupboards and the idea of light-weight, movable standardised units – such as the 100 soft square cushions – testified to these Japanese sources of reference.

Critical rhetoric and the 'consensus culture'

Certain features of the architecture of the Korsmo house, especially as put forward in the architect's own account, were also meant to be critical but entirely in a spirit that invoked shared values within the wider cultural context of Norway. In other words, the arguments set out by the design attempted to bridge the gap between the critique and the object of criticism, through an appeal to 'consensus culture'. Norwegian post-war society was a technocracy governed over by the Labour Party, an alliance between the political leadership and professional experts in health, economics, engineering, education and art, who formed corresponding hegemonies in their different fields. All these fields shared an optimism marked by a belief in progress and positivist science, and powerful egalitarian ideals permeated the pragmatism and secularisation of a predominantly Protestant culture. Despite the split in architectural viewpoints described above, it is generally agreed that Norwegian society has been relatively homogeneous and marked by a great degree of consensus.[13] Jonathan Hill is just one commentator who has remarked upon this 'consensus culture' in Norway, which he finds typically Nordic and thus essentially different from British 'adversary' culture.[14]

Korsmo's emphasis on ideas of standardisation and equality as the basis for the freedom of the individual to make his or her own combination of domestic units was hence totally in agreement with the common trend within mass industry in Norway at the time. The rather plain and 'neutral' exterior of the building complex alluded explicitly to egalitarian pragmatism. This aspect was further elaborated in Korsmo's writings, such as when he stressed the financial and social factors related to space restrictions as the reasons for adopting his 'Home Erector-Set' method of interior furnishing, which was aimed – just like Charles and Ray Eames in Los Angeles – at achieving maximum quality (and usability) with limited means. Moreover, he invoked the importance of making the inhabitants active in the process by offering them a furnishing method that encouraged experimentation, variety and change.[15] Even the term 'Home Erector-Set' alluded to the Erector-Set toy for children, which was very popular in Norway in the 1950s. This was a brilliant rhetorical move; it placed his critical interior design ideology within a broad socio-pedagogical movement of the time, allowing people to be educated in terms of their home furnishings on the new scientific grounds, as a means of social progress. Korsmo thus strengthened the democratic aspect of this Norwegian movement, and added a dimension of *homo ludens* by including and expanding upon the notion of children's playfulness.

The role of nature

Nature and one's relationship to nature marked another 'consensus' value in Norway, often implicitly charged with mythical strands. The first part of Korsmo and Norberg-Schulz's account in *Byggekunst* therefore dealt directly with nature:

> In Oslo we are still fortunate to have landscape that we can appreciate, so let us enjoy it fully as long as possible. A precondition for opening a house towards the environment must be that there is something to view. There-fore it is not at all certain that 'glass houses' are an unnatural solution in Norway. We just need to make sure that we are able to create the intimacy and warmth that is needed on a gloomy winter night! This was the simple reasoning behind the triple housing project at Vettakollen [the particular hill in the outskirts of Oslo].
>
> The glass made it natural to connect landscape and interior, while on the other hand no more than a curtain is needed to close the room. Thus we searched for a possibility of choice and adaptation, consequently an expanded spatial experience.
>
> (Korsmo and Norberg-Schulz, 'Tremannsbolig', p. 170)

The importance of nature, of access to nature and the view of nature from one's home, was – and is – entirely typical of Norway. It is a feature deeply rooted in Norwe-gian culture, as opposed to, for instance, Italy, as was so clearly pointed out later in a conference on Norwegian and Italian architecture held in Oslo in the autumn of 2004.[16] Both countries have beautiful landscapes that the inhabitants clearly appreciate. But whereas most Italians happen to live in dense urban settlements where the view from their homes is often of other historical buildings, Norwegians generally prefer to be able to view some aspect of nature – trees, hills or fjords. Even the latest Norwegian architecture presented at the conference featured designs that were framed by nature, as was remarked upon by contributors. It is relevant at this point to note that the contemporary North American houses that Korsmo usually referred to in his post-war lectures, such as Fallingwater, the Farnsworth House and the Eames House, all shared this quality of being situated directly in their natural surroundings.

An icon to resolve social contradictions

On the one hand, the critical quality of the Korsmo house exposed nature as an agent of the dimension of time – in the sense that nature endlessly changing with the hours and the seasons was mediated for the dweller, and was infinitely reverberated as reflections in the transparent and translucent construction, since the majority of walls were made out of glass. On the other hand, Korsmo succeeded in combining this transitory dimension of his house with an extraordinary atmosphere of warmth and rootedness. The quality of the dwelling was particularly apparent in the living room, which was situated four wide steps lower than the entrance level, a drop of 600 mm in height. In this manner the living room appeared like a wide well that had been dug down into the earth, with the hundred cushions providing a warm lining around its perimeter, and surrounded by magnificent views of the woods and sky outside through the glass walls. The hearth by the party wall was set even one step lower, and provided a place for sitting at a generous teak table in front of the fireplace. Since the living room was furnished along the walls, the central space seemed almost empty by comparison, and enhanced a calm atmosphere to which the hearth added the ultimate warmth and sense of dwelling.

> Beauty today can have no other measure except the depth to which a work resolves contradictions. A work must cut through the contradictions and overcome them, not by covering them up, but by pursuing them.
> (Hilde Heynen, *Architecture and Modernity: a Critique*, Cambridge, MA: MIT Press, 1999, p. 148)

Hilde Heynen reprints this quote by Theodor W. Adorno from 1965 in her book on architecture and modernity. When Arne Korsmo's house over the years became a frequently published icon, a positive image that represented the values of post-war modernism, this was due to the manner in which the architectural design was able to resolve the contradictions between modernity and dwelling, as analysed by Heynen. Although the latest publications on the Korsmo house, especially in popular magazines and journals, tend to emphasise the design objects in the house (vases, plates, chairs) in accordance with a sense of increasing reification, its role as a piece of critical architecture in post-war Norway is still evident and valid. Aware of the shortcomings of a return to traditionalist values, the architecture also negotiated and transcended the pragmatic efficiency of modernism to transmit a quietly vibrating poetry of existence.

Notes

1   The houses have been published/commented upon in Christian Norberg-Schulz, *Arne Korsmo*, Oslo: Universitetsforlaget, 1986, pp. 72–8, 102–9; Nils-Ole Lund, *Nordisk arkitektur*, Copenhagen: Arkitektens Forlag, 1991, pp. 33–4; Nicola Flora, Paolo Giardiello and Gennaro Postiglione (eds), *Arne Korsmo – Knut Knutsen: due maestri del nord*, Rome: Officina edizioni, 1999, pp. 54–71, 91–124; Gennaro Postiglione (ed.),

One-Hundred Houses for One-Hundred European Architects of the Twentieth Century, Köln: Taschen, 2004, pp. 202–5; Elisabeth Tostrup, 'Opposites on Common Ground', *Nordic Journal of Architectural Research*, 15, 3, 2002, pp. 71–86; Astrid Skjerven (ed.), *Arne Korsmo: arkitektur og design*, Oslo: Universitetsforlaget, 2004, pp. 171–5.

2   Hilde Heynen also points out this positive function of architecture as regards criticality in modernity. See Hilde Heynen, 'Architecture between Modernity and Dwelling: Reflections on Adorno's Aesthetic Theory', *Assemblage,* 17, April 1992, pp. 79–91, p. 88.

3   'The architects' could have been one category and 'society' the other, but my choice here is that architecture – the society of architects – is part of society and at the same time autonomous; hence the division reflects the complexity of interests and different movements within the field, in which critique plays a dynamic role.

4   'The New Empiricism: Sweden's latest style', *The Architectural Review*, 101, June 1947, pp. 199–204, is relevant for Norway too.

5   Knut Knutsen's houses are published in Flora, Giardiello and Postiglione (eds), *Arne Korsmo*, pp. 125–77; and Postiglione (ed.), *One-Hundred Houses*, pp. 192–7.

6   CNS was the group's most eloquent spokesman, and for the period 1963–78 editor of *Byggekunst,* the Norwegian architectural review.

7   Peter Davey, 'Norwegian Reflections', *Byggekunst*, 68, 4/5, 1986, pp. 226–8, p. 228.

8   Elisabeth Tostrup, *Architecture and Rhetoric: Text and Design in Architectural Competitions, Oslo 1939–1997*, London: Andreas Papadakis Publisher, 1999.

9   The grid module line runs along the exact inside of the posts of the external walls, where the posts are placed at 1.22 m c/c. Korsmo and Norberg-Schulz made a point of the grid being 4 feet = 1.22 m instead of the later-to-be standard 1.20 m. The 8 cm × 8 cm-thick steel columns, however, are placed 8 cm further in from the external walls, and consequently at 3.54 m c/c. Korsmo left out the centre pillar and achieved a span of 7.08 m c/c.

10 Anna Maria Norberg-Schulz, personal communication, 18 January 2005.

11 The article/presentation by Arne Korsmo and Christian Norberg-Schulz in *Byggekunst* 1955 titled 'Tremannsbolig ved to av dem' (Triplex houses by two of them) pp. 169–89, had a shared introduction on pp. 169–73. Then followed a (subdivided) section 'Hos arkitekt Arne Korsmo', pp. 174–83, very obviously written by Arne Korsmo himself ('me and my wife, etc.') and finally a section 'Hos arkitekt Chr. Norberg-Schulz', written by Christian Norberg-Schulz.

12 Additional light is provided by a skylight in the ceiling/roof.

13 Karl-Otto Ellefsen, 'Tendenser i norsk arkitektur 1986: sprekker i den norske enigheten', *Byggekunst*, 68, 7, 1986, pp. N1–N24, in which Ellefsen writes about the cracks in the Norwegian consensus in architecture; Rune Slagstad, *De nasjonale strateger*, Oslo: Pax forlag, 1998; Edgeir Benum, *Oslo bys historie, vol. 5: byråkratienes by*, Oslo: J.W. Cappelens Forlag, 1994.

14 Quote from Jonathan Hill at the Nordic *Landscapes of Architectural Research* conference in Ultuna, April 2002.

15 Arne Korsmo/PAGON, 'Hjemmets mekano', *Byggekunst*, 34, 1952, pp. 110–13. Korsmo also refers to Le Corbusier's system houses from 1916.

16 *Architecture: A Meaningful Link in Cultural Relations Between Italy and Norway. Exchange of Views on Trends in Contemporary Architecture in the Two Countries*, 16 November 2004, held in Oslo, the speakers included Marco Casamonti, Eva Madshus, Franco Purini, Reiulf Ramstad, Livio Sacchi, Gudmund Stokke and Jan Digerud.

Three Scenarios for a Critical Architecture of Desert Mobility

Gini Lee

An invitation to consider the existence of critical architecture has prompted me to present another way of looking at the 'hybrid' architectures that are often encountered in the Australian outback. In particular, the view that 'the term critical architecture implies a mode of architecture that opposes dominant economic and cultural strands, and hints at an alternative form of practice that does not reproduce prevailing values' becomes extremely pertinent.[1] Within this context, in this chapter I will examine certain small architectures and built landscapes in places remote from urban sensibilities, where people build and occupy marginal environments that reveal the site-specific ecological, economic and social conditions which are at play in the desert.

Notions of mobility – whether temporary, portable or transportable – frame this text, particularly with regard to works that try to embrace the intersections of art, architecture and landscape. Mobility has recently been described as a complex concept within the contemporary context, in which the need for mobility enforced through global communication and economic structures is seen to offer a particular challenge to architecture, since the latter is so predicated on ideas of site specificity.[2] And certainly in the relationship between some temporary and mobile architectures located in (extra)ordinary cultural landscapes, I have been able to discover a critical architecture that in this way reveals the artful tendency within the everyday pragmatics of remote inhabitations.

An analysis of the architectures that have emerged in the iconic landscapes of central Australia automatically infers the long tradition of the folly situated in the picturesque landscape. But even if these Australian 'follies' today create photo opportunities for tourists, they also indicate a distinct cultural approach to settlement, in that they are more obviously examples of necessity as the mother of invention. They are architectures of mobility that respond to an ecological imperative based upon scant resources, and insecure foundations characterized by chance results.

An introduction to certain remote places

**Oodnadatta: café –
closed for business.
Photograph: Gini Lee
(2002).**

Moving around towns in the middle of South Australia, such as Coober Pedy or Mintabie – located geographically in the heart of the sub-continent, a terrain otherwise known as the 'outback' – one is confronted by places formed by spatial and material coincidence; where compositions of artefact and reworked topography, and middens of discarded material, emerge from the desert and from architectures and landscapes in the mind. In these compounds, temporary settlers live and work within the day-to-day practices of existence in remote and largely unsustainable environments. People still come to try their luck, strike it rich and move on to greater comfort elsewhere. These 'mobile grounds' occur in many outback towns over Australia, where get-rich-quick opportunities seem to abound, but the reality is often something else.[3] Of course, many stay on forever, looking for that elusive find, blowing whatever is earned on a few big nights out, or else the place imprints in their souls, so that leaving never happens.

The places are also known for their concealed architecture – the dugouts, where activity occurs underground – and much that is visible above ground is simply a forest of air and exhaust chimneys. Yet there are other architectures here that also demonstrate the reality of occupying and building under conditions where the physical consequence of remoteness from the urban fringe, or the reality of climatic extremes, meet with the cultural conditions of mining, pastoral and tourist activities based upon global markets and a frontier mentality of hard work and hard play. These architectures and their material qualities are never documented in the tourist literature; perhaps it is because they are too handmade or hybrid, and their aesthetic too raw or mundane. But 'dirty realism' has ever required the eye of a 'curator' to emerge, and my photographic practice has been aimed at revealing these overlooked architectures, as valid architectures in their own right.

The narratives implicit in these 'hybrid' architectures have not been recognized by mainstream planners, builders and architects in Australia. Whenever these latter groups venture to build in remote places, they import their exemplars from elsewhere, yet the nature of mining claims generates an evolutionary and organic development of sites and dwellings. Despite this, the adjacent service towns are ultimately laid out within the particular planning framework fashionable during that stage of town development. Most are now populated by spectacularly poorly conceived and prefabricated suburban housing and servicing systems.

My recording of the intrinsic architectures in the 'vernacular' landscape, below and beyond these planned developments, was made over a number of journeys. The photographs I took on these journeys of the material qualities of rural places in South Australia resulted in postcards that sought to celebrate the cultural fabric of these places through their architecture. I was concerned to record the material coincidences arising from the nature of occupation, the availability of economic and material resources for settling, the qualities of site and services, and the building and site-marking practices that resulted. These recordings also uncovered attitudes that express architectural improvisation, evolution, and alternative approaches to dwelling and interaction with landscape in harsh environments.

Propositions on postproduction: revealing the architecture behind the seemingly ephemeral and transitory

In framing this work, I have been strongly influenced by Nicolas Bourriaud's essays on (the art of) postproduction.[4] He suggests that postproduction practices are essentially about the recycling of existing material into new material, and asserts that postproduced works contribute to the eradication of the traditional distinction between production and consumption, creation and copy, ready-made and original. These practices work with objects that are already in circulation through their material manipulation. Bourriaud questions current practices when he asks how we might make do with what we have, rather than make things new, when there is a wealth of material already available for manipulating and (re)presenting through an interrogation of existing forms to produce different results. In postproduction theory, the work itself functions as a narrative that extends and reinterprets the preceding narratives.[5] Regarding built works, (re)programming the existing is evident in the making and remaking of 'hybrid' architectures and landscapes in remote places.

There are hence architectural types that emerge in remote desert places in Australia that exhibit a unique visual aesthetic reflective of prevailing conditions and defining narratives. They are described through a spatial and material reading that also infers a range of actions such as transformation, evolution, improvisation, appropriation and mediation. These actions parallel those introduced in postproduction theory, where art and installation practices utilize the activities of insertion, occupation, manipulation of the 'original' and its subsequent re-appropriation.

In the following three scenarios I will suggest ways of reading the postproduction practices of the builders and makers of these desert architectures through the theoretical lens of (conceptual) mobile ground.

Mobile ground one: on architecture merging to landscape

Coober Pedy: hill (and garden) topography 1. Photograph: Gini Lee (2002).

A chronology of occupation and development, boom and bust, and use and obsolescence is evident in the spatial arrangement of mining compounds, constructed as the latter are in association with existing hill topographies. The caravan is the first act of occupation. In time and with the success of the mine, a range of sheds and shelter structures are built beside the caravan and then into and over the mine workings. Gradually, the space of the mine and the hill become fused – the relative plasticity of corrugated iron-clad framing allowing forms that mimic or even structure the working of soil and topography.

Socially, the house and the mine become interdependent. A miner's domestic arrangement is merged with their working life, and the living room is often also the entrance into the underground workings deep into the hill. These multi-purpose dwellings allow for an economy of scale and construction, for expanding and decreasing populations, and also for security. Surveillance and protection of valuable mining claims and gem storage is paramount to the safe workings of these places. Dynamite is readily available, demarcation disputes and robbery occurs, so a single entry reduces the availability of access: these places are also fortifications.

Here, the hill provides a framework for the spatial installation. Corrugated iron is easily transportable and relatively abundant as a protecting skin. Often appropriated or borrowed, corrugated iron sheeting folds into architectural forms and is moulded to extant topography. Many remote areas are 'out of council', which means that few building regulations exist; constructions can appear overnight, and just as quickly be abandoned as the need arises. And the rusting, discarded machinery lying about reflects an encompassing garden of dreams and aspirations, where the placement of this stuff defines the outer perimeter of the compound, and marks the territory alongside the active mine/house. These desert gardens serve as a spare-parts shop, available to all. This kind of 'mobile ground' appropriates existing topographies, spaces, and abandoned/unused and new materials. A new aesthetic and a new programme for dwelling and working arise from reworking sites of activity.

The first move that persists in such mining settlements is this principle of 'mobile ground'. It is particularly visible in the urban fabric of these remote places. The first construction or the original vehicle that provided shelter, a workplace, or a lockup against marauders and animals never appears to lose its influence as a foundation for future instalments of development.

Mobile ground two: on material (re)contextualization

Coober Pedy: the articulated shed. Photograph: Gini Lee (2002).

The next stage may emerge from many quarters; material may be ordered from town (in this context this means the nearest major city, some 800 km away) and transported up on road trains, or scrounged from a neighbour, or the components may be collected from an adjacent pile of redundant building materials. Nothing is discarded if it may be reused later: in these places, waste and rubbish piles are material 'commons' available for picking over, and not an affront to the city beautiful.

It is possible to read the history of building, rebuilding and reuse written on the weathered and patched walls of successive sheds, in successive locations, by successive builders. Buildings are connected through the archive of their materiality. Through a close inspection of corrugated iron profiles and colours, or of window frames, you can infer previous installations that existed on adjacent sites, or in other parts of town, or even in other towns. In Oodnadatta, there is a man called Adam who

Mintabie: material layering (on wheels). Photograph: Gini Lee (2002).

paints all his buildings a particular shade of bright pink. Wherever this pink is seen else-where along the track, it is thought that Adam has been there – either in reality or cer-tainly in the imagination.

Material layering becomes in this sense a spatial layering, when the first shelter, the physically mobile shelter, is parked within a temporary but less mobile enclosure. Mobility on wheels gradually moves towards fixity as people stay on; and, when shelter is built over a mobile shelter, the wheels are usually removed. These material layers reveal evolving attitudes to climate and protection of the settler, no longer a nomad; yet it seems that the potential to remobilize is always on hand.

Amusing juxtapositions of 'hybrid' architectures are really evidence of a serious culture of making-do, and the forging of narratives that deal with evolving and altered stages of occupation. This reprogramming of existing fabric and artefact into new or reworked and re-conceptualized dwellings is a material mobility, wherein the pragmatic reuse of material is fixed around a settler's first move, contributing to an unlikely but clearly articulated architectural intention.

Mobile ground 3: on the ephemeral inside/outside and adapting the mass-produced

The ubiquitous ATCO shed has replaced the caravan as the mass-produced shelter of choice in many remote places in the Australian desert. Little more than a glorified con-tainer, the ATCO is modular, fits on a semi-trailer, can be easily perforated to allow ways to get in or out, and can be connected to services (if they exist) in a jiffy. It can be readily moved from place to place, up and down the road; it can contain anybody and anything, and sit lightly upon the ground, although the sheds can be hard to shift without heavy machinery. There is little inherent charm in the bare-faced ATCO, and it

Parachilna: mobile
ATCO
accommodation
(with shade).
Photograph: Gini Lee
(2002).

pretends no site specificity. Its modularity allows for ATCO compounds and settlements to be set up wherever and whenever. As the use of the ATCO increases across
Australia, an experiential sameness is creeping into tourist facilities in the outback.

Despite the fine qualities and ready availability of the ATCO shed, it is
impossibly unrewarding to inhabit – you are either inside it or outside it, and there is no
obvious room for mediation in the mass-produced object. However, ATCO design
interventions are also evident in many remote places, devised to improve the living
environments for those unfortunate enough to live in them full time, or for the many
international backpackers, who find the landscape and the weather unrelenting. It is, in
reality, possible to hang anything off or cut any hole into an ATCO – it is the ultimate
mobile ground concept within a strict modular framework. Its ubiquitous flexibility has
produced a number of sheltering forms that allow for extensions to both the view and
to the immediate external spaces of the ATCO compound. In these adaptations, the
contained space of the ATCO shelter is opened up or extended to create a link
between inside and outside. For example, a single window punched through the container focuses views on to the landscape beyond, and a shade cloth enclosure or
veranda mediates one's exposure to sun, wind and dust.

Through the medium of this mass-produced product, a pragmatic mobility
coincides with spatial experimentation. The container, in every way an expressionless
uncomfortable box, an identifiable product of a universal solution to the need for a transportable shelter, is liberated from its limiting properties. Actions taken to allow for movement across the plane of the wall are mostly about making connections with the
landscape, with relieving a claustrophobic interiority, and with bringing the outside to the
inside. The alternative actions provide a spatial mobility, enclosing exterior space and
expanding interior space while also providing for climatic relief from sun, heat and flies.
The containment provided by translucent shade structures evokes other ephemeral
shade conditions, those that convey the temporal passage of sunlight and shadow.

Desert mobility: in three, if not more, ways

If, as suggested above, grounded space has become conceptually ephemeral in the Australian desert, then the methods of spatial occupation observed in these architectures are concerned primarily with physical and ephemeral mobility. 'Hybrid' architectures involving temporary and mobile insertions into the fabric of existing buildings and landscapes therefore express programmes where transportability and an evolutionary response to changing conditions are essential, resulting in these unrecognized architectural practices in those places most affected by cultural and physical remoteness.

People living in remote areas have always operated within communication and living systems based upon an improvisation on scarce materials, transforming their practices to suit transience, and mediating between local and external ecological conditions. The visible result of these operations resides in the use and reuse of materials and building forms that work to mediate and reprogramme the very relationship between architecture and landscape.

'Hybrid' desert architectures operate within social and cultural, as well as physical, ways of experiencing mobility. The shelters in remote South Australia – as myriad compositions of container, caravan and ATCO architectures – have been realised without any architect as author, and are certainly postproduced. These seemingly dissimilar projects are connected through shared degrees of mobility, in which the response to landscape context is linked to spatial and material mobility, and to the passing of time. Impermanence is evident in ways in which the ground is touched lightly, and in evolutionary adaptations to material and immaterial conditions; even the architectures that emerge from the topography appear as a temporary wrapping, such as might occur with a tarpaulin thrown over a gaping hole.

Yet, over time, each project tends to 'ground' itself towards at least the promise of permanency. Even in their ruinous state, such 'hybrid' architectures mutate from the caravan to the shed to the house/shelter, and they transform into structures where mobility and fixity coincide. Yet, there remains the sense that they could take off at any time, through demolition and rebuilding, or through a re-engagement of wheels, or even through the act of opening out the structure.

So, do I believe that a mobile and less-permanent architecture is more inherently suited to a critical theoretical position, or not? These desert architectures of Australia demonstrate alternative forms of practice that work outside the cultural and economic agendas of our dominant urban environment. Due to their remoteness, they are barely known. Whether a critical, theoretical perspective is relevant to these practices is probably not the point, since professional architectural practice will probably remain a distant concept in outback Australia. Yet the practices and narratives that emerge in these constructions may inform wider architectural practice – indeed across all places where the distinctions between architecture, art and landscape collapse.

Coober Pedy: hill topography 2. Photograph: Gini Lee (2002).

Notes

1   Quotation taken from original call for papers, 'Critical Architecture' conference, Bartlett, UCL, London, November 2004.

2   Anthony Hoete (ed.), *Roam: Reader on the Aesthetics of Mobility*, London: Black Dog, 2003.

3   Andrea Kahn, 'Defining Urban Sites', in Carol J. Burns and Andrea Kahn (eds), *Site Matters: Design Concepts, Histories and Strategies*, London and New York: Routledge, 2005, pp. 289–99.

4   Nicholas Bourriaud, *postproduction*, New York: Lukas and Sternberg, 2002.

5   Ibid., p. 11.

The Responsive City

Ana Betancour

Western cities are increasingly adopting strategies of branding, promotion and privatisation of public spaces. The construction of a staged official identity, and the choreographing/adjusting of this urban image, is having an extensive physical impact that is affecting, displacing and dislocating local identities – such as can be seen clearly in the case of the city of Barcelona.[1]

In these urban-regeneration projects in Barcelona, the demolition and insertion of newly privatised public spaces, and of new institutions, has largely redefined the nature of the areas in question. Design and surveillance technologies have been developed to prevent or exclude certain groups of people and uses, thereby increasing segregation and the predominance of single-purpose spaces.

Barcelona as an urban model, in its use of culture and the emblematic power of architecture as catalysts in the branding and regeneration of the city, is by no means a new phenomenon. It is a model that has also been developed in many other European cities in the past 20 years, and so, too, its problems are reproduced across continental Europe. Architectural interventions become, in these regeneration projects, a form of theme park – an event in itself in which the representations and rhetoric surrounding it becomes more real than its physical location. The culture industry is hard at work producing slogans, logotypes, mascots, souvenirs, books, maps, t-shirts, exhibitions, buildings and parks, all of them to create a corporate identity – the city as a logo.

> Unlike the authoritarian state, globalized capitalism does not seek control of desire, but control through desire, the channelling of experience and otherness in cycles of consumption and (increasingly symbolic) production. It seeks a kind of open, inventive, productive compliance […]. Under this new regime, each space of freedom you create is potentially open to colonization, manipulation. Disruptive gestures are not prohibited but studied, emulated.
>
> (Interview with Brian Holmes, as cited in Jordan Crandall, 'Drive: Technology, Mobility, and Desire', in Brian Holmes and Peter Weibel (eds), *Drive*, Ostfildern: Hatje Cantz Verlag, 2002, pp. 222–3)

In this chapter I will look at practices that lie at the intersections between public art and new social movements (NSM),[2] and which are being developed as responses and reactions that are critical of the processes of homogenisation, gentrification and corporatisation. My argument is that a closer examination of these modes of action, and the ways of working developed by certain collaborative art projects, social movement networks and direct actions in Barcelona in the period from 2000–2005, will not only trace a shift in the role of artistic work in the city but might also offer some answers to the questions as to what tools and tactics could be introduced to counter the deleterious effects of recent urban developments.

In recent years the advent of global protests, as has been seen since 1998 in Seattle, London, Prague, Genoa and Barcelona – not to mention the historically unprecedented demonstrations opposing the war on Iraq which brought onto the streets in February 2003 nearly 20 million people from over 60 nations – has shown that 'a sweeping critique of capitalist globalisation is possible – and urgently necessary'.[3] These grassroots NSM networks have catalysed a process of democratic renewal, and it is suggested this has led to a redefinition of what we see as global civil society.[4] The contention here is that these mass mobilisations and this process of democratic renewal have also led to the re-imagining of the production and distribution of culture, and of modes of working in artistic and spatial practices.

I define as tactical practices – such as political art, art activism, collaborative art and direct actions of civil disobedience – those specific artistic networks that occur in a process of interaction between a multitude of actors and spaces within the city. In this definition, networks are not simply an account or mapping of 'frozen' densities of people, ideas, events and resources, but instead form a cartography of networks that are always in process of, in the words of Graeme Chester, 'expanding and contracting across an "n"' dimensional space [...] [at] junctures in which a network is manifest and transformed simultaneously'.[5]

Direct action and communication space

> Reclaiming the streets, producing an emancipatory public sphere – how does that work in a society that many call in the information society, in which it seems that the spectacle has taken the place of political debate, in which urban space is progressively trimmed to neo-liberal/economic imperatives?
>
> (Marion Hamm, 'A r/c tivism in Physical and Virtual Spaces',
> www.republicart.net/disc/realpublicspaces/hamm02_en.htm (accessed 10
> October 2004))

Arriving in Barcelona in the early spring of 2003, I encountered a city covered in slogans, banners and graffiti against the Iraq War. With almost 90 per cent of the Catalan and Spanish population against the invasion, the response and reaction towards official politics took the form of mass demonstrations and singular representations of dissent. What was perhaps at first an initiative by individual citizens to hang a white flag of peace from windows and balconies was soon adopted by the entire city and by other cities across Spain. In Barcelona, this way of protesting was so widespread that it forced the regional government of Catalonia as well as the Barcelona city council to adopt it as an official policy for all municipal and institutional buildings, including the town hall. The power of the messages, however, was both visual and very loud: demonstrations and collective *cacerolazos* (the slamming of cooking pans) occupied municipal buildings, owned by the Municipality of Barcelona, and the public squares and parks of the city every day at 10 pm.

Such events were augmented by the various occupations initiated collectively and differentially by a number of individuals, groups, student organisations, collectives, communities, political parties and trade unions. These groups met in open public assembly to discuss strategies and actions of protests against the Iraq War. These gatherings grew to become known as the political platform and network against the war, the 'Plataforma contra la Guerra /Aturem la Guerra'.[6] Numerous collectives took part in this platform, consisting of independent group of artists, philosophers, media and video activists who carried out a series of daily occupations over a period of several weeks.

This pattern of direct action began in February 2003,[7] when the occupation of certain buildings evolved into a mass camping and squatting of squares and parks across the city. These open-air camps or *acampados* were not primarily preoccupied with the physical appropriation of specific spaces, but rather with the reclamation of the political significance of these public spaces. Such spaces were henceforth used for debates, meetings, screenings, cultural events and do-it-yourself technology workshops.

What came out of the anti-war occupations and liberation of the urban spaces was precisely the notion of the liberation of spaces so as to make them genuine public places and spaces that belonged to the city, open and available to the citizens of Barcelona. Espai Alliberat, an independent group of artists, philosophers, musicians and media activists even began to engage openly with the expression of 'liberating spaces' in their manifesto:

> Why the liberation of spaces? Millions of people in the world take to the streets against the war – and it doesn't change a millimetre the course of things. How do you stop this machinery? There is a void of open spaces for debate, reflection, cultural events, information, etc. – that are 'of' and 'for' everybody in the city. Why do we choose public places owned by the national or regional government? We choose to occupy spaces owned by the city council, because our governments have showed neither to be democratic or ethical. They implement policies of property speculation, and segregation making people homeless in the name of urban regeneration and cultural diversity.
>
> (Espai Alliberat, see www.espaialliberat.net (accessed 24 October 2004))

Here a strategic shift in the squatting movement occurred.[8] The strategic use of the tactic of occupying buildings (as an act of resistance by an alternative community to acquire living space) became now a representational political tool and media event: the reclamation of both a physical and a communication space.

DIY and free mobility of knowledge

Plaza St Jaime, the main square in Barcelona and the symbolic heart of political power in Catalonia – and indeed the location for the regional government of Catalonia and the regional delegation of the Spanish Government as a whole – was occupied in the spring of 2003. The square was turned into a focal point for the demonstrations opposing the Iraq War, a liberated space or *espai alliberat*, and it functioned as well as a school extension for academic activities by a large group of students and teachers from Bellas Artes, the School of Art at the University of Catalonia. The square was now used for seminars, workshops, assemblies and public lectures; an open-air working space, meeting point and lecture hall.

And here in the square, right in front of the regional and national government buildings, I along with colleagues in an international network of architects, graphic designers, film-makers and media artists working as the Architecture + Urban Research Laboratory (A+URL), together with a group of architecture students, were drawn into the open workshops and actions being organised by Bellas Artes, as part of a series of interventions around the city.[9] We had brought with us to Barcelona the concept of 'Intersections', a series of interactive installations, devices, prototypes, performative tools that are able to unfold and have an impact in various ways on physical urban space: whether by recording, producing and projecting sound, or by producing or measuring light, or by inflating temporary structures,[10] or by tracing graffiti, or else by occupying space. These interventions were originally intended to be exhibited in a local gallery of art and architecture, and thus displayed as public art installations. However, it

**A+URL/Architecture
+ Urban Research
Laboratory,
Inflatable Backpack,
Plaza St Jaime,
Barcelona.**

did not take long before we abandoned the plan to use an institutional space, instead moving out to the streets, where we became participants in the wider urban processes against the war.

The intention of the A+URL installations was to explore how we as artists and architects might be able to intervene in the public – as catalysts, users and designers. By developing ways of working and understanding how information technologies and social connectivity can function 'in and as public space', these projects involve the making of physical and electronic devices to link physical phenomena to virtual aspects. The focus is always on the relationship between mediated/responsive (virtual) spaces and physical spaces. The point of departure of A+URL is thus to understand architecture and the city as a dynamic system, and the design process as a field of experimentation and research, as a technique to create alternative strategies to direct and drive new forms of urbanity. In this working process, the prototyping and testing of full-scale installations are used for the development of innovative modes of action and communication.

'Intersections' has thus evolved into an ongoing project and workshops. The framework for these workshops is to make tools and devices connected to media communication and intervention in public space. The use of technology is based on a notion of collective shared knowledge, such as 'open source/open hardware' systems,[11] as well as on adopting a DIY (do-it-yourself) attitude in the making. Recycling obsolete materials and computer industry waste, as well as rubbish bags, car parts, backpacks, vacuum cleaners etc., is important, and the devices/tools produced thereby all use low-cost, renewable sources of energy. The attitude to technology is seen as a political process – a free circulation of knowledge, and a development and reconfiguration of the production process outside the multinational-driven 'free market'.

Disrupting everyday life and direct representation

The protests and actions against the Iraq War in Barcelona also reflected an ongoing discussion within social movements: that of the urgency and necessity for alternative channels of communication, representation and dissemination to rival those of the corporate media. As part of this discussion, the notion of direct communication and action as 'media events' become key tools in the construction of the physical representations. The use of direct representation as a tool was exemplified in the work of Las Agencias, an autonomous network of artistic groups in Barcelona. This network of photographers, graphic designers, artists and film-makers focuses on the construction of a 'bio-political antagonism', a notion that can be defined as a field concerned with the construction of culture and lifestyles that are seen as inseparable from the construction of a political body.

Established in 2000, the collective Las Agencias emerged out of a series of open workshops as part of the programme of events at MACBA, the Contemporary Art Museum of Barcelona. In the first year of activity, these 'permanent public workshops' produced more than 20 projects, 14 tactical workshops and five longer-term projects. The workspace also hosted the headquarters of the anti-World Bank Summit Campaign (2001) and the newborn Indymedia Barcelona. Out of these tactical workshops emerged the 'Pret-a-Revolter' project, a fashion line for use in protest and direct action which has a two-fold aim: a street function and a media function. On one hand, 'Pret-a-Revolter' aims to produce and design clothes suitable for actions of civil disobedience. On the other hand, these designs are intended as forms of 'direct representation'[12] – the construction of images of the activists by the activists themselves, functioning as counter images to the prevailing representations of activists spread by the corporate mass media. A common experience of activists is that 'during mass protests the images that come out in the media [portraying activists] are usually negative and violent'.[13] Images of 'Pret-a-Revolter' and its processes of production were thus released to the mass media several weeks before the planned World Bank meeting in Barcelona in 2001, creating 'fashionable images [that] can serve as a pre-emptive media strike, decriminalizing the protest and its participants, portraying them as individuals that put their body on the front line and putting the emphasis on the brutal police tactics'.[14]

The 'Show Bus' is perhaps the most developed communication tool, in terms of its construction and possible multiple uses, to be constructed by Las Agencias. It consists of a regular bus that is equipped with Internet connection, a detachable stage, and a video and slide projection screen, providing a versatile interior design suitable for work or travel. The 'Show Bus' was built to provide a powerful tool for use in the occupation of public space during key events, through the use of visual communication and music.[15]

The most recent project by Las Agencias, 'Yomango', is a brand name that is intended to promote an alternative lifestyle.[16] 'Yomango' meshes irony and clever actions to imitate the hegemonic, economically motivated phenomenon of global brands, whilst simultaneously exposing and evacuating the branding phenomenon itself as simply an advanced form of economic control over our personal desires and urban public spaces. To achieve this, 'Yomango' steals back the brand from the multinational corporations, and through this re-appropriation process, the 'tools' of branding are transformed into a variety of different uses and representations – thereby transforming, disrupting, subverting and constructing other ways of living. In the words of Las Agencias:

> The things we create can be on the one hand very invisible (meetings, exchanges, workshops, etc.) and, on the other hand, they can be for instance, visible manifestations. However, none of them have any meaning on their own. They are just empty signs and symbols. All the things we have collectively created, they obtain their meaning from their use in a context. Both the creation and the use of these tools are a collective process. Our projects always contain a concept of the manner in which tools are being spread, always in relationship to social movements, which are the ones using and giving these practices a political meaning.
>
> (Interview by author with members from Las Agencias, Barcelona, August 2003)

Networks and media events

> Public events are not merely markers in our private lives but they are also what form our lives, both private and public.
>
> (Eric Hobsbawm, *Age of Extremes: a History of the World 1914–1991*, New York: Vintage Books, 1996, p. 4)

In order to understand some of the background of these recent actions in Barcelona, it is perhaps important to mention an occupation that happened five years earlier, in 1998, which acquired a significant political reputation in terms of the local grassroots social movement. The squatting of Avinyo nr 15, an empty building that belonged to the city council, was not the squatting of just any building in the city. It was the building that had officially been announced to become a new headquarters for the public relations department for the city. The regional government had decided to create a new political body to promote the image of the city of Barcelona. These plans were unveiled at the same time as it was made official that Barcelona was going to host a Forum of Cultures in 2004, for which a number of large urban interventions in the city were projected. The occupation of the building in Avinyo in the event only lasted for a few hours, but the group that carried it out, Oficina 2004, had been able to proclaim the space as 'La Oficina' ('The Office'), a space for social diversity and thus a direct protest against the whole idea of the Forum of Cultures.

As a cultural event that has indeed since been organised by the Barcelona city council, the regional government of Catalonia and the Spanish government, all under the patronage of the United Nations Educational, Scientific and Cultural Organisation (UNESCO), the so-called Forum of Cultures has set itself up around three themes: peace, cultural diversity and sustainable development. But it is, in truth, sponsored by multinational giants such as Indra, the Spanish weapons manufacturing company, General Electric, Coca Cola, Nestlé and many others. Altogether some 1500 performances, cultural shows and concerts took place from May until September 2004 in connection with the event. An entire new urban quarter, and one of the largest regeneration projects in the city, on a 50-hectare site, has been developed on the banks of the polluted Besos river; it is a project that can be compared to the redevelopment and urban transformations surrounding the Olympic Games in the city back in 1992. The site was in a deprived old neighbourhood and industrial area called Poble Nou, now renamed as '22@', or 'the city of knowledge and new technologies'. This new quarter for IT industries and office functions is aiming to re-develop a large part of the district, and in the process demolishing housing, dislocating the local inhabitants, changing the morphology, ecosystem, demography and identity of the area.

The Forum of Cultures event and the real estate speculation that it encompasses has provoked a huge debate, and has provoked strong criticism from social movements, intellectuals, local residents and general public opinion in Barcelona. One writer cynically suggested:

It is nothing but an operation to rebuild that part of the city. It is a mask to hide this transformation. They invented the idea to get the population involved in the project of gentrification. It was not possible to organise another Olympic Games.

(Interview by author with an anonymous activist, in May 2006 at Miles de Viviendas, Poble Nou, Barcelona)

During the spring and summer of 2004, a series of actions and art projects were organised in Barcelona to protest against the Forum of Cultures. These projects were again carried out by various groups and counter-collectives: Fotut 2004, Plataforma contra el Forum 2004, Oficina 2004, to name just a few. Social networks, connecting groups and individuals and a policy of direct actions – aquatic demonstration, workshops, public talks, open-air screenings, photographic campaigns (fotomaton)[17] – made visible the existing conflicts and contradictions in the Forum 2004 event, the latter being represented as a wasteful festival and architectural theme park, commodifying the idea of culture as well as the citizens of Barcelona. These actions were aimed to function as media events to explore means of making an impact on public debate, as well as to function as catalysts for wider social and cultural processes.

Tactical practices

Tactical media [practices] is creative solidarity in the fight for justice and democracy: resistance to the rampant tendencies toward repression, exploitation, isolation, alienation and corporatization.

(Geert Lovink, 'What is Tactical?', 2002, at www.nyu.edu/fas/projects/vcb/contributors_edition911.html (accessed 28 October 2004))[18]

Why do I choose to define these artistic projects, actions, networks in Barcelona, whether against the Iraq War, or the Forum of Cultures, as tactical practices? It is because they act as parallels to the use in NSM of the broader notion of tactical media. These tactical practices are concerned with the process of creative production, using an interaction with and subversion of existing structures of control over the production and distribution of culture as their primary strategy. And through such strategies, the use of new media not only offers opportunities for re-mixing and re-appropriating mainstream culture, but also for redistributing culture and developing new models of urban spatial action.

In a work on *The ABC of Tactical Media*, David Garcia and Geert Lovink have offered a theoretical explanation of what distinguishes tactical media from the alternative media programmes of the 1960s and 1970s, by suggesting that the tactical media of today is the creation of

a class of producers who seem uniquely aware of the value of these temporary reversals in the flow of power. And rather than resisting these rebellions they do everything in their power to amplify them, and indeed make the creation of spaces, channels and platforms for these reversals central to their practice.[19]

> (David Garcia and Geert Lovink, *The ABC of Tactical Media*, in the introduction to the event *Next 5 Min*, at the De Waag, Amsterdam, September 2003)

Developing further this notion of 'a class of producers' who are now working tactically in media, Garcia and Lovink make reference in their argument to the analyses of Michel de Certeau in *The Practice of Everyday Life*, in which the latter defines popular culture not as a 'domain of texts or artefacts but rather as a set of practices or operations performed on textual or text-like structures'.[20] As Garcia and Lovink note, change therefore occurs here between what de Certeau calls 'the emphasis from representations in their own right to the "uses" of representations'.[21] In the words of Garcia and Lovink:

> How do we, as consumers, use the texts and artefacts that surround us? And the answer he [de Certeau] suggested was 'tactically', or: in far more creative and rebellious ways than had previously been imagined. He described the process of consumption as a set of tactics by which the weak make use of the strong. He characterized the rebellious user (a term he preferred to consumer) as tactical and the presumptuous producer (in which he included authors, educators, curators and revolutionaries) as strategic.
>
> (Garcia and Lovink, *The ABC of Tactical Media*, p. 1)

By establishing this dichotomy between the user and the consumer, de Certeau was hence able to develop a vast and comprehensive language of tactics, allowing him also to create a 'distinctive and recognisable aesthetic' for such events.

There are now many other definitions for tactical media – with, for example, Susan Braman in her contribution to *The Virtual Casebook Project* giving an in-depth overview when she suggests:

> Thus the phrase 'tactical media' might be defined in both narrow and general terms: The narrow definition refers to the nonideological, aesthetic, and humorous use of digital media as content. More generally, 'tactical media' may be used as an umbrella term to cover all four types of alternative media as they appear in the 21st century.
>
> (Susan Braman, 'Defining Tactical Media: an Historical Overview', www.nyu.edu/fas/projects/vcb/definingTM_list.html (accessed 28 October 2004))

Braman also points out the etymology of the word 'tactical', since according to its original military usage, tactics are short-term actions taken in pursuit of long-term strategies that have been designed in accordance with doctrine or overarching principles.

Notwithstanding this wide range of definitions, and the diversity of those involved in producing them, the tactics and strategies that can be used in tactical media suggest a further relevance to practices using media and digital technology. My argument is that these tactics and strategies have been, and are being, used by artistic practices in a variety of fields, and to support this contention I would cite a deeply inspiring book, *The Handbook of the Communication Guerrilla*, which has had a strong impact on the development of tactical media – and as much on tactical artistic practices.[22] As a strategic handbook it describes the basic principles, methods, techniques and practices, groups and actions, that can be used to intervene in social processes of communication. The range of examples in the book has also widened our understanding and definition of communication, not only making reference to mass media, but also the understanding of 'face-to-face communication' in everyday life.

Creative dissent

City Mine(d), *The Bubble*.

The proposed re-definition of artistic practices to those of tactical practices in the city, such as happened in Barcelona recently, can be indicated as a shift in the creative process; now the focus is not so much on the 'work of art', the 'piece' or 'object', but on the tools, strategies and the ways of doing things – the modes of working: 'The work itself, what we produce in these processes, is understood as an "artwork".'[23] These urban projects are not 'an object or a piece of art', in the sense that they don't acquire any meaning unless they are used or experienced, and it is precisely this use or experience that provides them with meaning.

Here the creative processes and artworks are defined as part of networks, and these networks, by extension, as a political subject; indeed the notion of the crowd, as seen in the writings of Michael Hardt and Antonio Negri, refers to a new political subject composed of multiple independent and diverse agents, as a multitude of networks, 'who are interconnected by a net and are able to produce creative convergences in specific circumstances'.[24] This is what I would like to term overall as the 'Responsive City' – it being a 'city' of networks, responses, actions and events, a mediated and constructed cartography that exists between geo-localities and wider communication and media spaces.[25] These networks of art activism, collaborative art projects and direct actions of civil disobedience also suggest a notable shift in the role of the artist. The artist, in this definition, becomes a cultural producer and a node within local and global social networks – and in their work contributes a generative part in the creation of a participatory political debate.

Notes

I would like to thank Murray Fraser for the opportunity to write this chapter; Nicola Kirkham and members from Las Agencias for their input, the team of A+URL for projects carried out in Barcelona, Marion Hamm, Brian Holmes, and City Mine(d) through Tom Deforce, for allowing me to use their material.

1   To be specific, I am referring to recent urban projects in the neighbourhoods of El Raval and Poble Nou. In the beginning of the industrial revolution in nineteenth-century Barcelona, El Raval (also known as Barrio Chino) and Poble Nou formed the industrial edge of the city – warehouses, factories and cheaply built working-class housing. Industry declined during the second half of the twentieth century in El Raval, which became instead the marginalised red-light district of the city. However, Poble Nou has remained one of the most vital industrial areas and traditional working-class neighbourhoods in the city. Both areas are gateways to the city, a place where newcomers and immigrants have settled, which is evident in recent years by the presence of North African immigration in the neighbourhood of El Raval. One of the main preoccupations when the regeneration of El Raval began in the 1980s was to change this sense of urban marginality, and the official strategy was to open up the area in a Hausmannesque mode. Through this urban regeneration project, new institutions such as MACBA (Museum of Contemporary Art of Barcelona) have largely redefined the area. For more readings on the impact of the Barcelona model of regeneration in the city, see Stefanie von Heeren, *La remodelacion de Ciutat Vella: Un analisis critico del modelo Barcelona*, Hannover: University of Hannover, School of Architecture, 2001; Horacio Capel, *El Modelo Barcelona: un examen critico*, Barcelona: Ediciones del Serbal, 2005; Taller VIU, *El Cielo esta Enladrillado*, Barcelona: VIU, 2005.

2   By the term 'new social movements' (NSM) I understand a heterogeneous range of collectives that include anti-militarists, anti-authoritarians, autonomous groups, ecologists, human and women's rights groups, as well as many other groups opposing neo-liberal politics.

3   Brian Holmes, 'The Flexible Personality: for a new Cultural Critique', presented at the *International Seminar on Class Composition in Cognitive Capitalism*, 15 and 16 February 2002, Faculty of Economics, University of Paris, Sorbonne. See www.geocities.com/CognitiveCapitalism/index.html and ut.yt.t0.or.at/site/index.html (accessed 25 October 2004). Included in a collection of essays, Brian Holmes, *Hieroglyphs of the Future: Art and Politics in a Networked Era*, Zagreb: Arkzin, 2003; Geoff Cox, Joasia Krysa and Anya Lewin (eds), *Data Browser no. 01: Economising Culture: on 'the (Digital) Culture Industry'*, New York: Autonomedia, 2004.

4   Mary Kaldor, of the Centre for the Study of Global Governance, London School of Economics, offers the following 'activist' definition of global civil society:

> a global public sphere comprising active citizenship, growing self organization outside formal political circles, and expanded space in which individual citizens can influence the conditions in which they live both directly through self organization and through pressure on the State.
>
> (Mary Kaldor and Helmut Anheier (eds), *Global Civil Society 2002*, Oxford: Oxford University Press, 2002)

In a further development by Graeme Chesters, it is 'a generative context that connects new social formations and base communities with established social movements networks and orthodox, non-governmental actors, NGO's etc.' (see Graeme Chesters, 'Shape Shifting: Civil Society, Complexity and Social Movements', *Anarchist Studies*, 11, 1, 2003, pp. 42–65).

5   Chesters, 'Shape Shifting: Civil Society, Complexity and Social Movements', p. 43.

6   'Platform against the [Iraq] War', translation from Spanish and Catalan by author.

7   The starting date of the occupations is considered to have coincided with the International Day of Demonstrations Opposing the Iraq War, held on 15 February 2003.

8   For a history of the active squatting movement in the past decades, occupations and the building of alternative communities in Spain, see Asamblea de Okupas de Terrassa, *Okupacion, represion y movimientos sociales*, Madrid: Diatriba/Proyecto Editorial Traficantes de Sueños, 2000.

9   A+URL (Architecture + Urban Research Laboratory) is an independent international network of artists and an academic course/research laboratory in architecture, urban, and media design which was co-established by author with Peter Hasdell in 1999 at the School of Architecture in Stockholm, KTH. See www.arch.kth.se/a-url (accessed 24 October 2004).

10 The A+URL team have developed a variety of inflatable prototypes in the past three years. The inflatable backpack and structures used in Barcelona (see figure on page 291) were the result of a collaborative workshop, and constructed by Alexander Lang and Thomas Scherzer.

11 Free/Libre and Open Source Software (FLOSS) production is source code made accessible, through specific licensing methods, challenging the legal structure of corporate privatisation that governs most software production and distribution. See www.opensource.org; lugww.counter.li.org; and echo.gmu.edu/freeandopen (accessed 10 April 2006); Makenzie Wark, *A Hacker Manifesto*, Cambridge, MA: Harvard University Press, 2004, paragraphs 126–39.

12 The notion of 'direct representation' was coined by Brian Holmes, in a 'direct action' workshop in Barcelona 2000, see www.sindominio.net/fiambrera/macba.htm (accessed 20 April 2006); Brian Holmes interviewed by Marcelo Exposito, 'Esteticas de la Igualdad: Jeroglificos del futuro', *Brumaria*, 5, Summer 2005, Arte: La imaginacion politica radical, Madrid: Asociacion cultural Brumaria, co-production with www.republicart.net and the European Institute for Progressive Cultural Policies (eipcp) in Vienna.

13 Street Rec, *Retooling Dissent: Creative Resistance Projects from the World Economic Forum Protests in New York City, February 2002*, a 22-minute video project by Institute for Applied Autonomy, Las Agencias/New Kids On The Black Block, Bikewriters and Street.Rec, see www.counterproductiveindustries.com/retoolingdissent (accessed 24 October 2004).

14 *Retooling Dissent* (accessed 24 October 2004).

15 Throughout the twentieth century, there are several examples of the construction of 'mobile' communication devices – for instance, the early Soviet propaganda trains,

Alexander Medevedkin's train in 1932, to the buses and vans used in the 1970s by independent groups for decentralised communication and counter-information through independent films, guerrilla television, community videos, etc.

16 'Yomango' is an expression that merges together the Spanish slang word for 'I shoplift' (yo mango) with that of 'Mango', a trendy Spanish clothing shop franchise.

17 Website for a campaign against the Forum of Cultures 2004, for images see www.fotumaton.net (accessed 10 October 2004).

18 'The term "tactical media" arose in the aftermath of the fall of the Berlin Wall as a renaissance of media activism, blending old school political work and artists' engagement with new technologies.' Geert Lovink continues, 'the early nineties saw a growing awareness of gender issues, exponential growth of media industries and the increasing availability of cheap do-it-yourself equipment creating a new sense of self-awareness amongst activists, programmers, theorists, curators and artists.' And in this, the role of the media was '[No] longer seen as merely tools for the struggle, but experienced as virtual environments whose parameters were permanently "under construction".' See also www.nyu.edu/fas/projects/vcb/contributors_edition911.html (accessed 28 October 2004). This is further elaborated in Geert Lovink, *Dark Fiber: Tracking Critical Internet Culture*, Cambridge, MA: MIT Press, 2002.

19 This manifesto was written for the opening of the website of the Tactical Media Network, hosted by De Waag, *The Society for Old and New Media*, see www.waag.org/tmn (accessed 28 October 2004). The manifesto was first distributed via Nettime in 1997, see project.waag.org/tmn/main.html (accessed 20 October 2004).

20 Garcia and Lovink, *The ABC of Tactical Media*, p. 1.

21 Garcia and Lovink, quoting Michel de Certeau, in Garcia and Lovink, *The ABC of Tactical Media*, p. 2.

22 a.f.r.i.k.a., Luther Blisset and Sonja Bruntzells, in *Manual de Guerrilla de la Comunicacion,* Barcelona: Virus Editorial Aurora, 2000.

23 Interview by author with a member of Las Agencias, Barcelona, August 2003.

24 Notes and common manifesto from a working meeting on 'Collaborative Art: Reu 03', 1–5 September 2003, Santa Maria de la Rabida, Spain.

25 This argument is based on the notion of networks as 'moments of brief but "intense stabilization" […] and re-configuration […] a plateau' (Gilles Deleuze and Felix Guattari, quoted by Graeme Chester in 'Shape Shifting: Civil Society, Complexity and Social Movements', p. 43). In this argumentation, the 'summit sieges', Seattle, Prague, Quebec, Genoa etc., and gatherings such as the People's Global Action, the World Social Forum in Porto Alegre, are meetings that can serve as examples of what constitutes a 'plateau':

> The concept of 'plateau' is most commonly associated with Deleuze and Guattari (2002) but originates in the work of Gregory Bateson (1973), in this, 'events are not nodes within the network of networks; they are separate, contingent and chaotic 'plateau of intensity' (Bateson, 1973: 86).

> (Quoted in Graeme Chesters and Ian Welsh, 'Reflexive Framing: An Ecology of Action', *Research Committee 24: Globalization and the Environment*, XV World Congress of Sociology, 6–13 July 2002, University of Brisbane, Queensland, Australia, pp. 5–6, see www.shiftingground.freeuk.com/isapaper.htm (accessed 28 October 2004))

See also Gilles Deleuze and Felix Guattari, *A Thousand Plateaus*, London: Continuum, 2002, p. 22; Gregory Bateson, *Steps to an Ecology of Mind*, London: Paladin, 1973, p. 86. For the significance of networks in a global age, see Michael Hardt and Antonio Negri, *Empire*, London: Harvard University Press, 2001; Tiziana Terranova, *Network Culture*, London: Pluto Press, 2004; Michael Hardt, 'Today's Bandung?', *New Left Review*, 2, 14, 2002, pp. 112–18.

China as a Global Site

In a critical geography of design

Jianfei Zhu

There are urban, social, and ecological issues that one has to deal with when analysing China. Yet it remains a central task for the profession to focus on design and design discourse to which other concerns may be related. In a mapping of design thinking in contemporary China, two factors seem the most important: a global geography, and also China's interaction with the classical powers of the world, the advanced 'Western' countries, as centred on the north Atlantic. Although China had always played a part in world affairs, the late-1970s witnessed China's substantial entry into a global scene dominated by the West, and a dramatic rise in China's interactions with other countries, including Western nations. In such a case, for any analysis of design thinking in China today, one has to consider, first, a global space in which China relates to others, and also a China that is being internally internationalised as global forces start to flow into and inside of China. We need to consider, in other words, a global space in which China is conceived within and without. Second, an historical asymmetry has existed since the mid-nineteenth century, when China depended on the West for ideas of progress, and continues today. Despite China's partial success and some 150 years of effort, design thinking in China today still depends upon learning from – or at least a mutual interaction with – the West. In this short chapter, to map design thinking in China, I would like to outline first a recent pattern of interaction between China and the West, and then look at a landscape of design positions in an increasingly globalised China from within and without.

Against a long history of asymmetrical relations, in which more ideas travelled from the West into China than those going in the opposite direction, in the mid-1990s a moment of 'symmetry' emerged, a moment when a two-way flow of ideas erupted. This is a pattern that appears to be ongoing and mutating today. On the one hand, a new generation of Chinese architects have brought Western ideas of reflexivity and autonomy into China, producing a tectonic purism to challenge the dominant tradition of social realism in the country. On the other hand, some Western architects and theorists – or at least some of the most 'edgy' ones – have begun to bring ideas of efficiency and 'constructivism' from China and Asia into the West, engendering a new pragmatism that has challenged the critical traditions of the previous, postmodern era. If Yung Ho Chang, Qingyun Ma, Liu Jiakun and Wang Shu represent those Chinese architects taking part in the first flow of ideas, then it is Rem Koolhaas who may be regarded as the best representative of the second trend.[1]

This second flow of ideas has been identified, to a certain extent, by writers such as George Baird, Michael Speaks, Robert Somol, and Sarah Whiting. In their discussion of a move towards a 'post-critical' pragmatism, they have identified individuals such as Koolhaas – although not the practices in countries and regions such as China or Asia. Somol and Whiting, for example, have contrasted Rem Koolhaas with Peter Eisenman in this regard.[2] They have suggested that if Eisenman's work is 'critical', then that of Koolhaas is 'projective', and that if the former is based on the logic of sign and index, representing a philosophical critique, then the second operates on the basis of 'diagrams' and 'abstract machines', and is aimed at a constructive practice of force and effect.[3] Baird seized on a statement by Koolhaas in 1994 as an early indication of the challenge to the postmodern critical tradition, where Koolhaas declared that 'there is in the deepest motivations of architecture something that cannot be critical'.[4] In fact, Koolhaas also said around the same date that we must 'dare to be utterly uncritical', to accept what exists and what is inevitable in the urbanisation of the world.[5] A closer reading of his writings from 1994 to 2005 reveals that there is often a deliberate use of certain terms to challenge the critical tradition of the West. Yet the real agenda of Koolhaas, it seems, is not to eradicate criticality altogether, but instead to develop a new critical spirit in which pragmatism and 'constructivism', much alive in Asia now, may also be incorporated into the equation.[6]

What needs to be emphasised here is that Koolhaas' interest in the operative and the constructive, in urbanisation and modernisation, overlaps substantially with his studies of Asia and China. The reason for this overlap is obvious: 'today', according to Koolhaas, 'modernization is at its most intense in Asia, in a city like Singapore or in the Pearl River Delta [in China].'[7] It is here, in a global comparison, that one finds the operative, the diagrammatic, and the constructive at their maximum intensity. In other words, China and Asia have to be included in any global picture of the move towards the 'post-critical' tendency. But there are specific dimensions that must be noted. If Koolhaas is indeed the main figure for the move to the 'post-critical', and if Koolhaas has been interested in mega-structures for their capacity to accommodate large quantities of the metropolis, then one can say that, in the rise of pragmatism around the world, as captured by Koolhaas, a new aesthetic category of quantity and 'bigness' is emerging, and a new interest in mega-structures and meta-forms. Again, it is in Asia and China that one witnesses a raw and real surge in this practice, fuelled by socio-economic urgencies.

If this represents a clear flow of ideas from China to the West, then there is a flow in the opposite direction as well. There is of course a much longer history here. It started at least in the 1920s when Beaux-Arts teaching and design methods were absorbed from the United States into China. The subsequent importation of Socialist

Realism from the Soviet Union during the 1950s, and then Post-Modernism from the West in the 1980s, all reinforced the decorative tendencies of the Beaux-Arts tradition. By the late-1970s, this social realism had already grown into the dominant tradition in modern Chinese architecture, and some of the most 'artistic' buildings were political monuments that celebrated nationalism or the triumph of socialism, as in Nanjing in the 1930s and Beijing from 1949 to 1977.

This inheritance has now been brought to an end, or at least it has undergone a major transition, due to the new sense of design purism that has arrived in China in the past decade. The latter consists of a tectonic modernism that emerged in the late-1990s in the hands of a younger generation of Chinese architects who had been educated in the post-Mao era after 1977–8. Western influence was significant for those of this generation who had studied for periods overseas, especially in America or Europe. Their agenda in China since then has been to develop, in Yung Ho Chang's terms, a 'basic architecture' or 'architecture-in-itself', with independent concerns of form, tectonic and space, set against the iconic demands of the state and society, which had been overwhelming values in twentieth-century China.[8] The use of theory or reflective research in design is another key dimension that this new generation introduced after returning to China. A third dimension is the emphasis on individual authorship in defining their design positions against certain mainstream practices or traditions. What has been transferred then from the West to China at this moment in time is not any particular theory or '-ism', but rather a reflexivity and a need for autonomy, and especially the autonomy of design in the use of tectonic form. Yung Ho Chang, Liu Jiakun, Qingyun Ma, and Wang Shu are some of the first to have made these breakthroughs, although it has to be said that Chang and Ma, having studied in the United States, have displayed a stronger interest in articulating ideas, in the critical use of forms, and in the analysis of urban conditions. It must be added that whether they have studied overseas or not, this generation have been influenced by ideas and books imported from abroad. The distinction, in other words, is not always important.[9]

If what is described above is correct, then we are witnessing today a tendency towards a symmetrical exchange between China and the West. Going in one direction, through the writings and designs of Koolhaas, operative pragmatism is being imported from China (and Asia as a whole) to the West for the move beyond the purely critical position. In the other direction, through the equally self-conscious writings and designs of Chang and others of his generation, reflexivity and the autonomy of architectural form are being imported into China, engendering a criticality that transcends the decorative social realist traditions of the country. Western nations are now absorbing 'material' energies, and pragmatism from China/Asia, for their revitalisation, and for a move beyond criticality. China/Asia, on the other hand, is accumulating reflexivity from the West, for its own transcendence beyond raw materialism.

This description however only outlines some of the flows of ideas between these two parts of the world. A large quantity of buildings in China are designed by architects with diverse national backgrounds. How then are we to define these buildings as

Book-Bike-Store,
Beijing, ground floor
interior (1996).
Architect: Yung Ho
Chang/Atelier
Feichang Jianzhu.
Photograph: Cao
Yang and Atelier
Feichang Jianzhu
(1996).

Design for the
headquarters of
China Central
Television (CCTV),
Beijing, currently
under construction
and due for
completion in 2008.
Architect: Rem
Koolhaas/OMA.
Digital Rendering.
Crystal CG Beijing
(2002).

nodes within the more general interflow of ideas between China, Western nations, and the world at large? A closer observation of China reveals a picture of overlapping positions, each with a certain level of intentionality and a certain impact in a specific context and direction.

This landscape can be understood as a spectrum of designs ranging from the smallest to the largest; size is here categorical rather than literal. At the one end of the scale are the designs of the Chinese architects of Chang's generation, and at the other those from the West as represented by Koolhaas. In between are three overlapping groups of projects: small designs by overseas architects from Asia, Japan, and Western countries, such as those for the much-publicised 'Commune by the Great Wall'; medium or large buildings by overseas architects such as I. M. Pei, Arata Isozaki, and Riken Yamamoto; and then the very largest mega-buildings, which include airports and stadiums mostly by European architects like Paul Andreu, Norman Foster, and Herzog and de Meuron. This last group extends to the design of the China Central Television (CCTV) headquarters by Koolhaas, whereas the first overlaps with the work of the Chinese architects of Chang's generation. There is, of course, a whole world of commercial and residential buildings as well, often immense in scale, designed by Chinese offices and overseas firms. In terms of critical innovation and design reflexivity, this grand landscape of super-blocks and high towers may be treated as a background, whereas the three groups of projects – with the work of the Chang generation and of Koolhaas marking the two ends – should be together regarded as positions of immediate importance for any reading of the architectural situation in China.

Within this spectrum of positions, the writings by Chang, Ma, Liu, and Wang, as well as those by Koolhaas, remain the most conscious and critical. Both camps have produced designs and a body of reflective writings that are aimed at questioning the status quo within the specific context, as described above, of the emerging symmetrical exchange between China and the Western world. What needs to be emphasised here is that even when we are examining projects physically located in China, the symmetrical pattern still clearly exists. A virtual world of global exchanges can therefore happen with buildings physically located in China. That is, the critical impact of designs located in China can be global, moving inwards or outwards, whether towards China or the Western world.

What makes these exchanges flow in one direction and not another? The cultural–linguistic background, latent images, and background references in written texts, and the very context from which the initial critical urgency arises, all help to secure a specific direction and a specific geo-cultural context in which the critical impact is most effective. For the Chinese architects of the Chang generation, their designs using autonomous tectonic forms, together with their self-conscious writings, are targeted at the Chinese context, and have arguably facilitated a subversion of decorative social realism within modern Chinese architecture. For Koolhaas, on the other hand, his writings on urbanisation and mega-structures in Asia, and his designs that use related ideas of strategic and programmatic planning, including the CCTV building in Beijing, seem to be targeted more to an audience in the West. They have certainly influenced theoretical circles in the West, as evidenced in the recent post-critical debate. Besides these two critical forces, positioned at the opposite ends of the debate, a more general interflow of ideas exists.

In terms of the impact upon the West, it is the magnitude of the projects, the overall surge of urbanisation, and the speed and scale of development in China that is much reported upon and regarded as most impressive. This impact, in turn, reinforces Koolhaas' message to the Western audience about quantity, bigness, and pragmatism, as seen in his studies and designs, such as the CCTV headquarters.

In terms of impact upon the Chinese, the CCTV and the National Olympic Stadium, as well as other large, medium or small projects by the overseas architects identified above, may be considered as 'post-tectonic' and 'post-purist'. These designs, that developed from a neo-modern interest in the 1980s, have extra messages beyond the classical modernism of 1920s Europe, yet they also share with the Chinese architects of this current generation a basic interest in tectonics and purism initially explored in inter-war modernism. They are united here, as it were, in opposition to their common 'enemy', the decorative realism of the Beaux-Arts and the Post-Modern traditions. In this sense, these designs by overseas architects in China assert a formal impact – both by reinforcing a local interest in purism and tectonic form, and also by propelling the Chinese to adopt a more radicalised, contemporary, and neo-modern position. Both the CCTV by Koolhaas, and the National Olympic Stadium by Herzog and de Meuron, despite their different formal approaches, fit this description well in terms of their impact upon the Chinese scene.

If the 'radical' architects from Europe offer a formal impetus in China at a large scale, then the 'poetic' and 'refined' architects from Asia – and especially Japan – are providing formal examples for the Chinese at a smaller scale. The medium-sized buildings, such as Jianwai SOHO by Riken Yamamoto and Shenzhen Culture Center by Arata Isozaki, are important cases here. Isozaki, Toyo Ito, and Yamamoto frequently participate in discussions and forums in China. Isozaki's criticism of design qualities in China, and his finely crafted buildings in China and Japan, seem particularly close to, if not supportive of, the Chinese agenda to improve formal and material qualities in design and construction. At yet a smaller scale, the designs for the 'Commune by the Great Wall', such as the Bamboo Wall by Kengo Kuma and the Club House by Seung H-Sang of South Korea, provide refined examples of the use of abstract forms, raw materials, and the creation of a tactile and phenomenological space.[10] The China International Practice Exhibition of Architecture (CIPEA) in Nanjing, coordinated by Arata Isozaki and Liu Jiakun, and currently under construction, is an exhibition of some twenty buildings by architects invited from China and around the world.[11] As the scope of selection has now moved beyond the 'Asian circle' used for the Commune buildings, CIPEA may produce a result that is more complex and diverse.

Of all the projects at this end of the scale, a building of particular importance is a gatehouse in Tongzhou near Beijing (2004), designed by Monica Ponce de Leon and Nader Tehrani from Office dA of Boston.[12] The 200 m² building displays a surprising richness and sensitivity in its use of bricks and construction details, as well as in a shifting interaction between skin and structure. This building, with the interest it has generated locally, is a perfect example to illustrate the current situation in microcosm: contemporary Western design, post-tectonic, and post-purist, is arriving in China to support and also propel tectonic modernism towards a more radicalised sensitivity.

All of these 'edgy' designs by overseas architects in China are thus supporting local interests. However, without a socio-ideological argument that is embedded in the local historical context, without the use of localised references and backgrounds, and without a cultural–linguistic basis, these contributions to the Chinese situation remain formal, even intellectual, but not as yet critical or ideological: the latter is a job that is being mediated only by the Chinese themselves. At the moment, despite rich formal influences, the actual critical-ideological forces flowing both ways across the Chinese borders are mediated by specific, localised agents: those from China to the West are enacted by or through Western voices, as represented by Koolhaas; whereas those from the West into China are enacted by or through Chang, Liu, Ma, and Wang, and others of this generation. Formal exchanges are smooth, fluent, and dynamic, whereas critical voices do not seem to flow so easily across geo-cultural distances.

So can critical ideas flow in *other* directions, overcoming geo-cultural-linguistic barriers? Could the ideas of Koolhaas be received in the Chinese world as a form of modernist 'social realism'? Could Peter Eisenman's idea of a critical architecture, one that is based on a reading that opposes the spectacular – a comment that he made in a recent Chinese publication[13] – be absorbed into Chinese intellectual circles? Will Isozaki's criticism of design in China, revealing a closer positioning of Japanese with Chinese interests, be acknowledged and embraced? Will Ma and Urbanus's practice in the use of mega-structures bring about a critical effect beyond China? Will Chang's idea of a 'basic architecture' develop into a new position on the tectonic, one that could be critical not only in China but also in the West? There are no answers as yet, but signs are emerging. The disadvantage of the historical asymmetry – when China depended on the West for ideas of progress – have gradually turned into an advantage: the Chinese world, including a modern Chinese subjectivity, has become hybrid, nomadic, often bi-lingual, and deeply bi-cultural. It is reasonable to expect that, in the global space of China, both within and without, and with different nationalities involved, such lines of flight across barriers are likely to happen; perhaps the transgression has already started.

Notes

1   This has been explored in an earlier article: Jianfei Zhu, 'Criticality in Between China and the West', *The Journal of Architecture*, 10, 5, November 2005, pp. 479–98. My purpose here is to summarise this 'symmetrical' relation between the two and to expand this framework to capture the larger scene of design positions in contemporary China.

2   See Robert Somol and Sarah Whiting, 'Notes Around the Doppler Effect and Other Moods of Modernism', in Michael Osman, Adam Ruedig, Matthew Seidel, and Lisa Tilney (eds), *Mining Autonomy*, a special issue of *Perspecta*, 33, 2002, pp. 72–7.

3   Ibid., 74–5.

4   George Baird, ' "Criticality" and its discontents', *Harvard Design Magazine*, 21, Fall 2004/Winter 2005; also available online, www.gsd.harvard.edu/hdm (accessed 5 November 2004).

5   For example, Koolhaas says in 1994 'we have to take insane risks; we have to dare to be utterly uncritical', when he is arguing for a realist understanding of the inevitable in urbanisation and modernisation. See Rem Koolhaas, 'What Ever Happened to Urbanism?', in O.M.A., Rem Koolhaas, and Bruce Mau, *S, M, L, XL*, New York: Monacelli Press, 1995, pp. 559–971.

6   Rem Koolhaas, 'Pearl River Delta', in Rem Koolhaas, Stefano Boeri, Sanford Kwinter, Nadia Tzai, and Hans Ulrich Obrist, *Mutations*, Bordeaux: ACTAR, 2000, pp. 308–35. Here Koolhaas says:

> today it is clear that modernization is at its most intense in Asia, in a city like Singapore or in the Pearl River Delta. These emerging cities teach us about what is in the midst of happening [...] To renew the architectural profession and to maintain *a critical spirit*, it is important to be aware, to observe these emergent conditions and to theorize them.
>
> (p. 309; my emphasis)

7   Ibid.

8   Yung Ho Chang, 'Pingchang jianzhu' ['A Basic Architecture'], *Jianzhushi: Architect*, 84, October 1998, pp. 27–37, especially pp. 28–9. See also Yung Ho Chang, 'Xiang gongye jianzhu xuexi' ['Learning from Industrial Architecture'], in Yung Ho Chang (ed.), *Pingchang Jianzhu: For a Basic Architecture*, Beijing: Zhongguo Jianzhu Gongye Chubanshe, 2002, pp. 26–32.

9   For a study on these architects, see Zhu, 'Criticality', pp. 485–95.

10   The architects invited to design for the villas in the 'Commune' as completed in 2002 were: Gary Chang (China–Hong Kong), Shigeru Ban (Japan), Cui Kai (China), Chien Hsueh-yi (China–Taiwan), Antonio Ochoa (China), Kanika R'kul (Thailand), Yung Ho Chang (China), Nobuaki Furuya (Japan), Kay Ngee Tan (Singapore), Kengo Kuma (Japan), Rocco Yim (China–Hong Kong), and Seung H-Sang (South Korea).

11   The architects are: Steven Holl (USA), Liu Jiakun (China), Arata Isozaki (Japan), Ettore Sottsass (Italy), Zhou Kai (China), Qingyun Ma (China), Kazuyo Sejima + Ryue Nishizawa (Japan), Zhang Lei (China), Mathias Klotz (Chile), Hrvoje Njiric (Croatia), David Adjaye (UK), Luis M. Mansilla (Spain), Sean Godsell (Australia), Odile Decq (France), Liu Heng (China-Hong Kong), Kris Yao (China-Taiwan), Gabor Bachman (Hungary), Tang Hua (China), Wang Shu (China), Ai Weiwei (China), Yung Ho Chang (China), Cui Kai (China), Alberto Kalach (Mexico), and Matti Sanaksenaho (Finland).

12   Huang Yuan, 'Zhezhou Jianzhu: Beijing Tongzhou yishu zhongxin menfang jiqita zuopin pingjie' ['Draped Architecture: the Gatehouse of the Art Center of Tongzhou Beijing and other works by Office dA'], *Shidai Jianzhu: Time + Architecture*, 1, 81, 2005, pp. 98–105.

13   See Peter Eisenman, 'Contro lo spettacolo: Dui "qiguan" wenhua de zhiyi' (in English and Chinese), *Shidai Jianzhu: Time + Architecture*, 5, 91, 2006, pp. 61–2.

Critical Practice

Sarah Wigglesworth

Sarah Wigglesworth
and Jeremy Till,
Dusk view (2000),
Stock Orchard
Street, Islington,
London. Photograph:
Paul Smoothy (2001).

As a rule, architecture is considered a necessity, housing functional activities which, by their nature, produce wealth. It is also a means of securing capital through investment growth (in the form of real estate). Additionally in our post-industrial economy, architecture is increasingly being used to provide 'symbolic' capital for a company or individual (as in the trophy architect used to 'brand' a client's business). In all these situations, architecture plays the role of handmaiden to the economy, and to institutional or personal interests. The association with money that attaches to architecture can be an opportunity, but also a curse, for in a service economy one is paid to furnish one's clients' desires, not to question them. A critical practice implies an act of criticism; and an act of criticism is designed to question the status quo, and to interrogate conditions that are contingent to a project. Art practice is, of course, based on an acceptance of this prior condition, but it is more difficult to practise critically in architecture, where the commercial relationship keeps the architect in service to their client's interests. Most clients appoint architects that mirror their value system, and as a result, the opportunities for critical practice exist in relatively rare circumstances.

Practising architecture 'critically' implies working with the status quo, but at the same time exploring ways of critically adjusting the status quo in order to be able to make a critique. The 'critical' architect makes readings of existing situations and reveals their findings as a way of moving knowledge forward. The dilemma posed by attempting to practise critically is to balance the demands of the commercial imperatives (and clients' wishes) that permit a practice to take place at all, with the possibilities of critique and change. The practitioner, and especially the critical practitioner, decides where s/he stands in relation to the issues that surround the production of architecture – its ethics, its knowledge, its people, and its economics – and takes up a conscious position.

It is important to note that genuine criticality does not come about through a simple instrumental opposition to existing conditions; rather, it involves a disciplined training in a way of thinking that is entirely contingent and responsive to the opportunities presented by each project. A genuinely critical architecture has to develop ways of acting critically, and this in turn demands an engagement with its own production in a critical way. This requires judgement about situations the architect hasn't met before. Every project offers its own unique set of challenges and demands, so the critical practitioner needs to respond flexibly; such an architect cannot approach the problems of practice using a set of rules or formulae to be applied (as in causal or instrumental approaches). A critical architecture depends on critical thinking, but thinking critically does not guarantee a critical outcome. Many other factors must come into play to ensure a critical practice.

Whether you join the system, act unilaterally on your own principles, or choose a collective resistance becomes the vital issue. One example is where the architect makes an architecture that sets out to question existing political and social structures (such as in Paolo Soleri's Arcosanti, communes, travellers, squatters). Equally the architect can sometimes act unilaterally to question the values of their client (implying that they probably do it clandestinely). The tactic of being oppositional to a client's wishes can cause confrontation, and is likely to result in ill-feeling and a poor working relationship. It is a brave architect that bites the hand that feeds them, so the critical practitioner must be far more devious and/or subversive if they are going to survive.

The more complex and the more public a project is, the more problematic it is for the architect to be critical. Public projects by definition aim to express shared cultural values, and these can become dysfunctional – even meaningless – because a critical approach may be openly misconstrued. For this reason, critical practice within the public realm tends to be limited to formal manipulation, an anodyne version of true critical action because it engages so minimally with the political or social issues that lie at the heart of architecture. The critical practitioner will instead most commonly be found on the margins of mainstream practice, which is, by definition, a political position to adopt.

Superficially, critical architecture looks like normal architecture: you have to examine its production to discover where the critical position lies. Formal and technical critiques are almost always a smokescreen, because within architecture the issue of technology is regarded as politically neutral and form as progressive. Formal novelty as a response to a client's desire for added cultural capital – a signature building by an 'iconic' architect for example – is not a critical practice. Equally, enquiries made possible by instrumental drivers and/or technologies (such as in new computing techniques or new materials, for example) come under the category of 'innovative' as opposed to critical. Accordingly, formal or technical novelty can rarely ever be categorised as questioning cultural conditions; rather, they are manifestations of the status quo. The avant-garde is simply the revelation of a historicist consciousness.

Far more interesting are the possibilities offered by programmatic or professional critiques, where, if given scope to interrogate a brief (with or without the full knowledge of the client), the critical architect can begin to play. Where an architect adopts an unconventional role, such as becoming a developer, being their own client, or developing a building product, then the possibilities of making a critique of existing working practices or products are opened up. In collaborating with other people to develop new working methods, the opportunity arises to use techniques of enquiry that are alien to – and possibly critical of – normative architectural processes. For example, it could imply a new analytical approach (philosophical, mathematical), or an innovative form of collaboration (interdisciplinary working), or the development of new forms of etiquette or association (such as cooperative working) to address a problem. Yet perhaps the greatest freedom to practise critically lies in the service of one's own interests, since here the role of client and architect are almost certainly closely aligned. And this is what happened in designing, along with Jeremy Till a project, for our own use at Stock Orchard Street in Islington, north London.

In this design, for a house and an office on the same site, we seized the opportunity to critique the brief, especially the idea of the separation that exists between home and work, as well as other specifically architectural conventions.

In exploring the differences between home and office, we wanted to raise awareness of the received assumptions of what 'home' and 'office' mean, and did so

Sarah Wigglesworth and Jeremy Till, The living room (2000), Stock Orchard Street. Photograph: Paul Smoothy (2001).

Sarah Wigglesworth and Jeremy Till, The office (2000), Stock Orchard Street. Photograph: Paul Smoothy (2001).

by adopting the surrealist strategy of juxtaposing unexpected combinations of elements. Accordingly the house element of the building adopts the spatial typology most often associated with offices, while conversely the office adopts characteristics usually associated with houses. The house occupies a volume that is 7 m deep (the limit for natural cross-ventilation) and which is spatially undifferentiated, as in a typical open-plan office. Perimeter columns permit any organisational arrangement. This degree of openness allows the furniture in the living room to be rearranged in different configurations according to desire. Meanwhile, the office occupies spaces that are defined by a module of 5.5 m – or 16.5 feet in old imperial measurement – this being the cross-wall dimension typical of London terraced housing for those of moderate income. Modest in depth (ranging from 4.5 m to 6 m), the office spans over the cross-walls below to suggest a sort of lateral conversion, and the scale of its two-storey composition is identical to the adjacent nineteenth-century terraced houses. The different functional elements of the building are organised at right angles to one another, so from both parts one is always made aware of the presence of the other, a condition denied under capitalism but prevalent in everyday life. Capitalism requires the separation of life's activities into categories in order to ensure the efficiency of production. Our project questions the location and expectations of work and acknowledges that home can be as productive as the workplace, while office life can be social, pleasurable, and emotional, just like home.

The dining table is a metaphor for the confusion of life and work. It is a place of domesticity (for family gatherings and special meals), as well as functioning as

Sarah Wigglesworth and Jeremy Till, The dining/conference room (2000), Stock Orchard Street. Photograph: Paul Smoothy (2001).

a conference room for the office during the weekday. Six metres tall and overlooked by two balconies, this space has formality and pomp; it is also the only room in both buildings directly to address the street, through a large window that acts as a proscenium and a frame. This emphasises the performative aspect of the space, reminding us that we are always playing roles, particularly in an office setting – but also perhaps when we are on our best behaviour during special occasions. And the dining table is a proper dining table, not a conference table. It comes apart in several sections and has specific dimensions that are to do with the intimacy surrounding conversation over food, rather than the dimensions often inscribed in the conference table where the distance across the table is a sign of power and professional neutrality. These subtle signs challenge our behaviour and remind us that we live in a hybrid world. The distance between domesticity and work is very small.

An important aspect of the critical enquiry contained in the Stock Orchard project was a questioning of the categorisations of what a home or what an office should look like. We were interested in exploring what is actually meant by phrases such as 'high tech' and 'low tech'. Fascinated by why architectural culture in Britain loves minimalism, we sought out alternatives to these rigid categories. And we wished to encourage a demystification of the building process itself, since this is an area of expertise that wrongly allows 'experts' to claim knowledge and keep it out of reach of those wishing to participate more fully in the design–build axis, such as self-builders.

In line with the surrealist techniques mentioned earlier, we developed cladding systems for the walls of the house and the office wing that would confound

Sarah Wigglesworth and Jeremy Till, Straw walls (2000), Stock Orchard Street. Photograph: Paul Smoothy (2001).

Sarah Wigglesworth and Jeremy Till, Quilted rainscreen to the office (2000), Stock Orchard Street. Photograph: Paul Smoothy (2001).

expectations. We again swapped expected types, cladding the house in the industrial corrugated steel sheeting normally associated with factories and workshops, and clad the office in a quilted fabric reminiscent of domestic upholstery. The north walls of the house are made of straw because straw is simple to build with, has excellent insulation properties, and is very cheap. It is a beautiful colour too. Consistent with our plans to demystify the building process, we wanted to demonstrate how the straw walls were made – so we cut a large square hole in the corrugated steel and replaced it with transparent polycarbonate of the same profile. In this way the hairiness of the straw bale wall is exposed beneath the slickness and shininess of the polycarbonate. The effect of bringing together the slick and hairy reveals how architecture generally tries to conceal the hairy (rough, poorly built, messy) beneath a seductive surface, eliding the reality (chaos, mistakes) of building construction under the appearance of perfection.

The wattle hurdles that form the fence in front of the property have a tolerance of about 50 mm. The steel frame for the fence posts has a tolerance of about 1 mm. We brought these two together to signify our preference for the eclectic rather than the exclusive. Here we also wished to contrast the hand-crafted with the machine-made, although in reality both steel and wattle are largely hand-made in their own ways. It is only the origin of the base material that differs (one is grown, the other is manufactured). Hurdles are domestic items, while steel is industrial. The cross-categorisation of technologies suggested by these two materials united in a single detail questions current orthodoxies concerning manufacturing techniques, aesthetic combinations, and iconography.

Sarah Wigglesworth and Jeremy Till, Wattle/steel fence (2000), Stock Orchard Street. Photograph: Paul Smoothy (2001).

Sarah Wigglesworth and Jeremy Till, Gabion walls (2000), Stock Orchard Street. Photograph: Paul Smoothy (2001).

Since one of architecture's current concerns is the striving towards control of excess, we wanted the design for Stock Orchard Street to be something other than minimal: fat, in fact. Architecture that is fat and wobbly. The solution arose because we needed to demolish a number of structures that were on the site to make way for the new building. Presented with a lot of material that would normally go into landfill sites, the original plan had been simply to tip it all into gabion cages and reuse it. Our structural engineer argued that the fill would have no structural integrity, so we were obliged to think again. How could we avoid contributing to further landfill? By swapping our fill for other fill. So we found a source of crushed concrete recycled from previous buildings and filled the gabions with this instead. It proved cheaper to buy recycled concrete than to take away the demolished material. That is exactly how it should be.

Sandbags were another response to the aesthetics of clean, sharp arrises and perfect masonry coursing in contemporary architecture, and of factory-produced materials whose performance can always be predicted. The sandbags provide mass to the office wall that faces the railway and its rhythm of passing high-speed trains. Seeking a way of providing a heavy façade that did not rely on brick or blockwork (high in embodied energy), this seemed a simple solution that could be home-made.

In conclusion, this is a project in which critiques are made on a range of issues: the separation between aspects of our lives as dictated by social, economic, and cultural forces beyond our individual control; architecture's own concerns (aesthetic categorisations, architectural identity, fashion); expertise, knowledge, and techniques (who or what determines how we build); and ecology and responsibility. Our

Sarah Wigglesworth and Jeremy Till, Sandbag wall (2000), Stock Orchard Street. Photograph: Paul Smoothy (2001).

expectations of how familiar and everyday places should feel, look, and service us is revealed as something that is simultaneously robust and long-lasting, but also capable of reinvention. Typical photographs of new buildings illustrating a frozen moment are powerful evocations of the myth of architecture's power to renew. Yet in reality all buildings weather and decay, and cities constantly change. Being ubiquitous and obvious, these are conditions we often take for granted. In the gabions that integrate existing buildings into new ones, in the sandbags that decay and crumble, in the juxtaposition of farm and industrial products, in the diverse aesthetics and simple constructional techniques, Stock Orchard Street reveals and embraces the processes that determine our expectations and the metamorphosis at work in the city, and asks us to reassess old ways of making sense of them.

Architecture for an 'Active Edge'

The Gateway, Derby

Steve McAdam, Fluid

This is a short story about a particular building in Derby, which traces the routes and trajectories of change that the building has both nestled within and caused by its presence. The political and social context for the tale unfolds as part of the Labour Government's New Deal for Communities (NDC) programme, focused as that is on the regeneration of deprived neighbourhoods across England. To start the process, a variety of NDC Boards[1] – which were composed of local authority and agency officers, councillors and local residents – mounted bids for government funding through the submission of ten-year 'delivery plans' to collectively tackle the social, economic and environmental issues outlined in the official figures used to identify areas of maximum deprivation.[2] The successful bids attracted government money in the region of £50 million, with the expectation that 'match funding' from project partners and the private sector would also significantly boost local coffers.

By the turn of the millennium, some 39 of these NDC 'pathfinder' projects had been identified. They were meant to test new methods of bottom-up design and delivery, holistic regeneration and 'mainstream bending', whereby health, crime control and educational mainstream funds would be drawn together to develop prototypes for hybrid service delivery agencies. It was – and indeed remains – an ambitious political and socio-spatial programme.

Planning a neighbourhood

In 2001 the Derwent Community Team, a NDC group in Derby, commissioned Fluid, the Bartlett's Space Syntax Laboratory[3] and the Nottingham-based agency Tanc[4] to assemble a 'neighbourhood plan'. This was carried out in partnership with a wide range of bodies and organisations, and through an extensive process of consultation and engagement with local stakeholders and residents. The plan was to deliver locally tailored, and hence collectively 'owned', solutions and projects. Fluid used a series of new tools – ranging from 'walk-and-talk' excursions with residents and officers, daily

Tools and 'what if's' for consultation and engagement: Fluid (2004).

diaries and route mappings, to 'what-if' visualisations – in order to build up a clear understanding of life as lived in the Derby area, and also to identify a set of environmental and social initiatives through an iterative process involving the NDC team and local residents. The approach valued the importance of local memories, social mores and psycho-geographies[5] in the generation of nuanced and site-specific design responses. After three months of dialogue, over 50 projects of various shapes, sizes and durations had been pinpointed.

A strategy for regeneration

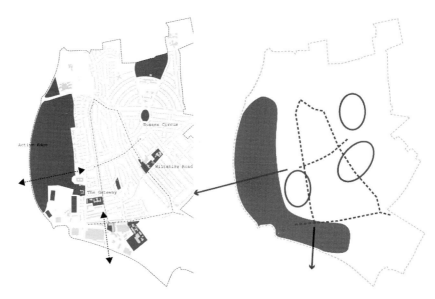

Regeneration concept: Fluid (2002).

To build synergy between the individual projects, and to provide overall coherence in urban design terms, it was necessary to devise a strong but simple regeneration concept. We shaped a strategy that focused regeneration in two directions. The first part tackled the dormant industrial estates and abandoned parks that bordered the western and southern margins of the site, so as to build an 'active edge' in social, economic and physical terms, and to project the growing level of local confidence and pride in the neighbourhood. The second part of the strategy drew together clusters of projects into three 'neighbourhood centres', each providing a complimentary 'offer' for the community in the form of retail, sports, health, open space and so forth. The wider strategy enfolded the emerging projects and in doing so added purpose and greater volition. It provided a clear strap-line that underpinned the project vision and focused the process of decision-making.

Scale shift 1

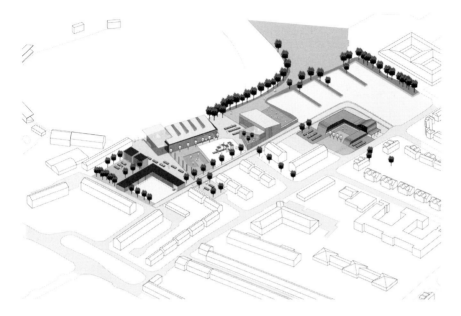

Initial urban design schematic for The Gateway: Fluid (2003).

Fluid was retained to update the neighbourhood plan, since it was generally understood that the proposal always needed to be provisional, organic and subject to change, rather than a fixed, immutable blueprint. A by-product was the commission for Fluid to design a new community hall and indoor-cricket academy: a landmark project for the 'active edge'. The commission relied on successful negotiations between the NDC Board, which had, at best, a troubled relationship with the project partner, Derbyshire County Cricket Club. The latter, for their part, had already gained planning permission for a new cricket academy, but in a different location, and was about to realise its goal via subsidies achieved by selling off a key site on the edge of the park for private housing – a move that ran counter to and threatened aspects of the overall neighbourhood plan. The difficulties ran deeper than those of just a clash of master-planning objectives, or even of cultures and social classes, as the cricket club had recently demolished an historically significant grandstand building that had previously provided an important social venue for the community in the surprising form of a bar and dance hall. Project sponsorship from Sport England depended on clear agendas which, unsurprisingly, put sport at the heart of the project. The commission for the new joint-use building was therefore akin to a process of healing and negotiation in which the separate and often competing voices had to be joined in conversation.

The Gateway

The resulting architectural project, known as The Gateway, accepted its landmark role but refused to take on the status of either a self-referential icon or a sporting institution. Instead, the design team set out a playful and irreverent response, arriving at a

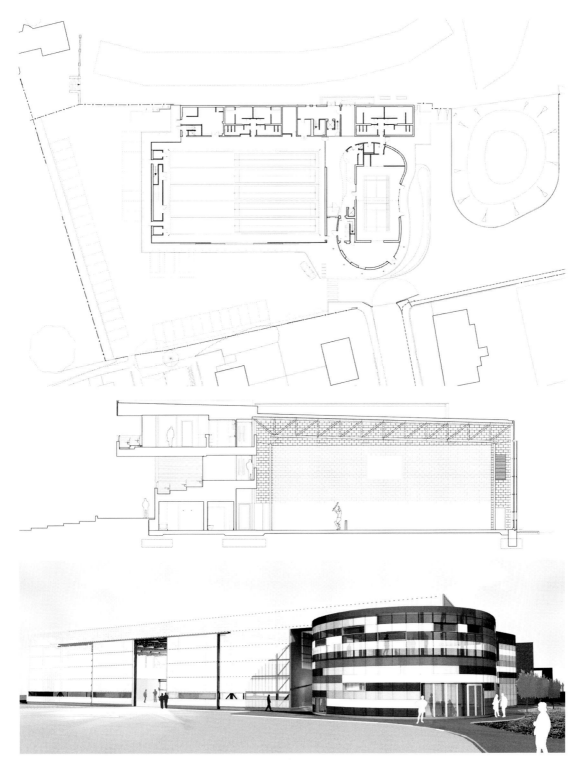

Plan, section and visualisation of The Gateway: Fluid (2004).

kind of *architecture parlante* in which the origins and configuration of the various agendas could be traced, and the sum of the parts judged against each other.[6]

A balance of funding pledges and management protocols eventually underpinned the development of the project. Sport England's support for the provision of a non-institutional 'gateway' to sport added further impetus, and so the basic design concept began to take shape. The Gateway was to be a collection of different structures, each with their own signification and resonance, their own fiefdoms, materials and atmospheres, but a subtler and key move – as detected by architectural critic Jeremy Till in his review of the building – was the blurring of these territories inside the centre along axes of movement, major sightlines and related sections.[7]

The three principle parts of the design consisted a vast polycarbonate clad steel-framed academy hall for the indoor practice nets; a cedar-lined stand containing the kitchens, bars, hospitality suites and changing facilities; and the playful amoeba of the community hall, gym, toddlers' room and chill-out gallery, whose colourful strips emerged in collaboration with the specially formed residents' group and the artist Marion Deuchars. The spectrum of colours chosen referred to the greens and blues of the adjacent park, the blurred reddish colour of a cricket ball in flight, the burnt umber of the local brickwork, and the painted lines which are used to define fields of sport and play.

The Gateway 'parts' – the 'peanut', academy hall and stand: Fluid (2004). Photographs: Hélène Binet and Kim Trogal (2004) (Fluid).

The dumb box of the academy sailed deliberately close to the wind, only to be countered by the glazed slit that was detailed with scientific precision against the 'pale grey cliff-face' of the walls of the main hall, so as to deliver what another critic described as a 'moment critique'.[8] The attentive new stand jostled with the sightlines and memories of the previous stand to create a thing, rudely sketched, both of the future and the past. The amoeba section, affectionately known locally as 'the peanut', announced the entrance to the building from the 'community side', here with a sightline aligned on the scoreboards on the other side of the cricket pitch. The playful interior volumes, whilst containing the multi-purpose sports hall, eschewed the science of

The Gateway – controlled collisions and interior views: Fluid (2004). Photograph: Hélène Binet (2004).

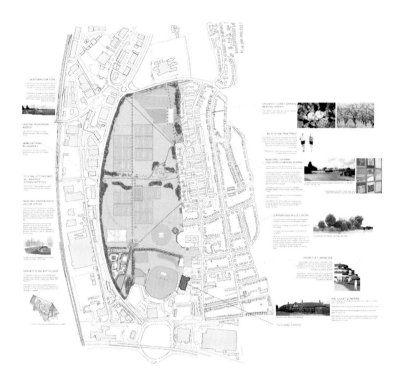

**Park masterplan:
Fluid (2005).**

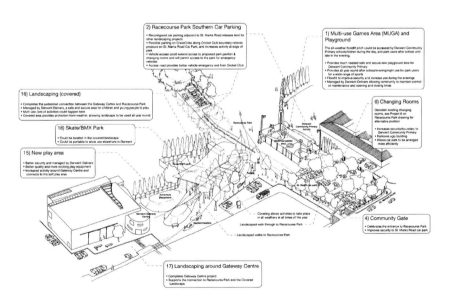

**Sketch axonometric
of The Gateway area:
Fluid (2005).**

sport for the feel of a provisional and adopted space, equally at home with tea dances as with badminton tournaments. Inside, circulation routes attempt to cross-pollinate the interests of the building's users, and expose 'exotic' and 'everyday' worlds to visitors in a manner that is both purposeful and casual. At night the halls glow, casting shadows of their strange cargoes.

Scale shift 2

Although the project achieved its presence without undue claim for authorship, and met its goals of assembly and blur, delivery of the project was always seen as a point on a line, and not as a final utterance. As hoped, The Gateway is now beginning to act as a catalyst for further change in the form of multifarious landscaping projects in the adjacent park, or for changing rooms for weekend football matches, or herbal gardens for the surrounding schools, or a car park for the Midlands populace who arrive to run their land yachts along clear and uncluttered flatlands. A local visitor centre will remind us all that unique ancient Roman remains still lie buried below the park, and may some day surface. This short story of The Gateway project is leading to a longer story of change, as yet to be told.

Notes

1   In 1998, the UK Government set up the NDC initiative targeting just under £2 billion of government funding to pilot 'bottom-up' regeneration in some of England's most deprived neighbourhoods. The ambition was to 'close the gap' between these neighbourhoods and United Kingdom norms in a holistic manner, tackling health, education, employment and crime-related issues alongside environmental improvements of all kinds. Bids were mounted in two stages. Successful first round 'shadow board' bidders, composed of a mix of local residents, councillors, health agency and police representatives, were given the go-ahead and financial assistance to work up a full bid. Shadow Boards became full NDC boards on government-approved stage-two bids, with board members often being voted in by local residents. Theme teams focusing on education, crime, employment and health supported the Boards, and were themselves composed of NDC officials (often seconded from other public-sector, health or policing posts) and local residents. Decision-making regarding the expenditure of budgets – typically underpinned by £40–50 million of Government funding – was the business of the Board, although significant levels of expenditure had to be approved by local Development Agencies. In Derby's case, this was the East Midlands Development Agency.

2   The National Index of Multiple Deprivation (IMD) is based on a range of educational, health and economic readings at council ward levels.

3   The Space Syntax Laboratory was founded by Professor Bill Hillier at University College London in the mid-1980s to explore the use of techniques for the analysis of spatial configurations of all kinds, especially in connection with architecture, urban design and transportation.

4   Tanc (Technical Aid for Nottingham Communities) is a Nottingham-based community regeneration consultancy.

5   A term used by the Situationist International to denote personal and psychological readings of place.

6   The design team comprised Christina Norton (Director and Project Architect), Steve McAdam, Peter Morris, Nicholas Laurent and Afolabi Spence.

7   Jeremy Till, 'Class Collaborators: Fluid's Derwent Gateway Centre; Architects: Fluid', *Architecture Today*, 152, October 2004, pp. 44–55.

8   Jay Merrick, 'On the Street Where We Live', *Independent*, 11 October 2004.

Neuland

Disenchanted utopias for Tel Aviv[1]

Alona Nitzan-Shiftan, Ganit Mayslits Kassif and Udi Kassif

White City – White Land

Numerous street banners and huge advertisements in all major Israeli newspapers recently announced that 'The people of Tel Aviv are walking around with their heads held high'. And, the message continued triumphantly, 'Now the whole world knows why!'[2] The secret happened to be the modernist core of 1930s Tel Aviv, and the stamp of authentication was UNESCO's declaration of the downtown 'White City' as a World Heritage Site. The celebrations were undoubtedly grand. A week of official ceremonies, exhibitions and cruises inaugurated a campaign whose joy and pride testified to an almost desperate desire to remould the history of the Zionist project, to choose from it the virtues the world should see – the dream, the utopia, the white fleeting vision, the Bauhaus imprint.

Implicit in these celebrations was a plea to forget the painful cost of implementing the Zionist dream. It was a quest for pause, for beauty, for making news out of modernist urbanism and enlightened preservation, rather than occupation and terror. In the midst of the second Palestinian Intifada, at a time when the world was condemning Israel for crushing the houses of Rafiah, ordinary Israelis suddenly heard a different message. The world was praising their state for having constructed rather than destroyed, for embodying a great utopia rather than shattering hope. The breach between Rafiah and Tel Aviv indicates and continuously demarcates the tensions in which Israelis are caught – the anxiety-ridden friction between Zionist redemption and oppression.

The collaborative project of *Neuland Island*, conceived as an 'ironic utopia', is located within this tense zone. The *Neuland* project was exhibited in the Israeli Pavilion at the 9th Venice Architecture Biennale in 2004; as created and curated by Ganit Mayslits Kassif and Udi Kassif, it featured design proposals by six teams of architects. Rather than concentrating on the political conflict, in which news and public debate assault life with firm and inescapable 'facts', the *Neuland* project looked at how these conflicts and public debates are replicated internally. Disillusioned with simplistic solutions, and painfully aware of the inseparability of centre and border, we chose to open windows onto Israeli interiority – a zone where 'nation' and 'state', their history and identity, are constantly challenged. More poignantly, we sought to explore, through the images and texts of the *Neuland* project, the ambivalent and urgent plea to break away from the Zionist vision, to split the national body and escape its eccentric ends.

This chapter will deal with the growing tension between the Zionist utopia and its costly implementation by focusing on two conditions of modern nationalism which Israel not only exemplifies, but in fact accentuates to absurdity. One is the definition of the national 'self' versus the 'other'; the second is the meshing of the concept of nation and state. The impediments to these nationalist programmes will be illustrated via two episodes – one a cartoon, and the other a manifesto. Both clarify how the Zionist dream of a Jewish revival in the holy land of Palestine is necessarily trapped in the national logic of territorial settlement. The resultant fractured terrain is the one that the curators adopted as the paradoxical starting point for constructing *Neuland*. And, in doing so, they reminded all of us of the extent to which the Zionist project was already ambivalent at its inception.

Arab Line – divided land

Dudu Geva, 'Yosef the Hero', Zoo Eretz Zoo, Jerusalem: Domino Press (1975).

A 1975 cartoon by the Israeli artist Dudu Geva portrays a typical Zionist settlement, a socialist workers' housing estate designed in the modern paradigm: separate, clean-lined towers with punched-out windows. The buildings occupy only the upper part of the cartoon. These light, airy buildings, drawn on empty white paper, rise above a narrow, dense, black area below. Carved out of this black entity is another series of houses – low, bulky, arched, and domed – it presents an inverse image from the bisecting line downwards. The modernist buildings, we are thus reminded, did not emerge from a *tabula rasa*, on a land without people for a people without land, as Ben Gurion famously put it. The houses of the Palestinian village, on the ruins of which the Zionist settlement was built, indicate the histories and memories embedded in the land.

Imagining a national community is contingent on the logic of boundedness – on a clear boundary that separates a horizontally defined group from another across the border, against which it takes its form. The 'other' of Jewish Israeli culture, however, is not only the menacing Arab across the border. An even more immediate 'other', the Palestinian Arab, constitutes a border that runs underneath the Israeli polity in the form of a tangible recent past which is impeding the effort to naturalise Jewish nativeness. Thus, the land that Zionists prefer to consider primarily for its fertility and real-estate potential becomes the ultimate mirror image of the Israeli ideal. Geva's cartoon line between the village and the settlement suggests the cultural spatiality of the Green Line. It seems as if the latter runs not only horizontally between the territories of Israel and Palestine but, more subtly, between the layers of Israel and its Palestinian past. It becomes the inescapable shadow attached to every Zionist dream, an iron weight on the vision of the Zionist utopia.

Tel Aviv State – a city-land

Also recently, a group of frustrated residents of Tel Aviv composed a heartening proposal. Why not, asked the rebels, separate Israel like in biblical times, and establish a new state around greater Tel Aviv? Citizens of the State of Tel Aviv would enjoy complete civil freedom without ethnic tension. They would rise an hour later, in the European time zone, and would use a 'Danro' currency (derived from the Dan region, where Tel Aviv is situated) to match the Euro of their Western neighbours. Relieved from the financial burden of the Israeli settlements and the huge security budget these entail, they would be able to enjoy economic prosperity for the pursuit of education, welfare, and culture. 'It may sound like wishful thinking,' they admitted. 'Perhaps it is. But what a pleasure it would be to hear the right-wing leader speaker of the Knesset, Reuben Rivlin, speaking from a "stable and glorious Jerusalem which is united forever", and to know that he is now a minister in a different, faraway land' – the foreign country known as Israel.[3] Such statements bluntly expose the current disenchantment with the aims of Jerusalem and its surrounding territories. Geographically biased, they indicate the damaged form of the nation-state – the failure to consolidate 'the political space of the sovereign state and the cultural space of the nation'.[4]

Poster, Israel's Ministry of Tourism, 1950s, The Zionist Archive.

The Israeli nation-building project was predicated on meshing the two sides, as could be seen in a poster of the period: the primordial sentiments of the nation, the authentic and timelessly Jewish Jerusalem, on the left; and the civic sentiments of the state, the progressive and modernist settlement, on the right. Once realised, this nation-building project embarked on its colonial complement in the form of the Israeli occupation of Palestinian territories. After the 1967 Arab–Israeli War territorially unleashed the spirit of Israeli nationalism, the Israeli state could no longer conceal the ambiguity of its national–colonial practices, even from its own citizens. Haunted by the distractive force of the Jewish primordial sentiments, many Israelis started to focus their desire instead on Tel Aviv. Let Jerusalem have its nationalism, the manifesto suggested. Tel Aviv wants to be a modern, Hebrew-speaking city-state.

Dissociating Tel Aviv from Israel, however, cuts to the heart of the modernist project that had brought Jews to Palestine during the Ottoman and British Mandate eras. This project advanced a liberating national cause, while participating in the oppressive enterprise of settling the land of the 'other'. Both the acts of nation-building and settlement 'developed at one and the same time on a single colonial terrain', with no metropole to recede to.[5] In the context of Israeli settler society, the wish to retreat from the project of colonisation into its own modernist body thus required an operation of greater magnitude. The celebrations of the 'White City' and the wider Tel Aviv manifesto attempted not only to undo the seam between nation and state, but, more urgently, to split the national body itself – to detach the dream from its authentication, the 'neuland' from its 'altland', the utopia from the settlement.

Split body – *Neuland*

Neuland Island is thus seen as a state without a nation, a fantastic utopia without solid ground, Zionism without history. It is a clone made out of virtual land, one that offers internal views into a conflicted national body. Wishfully neither holy nor contested, Tel Aviv is itself the ultimate clone, because its genes, so to speak, are made of sand. There is no claim to landed rights within its 'genetic code' – it is presumably a purely Zionist creation. Modernists dwell on sand. In Tel Aviv, Israelis want to believe, there are no shadows, no chains on the wings of white balconies, no past beneath them. The obstacle that must be removed in order to achieve pure statehood is territorial continuity with the rest of the nation-state of Israel.

The island of *Neuland* challenges the aspiration to break from Geva's subterranean Palestinian village, and from the strong foundations of Jaffa – the city to which Tel Aviv was initially appended as a suburb.[6] Clean and weightless, *Neuland* is sent out into the purifying waters of the Mediterranean. Close to the shore it resembles a crowd of holiday bathers, immersed to the waist, freed of the gravity of the everyday. It suggests a displacing of the older 'White City' of Tel Aviv. If the 'Bauhaus Style' containers, the modern structures for new Jews, were built on sand, *Neuland* is to be built on water, the ultimate expression of rootlessness. Released from the internal conflicted landscape of utopia and oppression, *Neuland Island* suggests an ironic, speculative, and of course an utterly impossible escape. Theodore Herzl, the acclaimed founder of political Zionism, envisioned the state in his 1902 novel *Altneuland* – in the Neuland project it could finally find its appropriate setting. On a land that is the result of cartographic manipulation, *Neuland* clones a vision without the nastiness of its implementation.

Neuland

Ganit Mayslits Kassif and Udi Kassif, *Neuland*.

Neuland was thus conceived in an act of irony – as the ultimate site of our yearnings, a harmless territory for dreams and speculations. Formed as an inverted mirror-image of Tel Aviv, the fictitious island of *Neuland* is placed opposite the real city as a provocative or inspiring alternative. *Neuland* offers a platform for self-reflection. It takes a break from reality, yet uses its actuality both as resource and objective. *Neuland* sprouts out of the moral paradox of its implementation. Living this inherent paradox, we got weary of shattered dreams, fed up with bloody utopias. We can no longer serve as the operating arm of one great vision or another. And so we created *Neuland Island*.

Six teams of young architects were invited to use *Neuland* as a site for critical observations, an opportunity to juggle with the notions of utopia, and to rethink urbanism. Using the polluted utopia as a starting point, *Neuland* becomes a breeding ground for new viewpoints, a site for irresponsible urbanism, alternative histories, seeds of hope, catastrophic scenarios, ironic oppositions, wild operations, and critical interventions. The *Neuland* project is an attempt to explore the potential of a pseudo-utopian gesture as a critical tool. It proposes an alternative site of research for a culture in which architecture operates as an institutionalised profession, primarily serving the nationalist agenda. Sometimes it aims to negate this agenda, but only rarely does it develop any cultural input that questions its own tools and motivations.

The six projects reflect the tremendously varied motivations, backgrounds, and passions of their creators. While all operate within a politically charged and highly conflicted context, they attempt to go beyond the exteriority of the conflict, and to develop a cultural critique that challenges the institutional practices of both the state

and the profession. Instead of turning to the 'problem-solving' methods used in professional practice, they carve out instead a space for critical reflection, peering into the very heart and interiority of the conflicted Israeli culture in order to speculate about alternative tools of action.

'Alt/Neuland', the first project, by Dan Koniak, Karina Tollman, Philipp Misselwitz, and Philipp Thomanek, is an investigation into the heterotopic nature of Tel Aviv, based on an analogy between *Neuland*, the fictitious island created in 2004, and the empty dunes of 1909, upon which Tel Aviv was originally founded. The famous myth of the lottery scene in which the first plots of Tel Aviv were supposedly handed out was restaged by a random group of founding members for the new island. The project book that maps the desires of these founders provides a fascinating self-reflective document of a grassroots set of fantasies which were to become the building stones of the new island.

The second project, 'Neuland rECOvery', by Galila Yavin and Tamar Zacharovitch, uses *Neuland* as an opportunity to push Tel Aviv's ecosystem to its inevitable collapse, and floods its coastal strip in order to envisage an alternative future for the city. The experiment exposes the vulnerability of our environment while exploring the potential of healing processes. In a reality-cum-fantasy setting, sea salt is proposed as the new building material for *Neuland*'s construction.

The third project, 'urban-shift.net', by Gaston Zahr, Noa Pasharel-Haim, Alasdair Ross Graham, Oded Kidron, Birgit Glaetzel, and Omer Weissbein, takes the symbolic aspect of twinning cities and the familiar concept of ex-territorial spaces several stages further, to develop the possibilities for the transplant and exchange of urban branches of one city within another. Allowing for varying degrees of permanence, interaction, and connection, the project examines the probability of creating branches of Amman, Tokyo, Kiev, Frankfurt, and Bat Galim in a new settlement next to Tel Aviv.

The fourth project, 'Insomnia', by Tamar Navon, Ifat Hollender-Emmer, and Michal Ilan, takes as its starting point the highly vibrant and dominant night scene in Tel Aviv, and focuses on the night's inherent power of creation. The project takes the imaginary island as an opportunity to challenge the supremacy of daytime practices within normal planning procedures. While illuminating the unique, dreamy, nightmarish, and sensual facets of night time, the project rethinks their position within the planning agenda, and suggests, as a result, an alternative index of materials and programmes.

The fifth project, '*Suede!*', or 'Variations on a Fucked-Up Situation', by Roee Hemed and Jonathan Dror, states that the citizens of *Neuland* can no longer exist as an all-Jewish society within the land of Israel, and so the project offers the citizens of *Neuland* a choice – either to live on the street and concede the indoor spaces, or to create a new land in an upper-floor territory and renounce all of the outdoor spaces. By flipping and reversing inside and out, '*Suede!*' manipulates the Zionist existence and divides it, ironically, into two states: JEWGANDA, an all-indoors land; and ZIONSTINE, an all-outdoors land.

Finally, the sixth project, 'Urban Quilt', by Maor Roytman and Oren Ben Avraham, suggests Israel's most infamous underprivileged neighbourhood as a ground for the inspection and challenge of urban renewal methods. In the process of mapping the neighbourhood's laundry practices, deep-frying policies, or loitering routes, as well as its physical assets, the project offers a fresh outlook on means of intervention in the urban environment.

Notes

1   This chapter was written in conjunction with the *Neuland* project that was exhibited in the Israeli Pavilion at the 9th Venice Biennale of Architecture, as part of the exhibition *Back to the Sea* by the curators Yael Moria-Klain and Sigal Barnir. *Neuland* was created and curated by Ganit Mayslits Kassif and Udi Kassif and featured projects by six teams of architects.

2   For recent studies on Tel Aviv's 'whiteness', see A. Nitzan-Shiftan, 'Whitened Houses', *Theory and Criticism*, 16, 2000, pp. 227–32; Sharon Rotbard, *White City, Black City*, Tel Aviv: Bavel Publishers, 2005.

3   E. Zvuluni, 'Medinat Gush Dan' ['The State of the Dan Block'], *Ha'aretz*, 25 June 2002.

4   Adriana Kemp, 'Borders, Space and National Identity in Israel', *Theory and Criticism*, 16, 2000, p. 17.

5   Nadia Abu El-Haj, *Facts on the Ground: Archaeological Practice and Territorial Self-Fashioning in Israeli Society*, Chicago: University of Chicago Press, 2001, p. 5.

6   See, for instance, Mark Levin, *Overthrowing Geography: Jaffa, Tel Aviv, and the Struggle for Palestine, 1880–1948*, Berkeley and Los Angeles: University of California Press, 2004.

Beyond Koolhaas

Murray Fraser

We need urgently to discover a new kind of critical architecture. By this I refer to an approach that can reinvigorate the level of critique amongst architects in developed Western countries, where the tradition of oppositional design has lain moribund for years. Equally importantly, the new approach needs to be capable of being adapted in other regions of the world, where opportunities to speculate about alternative social and economic realities, through the medium of architecture, are still taking root. Even to make such an appeal, however, is to recognize that we have reached a particular moment in architectural discourse.

Now that the post-critical stance – as pulled apart elsewhere in this book – seems to be abandoned even by its erstwhile exponents, the shortcomings of previous models of critical architecture have also become evident. The most notable figures in the earlier generation of critical architects were Rem Koolhaas and Bernard Tschumi, both of whom had developed their stance in response to the intellectual challenge made to architects in the late-1960s and early-1970s by Manfredo Tafuri, the celebrated Italian Marxist critic and historian.[1] It was Tafuri who asked how it could ever be possible to use architectural design in any positive sense to transform the lives of ordinary people, so long as the exploitative nature of the capitalist system – masked by false consciousness – still prevailed. Tafuri exposed the delusions of the modernist pioneers in the inter-war era, with their belief that they could harness the resources of industrial capitalism and point it towards a social goal. Equally, he argued that the efforts of Welfare State architects in European countries after the Second World War were also futile, and if anything were only adding to the growing immiseration of the working classes. It was a dilemma that prompted Tafuri to retreat into a condition of 'pure' criticism; he defined his task as being that of exposing ideological falsehoods, and above all of showing up the follies of what he termed 'anachronistic hopes in design'. This hit a raw nerve for architects, particularly amongst those who were radically opposed to the values of capitalism and yet still believed it their duty to ameliorate social conditions. Hence it was the dilemma set out by Tafuri – as well as the smug confidence, bland utopianism and unambitious design of Welfare State architecture itself – that Koolhaas and Tschumi were reacting against. They let it be known, albeit subtly and using the latest terminology of continental critical theory, that their projects encapsulated ideas that were critical of the dominant economic and social order, while being framed within an approach that could nevertheless accept and operate inside the realities of capitalist development. As Tschumi later explained:

> Architects act as mediators between authoritarian power, or capitalist power, and some sort of humanistic aspiration. The economic and political powers that make our cities and our architecture are enormous. We cannot block them but we can use another tactic, which I call the tactic of judo, that is, to use the force of one's opponent in order to defeat it and transform it into something else.
>
> (Comment by Bernard Tschumi in Cynthia Davison (ed.), *Anyplace*, New York: Anyone Corporation/Cambridge, MA and London: MIT Press, 1995, p. 229)

While his analysis was as spot-on as ever, the problem with Tschumi's tactic was making it work in practice. How could one ensure that even the cunning judo artist would not simply end up flattened on the ground themselves? The *leitmotif* of the brilliant early essays by Tschumi was a forensic deconstruction of the dual mantras of architectural modernism, functionalism and zoning, now accepted as the principles for capitalist development.[2] But Tschumi had already fully articulated his counter-position by the late-1980s, and since then he has added little of substance to his initial polemic. In the case of Koolhaas, the target of attack was always somewhat larger, being that of Western architecture as an entirety. Using the emerging realities of globalization as the ammunition for attack, Koolhaas ridiculed the slowness of Western architects to adapt their thinking and modes of practice to suit the new global conditions. It proved fertile ground, but after superb direct hits with *Delirious New York* (1978) and then a few stand-out essays collected into *S, M, L, XL* (1995), his fount of inspiration has notably dried up as well.[3]

Paradoxically, this relative decline in his theoretical writings has enabled Koolhaas to focus ever more on his architectural designs, which for most observers have improved greatly in quality as a result. But as far as any implicit social critique is contained in the latest Koolhaas projects, it does not have the intended impact. For example, the designs for Prada stores in SoHo in Manhattan and Rodeo Drive in Los Angeles might contain copious amounts of superfluous space with no possible commercial use, with an intention of turning them into places as much of free public promenade as hard-nosed retail outlets, but within a deluxe shopping environment the absence of spatial functionality matters little. Conspicuous waste becomes a quality that merely reinforces the brand image of Prada, which after all is based brazenly on conspicuous, empty-value consumption. Likewise, the fact that the scheme for the Chinese Central TV headquarters by Koolhaas – sculpted dramatically with the help of the engineer Cecil Balmond at Arups – contains a public right of way snaking through its contorted form does not as such challenge the notorious secrecy and authoritarianism of that state-controlled institution. It offers at best an isolated symbol of critique, rather than a critical architecture that can hint at changes in meaning through radical aesthetics and a thoroughgoing spatial manipulation of the building programme.

The resulting feeling, therefore, is of a critical discourse started by figures like Koolhaas and Tschumi that has needed to go undercover for so long that it has become dissipated and lost its bearings. At the time, by reacting against the banal complacency of Welfare State modernism – and the backdrop of an essentially positivist architectural discourse – they played a vital role. But now their tactics come across as a resigned reaction to the impossibility of ever challenging the dominant economic forces of capitalism. While these capitalist forces are undoubtedly powerful, and are making life ever more miserable for billions of people across the globe, it cannot be right to retreat into a cynical worldview, nor does the stealth tactic seem workable any more. Two events held recently in London at the Royal Institute of British Architects – the speech given by Koolhaas on receiving the RIBA Gold Medal in February 2004, and the participation by Tschumi in a misguided panel discussion on globalization in February 2006 – have simply demonstrated that the tactic of blending into the corporate world has clipped both of their wings, eroding the ability now to be critical. Having added so much to the spirit of critical architecture in the 1970s, 1980s and early-1990s, the widespread impression is that neither Koolhaas nor Tschumi are any longer able to lead the way in future; instead, they will likely continue on their path to becoming mainstream architectural superstars. Given such a reality, it is now time to move beyond figures such as Koolhaas and Tschumi, and to search elsewhere for answers.

So where can one find more useful examples of critical practice going on? As well as examples contained in this book, or already well-known practices such as Rural Studio in the southern states of the United States, one of the brightest hopes today in Britain has to be Peter Barber. He is an architect who has been earning much attention lately in the press and television, even being invited to speak on housing and urban design policy at the New Labour party conference in Manchester in September 2006. Barber first came to note for the design of the Villa Anbar in Saudi Arabia in the early-1990s, a neo-Corbusian house that played knowingly on the gender separations in the Middle Eastern home, and which was designed for an independently minded female novelist.[4] This dwelling was designed around the typical Islamic division of male and female space, but – at the urging of the client – a slot was cut into the wall separating the two gendered zones. When the men of the household protested about the presence of this slot, Barber was then asked to put a shutter over it; he did so, but with the handle on the female side so that the women occupants could control whether it was open or not.

Barber has since returned to practice in Britain, and has taken up a crusade on an issue that serves to divide classes and social groups in his native country: that is, the relationship of private domestic environments to the public urban spaces that lie outside. He has taken up the challenge of re-establishing a sense of street culture within architectural discourse, and this goal – along with the concomitant of increased housing density – now represent the twin prongs for the urban regeneration schemes he is engaged upon. It should be noted that Barber is not just mildly critical in his atti-tude; he is intensely angry at the ways in which society is being controlled, and in which cities are being designed as a result. He is an advocate of dense and vibrant urban spaces, championing the qualities of pedestrian movement and social convivial-ity that were praised so evocatively years ago by figures as diverse as Walter Benjamin and Jane Jacobs. Creating a heightened degree of visual permeability and overlooking is, in his view, a positive design device, not only for mutual self-policing, but also to militate against the artificial creation of social barriers between urban inhabitants. There is still no alternative on the horizon, and so only the proper design of the street as a spatial movement device can allow social mixing to happen – a truism that urban analysts such as Bill Hillier have long been pointing out.[5] It is a crucial issue that most architects, overly obsessed with visual aesthetics, still do not fully grasp. 'Buildings are used as a popular stage', wrote Benjamin in an essay on street culture back in the 1920s. 'They are all divided into innumerable, simultaneously animated theatres. Balcony, courtyard, window, gateway, staircase, roof are at the same time stages and boxes.'[6] Barber warms to this insight, noting of Benjamin's text that it:

> captures fleetingly but beautifully the idea of a city and of architecture ani-mated and activated by the business and activity of its occupants, and of space as being inert without people and culture. He sketches for us the colour and frantic activity made possible by spatiality that is 'permeable', which invites occupation. He gives an intimation of the fragile and complex reciprocal relationship that exists between people and space, between culture and architecture. My belief is that space conditions – and is in turn conditioned by – society and culture, and that architecture can therefore create the potential for social action and activity.
>
> (Peter Barber, manifesto text, as sent in email correspondence to Fraser, 10 October 2006)

By adopting this approach, Barber is consciously asking a provocative question: if the notion of the shared public street is in fact a spatial device initiated in the very first cities nearly five millennia ago, then is the reassertion of the pedestrian street within a condition of advanced capitalism a conservative or a radical act? His view is very much that it offers a radical critique, one that taps into a consistent human need across the ages to participate daily in a lively and shared urban environment. We are social animals, and no amount of the privatization of wealth can erode the basic need for visual and physical interaction amongst humans. This idea has also turned Barber into a vocal critic of suburbanized values in British architecture, seeing these just as a veiled excuse for class and ethnic exclusivity. 'Suburbia is crap', he has claimed recently. 'A lot of contemporary suburban visions are very sad and contribute to all sorts of [social] problems.'[7]

In terms of actual schemes, Barber's response is to design a series of high-density, low-rise housing projects that are organized around re-stitching the existing street pattern in areas where this sense of historical spatial continuity has been eroded, either by post-war planning or the inroads of the motor car. Working at first on a number of small schemes of this type in Hackney, a poor borough in east London, in 2002 Barber won a competition run by a housing association to design a prototypical urban quarter of the future. The result is the Donnybrook Estate in Bow, bang in the East End of London, and a scheme that is already attracting much critical acclaim and awards – while, it has to be said, also being bitterly attacked by others.[8] Here the mixture is of Le-Corbusier-meets-the-Casbah, designed at a density that is almost triple the norm for local housing development in that area. There are 42 houses and apartments in the scheme, at a level of 111 dwellings to the hectare; for comparison's sake, this is about four times the recommended density of the traditional garden city. Housing is provided in four terraces of between two-to-four storeys in height, with the street spaces in between for circulation and children to play in. A profusion of asymmetrical windows and balconies dotted into the smooth white rendered facades provide views into and out of the homes. With dwellings either for sale or for renting through the housing association, it creates a mixed social use. When the client at one point felt it necessary to segregate the private and the rented dwellings in the design, with a dividing wall between them, Barber threatened to walk off the job; not as a prima donna, but simply because getting his way on this issue was essential for the urban proposition to work. In the end, the client relented. The scheme also implies a genuine critique not just of the boring monocultures of the vast majority of urban areas designed under capitalism, but also of the need for people to be given a chance to shape and create their own parts of the city – not have these handed down to them by the state (New Towns, prefabricated housing and all that) or have their living environments pre-commodified (suburban estates, lofts) and sold to them through the frankly sinister workings of consumer capitalism. Within the fixed built framework for the

All figures are Peter Barber Architects, Donnybrook Quarter, London. Photographs: Peter Barber Architects (2006).

Donnybrook estate, Barber has given the maisonettes on the first floor their own open courtyard area, leaving it to occupants to decide later how they want to infill and protect this area from the weather. Nor is there any attempt at simplistic visual contextualism in the external appearance of the project. Barber rejects the British habit of copying the surrounding forms and building materials for the spineless ethos that this represents. Fantastic cities are only good because they contain many different types of buildings, and it is rather the linking of lively social spaces that gives them a sense of urban context, not sterile design codes.

An architect such as Barber does not want to act as a would-be 'fifth colum-nist' like Koolhaas or Tschumi, entering equipped with a hidden agenda into the inner circles of capitalist corporations, nor does he depend on coded or ambivalent terminol-ogy for his critical stance. Instead, his tactic is to address social problems directly, without any trace of cynicism, and with absolutely no intent at irony or of playing up to the fashion brigade. Architecture for him is a supremely serious business, and he regards the role of the architect as very much a public intellectual who is tasked – as far as possible within the limitations set by the brief, budget and general social system – to affect urban improvements that will improve everyday life for citizens with the least power and opportunity. And, in the end, this surely has to be the telling point. Criticality does not come from any inherent condition of architecture, which if anything tends towards the support of dominant power structures, as history shows us. Instead, criticality springs from the persistence of social inequality, and given there is no hope of a utopian future, then the critical function will always need to be sustained and replenished as part of architectural practice. The question therefore is not whether critical architecture is needed, but how to frame it. Here lies the importance of cultural readings from across the world. As writers such as Edward Said and Homi K. Bhabha have argued so eloquently, cultural identity offers the location for identifying what might be considered as critical practice, not the other way around.[9] Playing on these issues becomes the way forward in an age of increasing globalization. And what all of this analysis signals is a renewed sense of the importance of critical architecture: no longer blind or arrogant like the pioneers of early modernism, and definitely not equivo-cal or cynical like later adherents who masked themselves up behind critical theory. So let us now move on from Koolhaas, and even more so from the futile gesture of post-critical theory; let's look instead to Barber and others like him, wherever they happen to be operating around the world.

Notes

1   Manfredo Tafuri, *Architecture and Utopia*, Cambridge, MA and London: MIT Press, 1976. See also Murray Fraser, 'The Cultural Context of Critical Architecture', *Journal of Architecture*, 10, 3, June 2005, pp. 317–22; K. Michael Hays, 'Critical Architecture', *Perspecta*, 21, 1984, pp. 15–28; Fredric Jameson, 'Architecture and the Critique of Ideology', *The Ideologies of Theory: Essays 1971–1986*, vol. 2, Minneapolis: Univer-sity of Minnesota, 1988, pp. 35–60.

2   Bernard Tschumi, *The Manhattan Transcripts* [1981], London: Academy Editions, 1994; Bernard Tschumi, *Architecture and Disjunction*, Cambridge, MA/London: MIT Press, 1994.

3   Rem Koolhaas, *Delirious New York: a Retroactive Manifesto for Manhattan* [1978], New York: Monacelli Press, 1994; Rem Koolhaas, 'Singapore Songlines' and 'The Generic City', in *S, M, L, XL*, New York: Monacelli Press, 1995, pp. 1008–89, 1251–2.

4   Peter Barber, 'Villa Anbar, Dammam, Saudi Arabia', in Murray Fraser (ed.), *Culture and Technology Issue: the Oxford Review of Architecture*, vol. 1, Oxford: Oxford Brookes University, 1996, pp. 10–19.

5   Bill Hillier, *Space is the Machine*, Cambridge: Cambridge University Press, 1995; Jane Jacobs, *The Death and Life of Great American Cities* [1961], London: Cape, 1994; Richard Sennett, *The Fall of Public Man* [1974], London: Penguin, 2003.

6   Walter Benjamin, 'Naples' [1925], in Marcus Bullock and Michael W. Jennings (eds), *Walter Benjamin, 1913–26: Selected Writings,* vol. 1, Cambridge, MA: Harvard University Press/Belknap Press, 1996, p. 417.

7   Quote from Peter Barber, in Ellen Bennett, 'Welcome to "Superbia"', *Building Design*, 29 September 2006, p. 1.

8   Eleanor Young, 'Neighbourhood Watch', *RIBA Journal*, April 2006, pp. 32–40; Ellis Woodman, 'Streets Ahead', *Building Design*, 24 February 2006, pp. 12–15; Fionn Stevenson, Letter in *Building Design*, 3 March 2006, p. 10.

9   Homi K. Bhabha, *The Location of Culture*, London: Routledge, 1994; Edward Said, *Culture and Imperialism*, London: Chatto and Windus, 1993.

Index